ICONS OF MYSTERY AND CRIME DETECTION

ICONS OF MYSTERY AND CRIME DETECTION

From Sleuths to Superheroes

VOLUME 2

Mitzi M. Brunsdale

GREENWOOD ICONS

 GREENWOOD

AN IMPRINT OF ABC-CLIO, LLC
Santa Barbara, California • Denver, Colorado • Oxford, England

Library of Congress Cataloging-in-Publication Data

Brunsdale, Mitzi.
  Icons of mystery and crime detection : from sleuths to superheroes / Mitzi M. Brunsdale.
    p. cm. — (Greenwood icons)
  Includes bibliographical references and index.
  ISBN 978-0-313-34530-2 (alk. paper)—ISBN 978-0-313-34531-9 (ebook)—ISBN 978-0-
313-34532-6 (v. 1, hard copy)—ISBN 978-0-313-34533-3 (v. 1, ebook)—ISBN 978-0-313-
34534-0 (v. 2, hard copy)—ISBN 978-0-313-34535-7 (v. 2, ebook)
  1. Detective and mystery stories—History and criticism. 2. Detective and
mystery stories—Authorship. I. Title.
  PN3448.D4B77   2010
  809.3'872—dc22   2010005083

ISBN: 978-0-313-34530-2
EISBN: 978-0-313-34531-9

14 13 12 11 10   1 2 3 4 5

This book is also available on the World Wide Web as an eBook.
Visit www.abc-clio.com for details.

Greenwood
An Imprint of ABC-CLIO, LLC

ABC-CLIO, LLC
130 Cremona Drive, P.O. Box 1911
Santa Barbara, California 93116-1911

This book is printed on acid-free paper (∞)

Manufactured in the United States of America

For Rex and Drake, and in loving memory of Duke:

. . . if the while I think on thee, dear friend,
All losses are restor'd and sorrows end.
—William Shakespeare

Contents

List of Photos

Christian Bale as Batman in *Batman Begins* (page 1). © David James/Warner Bros./Bureau L.A. Collection/CORBIS.

Sean Connery as James Bond in *From Russia, With Love* (page 35). Used by permission of the Motion Picture & Television Photo Archive. http://www.mptvimages.com/

Book Cover, from *Father Brown: The Essential Tales* by G.K. Chesterton, edited by P.D. James, copyright © 2005 (page 71). Used by permission of the Modern Library, a division of Random House, Inc.

Warner Olan as Charlie Chan (page 103). Photo by Hulton Archive/Stringer/Getty Images.

Agatha Christie (page 135). Courtesy of PA Photos/Landov.

Peter Sellers as Inspector Clouseau (page 169). Photo by Evening Standard/Hulton Archive/Getty Images.

Peter Falk as Columbo (page 199). © Douglas Kirkland/CORBIS.

Dragnet (NBC) 1951–1959 (page 229). Shown: Ben Alexander (as Officer Frank Smith), Jack Webb (as Sergeant Joe Friday). Courtesy of NBC/Photofest.

Cover illustration from *The Secret of the Old Clock* by Robert D. San Souci, illustrated by James Ransome, published by Grosset & Dunlap (page 259). Used by permission of the Penguin Group USA.

Angela Lansbury as Jessica Fletcher (page 289). Courtesy of CBS/Landov.

Mickey Spillane pretending to slap an actress (page 321). © Bettmann/CORBIS.

Clint Eastwood as Dirty Harry (page 351). Photo by Warner Bros./Archive Photos/Getty Images.

Tony Hillerman (page 383). Photo by Kelly Campbell. Used with permission.

Alfred Hitchcock (page 415). Courtesy of CBS/Landov.

Illustration by Sidney Paget for "The Greek Interpreter" (page 447).

Georges Simenon with statue of Inspector Maigret (page 483). Photo by Keystone Features/Getty Images.

Humphrey Bogart as Philip Marlowe in *The Big Sleep* (page 513). © John Springer Collection/CORBIS.

Raymond Burr as Perry Mason in "The Sardonic Sergeant" (page 545). Courtesy of CBS/Landov.

Edgar Allan Poe (page 575). Courtesy of the Library of Congress.

Dorothy L. Sayers, 1926 (page 605). Used by permission of the Marion E. Wade Center, Wheaton College, Wheaton, IL.

Humphrey Bogart as Sam Spade in *The Maltese Falcon* (page 637). Courtesy of Reisfeld/DBA/Landov.

"Listen, there's got to be more action . . . ," by Chester Gould, 1942 (page 669). © Tribune Media Services, Inc. All Rights Reserved. Reprinted with permission.

Photograph from "The Golden Spiders: A Nero Wolfe Mystery," A&E TV Movie, March 5, 2000 (page 699). Directed by Bill Duke. Shown from left: Maury Chaykin (as Nero Wolfe) and Timothy Hutton (as Archie Goodwin). Courtesy A&E Television Networks/Photofest.

Matt Rawle as Zorro on poster from *Zorro the Musical* (London) (page 731). © Robbie Jack/CORBIS.

Tony Hillerman. Photo by Kelly Campbell. Used with permission.

Tony Hillerman: Creator of Ethnic Detectives Joe Leaphorn and Jim Chee

Earth's voice has become my voice.
By means of this I shall live on.

—from the "Blessing Way" of the Dineh

The ethnic detective is a relatively recent phenomenon in crime and mystery writing, although "Anyone . . . writing fiction about the friction in crime and punishment between one culture and another is an ethnic crime writer." Ethnic crime fiction provides powerful cultural insight, dramatizing intercultural conflicts and the fears of the dominant society, offering humor, and reestablishing "the reader's feeling of safety from and superiority over other people or groups of people"; and as "a kind of affirmative fiction, it demonstrates remorse and atonement for former and present social injustices" (Browne 1029). Despite its potential for social commentary and anthropological insights into exotic cultures, however, ethnic crime fiction took a long time to become an established subgenre of its field, possibly because of deep-rooted prejudices against nonwhites, and white authors initially invented the earliest ethnic detectives, like Earl Derr Biggers's Charlie Chan, to embody "mainstream" stereotypes (Freese 10). In 1946, Manly Wade Wellman's short story "A Star for a Warrior" introduced David Return, a Native American who solved a murder case through his "deep understanding of Indian character, tradition, and ceremonials" (Greenberg 4), but not until Tony Hillerman's *The Blessing Way* (1970) did the mystery genre begin to explore a Native American culture extensively. In 18 novels, a handful of short stories, and several handsome travel volumes, Hillerman, "the dean of advocacy literature on Native [American] rights today" (Browne 1031), celebrates the harsh grandeur of the American Southwest and the Dineh (Navajo) who then and now and always "walk in beauty," their metaphor for the Navajo Way central to Hillerman's distinguished mystery series.

HISTORICAL/CULTURAL CONTEXT

To appreciate ethnic mystery novels as multicultural, readers need to understand the customs, creeds, and ethnic history such fiction takes for granted (Freese 13), such as the Navajo anthropology in Hillerman's work. From the 1300s to the 1600s, the Navajo, who call themselves the "Dineh" ("The People"), an Athabaskan tribe of formidable nomadic warriors related to the Apache, migrated from west central Canada into the Southwest, trading bison meat, hides, and stone tools for corn and woven goods with the long-established Pueblo Indians. About 1750 the Dineh settled in the mountains and valleys surrounding Arizona's Canyon de Chelly, keeping sheep and raising corn, squash, and beans in areas 17th-century Spanish settlers called *Nabajo*, "great planted fields," living a distinct life separate from

We Navajo are always learning.
—Jim McGrath, written about Navajo artist R.C. Gorman

other tribes in that high arid country. Today the Navajo Nation numbers about 300,000, the largest U.S. Native American jurisdiction, about 27,000 square miles, an area larger than New England, in the "Four Corners" of northeastern Arizona, southeastern Utah, southwestern Colorado, and northwestern New Mexico, "an island in a white ocean" (Murphy 245). The Navajo Nation requires a blood quantum of one-fourth for enrolled tribal membership, though other tribes only require a one-thirty-second blood quantum for official membership.

Until 1848, the Dineh fought continuously with other tribes, the Spanish, and later the Mexicans, to live on their land. After the Mexican War, Americans claimed Dineh land in 1848, and the fierce Navajo Wars began, lasting until the early 1860s when Americans built Fort Defiance near Window Rock, Arizona, now the capital of the Navajo Nation. Eventually Americans under the Navajos' "friend" General Kit Carson killed or captured thousands of the Dineh, burning their crops and hogans, slaughtering their sheep, and forcing them on "The Long Walk" some 300 miles to Bosque Redondo (Fort Sumner) in eastern New Mexico, where 7,000 Navajo endured four years' harsh confinement. Finally in return for their promise to war no more, the American government offered them the choice of a fertile Oklahoma reservation with good grazing, a reservation at Basque Redondo—or their Four Corners land, the Colorado Plateau high desert country, "desolate, infertile and generally worthless"—as General William Tecumseh Sherman assured President Andrew Johnson, "as far from our future possible wants as is possible to determine." Borboncito, the Dineh war leader, speaking for the Dineh and "for the animals, from the horse to the dog, and also for the unborn," gave General Sherman his people's answer: "They would go home" (*Indian Country* 15–16).

The Dineh doubled in population by 1900, farming, raising sheep, weaving, and producing the silver smithing they had learned at Fort Sumner. Even after the brutal Long Walk and the slaughter of their animals by the U.S. government in a deliberate "stock reduction" from 1923 to 1941, the Dineh served proudly as U.S. Marine front-line "code talkers" whose Navajo language proved the only unbreakable code used during World War II.

In 1946, a Dineh healing ceremony Tony Hillerman witnessed while recuperating from his own war wounds profoundly captured his imagination and his heart, and 20 years later he began writing mystery novels that "are like windows that look out into Dinetah, the holy Navajo landscape" (Parfit 92). Nearly all of Hillerman's fiction involves the blend of traditional Dineh spirituality and modern Navajo economics seen in today's flag of the Navajo Nation: a rainbow, symbol of Navajo sovereignty, surrounds an outline of the present reservation, itself bounded by the Four Sacred Mountains and containing symbols of agriculture, oil, wild animals, and the lumber industry. To this day, poverty and a lack of infrastructure due to U.S. Bureau of Indian Affairs' refusal to allocate funds for rehabilitation afflict 700,000 acres of the Navajo Reservation that had been "frozen" for 40 years in a dispute with the Hopi Nation.

Hillerman, a Roman Catholic, has commented, "Our genesis, the Judeo-Christian story of creation, teaches that God said that man should have 'dominion over all this earth.' But this country [the American Southwest] puts man on a scale in which he is not comfortable—a tiny insignificant creature surrounded by emptiness" (*Indian Country* 11). "New Mexico offers much that makes him [Hillerman] 'want to write': its peoples, its strange, empty geography, and, most of all, its compelling embodiment of a Navajo creation myth" (Erisman 12). That myth develops a view of man's place in the universe in which "spirituality is not a side aspect . . . it is tightly woven together with everyday life," so that the Dineh experience a "deep joy of living immersed in a world of connection" (Heffern 13). For them, the universe is of a single piece; "it is all natural, and man is a part of that universe and must adhere to its many laws (which the Navajo know)" (Downs 95).

The Dineh creation myth begins with the First/Black World, symbolized by the sacred stone of jet, and its many *yei,* spiritual beings associated with natural features and aspects of weather, vegetation, minerals, and certain animals. Altse Hastiin (First Man) and Altse Asdzaa (First Woman) defy natural law and produce monsters that must be slain by the Hero Twins born of the most important figure in Dineh myth, Changing Woman. Overcoming these monsters is "the Navajo metaphor for salvation—of human ability to transcend unhealthy appetites that disrupt the harmony of the Navajo Way" (*Indian Country* 55). "When the Hero Twins . . . slay the monsters of Dinetah, they allow Hunger to live as a reminder to The People that there is more to life than material things" (Erisman 12), the Dineh explanation for the centrality of spirituality in their lives.

First Man and First Woman then pass through the east to the Second/Blue World, symbolized by the sacred stone turquoise; then through the south into the Third/Yellow World, symbolized by abalone, with Bluebird, Coyote, and other *yei.* After a huge flood, First Man orders everyone to climb up for safety into the Fourth/White World, symbolized by white shell, where they settle, forming the Four Sacred Mountains from dirt brought from the First World. The Sacred Mountains bound the Dinetah or Diné Bikeyah, the Navajo's Sacred Land, given to the Dineh by Changing Woman, who created the four original Navajo clans from the skin of her bosom. Away from the Dinetah, Borboncito told General Sherman, "whatever we do causes death" (quoted in *Indian Country* 26).

It is the very form of Earth that continues to move with me, that has risen with me, that is standing with me, that indeed remains stationary with me.

—from *The Blessing Way of the Dineh*

Like the Dineh, Tony Hillerman believes "The magic is indeed in the land itself," and "for those of us whose culture grows from the law of Moses instead of the teachings of Changing Woman . . . such harsh inhospitable beauty reminds us that man is not as much master of his planet, or of his destiny, as he likes to think" (*Indian Country* 40). The Dineh geographic metaphor for their life in harmony with nature is the Dinetah, enclosed by the Sacred Mountains: Mt. Blanca in the east, Mt. Taylor in the south, the San Francisco Peaks in the west, and Mt. Hesperus in the north. East is the direction of the dawn, their thinking direction: "We should first think before we do anything." After the sun rises, they look South, the planning direction, then when the sun sets, to the West, the direction of action, and finally to the North, where they evaluate the outcomes of thought and planning, and determine either to remain on that path or to make things better. The cycle repeats each day with a new lesson, since the Dineh believe "early dawn is when you can start a new life again. This is how much Mother Earth and Father Sky love us" (www.crystallinks. com/navajo).

The Dineh's four original clans, "Towering House," "Bitterwater," "Big Water," and "One-Who-Walks-Around," established the pattern of their extended family life; they believe that "only with one's close relatives can one feel safe and only to them can one turn for comfort, aid, and protection" (Downs 112). Today the Dineh recognize nearly 130 clans, identifying one another by the clans of their parents and ancestors. Their society is matrilineal, with men moving into their brides' clans and daughters inheriting property. A child belongs to its mother's clan, being "born for" the clan of its father. Traditionally, marrying or even dating someone from any of a person's four grandparents' clans is usually considered a form of incest.

The Navajo Way centers on harmony, because the Dineh consider everything on earth is alive and sacred. They have no separate word for religion because all life is lived in sacred relationship to the land, as their *Yei*, "Holy People" or spiritual beings who live in the Four Sacred Mountains, taught their ancestors, the "Earth People," centuries ago. To live in harmony, to "walk in beauty," a Navajo develops equally in the four essential values: the values of Life, the values of Work, the values of Social/Human Relations, and the values of Respect/Reverence, each analogous to the four essentials that corn must have to grow: sunlight, water, air, and soil.

To the Dineh, thought is inseparable from speech, and if a person thinks of good things and good fortune, good things will happen; if that person thinks of bad things, bad fortune will occur. When disharmony such as illness strikes, a supernaturally gifted *hataalii* (medicine man) sings songs, creates sacred sand paintings, and conducts ritualistic healing prayer ceremonies, today sometimes in conjunction with modern medical care. Two major "sings" or ceremonies are the Blessing Way to keep the people on the path of happiness and wisdom, and the Enemy Way to help cure an individual who has become ill after going to war and to eliminate ghosts and discourage evil spirits. As the *hataalii* sings, he creates sand paintings with his hands by trickling fine grains from crushed pollen, cornmeal, charcoal from burned trees, and other powdered minerals to depict detailed figures of the Holy Ones. Scores of Dineh healing ceremonies reenact the creation myth; the principal ones last nine days and nine nights, each with its appropriate music and four sand paintings based on mythic stories, while

They walk with beauty.
—from "Navajo People"

lesser rituals require four days and some only one, each with a sand painting. The beginning *hataalii* must study for years with a master to perfect these ceremonies, since "the effectiveness of the performance is based on the skill of the singer, who must know the proper songs in word-for-word perfection, as well as the ritual acts" (Downs 102). The ceremonies sustain the Dineh culture by teaching about the universe and the Navajo's place in it; healing returns the individual to communion with the Holy Ones and the Creator.

AUTHORSHIP

Born in 1925 in Sacred Heart, Oklahoma, population about 60, to parents who farmed and ran a little store, Tony Hillerman grew up during the harsh Dust Bowl years of the Great Depression. Hillerman was proud of his happy childhood, though he had nothing but "a lot of love" (Herbert 94). He recalled, "My mother used to tell us kids when we were whining: Blessed is he who expecteth little. He is seldom disappointed" (OKT Profile 22). Their farm had no tractor, no electricity, no indoor plumbing, not even radio batteries, but Tony loved reading and listening to stories told at his parents' store. Being a storyteller in Sacred Heart "was a good thing to be" (Winks 129), and Hillerman's mother could spin tales with the best, where Hillerman learned "pacing, timing, and the importance of detail," and though "poor in money," like many of today's Native Americans, he became "rich in the tools of a future writer" (*CA Online*). When he attended a Sacred Heart boarding school run by the Sisters of Mercy for Potawatomie Indian girls, though, Hillerman also learned "what it meant to be an outsider"; "the nuns forgave us," he later recalled, "for not being Indians, but they never forgave us for not being girls" (Herbert 86).

As a Roman Catholic "country boy," too, Hillerman was an outsider. "Town kids," mostly fundamentalist Baptists he met when he rode the bus to Konawa High School, seemed unimaginably sophisticated, with their movie theater, their pool hall, their telephones; Hillerman made his first telephone call at the age of 21, back from the war. "Country boys," either German-American like Hillerman and his brother and sister or Native Americans, wore the same kind of overalls and knew all about hard farm work, shooting, and riding horses. The struggle that small farmers of all ethnic backgrounds shared just to survive in rural Oklahoma's exhausted wind-scoured landscape indelibly reinforced the lesson Hillerman's father taught his children: that despite racial differences all people are fundamentally the same.

Hillerman's father died in 1941 when Tony was 16. His brother Barney farmed while Tony tried chemical engineering at Oklahoma A & M, but he lacked the necessary mathematics and had to work three jobs. After Pearl Harbor, Barney enlisted in the Air Force and then Tony joined the U.S. Army, so the Hillermans auctioned off their farm. He spent two years in C Company of the 410th Infantry, becoming one of only eight of their 212 original members who survived the war. After he took part in the D-Day invasion, either a concussion mine or a grenade blew up under him in Alsace, and he spent seven months in the hospital with two broken legs and partial blindness that earned him a Purple Heart, a Bronze Star with Oak Leaf Cluster, and a Silver Star.

While Hillerman was recuperating at home in 1945 trucking oil drilling equipment, he happened on a party of ceremonially clothed Indians on horseback. They were conducting the "Enemy Way" ceremony, ritually cleansing two young Navajo Marines of destructive influences acquired during military service (Reilly 4). "I was given a glimpse," Hillerman later wrote, "of people who had kept their religion and cultural values strong, welcoming home two of their warriors with a ceremony of love and healing. I liked that idea a lot" (Linford xiii). It became one of two cornerstones of his future literary success.

From where threatens the weapon of the white man's ghost, its sorcery, its indispensable power, its parts naturally affected by evil, all of which bother me inside my body, which make me feverish. . . . Far away with its evil power it has gone.

—from *The Enemy Way of the Dineh*

The other cornerstone also surfaced during Hillerman's return to Oklahoma. While in the service he had written lively letters home, and feature writer Beatrice Stahl had done a story about them for *The Daily Oklahoman.*

She encouraged Hillerman to pursue journalism, and he graduated with a BA in that field from the University of Oklahoma in 1946. He married Marie Unzner, a Phi Beta Kappa in bacteriology, in 1948, and over the next 14 years, Hillerman's journalistic career steadily flourished. After a few weeks of writing Purina Pig Chow radio commercials in Oklahoma City, he became a police reporter for the Borger, Texas, *News-Herald,* encountering "every sort of crime and violence mentioned . . . in the Bible and the Glossary of Psychopathy" (Anderson 48). Later he joined the Oklahoma City United Press International bureau, and in 1952, the Hillermans moved to Santa Fe, where in 11 years he rose from political reporting to the executive editorship of the *New Mexican,* the capital city's newspaper.

Dealing only with facts, however, didn't satisfy Tony Hillerman. He later observed,

> Truth has its beauty, but it doesn't bend. In the seventeen years I spent covering crime and violence, politics, and that "deviation from the normal" which journalism defines as news, the longing grew to take a vacation from the hard rock and move into the plastic of fiction. (Quoted in Reilly 5)

The move took him 20 more years. He received his MA from the University of New Mexico

You can have a lot more impact if you go on to college and go into politics.

—Tony Hillerman

*Nothing bristles my hair
more than the damn ruling
class.*
                 —Tony Hillerman

(UNM) in 1966 with a collection of experimental descriptive essays as his thesis displaying just the right amount of detail, a technique he learned from Professor Morris Friedman.

Hillerman then joined the UNM faculty and after only a year was promoted to professor of journalism, chairing the University's Department of Journalism from 1966 to 1973. In 1985, at 60, Hillerman says, he delivered "a lecture so bad even I knew it was boring," so he decided "to quit academia and return to the real world" (*Seldom Disappointed* 250), the world of his Navajoland novels.

Around 12, Hillerman had devoured the works of Australian ethnic mystery novelist Arthur W. Upfield, serialized in the *Saturday Evening Post*. After surviving World War I, Upfield returned to the outback, doing odd jobs like gold mining and fence riding on a sheep station. After meeting Tracker Leon, a part-aborigine who worked for the police, Upfield created "Bony," his mixed-race detective hero Inspector Napoleon Bonaparte, as a bush version of Sherlock Holmes, who uses his traditional aborigine skills and knowledge, uncanny patience, and native sense of time to trap villains. "The white detective lives with modern time pressures, races against them, and becomes discouraged; [but] like a mystical philosopher, Bony sees the moment as the flowering of the seed of eternity, and has a capacity for total absorption" (Murphy 56). Upfield neither patronized nor romanticized the aborigines, even Bony, and made Australia itself the real star of his detective series: like Hillerman's portrayal of the rugged Southwest, Upfield's evocation of "its sometimes cruel beauty and desolation alone makes the novels worth reading" (Murphy 501).

In his introduction to a reprint of Upfield's *A Royal Abduction*, Tony Hillerman couldn't say whether Upfield and his books were consciously in his mind when he began writing his own mysteries, but

> Subconsciously, he certainly was. Upfield had shown me—and a good many other mystery writers—how both ethnography and geography can be used in a plot and how they can enrich an old literary form. When my own Jim Chee . . . unravels a mystery because he understands the ways of his people, when he reads the signs left in the sandy bottom of a reservation arroyo, he is walking in the tracks Bony made fifty years ago. (Quoted in Winks 1031)

Hillerman also credits Upfield with awakening him "to the complementary nature of place and events" (Holt 6–7). Other authors influenced Hillerman, too, especially Eric Ambler, "because he never wrote the same book . . . twice"; Raymond Chandler, "a master of setting scenes which engage all the senses and linger in the mind"; Graham Greene; Ross Macdonald, who "taught every one of us that, given enough skill with metaphorical language, one plot is all you ever need for as many books as you want to write"; George V. Higgins; and Joan Didion for her "superb journalism" (quoted in

Talking Mysteries 27–28). Ray B. Browne also quotes Hillerman to this effect (Browne 1031).

While teaching at UNM, Hillerman developed *The Blessing Way* (1970), creating a new subgenre, the anthropological mystery. He had been informally studying cultural anthropology, the science of man and his works primarily concerned with the origin, development, and varieties of humanity and their cultures, emphasizing data from ancient and primitive peoples and their artifacts, research especially important to the American Southwest and a major motif in Hillerman's novels. Hillerman made Bergen McKee, the co-hero of *The Blessing Way*, a professor of anthropology accidentally involved in Reservation crimes, and both his Navajo policemen Joe Leaphorn and Jim Chee had academic training in anthropology. The widowed Leaphorn's lady friend Dr. Louisa Bourbonette is also a practicing anthropologist. Hillerman's anthropological focus allows him to explore "the intricacies, subtleties, and differences of various Native American cultures— Navajo, Hopi, Zuni, and others—as well as the Spanish and Southwest Anglo cultures" (Browne 1031), though he always insisted "The name of the game is telling stories; no educational digressions allowed" (quoted in Roush, 468).

In his essay "Mystery, Country Boys, and the Big Reservation," Hillerman detailed his slow three-year progress on what eventually became *The Blessing Way*. He really wanted to write a "big" novel based on his experiences as a political reporter, but he thought writing a mystery might be easier (Greenberg 71), so he began with the Navajo ritual he had encountered in 1945, initially making McKee the white hero of the story. He mailed it to an agent who had advised him to write fiction as being more lucrative than essays, but she suggested he "get rid of all that Indian stuff" (Parfit 260). He then sent the manuscript to Joan Kahn at Harper & Row, who liked the "Indian stuff" and agreed to publish it in 1970 with only a few non-Indian-related revisions (Reilly 6). *The Blessing Way* won Hillerman immediate critical acclaim as a finalist for the Mystery Writers of America Best First Novel award and options for screen production and paperback publication. Interestingly, Harper & Row insisted on changing Hillerman's original title, "The Enemy Way," which was the correct title for the Navajo cleansing ceremony that Hillerman had encountered in 1945, to "The Blessing Way," which is the name of a completely different Navajo ritual. Hillerman's first novel contains no Blessing Way ritual at all.

Only two of Hillerman's novels depart from the Native American Southwest world. The "big novel" about politics he originally wanted to write, *The Fly on the Wall*, appeared in 1971, and *Finding Moon*, a mystery about Southeast Asia with another accidental detective, in 1995. Hillerman's other fiction, including two children's books, *The Boy Who Made Dragonfly: A Zuni Myth* (1972) and *Buster Mesquite's Cowboy Band* (1973), as well as most of his nonfiction, celebrates his appreciation of the Southwest and its peoples, who return his affection. According to one Native American activist, members of his tribe give Hillerman's book to their children, to encourage them to love their land. The Navajo gave Hillerman their "Special Friend of the Dineh" Award in 1987.

TONY HILLERMAN'S NAVAJO DETECTIVES

Tony Hillerman takes his time—"Indian time"—developing the characters of Joe Leaphorn and Jim Chee. "Hillerman's fiction moves with the rhythm of Indian attitudes and life," and the reader has to accommodate to it (Browne 1032). Hillerman also shows his readers only a few of Leaphorn's and Chee's physical attributes and tantalizing flashbacks to the ancestral lore each man learned in his youth. Their Dineh souls matter most to Hillerman.

Hillerman usually begins his Navajoland novels by immersing readers in "the exotic background of a Native American ritual" (Greenberg 16) and then shifts his focus to the detective assigned to investigating a crime loosely connected to that ritual, a crime that usually appears to have a supernatural cause. Only through the detective's patient unraveling of clues in "Indian time" and his intimate knowledge of tribal traditions—in which he may fully believe, like young Jim Chee, or doubt, like world-wearier Joe Leaphorn—can the crime, generally the result of human greed, be solved.

Important Navajo Terms

Biligaana: A white man

Bik'eh Hózhó: Speech

Chindi: A ghost, which the Navajo believe can contaminate the living

Dineh: The (Navajo) People; "People of the Surface of the Earth"

Dinetah or Diné Bikeyah: The (Navajo) homeland between the Four Sacred Mountains

Doot kl'izhii: The turquoise, a valuable safeguarding talisman

Ééhózin: Knowledge

Hosteen: "Old Man," a title of respect

Hózhó: To be in harmony with the circumstances that surround you; to walk in Beauty; the central concept in Navajo religious thinking

Hózhóogo nanináa doo: Goodbye; may you walk or go about according to *hózhó*

Hataalii: A singer-medicine man (also *yataalii*)

Sa'ah naagháii: Thought

Yei: Spiritual beings, Holy People, each associated with some element of nature: an animal, a weather feature, vegetation, or a mineral

Note: Spellings of Navajo terms vary, even between Hillerman's novels.

Joe Leaphorn's Background

In Hillerman's first draft of *The Blessing Way*, anthropologist Bergen McKee's "blue policeman" friend Lieutenant Joe Leaphorn of the Navajo Tribal Police, stationed at Window Rock, the Reservation's capital, was originally a very minor character. Hillerman based Leaphorn, whose name he adapted from Mary Renault's mythic Cretan novel *The Bull from the Sea*, on a Hutchinson County Texas sheriff he'd met when he was a green-horn reporter in the violent Texas panhandle. The smart and humane sheriff impressed Hillerman because, as he said, "He knew where the law began and where common sense ended" (*Mystery!* Interview). Hillerman turned the sheriff into a Navajo, but by the time *The Blessing Way* had begun to jell, Hillerman said, he had "kind of fallen in love with the guy," so he "beefed up" his role, realizing "this Leaphorn guy was a much better character than my plot gave him a chance to be," later claiming that "the only worthwhile part [of *The Blessing Way*] was the Navajo Nation and its culture (*Seldom Disappointed* 271). Hillerman made Leaphorn and McKee equally important in the early part of the book, but as many Native Americans observe and Hillerman readily admits, some tribal details in *The Blessing Way* are askew. When he finished the novel he told himself, "I've got to do another book and do the Navajo part right" (quoted in Greenberg 68).

Joe Leaphorn's Career

In *The Blessing Way*, Leaphorn, a middle-aged Slow Talking Dineh, has been married to Emma of the Bitter Water clan for about 30 years. Leaphorn traces his ancestry to the defenders of the sacred land, and his family traditions have shaped his life. His family tree is also "rich in ceremonial people" (Greenberg 188); his grandfather Hosteen Klee and two of his uncles had been *hataalii*, shaman-ritual singers. As an anthropology major at Arizona State University, Leaphorn lost his boyhood belief in Navajo witches, bad medicine men who have paid and labored to learn evil chants enabling them to bring illness and disaster on their enemies. Leaphorn also became comfortable enough with Anglo ways so that he might have settled into white academia, but he joined the tribal police and became a "cultural mediator . . . able to absorb, reconcile, and employ aspects of two vastly different cultures for the benefit of both" (Strenski and Evans 207–208). Over the series, Leaphorn grows older, becomes a widower, gains weight, acquires gray hair and a stiff back, and retires from the tribal police. He suspects nearly everyone's motives, including those of some Navajo, and he turns grouchy in his later years, but he never loses his fine-tuned "Navajo sensitivity to land and landscape" or his Dineh ability to see their beauty. Like the Anglos, especially the FBI agents with whom Leaphorn frequently finds himself in conflict, Leaphorn also recognizes the Navajo homeland as "a sparse stony grassland ruined by overgrazing and now gray with drought" (*Listening Woman* 92).

Though he might like to shake off some Navajo traditions, Leaphorn can't do so completely. In *Dance Hall of the Dead*, Anglo priest Father Ingles asks Leaphorn if he believes in witches. Leaphorn replies, "That's like me asking you if you believe in sin, Father" (262), either mildly reproving the priest for asking him to confront the issue, or simply assuming that since Leaphorn is Navajo, he must believe in witches, the Navajo explanation for the presence of evil in the world. In *Listening Woman*, Leaphorn asserts, "I am one of the Dinee. I know that the same thing that makes a man sick sometimes makes him die" (95), spiritually more than physically. When Leaphorn solves crimes by finding their concrete causes, he is metaphorically discovering a "witch," who then will "die," because his evil powers can be reversed (Witherspoon 40), but sometimes he feels his thinking has become "unNavajo," because "He had been around white men far too long" (*Skinwalkers* 38). He finds life is "changing and there were more . . . souls lost somewhere between the values of the People and the values of the whites"; what the white man sees as desirable progress for the Navajo becomes "a matter of deep social and spiritual distress" (*Blessing Way* 72) that Leaphorn can both witness and experience in himself, but never heal.

Jim Chee's Background

After selling the television rights to the character of Joe Leaphorn and experiencing a Hollywood movie option for *The Dance Hall of the Dead*, Hillerman felt he could not make the "skeptical, sophisticated" Leaphorn fit the concept he was developing for his next novel (Roush, 470), so he introduced Jim Chee, a "country boy" younger than Leaphorn, less sophisticated and more torn between his attraction to white culture and his Dineh spiritual calling. Chee, also of the Slow Talking clan and born for the Bitter Water people, generally seems more appealing than Leaphorn (Browne 1033). Chee earned his anthropology degree from the University of New Mexico and graduated "with distinction" from the FBI Academy in Virginia, but he joined the Navajo Tribal Police at 25 because he yearns to become a *hataalii* like his mother's brother Hosteen Frank Nakai.

Jim Chee's Career

As the sole hero of *People of Darkness* (1980), *The Dark Wind* (1982), and *The Ghostway* (1984), Chee solves Navajo-related crimes in the white world through ties to Navajo traditions that he cannot and will not break. Those ties also eventually lose him his white schoolteacher lover Mary Landon, who wants him to join the FBI and leave the Navajo world for her home state, Wisconsin. In *People of Darkness*, Chee exercises his intense curiosity about everything in the white world, comparing Anglo customs with the Dineh's, especially those involving death and witches, and questioning contradictions between contemporary American society and the Navajo Way. In two short stories written around this time, "The Witch, Yazzie, and the Nine of Clubs" and "Chee's Witch," Chee investigates witchcraft rumors on the Rainbow Plateau while becoming involved in the plot device of switching a protected witness under the FBI's nose. In *The Dark Wind*, Chee again encounters similar supernatural rumors and detects from physical evidence, as Holmes did, but he cannot fathom the Anglo motive of revenge:

> Someone who violated basic rules of behavior and harmed you was, by Navajo definition, "out of control." The "dark wind" had entered into him and destroyed his judgment. . . . But to Chee's Navajo mind, the idea of punishing . . . [him] would be as insane as the original act. (109)

Joe Leaphorn and Jim Chee: Strength from Spirit

After completing *The Ghostway* (1984), Hillerman bought back his rights to Leaphorn and brilliantly paired him with Jim Chee in the rest of his Navajoland novels, beginning with his "breakthrough book," *Skinwalkers* (1986), which won Hillerman a Golden Spur Award from the Western Writers of America. It sold 40,000 hard cover copies and 100,000 paperbacks (Neill 85), and before 1990, Hillerman received a $400,000 advance for his next book (Parfit 94). "The two investigators act as foils to one another: Leaphorn the older, more mature and methodical detective, and Chee the more quixotic, impulsive loner" (*CA Online*). Their views about Navajo tradition collide strikingly about "skinwalkers," the most malignant form of Navajo witch. Though Chee acknowledges Leaphorn is a Very Important Navajo Police Person,

> Everybody knew he [Leaphorn] had no tolerance for witchcraft or anything about it. . . . when he was new on the force in the older days he had guessed wrong about some skinwalker rumors. The other story was that he [felt] . . . belief in skinwalkers had arisen during the tribe's imprisonment at Fort Sumner and had no part in the Navajo culture. (*Skinwalkers* 58)

As an apprentice *hataalii* learning to sing the Blessing Way, Chee "knew that witchcraft in basic form stalked the Dinee . . . he saw it every day he worked as a policeman—in those who sold whiskey to children, in those who bought videocassette recorders while their relatives were hungry, in the knife fights in a Gallup alley, in beaten wives and abandoned children" (*Skinwalkers* 57, 193).

Leaphorn and Chee gradually accept each other's position about their shared native culture. Hillerman's favorite among his books, *A Thief of Time* (1988), which contains a new motif, the influence of the past through the ancient Anasazi culture, propelled Hillerman onto national bestseller lists for the first time and has been translated into 17 languages. It links Leaphorn, now mourning Emma's death and due to retire from the Tribal Police in 10 days, and Chee, becoming involved with tough-as-nails Navajo Legal Aid lawyer Janet Pete, at a revival meeting where a Navajo evangelist denounces white incursions into Dineh holy places: "I can't pray to the mountain no more . . . not after the white man built all over the top of it" (*Seldom Disappointed*, 49), allowing Hillerman to explore "religious values and the varieties of religious belief and expression" (Greenberg 50), the issue that implicitly dominates all of his Navajoland novels.

At the close of *A Thief of Time*, Hillerman modulates the working relationship between Leaphorn and Chee from tension to lasting mutual respect based on Dineh spirituality. Earlier Chee's personality and cultural shaping made him defer to the older detective's authority, even though he knew Leaphorn suspected that Chee's religious sensibilities affected his professional and personal judgment. Chee cannot relinquish his calling, and when Leaphorn decides to remain on the Tribal Police Force, "their professional association becomes spiritual":

> [Leaphorn] had another thought. . . . Why not? "I hear you're a medicine man.
> I heard you are a singer of the Blessing Way. Is that right?"
> Chee looked slightly stubborn. "Yes, sir," he said.
> "I would like to ask you to sing for me," Leaphorn said. (Quoted in Browne 1034)

Leaphorn's and Chee's Shared Nemesis: The Feds

According to Jack Batten, a Canadian journalist, "Not since it was revealed years ago that J. Edgar Hoover had a fancy for dressing himself in women's gowns has anyone done more to smudge the image of the FBI as upright citizens and efficient crimebusters than Tony Hillerman" (Batten D14). In *Seldom Disappointed*, Hillerman declared that his goal was "to make my policemen as real as I could—based on cops I'd known covering law enforcement and the courts." As his books' popularity grew, Hillerman said that his contacts with fans at book-tour tables affected "the attitude of Leaphorn—and particularly Chee—toward the FBI and the Drug Enforcement Agency." Hoping that the anecdotes he heard would "counterbalance the half century of abject hero worship for G-men that the movies (and now TV) have piled upon the taxpayers," Hillerman incorporated them into his detectives' views about U.S. federal policies and the lawmen who are supposed to enforce them (*Seldom Disappointed* 300).

Hillerman admitted that real-life street cops generally see FBI agents as "honest, intelligent, and diligent" policemen backed up by efficient technical support, but they also felt that the same agents are usually clueless in dealing with real crime and handicapped by "a huge, overstaffed, and mindless 'by the books' bureaucracy that injects Washington politics into law enforcement" (*Seldom Disappointed* 301). He also claimed that real policemen tell him, "Man, you haven't scratched the surface" of the "pure politics" of overlapping federal agencies—especially now that Homeland Security has added another thick layer of political patronage for real cops to cope with (Bates 52).

Hillerman made Leaphorn and Chee far savvier about real-life crime than their FBI counterparts, who even today consider Navajo country as a "hardship posting." Leaphorn recalls the 1950s when "Hoover loyalists in Washington exiled unpopular agents to distant New Mexico as a form of punishment" (Batten D14), and Chee and his Tribal Police colleagues refer to "the Federal Bureau of Ineptitude." Hillerman based *Hunting Badger* (1999) on a colossal real-life FBI bungling of a Southwest manhunt, when heavy wheeled-in manpower and equipment produced no arrests at all. In his fictional version, Leaphorn and Chee instead use their native lore to get their men. In *The Sinister Pig* (2003), the Navajo detectives methodically investigate a murder near a Reservation oil patch while the FBI thrashes the brush after Apaches supposedly hunting deer—even though, as Leaphorn and Chee well know, deer aren't in season then. Hillerman concludes that the federally choreographed crimebusting "circuses" brought to the Southwest Indian country are laughable buffoonery at best, destructive meddling at worst, and overall a "Keystone Copish squandering of our tax dollars" (*Seldom Disappointed* 304).

Romantic Interests

Hillerman handles romance realistically, but with dignity and charm, generally incorporating love stories into his novels "with no explicit sex but a sensitive probing of feeling" (Greenberg 13). Leaphorn adored his wife of many years, Emma Yazzie; he often discussed his cases with her and was influenced, Hillerman says, by her advice, while in the early novels her headaches and memory loss frightened them both by hinting at Alzheimer's. In *Skinwalkers*, Emma's sister Agnes comes to take care of her, unnerving Leaphorn because Navajo tradition would insist he take another Yazzie wife if Emma should die. After he tragically loses Emma following surgery for a treatable brain tumor, her presence lives on for a more vulnerable and poignant Leaphorn, but he and American Studies professor Louisa Bourbonette in later novels establish a mutually satisfactory quasi-platonic relationship.

Jim Chee's succession of girlfriends—from the first, Anglo teacher Mary Landon, then "city Navajo" Janet Pete, to Bernadette Manuelito of the Tribal Police—counterpoints his journey toward full acceptance of his Dineh heritage. In *The Ghostway*, Mary urges Chee to mail his FBI application, but when he chooses not to, she dismisses him as "another unambitious Navajo," and their stinging argument, presented in flashbacks, lasts throughout that novel (Greenberg 38). Although Chee keeps a plane ticket to Wisconsin, his thoughts turn to attractive Janet Pete, a lawyer with the Navajo Nation's public defender organization. While Leaphorn struggles with his grief after Emma's death, Chee decides that his world and Mary Landon's will never be compatible. Mary can't understand either the clash between the Anglo attractions of money and prestige and the Navajo Way of cohesion and identity, or the white concept of identity as "what they had done as individuals" versus "the Navajo knowledge of his place in the interlocking bonds of family and clan" (Erisman 27). Chee finds he cannot tell an elderly relative that he is going to join the FBI and leave The People and give up his idea of being a *hataalii* like his uncle. "He didn't want to see the sadness in that good man's face" (*Ghostway* 182), so his feelings for Mary are doomed.

Chee's interest in Janet Pete grows throughout *Talking God* (1989), but her lack of interest in her Navajo roots bothers him, and he denies she is his girlfriend. In *Sacred Clowns* (1993), Chee tries to establish whether his relationship with Janet might violate the elaborate Navajo incest taboos, since she doesn't even know her father's clans, but eventually Janet's ambition and Chee's desire to become a *hataalii* clash irrevocably. Intrepid and attractive Officer Bernadette Manuelito, born to the Bead People, however, proves the charm for them both. Eventually she becomes a Customs Patrol Officer and she and Chee marry, leaving Leaphorn to struggle in *The Shape Shifter* (2006) with a cold case that has bothered him for years.

THE ENDURING APPEAL OF TONY HILLERMAN'S NAVAJOLAND NOVELS

Hillerman's Navajoland novels present the eternal appeal of the underdog, a constant of Western culture since that old master storyteller Homer immortalized doomed Hector, a good man defending his family and home against implacable fate in the *Iliad*. As Hillerman himself puts it, he felt at home with the Navajo because "hardscrabble rural folks, Indians and whites . . . folks I grew up with," were in the same category, contrasted with "urban folks who had money" (*Seldom Disappointed* 251). "Hillerman doesn't just understand this kind of tension, he has lived it" (Parfit 93). To experience exotica," Hillerman noted, "I attended a College of Arts and Science faculty meeting" (*Seldom Disappointed* 251). Hillerman admits to a "self-made man syndrome," describing how on university search committees he favored "the graduate of North Dakota State," over Ivy Leaguers who had "a huge head start" with "family, money, the good-old-boy networks plus the inherent snobbishness of academia" (*Seldom Disappointed* 308).

Selected Native American Fictional Sleuths and Their Authors

Part-Navajo State Trooper Sam Watchman (Brian Garfield)
Modoc FBI Special Agent Anna Turnipseed (Kirk Mitchell)
Navajo Special Investigator Ella Clah (Aimee and David Thurlo)
Half-vampire Navajo lawman Lee Nez (Aimee and David Thurlo)
Arapaho Vicky Holden (Margaret Coel)
Part-Blackfoot paleoartist Ansel Phoenix (Christine Gentry)
Part-Ojibwa detective Cork O'Connor (William Kent Krueger)
Part-Seneca Jane Whitefield (Thomas Perry)

As Native Americans, Joe Leaphorn and Jim Chee represent one of the most "underdog" subcultures in the United States. Like other tribes, the Navajo have inherited a long warrior tradition and memories of tragic removal from their land, even economically motivated near-genocide. During their imprisonment at Fort Sumner, unscrupulous white contractors often loaded up flour sacks with "bits of slate, broken bread and something that resembled plaster of paris," so that many Dineh died of dysentery (Iverson 59). The unique Dineh religious sensibility, however, sustained them with rituals that promoted harmony and balance among the people, like a poignant account recorded by Mose Denejolie: at Fort Sumner, the Navajo leader Borboncito performed the *Ma'ii Bizéé'nast'áán* ("Put Bead in Coyote's Mouth") ceremony. A captured coyote was faced east, Borboncito put a specially prepared white shell into its mouth and freed the animal—which timidly then walked west. Borboncito concluded, "'There it is, we'll be set free.' Four days later, they learned they would be able to go home" (cited in Iverson 60).

Many of today's Navajo, like Leaphorn and Chee, live in two worlds, the Dineh world that insists on harmony and the ethnocentric Anglo world that so often preys on it. Hillerman's novels translate "Navajo values into attitudes and motives Anglos and Navajos can both understand . . . bridg[ing] cultural sensibilities and grappl[ing] with the darker side of human experience" (Bencivenga 13). Finishing *Sacred Clowns* after a bout with cancer in 1993, Hillerman declared that he shared the Dineh belief that "each human has this special relationship with God who will take care of meting rewards and punishment" (*Seldom Disappointed* 327).

Because Hillerman recognized "the universal ignorance on the part of the great American public of Indian religions, tribal value systems, all things foreign to our dominant system" (Hillerman's Foreword to Linford), he intended his Navajoland novels to be "the ideal way to teach the cultures and life values of a people" (Browne 1031) in sentences "as lucid, yet subtle, as sunlight in the high desert" (Bencivenga 13). Hillerman's principles are unabashedly traditional; he believes his novels are popular because they don't contain "gratuitous violence or sex scenes." He remarked in 1989, "I have a feeling a lot of librarians are like I am and are sick and tired of that stuff. They recognize it's as easy as hell to write that way, to expand a chapter by having someone get their hand caught in a meat grinder" (quoted in Quirk 108)—or, as a reader remarked about one of Hillerman's novels, "My God, he's moving toward eroticism: he's got them shaking hands" (quoted in Parfit 95).

Hillerman's work thus exhibits two facets of "the tension between the desire to assimilate and the need to retain native traditions" (*CA Online*) through Leaphorn's gradual re-acceptance of his Navajo heritage and Chee's interior struggle to balance his *hataalii* vocation with his police work. They illustrate Hillerman's overarching theme: identity can be maintained only by achieving spiritual harmony with an environment that often hides its beauty under an unforgiving exterior that can only be penetrated by human humility, dedication to principle, and shared joys and sorrow.

The cases of Tony Hillerman's Navajo detectives Joe Leaphorn and Jim Chee provide a world of interesting characters, beautiful landscapes, and a people who see things in different terms than Anglo-Americans do. Hillerman's honestly presented perseverant theme, however, transcends even the powerful Southwestern landscape that many readers feel dominates Hillerman's fiction.

> Leaphorn and Chee, as Navajos, give readers a sense of the demands of Southwestern life. In a larger sense, though, that they are Navajo is incidental; "they are human as well as Navajo, and as they . . . grapple with the realities of their people, their place, and their time, their responsibilities help all readers to decipher the palimpsest of human life in all its complexity and all its majesty." (Erisman 48)

ADAPTATIONS

Audio Versions

In 1989, Tony Hillerman's Navajoland novels began to be transposed into other media when Harper & Row released *Talking God* simultaneously with an author-narrated version by Caedmon. "I'd rather they read the book," Hillerman commented, "but let's face it, a lot of people fill up those empty miles by listening to a tape on the car radio" (quoted in Quirk 108). He felt that taping *Talking God* kept his writing honest, even though he had to admit that the condensation of his novel "was humiliating in one sense" because after cuts totalling 40 percent of the original text he found it just as good as his original.

Telefilms

In his autobiography *Seldom Disappointed,* Tony Hillerman wryly described one "classical stupidity" when he was disappointed—his initial contact with the film industry, which he felt assumed "A handful of city yuppies are worth half the elderly farmers in Iowa to the [television] marketing people." Optioned to write the script of *Dance Hall of the Dead* for a television production company, Hillerman went on "an adventure in tinsel town." At a posh lunch, he received the producer's successive requests to change to an "upbeat ending"; to change Leaphorn's Navajo Tribal Police affiliation to "some ambiguous agency"; to provide "a shapely blue-eyed blonde" heroine and a Gabby Hayes comic relief; to give the film an urban rather than the Southwest setting; and finally "a very traditional, unwise-in-white-ways assistant for Leaphorn, whom the audience and I [Hillerman] "will think of as Tonto." After the project evaporated Hillerman learned to his dismay that the producer, by mailing him his final renewal check, had bought the television rights to Joe Leaphorn, and years later, when Robert Redford decided to option the Leaphorn-Chee novels, Hillerman had to ransom Leaphorn for $20,000.

Dealing with actor-filmmaker Robert Redford proved different. In 1989 Redford attempted a low-budget three-film Hillerman series starting with *The Dark Wind*, with as many Native American actors as possible to accurately portray tribal culture, but financial problems and Reservation factionalism delayed the film until 2000, when it appeared with Lou Diamond Phillips as Jim Chee and Fred Ward as Joe Leaphorn. Hillerman, who had not worked on the script, had found its plot "too complicated, twisted, and convoluted" and suggested cuts, but not enough were made. *The Dark Wind* was not released in the United States, but it received reasonably good reviews in France and England.

Hillerman was better pleased with Redford's next efforts to bring Navajoland to the small screen, which Redford called "a passion [sic] project of mine for 14 years. . . . The chance to elevate the issues surrounding our Native American culture, and to do it through the vehicle of solid entertainment is our hope and purpose" (quoted in "Holmes on the Range"). Redford had bought the rights to *Skinwalkers* and *Coyote Waits* and his son Jamie had written the *Skinwalkers* script, but he had a hard time financing a movie about Indian culture. PBS's president Pat Mitchell, who had worked with Redford on an earlier Native American documentary, and Rebecca Eaton, executive producer of the PBS *Mystery!* series, approached Redford to use *Skinwalkers* as a pilot for a possible ongoing series within *Mystery!* With Cheyenne-Arapaho director Chris Eyre whom Redford knew through Redford's Sundance program that cultivates Native American filmmakers, and Native Americans Adam Beach as Chee and Wes Studi as Leaphorn, the film went into production outside Phoenix as *Mystery!*'s first made-in-America feature.

Hillerman liked this television adaptation's economy and resourcefulness. The script changed Leaphorn to "a grouchy urban cop who has lost touch with his Navajo roots and returns to the Reservation with his ailing wife." Studi commented that

Leaphorn is a figure that a lot of people can identify with—Indian and non-Indian—in terms of having left behind the world he grew up in to pursue interests in the urban world . . . he begins to see how much his roots, his culture, have to do with who he's come to be . . . a presence of mind that is not necessarily a hoot-before-you-think kind of thing. ("Native Arts")

Chris Eyre, who had been adopted into a white family, put his knowledge of both worlds into the film, declaring "I don't romanticize Indians," and avoiding stereotypical situations and performances ("Native Arts"). *Coyote Waits* and *A Thief of Time* appeared on *Mystery!* in 2003 and 2004, respectively, with different scriptwriters but again starring Studi and Beach. The critical consensus on the *Mystery!* Navajoland films (*Jim Chee and Joe Leaphorn Mysteries*) was that rather than faithful versions of their original novels, the PBS movies offered new and very good Chee/Leaphorn mysteries.

PARALLEL CHRONOLOGY

Major Events Related to Tony Hillerman	World Events
	ca. 11,200 BCE Navajo ancestors migrate from Siberia to western Canada
	ca. 1000 BCE Maize and squash arrive in Southwest from Mexico
	ca. 200 BCE Beans arrive from Mexico
	ca. 700 CE Ancient Puebloans spread through Southwest (cliff-dwelling ancestors of the Hopi)
	1050–1125 Height of Puebloan culture
	1000–1400s Navajo migrate southward to "Four Corners" (Utah, Colorado, Arizona, New Mexico)
	Late 1200s Navajo displace native Anasazi culture, raid neighboring Hohokam tribe
	Oct. 12, 1492 Columbus lands in the Bahamas
	Early 1500s Navajo and Apache appear substantially in Southwest as nomadic hunters
	1522 Magellan circumnavigates the World
	1535 Cortez reaches Baja California
	1540 Coronado attacks Pueblo peoples; returns to Mexico in 1542

Major Events Related to Tony Hillerman	World Events
	1565 Spanish establish first colony in N. America—St. Augustine, Florida
	1598 Juan de Oñate colonizes New Mexico for Spain
	ca. 1600 Horses introduced to Southwest by Spanish
	Early 1600s Beginning of Spanish missions among Navajo; Navajo and Apache use horses for raids
	1607 English found Jamestown, VA
	ca. 1609 Contact with Spaniards; trade with Pueblo peoples
	1610 Santa Fe founded as capital of New Mexico
	1620s Spanish first use term "Apachu de Nabajo"
	1620 *Mayflower* reaches Cape Cod
	1680 Navajo, Pueblos, and Apache unite to drive Spanish out of New Mexico in Pueblo Revolt
	1683 Spanish retake Santa Fe
	1700s Navajo weavers create intricate blankets
	ca. 1750 Navajo settle around Canyon de Chelly (N.W. Arizona), growing crops and raising sheep
	1775 Outbreak of the Revolutionary War
	1776 The Declaration of Independence
	1780s Spanish send military expeditions against the Navajo
	1788 U.S. Constitution ratified
	1803 Louisiana Purchase
	1821 Spain accepts Mexican independence
	1836 Texas declares independence from Mexico
	1845 Texas joins United States
	1846 American General Stephen Kearny invades Santa Fe
	1846–1848 U.S.-Mexican War and claims New Mexico for the U.S.
	1848 Americans claim Navajo land; Navajo Wars begin; Mexico cedes California, most of New Mexico and Arizona, plus much of Utah and Nevada to the U.S.; gold discovered in California

(Continued)

Major Events Related to Tony Hillerman	World Events
	1858 First Overland Mail stagecoach, St. Louis to San Francisco
	1859 Discovery of silver in Nevada's Comstock Lode and gold at Pike's Peak triggers increased westward migration
	1860s Americans build Fort Defiance near Window Rock, AZ; slaughter Navajo and their sheep
	1861–1865 The Civil War
	1861 Outbreak of the Apache War under Cochise
	July 20, 1863 General Kit Carson receives Navajo surrender
	Spring 1864 The "Long Walk" to Fort Sumner (Bosque Redondo); forced confinement there; Navajo learn silversmithing
	1866 Sioux under Crazy Horse massacre U.S. cavalry in Wyoming
	1868 Navajo allowed by treaty to return to Four Corners homeland and form their own nation of Cheyenne women and children
	1868 George Custer allows massacre
	1869 Completion of the transcontinental railroad; Manifest Destiny appears unstoppable
	1869–1915 Navajo reservation increases from initial 3.5 million acres to current 16 million acres; economic conflicts with non-Navajos; U.S. government enacts "Navajo Livestock Reduction"
	1873 First barbed wire demonstrated to Texas cattlemen
	1873 Custer's survey party finds gold in the Black Hills of Dakota
	1876 Custer defeated at the Little Big Horn; Chiricahua Reservation (Apache) abolished; their leader Geronimo battles U.S.; U.S. tries to eliminate Indian way of life
	1881 Gunfight at the OK Corral, Tombstone, AZ

Major Events Related to Tony Hillerman	World Events
	1883 Nearly all buffalo wiped out by that year
	1886 Geronimo and followers surrender; Statue of Liberty inaugurated in New York harbor
	1889 Congress forces Creek and Seminole to renounce $4.19 million land claim
	1890 The Ghost Dance; massacre of Sioux at Wounded Knee; last of Indian resistance
	1900 By that year, Navajo population doubled; silversmithing, weaving, and trade major economic factors
	1901 U.S. oil boom begins at Spindletop, Texas
	1912 New Mexico and Arizona admitted to statehood
	1914–1918 World War I
	1924 The American Indian Citizenship Act gives Native Americans the right to vote
May 27, 1925 Tony Hillerman born in Sacred Heart, OK	
	1929 The U.S. Stock Market Crash
1938 Hillerman attends St. Mary's Academy	
1939–1942 Hillerman rides bus to Konawa High School	**1930–1939** The Great Depression
1941 Hillerman's father dies after long illness	**1941–1945** Navajo "code talkers" serve the U.S. in World War II
1942 Hillerman enrolls at Oklahoma A & M College; works at several menial jobs; his brother joins the U.S. Army and goes back to farming	
1943 Hillerman enlists in U.S. Army (Infantry); gains PFC rank; awarded Silver Star and Bronze Star with Oak Leaf Cluster	
1945 Hillerman seriously wounded; receives Purple Heart; makes first telephone call	
1946–1948 While furloughed for convalescence Hillerman observes a healing ceremony for Navajo Marines;	

(Continued)

Major Events Related to Tony Hillerman	World Events
1946–1948 Hillerman receives BA from Univ. of Oklahoma; marries Marie Unzner	
1948–1962 Hillerman works as journalist and editor in Texas, Oklahoma, New Mexico; he and Marie have one child and adopt five more	
1963 Hillerman enrolls at the Univ. of New Mexico	
1966 Hillerman receives MA from Univ. of New Mexico	
1966–1987 Hillerman teaches journalism at Univ. of New Mexico; begins writing fiction in the late 1960s	
1970 *The Blessing Way*, Hillerman's first novel, published	
	1973 American Indian Movement begins members occupation of Wounded Knee, SD; ends on May 8 in shoot-out with FBI and Federal marshals
	1980s Navajo dispute over "shared lands" with Hopi; U.S. govt. attempts relocation of Navajo people in Navajo/Hopi Joint Use Area
1988 Hillerman named "Special Friend of the Dineh" by the Navajo Nation	**1988** Indian Gaming Regulatory Act legalizes gambling on Indian reservations
1991 Hillerman receives Grand Master Award, Mystery Writers of America	
Oct. 28, 2008 Tony Hillerman dies	

WORKS OF TONY HILLERMAN

Mystery Novels

The Joe Leaphorn Novels, published together as *The Joe Leaphorn Mysteries*. New York: Harper, 1989

The Blessing Way. New York: Harper, 1970

Dance Hall of the Dead. New York: Harper, 1973; rpt. 2003

Listening Woman. New York: Harper, 1978

The Jim Chee Novels published together as *The Jim Chee Mysteries* (1992)

People of Darkness. New York: Harper, 1980

The Dark Wind. New York: Harper, 1982

The Ghostway. New York: Harper, 1984

The Leaphorn and Chee Novels, published severally as:

Leaphorn and Chee: Three Classic Mysteries Featuring Lt. Joe Leaphorn and Officer Jim Chee. New York: Harper, 1992

The Leaphorn and Chee Novels. New York: HarperCollins, 2005

Leaphorn, Chee and More. New York: HarperCollins, 2005

Skinwalkers. New York: Harper, 1987

A Thief of Time. New York: Harper, 1988; New York: ImPress, 2005

Talking God. New York: Harper, 1989

Coyote Waits. New York: Harper, 1990

Sacred Clowns. New York: HarperCollins, 1993

Fallen Man. New York: HarperCollins, 1996

The First Eagle. New York: HarperCollins, 1998

Hunting Badger. New York: HarperCollins, 1999

The Wailing Wind. New York: HarperCollins, 2002

The Sinister Pig. New York: HarperCollins, 2003

Skeleton Man. New York: HarperCollins, 2004

The Shape Shifter. New York: HarperCollins, 2006

Detective Short Stories

"Chee's Witch." *The New Black Mask* 7 (1986); rpt. in *The Tony Hillerman Companion,* 366–375.

"First Lead Gasser." *Ellery Queen's Mystery Magazine,* April 1993; rpt. in *The Tony Hillerman Companion,* 355–365.

"The Witch, Yazzie, and the Nine of Clubs." *Crime Wave.* London: Collins, 1981, rpt. in *The Tony Hillerman Companion,* 341–354.

Other Works Related to the Southwest

The Great Taos Bank Robbery and Other Indian Country Affairs. Albuquerque, NM: University of New Mexico Press, 1973.

Hillerman Country: A Journey through the Southwest with Tony Hillerman. New York: HarperCollins, 1991

Indian Country: America's Sacred Land. Flagstaff, AZ: Northland Press, 1987

"Making Mysteries with Navajo Materials." *Literature and Anthropology.* Ed. Philip Dennis and Wendell Aycock. Lubbock: Texas Tech University Press, 1989, 5–13

"Mystery, Country Boys, and the Big Reservation." *Colloquium on Crime: Eleven Renowned Mystery Writers Discuss Their Work.* Ed. Robin W. Winks. New York: Scribner's, 1986, 127–147.

New Mexico. Portland, OR: C.H. Belding, 1974.

New Mexico, Rio Grande, and Other Essays. Portland, OR: Graphic Arts Center Press, 1992.

Rio Grande. Portland, OR: C.H. Belding, 1975.

Talking Mysteries: A Conversation with Tony Hillerman. With Ernie Bulow. Albuquerque, NM: University of New Mexico Press, 1991 (originally published by Bulow as *Words, Weather, and Wolfman: Conversations with Tony Hillerman*).

Other Fiction

The Fly on the Wall. New York: Harper, 1971. Novel.

Finding Moon. New York: HarperCollins, 1995. Novel. (With others) *The Perfect Murder: Five Great Mystery Writers Create the Perfect Crime.* New York: Harper Prism, 1991.

Children's Books

The Boy Who Made Dragonfly: A Zuni Myth Retold by Tony Hillerman. Albuquerque: University of New Mexico Press, 1972.

Buster Mesquite's Cowboy Band. Albuquerque, NM: University of New Mexico Press, 1973.

As Editor

The Best American Mystery Stories of the Century. Boston: Houghton Mifflin, 2000.

Best of the West: An Anthology of Classic Writing from the American West. New York: HarperCollins, 1991.

The Mysterious West. New York: HarperCollins, 1994.

With Rosemary Herbert:

The Oxford Book of American Detective Stories. New York: Oxford University Press, 1996.

A New Omnibus of Crime. New York: Oxford University Press, 2005.

The Spell of New Mexico. Albuquerque, NM: University of New Mexico Press, 1976.

Autobiography

Seldom Disappointed: A Memoir. New York: HarperCollins, 2001.

Other

Kilroy Was There: A GI's War in Photographs, photographs by Frank Kessler. Kent, OH: Kent State University Press, 2004.

Tony Hillerman has written introductions and forewords to books, including Erna Fergusson's *Dancing Gods: Indian Ceremonials of New Mexico and Arizona;* Ernie Bulow's *Navajo Taboos;* and *Robbers, Rogues and Ruffians: True Tales of the Wild West,* ed. Howard Beyan. He has also contributed to books, notably *Crime Lovers Casebook,* ed. Jerome Charyn (New York: Signet, 1996), and to many periodicals, including *New Mexico Quarterly, National Geographic,* and *Reader's Digest.*

Media Adaptations

Audio versions

Talking God, with Hillerman as narrator, was produced by Caedmon. *The Ghostway* and *People of Darkness,* narrated by George Guidall, were produced by Recorded Books in 1991.

Telefilms

The Dark Wind. 1991. Executive producer, Robert Redford; non-Native Americans Lou Diamond Phillips as Jim Chee and Fred Ward as Joe Leaphorn.

Skinwalkers. 2002; PBS, *Mystery!* First made-in-America *Mystery!* selection; Robert Redford, executive producer; Jamie Redford, writer; Chris Eyre, director; starring Native Americans Wes Studi as Joe Leaphorn and Adam Beach as Jim Chee.

A Thief of Time. 2004; PBS, *Mystery!* (DVD) (Personnel as above, except for Alice Arlen as writer).

Coyote Waits. American Mystery (DVD) (Personnel as above, except with Lucky Gold as writer and Jan Egleson as writer.)

The Silence of Cricket Coogler. Historical documentary by lafilm (production company of the Los Angeles Film School); Hillerman provided commentary. Charlie Cullin, director.

WORKS CITED

Anderson, Marc Duane. "Hillerman Reflects on the Long, Hard Road to Success." *The Writer* 115 (February 2002): 48.

Bates, Judy. "Politics and the Reservation" (interview with Tony Hillerman). *Publishers Weekly* 250 (April 14, 2003): 52.

Batten, Jack. "Hillerman Stumbles." *The Toronto Star* (August 24, 2003): D14.

Bencivenga, Jim. "This Author Seeks Healing Where World Views Collide." *Christian Science Monitor* 89 (July 31, 1997): B3.

Browne, Ray B. "The Ethnic Detective." In *Mystery and Suspense Writers,* edited by Robin W. Winks. New York: Charles Scribner's Sons, 1998.

Bulow, Ernie, and Tony Hillerman. *Talking Mysteries: A Conversation with Tony Hillerman.* Albuquerque: University of New Mexico Press, 1991. Cited as *Talking Mysteries.*

Downs, James F. *The Navajo.* New York: Holt, Rinehart and Winston, 1972.

Erisman, Fred. *Tony Hillerman.* Boise, ID: Boise State University, 1989.

Freese, Peter. *The Ethnic Detective: Chester Himes, Harry Kemelman, Tony Hillerman.* Essen: Verlag Die Blaue Eule, 1992.

Greenberg, Martin. *The Tony Hillerman Companion: A Comprehensive Guide to His Life and Work.* New York: HarperCollins, 1994.

Heffern, Rich. "Spirit in a World of Connection." *National Catholic Reporter,* May 2, 2003: 13.

Herbert, Rosemary. *Whodunit? A Who's Who in Crime and Mystery Writing.* New York: Oxford University Press, 1999.

Hillerman, Tony. *Indian Country: America's Sacred Land.* Flagstaff, AZ: Northland Press, 1987. Cited as *Indian Country.*

"Holmes on the Range: Navajo Police Join PBS' 'Mystery.'" *Daily News* (New York), Feb. 22, 2003.

Holt, Patricia. "PW Interviews Tony Hillerman." *Publishers Weekly* 218 (October 24, 1980): 6–7.

"Interview [2002] with Tony Hillerman." *Mystery!* http://www.pbs.org/wgbh/mystery/american/navajoland/hillerman, accessed 10/14/2007.

Iverson, Peter. *Diné: A History of the Navahos.* Albuquerque: University of New Mexico Press, 2002.

Linford, Laurance D. *Tony Hillerman's Navajoland.* Salt Lake City: University of Utah Press, 2001.

Murphy, Bruce F. *The Encyclopedia of Murder and Mystery.* New York: St. Martin's Press, 1999.

"Native Arts." http://www.aaanativearts.com/article553.html/, accessed 10/14/2007.

"Navajo." http://www.crystallinks.com/navajo.html, accessed 10/14/2007.

"Navajo People." http://library.thinkquest.org/J0020731/thinkquest/Navajo_people.htm, accessed 10/14/2007.

Neill, Michael. "A Keen Observer in a World Not His Own." *People,* July 18, 1988: 85.

"The OKT Profile: Tony Hillerman." *Oklahoma Today* 51 (November/December 2001): 22.

Parfit, Michael. "I Think You Should Take Out the Indian Stuff." *Smithsonian,* December 1990: 92–105.

Quirk, Thomas. "Justice on the Reservation." *The Armchair Detective* 18 (Fall 1985): 364–370.

Reilly, John M. *Tony Hillerman: A Critical Companion.* Westport, CT: Greenwood Press, 1996.

Roush, Jan. "Tony Hillerman," in *Updating the American West.* Fort Worth: Texas Christian University Press, 1997, 468–474.

Strenski, Ellen, and Robley Evans. "Ritual and Murder in Tony Hillerman's Indian Detective Novels." *Western American Literature* 16 (Fall 1981): 205–216.

"Tony Hillerman." *Contemporary Authors Online.* http://web2.infotrac.galegroup.com.

"Tony Hillerman's Jim Chee and Joe Leaphorn Mysteries." http://www.dancing badger.com/tony_hillerman.htm, accessed 10/14/2007.

Winks, Robin. *Colloquium on Crime: Eleven Renowned Mystery Writers Discuss Their Work.* New York: Charles Scribner's Sons, 1986.

Witherspoon, Gary. *Language and Art in the Navajo Universe.* Ann Arbor: University of Michigan Press, 1977.

FURTHER READING

"American Thief." http://www.pbs.org/whbh/mystery/american/thief/ntof2.html, accessed 10/14/2007.

"Anthropological Thrillers." *The Economist* (London), August 14, 1993: 83.

Bailey, L.R. *The Long Walk: A History of the Navajo Wars, 1846–1868.* 1964.

Bakerman, Jane S. "Cutting Both Ways: Race, Prejudice, and Motive in Tony Hillerman's Detective Fiction." *MELUS* 11 (Fall 1984): 17–28.

———. "Joe Leaphorn and the Navajo Way: Tony Hillerman's Indian Detective Fiction." *Clues* 2 (Spring/Summer 1981): 9–16.

———. "Tony Hillerman's Joe Leaphorn and Jim Chee." *Cops and Constables,* ed. Earl Bargainnier and George N. Dove. Bowling Green, OH: Popular Press, 1986.

Bernell, Sue, and Michaela Karni. "Tony Hillerman." In *This Is about Vision: Interviews with Southwestern Writers,* edited by William Balassi, John F. Crawford, and Annie O. Eysturoy. Albuquerque: University of New Mexico Press, 1990.

Breen, Jon L. "Interview with Tony Hillerman." In *The Tony Hillerman Companion,* edited by Martin Greenberg Jr. New York: HarperCollins, 1994: 65–90.

Breslin, Catherine. "PW Interviews Tony Hillerman." *Publishers Weekly* 223 (June 10, 1988): 57–58.

Chapman, G. Clarke. "Crime and Blessing in Tony Hillerman's Fiction." *Christian Century* 108 (November 13, 1991): 1063–1065.

———. "Tony Hillerman's Fiction: Crime and Common Grace." *Christianity and Literature* 48 (Summer 1999): 473–486.

Cleveland, Carol. "Tony Hillerman." In *Twentieth Century Crime and Mystery Writers,* 2nd ed., edited by John M. Reilly. New York: St. Martin's Press, 1985.

Doerry, Karl W. "Literary Conquests: The Southwest as a Literary Emblem." *Journal of the Southwest* 32 (Winter 1990): 438–450.

Donaldson, John K. "Native American Sleuths." In *Telling the Stories,* edited by Elizabeth Hoffman Nelson. New York: Peter Lang, 2001.

Engel, Leonard. "Landscape and Place in Tony Hillerman's Mysteries." *Western American Literature* 28 (Summer 1993): 111–132.

Erisman, Fred. "Tony Hillerman's Jim Chee and the Shaman's Dilemma." *Lamar Journal of the Humanities* 17 (Spring 1992): 5–16.

———. "Tony Hillerman's Southwest." *The Roundup Quarterly.* Summer 1989: 9–18.

Fitz, Brewster E. "Ethnocentric Guilt in Tony Hillerman's *Dance Hall of the Dead.*" *MELUS* 22 (Summer 1997): 91–204.

Forbes, Jack D. *Apache, Navajo and Spaniard.* Norman: University of Oklahoma Press, 1960.

Fredrikson, Karl G., and Lilian Fredrikson. "Tony Hillerman." *Twentieth Century Crime and Mystery Writers,* 2nd ed., edited by John M. Reilly. New York: St. Martin's Press, 1985: 519–520.

Gaugenmaier, Judith. "The Mysteries of Tony Hillerman. *The American West* 26 (December 1989): 46, 56–58.

Goeller, Allison D. "The Mystery of Identity: The Private Eye in the Detective Fiction of Walter Mosley and Tony Hillerman." In *Sleuthing Ethnicity,* edited by Dorothea Fischer-Hornung and Monica Mueller. Madison, NJ: Fairleigh Dickinson U. Press, 2003.

Gold, Peter. *Navajo & Tibetan Sacred Wisdom: The Circle of the Spirit.* Rochester, VT: Inner Traditions International, 1994.

Grape, Jan. "Tony Hillerman." In *Speaking of Murder,* edited by Ed Gorman and Martin H. Greenberg. New York: Berkley Prime Crime, 1998.

Herbert, Rosemary. "Tony Hillerman." *The Fatal Art of Entertainment.* New York: G.K. Hall, 1994: 85–111.

Hieb, Louis A. *Tony Hillerman: From the Blessing Way to Talking God: A Bibliography.* Tucson, AZ: Press of the Gigantic Hound, 1990.

Hirshey, Gerri. "Murder, Mayhem, and Mythology." *GQ (Gentlemen's Quarterly),* September 1993: 133, 136–140.

Keveney, Bill. "'Skinwalkers' Follows Trail of Unusual Killer." *USA Today,* November 22, 2002; "Life," 11e.

Kluckholm, Clyde, and Dorothea Leighton. *The Navajo.* Cambridge, UK: Cambridge University Press, 1946.

Knepper, Paul, and Michael B. Puckett. "The Historicity of Tony Hillerman's Indian Police." *Journal of the West* 34 (January 1995): 13–18.

Krumrey, Diane. "Subverting the Tonto Stereotype in Popular Fiction." In *Simulacrum America,* edited by Elizabeth Kraus and Carolin Auer. Rochester, NY: Camden House, 2000.

Langewiesche, William. "Sense of Place." *Atlantic Monthly,* January 9, 1999: 36.

McNitt, Frank. *Navajo Wars.* Albuquerque: University of New Mexico Press, 1972.

Mystery! Interview with Tony Hillerman, http://www.pbs.org/wgbh/mystery/american/navajoland/hillermanintv.html, accessed 10/14/2007.

Neary, John. "Dilettantes in the Game of Life." *Archaeology* (March/April 1995): 58–62.

Nolan, Tom. "Hillerman Country." *Mystery Scene* 87 (2004): 14–17.

O'Sullivan, Maurice J. "Tony Hillerman and the Navajo Way." In *Bad Boys and Bad Girls in the Badlands,* edited by Steve Glassman and Maurice J. O'Sullivan. Bowling Green, KY: Bowling Green State U. Popular Press, 2002.

Parker, Betty, and Riley Parker. "Hillerman Country." *Armchair Detective* 20 (Winter 1987): 4–14.

Pierson, James C. "Mystery Literature and Ethnography: Fictional Detectives as Anthropologists." In *Literature and Anthropology,* edited by Philip A. Dennis and Wendell Aycock. Lubbock, TX: Texas Tech University Press, 1989.

Plog, Stephen. *Ancient Peoples of the American Southwest.* London: Thames and London Ltd., 1997.

Ross, Dale H., and Charles L.P. Silet. "Interview with Tony Hillerman." *Clues* 10 (Fall/Winter 1989): 119–135.

Roush, Jan. "The Developing Art of Tony Hillerman." *Western American Literature* 28 (Summer 1993): 99–110.

Schneider, Jack W. "Crime and Navajo Punishment: Tony Hillerman's Novels of Detection." *Southwest Review* 67 (Spring 1982): 151–160.

Schuit, Kathy Louise, and Wayne Rowan. "Leaphorn's Blessing." *New Mexico Business Journal* 30 (June 2006): 8–9.

Schwartz, Benjamin. "Senses of Place." *Atlantic Monthly,* January 1999: 36–40.

Sobol, John. *Tony Hillerman: A Public Life.* Toronto: ECW Press, 1994.

Stasio, Marilyn. "What's Happened to Heroes Is a Crime." *New York Times Book Review,* October 14, 1990: 1.

Tapply, William G. "Mystery Writing: Pick a Good Setting and Bring It to Life." *Writer* 120 (January 2007): 13.

Taylor, Bruce. "Interview with Tony Hillerman." *Armchair Detective* 14 (Winter 1981): 93–95.

"Tony Hillerman Illuminates a Mystery: Himself." *Fort Worth Star-Telegram,* October 31, 2001.

Van Deventer, M.J. "Tony Hillerman's West." *Persimmon Hill* 21 (Summer 1993): 36–43.

Ward, Alan. "Navajo Cops on the Case." *New York Times Magazine.* May 18, 1989: 38–39.

WEB SITES

http://www.tonyhillermanbooks.com (Tony Hillerman Home Page)

http://www.umsl.edu/~smueller (Unofficial Home Page)

http://wiredforbooks.org/tonyhillerman (1988 audio interview of Tony Hillerman by Don Swain)

http://members.aol.com/Donh523/navapage/Navajo.htm

http://www.navajo.org

http://navajocentral.org

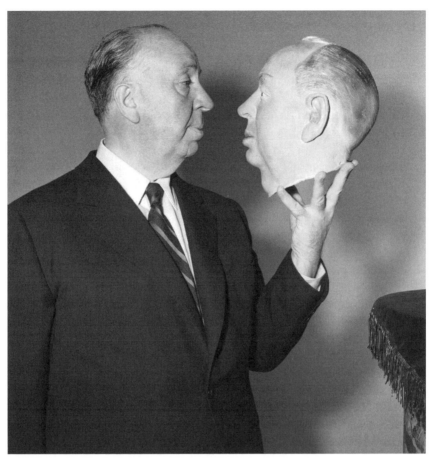
Alfred Hitchcock. Courtesy of CBS/Landov.

Alfred Hitchcock: Cinema's Master of Suspense

There are no secrets—just problems that need solving.
                                    —Alfred Hitchcock, quoted in Gottlieb 173

Alfred Hitchcock, one of the most successful filmmakers of all time, has become a household name, the subject of academized film studies, and a worldwide industry. Hitchcock's vast box office success brought him instant recognition and a multimillion-dollar net worth. More books have been written about him than about any other film director; when he died in 1980, 540 articles and books, including his own essays and articles, had already appeared about him, and at present around 200 books on him in English are in print and available; university Hitchcock courses and scholarly analyses have become "a particular lunacy of academics" (McGilligan 749); DVDs of 40 of his 53 feature films are available online; and both *Rear Window* and *Vertigo* have been restored and reissued at enormous cost. Often dismissed in his own time as a sensationalist, Hitchcock has even been compared with Shakespeare as "a major artist in an art form—the cinema—that has become the major artistic medium of the last century" (Belton 16).

HISTORICAL/CULTURAL CONTEXT

The development of cinema began before 1900 when European and American experiments using multi-image stop-action devices recorded minute stages of a continuous movement. A French physician, E.J. Marey, made the first motion pictures with a single camera in the 1880s, and American inventor Thomas Edison developed both the kinetograph, using rolls of celluloid film in 1889, and shortly after, the kinetoscope, allowing a single viewer to view a "peep show" lasting less than one minute. In 1895 French inventors Louis Jean and Auguste Lumière patented and demonstrated the cinématographe, the first documented device for photographing, printing, and projecting films, and the next year U.S.-developed projection machines sprang up in New York City. "Movies" immediately captured the popular imagination.

Alfred Hitchcock left no formal autobiography. His life paralleled the rise of the motion picture industry, and his creative career ascended during the "Golden Age" of British mystery fiction in the 1920s and 1930s. Hitchcock was born in Leytonstone, now a suburb of London, in 1899, a few years before the "nickelodeon," the first movie theater, appeared in Pittsburgh, Pennsylvania. His lower middle-class parents, William and Emma Hitchcock, ran a small grocery store and raised him and his two older siblings as strict Roman Catholics. As "a pat psychological explanation for his later filmic obsessions," Hitchcock liked to insist on a story, true or not, that his father had once had him locked up in a police station to teach him a lesson (Haeffner 2). When he was nine, his parents sent him to St. Ignatius College, a London Jesuit-run school whose educational tactics, draconian by today's standards, probably resembled those James Joyce depicted in *A Portrait of the Artist as a Young Man*—awful food, rigid discipline, frequent canings, spiritual "retreats" centered on horrifying visions of hellfire and damnation. "The Jesuits," Hitchcock commented much later, "used to terrify me to death, and now I'm getting my own back by terrifying other people in my films" (quoted in Leitch xi). Young Hitchcock took refuge in practical jokes—his life-long hobby—and in fiction, especially Edgar Allan Poe's macabre stories. He also relished Oscar Wilde's *The Picture of Dorian Gray,* Flaubert's *Madame Bovary,* and Dickens's *Bleak House* "with its dark atmosphere and memorable characters" (Haeffner 3).

While Hitchcock was at St. Ignatius, movie making in the United States blossomed, and by 1908 actors, producers, cinematographers, writers, editors, designers, and technicians were working interdependently, their efforts overseen and coordinated by a director exerting considerable authority over each film. After Hitchcock's father died in 1914, Alfred's bond with his mother strengthened, and the following year to help his family financially he began working at the Henley Telegraph Company, first as a clerk and then in the advertising department, where he exercised his talent for drawing. He also attended evening art classes at the University of London, and he kept up the sketching he learned there throughout his filmmaking career, a living example of the movie business' interrelation between art and industry. The movies' immediate appeal meant quick money for investors, but they also became an artistic medium to chronicle and comment on contemporary attitudes, fashions, and events. Cameras were initially stationary, but soon at the director's discretion they panned from side to side and either moved in for close-ups or back for longer shots, allowing considerable directorial latitude. Like most of his generation, Hitchcock fell in love with the movies, a love affair that eventually brought forth his stellar filmmaking career.

The United States soon dominated the world of film production. The "star system" was entrenched by 1910, and directors who could stamp their films with their individual trademarks were nearly as famous as their leading ladies and men. After 1913, major filmmaking moved from New York to Hollywood, turning that little California town, a former temperance colony, into the world's glamorous film capital. American filmmakers like Cecil B. DeMille and D.W. Griffith, whose *Birth of a Nation* earned a breathtaking $18 million in 1915, made epic silent feature films while Britain and Europe suffered through the horrors of World War I; British film production resumed shortly after the 1918 Armistice. In 1920, Hitchcock took an entry-level job designing titles for Famous Players-Lasky, an American studio in north London, and swiftly became head of its titles department, creating the written text that accompanied the silent pictures. Talent and luck made him British director Graham Cutts's assistant. Between 1922 and 1925 Hitchcock designed sets and wrote the scenarios of four films, and after Famous Players-Lasky rented their London premises to Gainsborough Pictures, formed by Michael Balcon and Victor Saville, Balcon pressured Cutts to allow Hitchcock to follow his "celluloid whims" and try directing (Gottlieb 249). Balcon also introduced Hitchcock to the highly talented film editor and scriptwriter Alma Reville. Hitchcock proposed to her in 1923 and they were married three years later. Alma subordinated her own career to Hitchcock's, remaining his "closest adviser and working associate throughout his career" (Haeffner 4). Their only child, Patricia, was born in 1928, and Hitchcock remained a lifelong devoted family man.

The Movie Director's Chief Responsibilities

- To plan the "shoot" to use actors for the shortest possible time in the most effective and economical location(s)
- To give "treatment" so the screenwriter can produce the screenplay
- To work out lighting and camera direction with cinematographer(s)
- To arrange action and control acting, dialogue, and all other creative work on the set

Hitchcock debuted as a director and made the first of his trademark cameo appearances in the thriller genre with *The Lodger* (1926), based on tales of Jack the Ripper, and a year later, by the age of 28 his celluloid whims and his painstakingly cultivated penchant for self-advertisement had made him the highest paid director in Britain. He spared no effort to promote himself and his work; in the 1930s, he often spent "his entire weekly salary on elaborate [self] promotional parties for London's film critics" (Belton 16). He also enthusiastically pioneered and adopted new filmmaking technology and techniques. After sound joined film in *The Jazz Singer* (1927), Hitchcock made the first British "talkie," *Blackmail* (1929) (Kenworthy 28), hailed as a product of his "sensitivity to the social and cultural currents of his time and place, and his ability to dramatize these at a profound level, particularly in terms of sexual politics" (McBride 81).

Following *Blackmail,* Hitchcock briefly experimented for British International Pictures (BIP) with comedy, romantic melodrama, and even a musical, but he found his artistic niche, suspense films, using revolutionary camera work that could manipulate space through creative camera placement, time through skillful editing, and psychology through inserting subjective shots. These key techniques allowed his innovative adaptations of works by some of the period's most powerful crime and mystery writers: John Buchan's *The 39 Steps* (1935), Daphne DuMaurier's *Rebecca* (1938), Patricia Highsmith's *Strangers on a Train* (1951), and Cornell Woolrich's *Rear Window* (1954). Between 1934 and 1938, Hitchcock established his technical, aesthetic, and entrepreneurial strategies with his "thriller sextet," including *The Man Who Knew Too Much* (1934), which he remade in 1956 using American settings. The Technicolor process was developed in 1932, but Hitchcock did not make his first color motion picture, *Rope,* until 1948, preferring in the

1930s and 1940s to direct stars like Ingrid Bergman, Cary Grant, Laurence Olivier, and Joan Fontaine in black and white.

During the 1920s, the "Big Five" American film studios—Warner Brothers, MGM, Paramount, Twentieth Century Fox, and RKO—virtually monopolized the film industry. Besides their production facilities, the studios owned theaters and controlled distribution, and Hitchcock, realizing Hollywood's potential for advancing his career, left Britain for the United States in 1939 and contracted to David O. Selznick for eight years. He made only three films for Selznick: *Rebecca* (1939), *The Paradine Case* (1947), and *Spellbound* (1948), in part because he found Selznick's ideas "crass and corny." For the climax of *Rebecca,* Hitchcock recalled, Selznick wanted the manor house to go up in smoke forming the letter "R" (Bogdanovich 508). Selznick frequently loaned Hitchcock out to other studios, and in 1941 Hitchcock for the first time both produced and directed a film, *Suspicion,* starring Cary Grant and Joan Fontaine. During 1942, Hitchcock's mother died and his brother apparently committed suicide, and his own struggles with a serious weight problem began. He followed *Lifeboat* (1942) with *Shadow of a Doubt* (1943), and acquired his powerful agent Lew Wasserman in 1946.

In 1948, U.S. antitrust legislation dismantled the "Big Five" studios' stranglehold on movie production they had enjoyed since the 1920s, and soon television began to cut into movie profits, necessitating technological innovations to attract audiences. Hitchcock assembled a regular production team with famed Hollywood specialists like costume designer Edith Head and composer Bernard Herrmann to showcase glamorous stars like Grace Kelly, James Stewart, and Kim Novak and highlight exotic locations like Marrakesh and the French Riviera. *Rear Window* and *To Catch a Thief* (1955), the remake of *The Man Who Knew Too Much* (1956), *Vertigo* (1958), and *North by Northwest* (1959), date from this period.

Hitchcock made four of the 2008 American Film Institute-ranked 10 best mystery films of all time during the 1950s: #1: *Vertigo* (1958); #3: *Rear Window* (1954); #7: *North by Northwest* (1959); and #9: *Dial M for Murder* (1954).

In the early 1960s, the movie industry, hit hard by television, was changing radically. Studios were turning to made-for-TV films, and independent filmmakers were starting to produce low-budget movies. The careers of "big names" like Hitchcock began to decline, and his films *Marnie, Torn Curtain,* and *Topaz* all failed at the box office. Hitchcock never received an Oscar for his directing, but the Academy of Motion Picture Arts and Sciences did give him the Irving A. Thalberg Memorial Award in 1967, five years before his last major film, *Frenzy*. Queen Elizabeth made Alfred Hitchcock a Knight Commander of the Order of the British Empire in early 1980, a few months before his death.

AUTEURSHIP

From the outset, a film's director could exercise considerable authority over its personnel and all its production details, inspiring the film studies term "auteur." The original 1950s French term *politique des auteurs* is probably best translated as "the policy of authors," fulfilling a need to divert attention away from the script and toward the art of the director, then little understood or appreciated. In the late 1960s, however, the phrase *politique des auteurs* was mistranslated as "the *auteur* theory," in order to claim that "great films come about solely because of great directors" (Haeffner 41) who so dominate the entire filmmaking process that they are the movie's "authors."

Hitchcock believed the term "director" was incorrect and preferred to be called a "filmmaker," because he believed that few "directors" exhibit individual and personal style. Currently film critics apply "auteur" in its newer sense to Hitchcock's unique directorial style and provocative personal vision where, in spite of deriving most of his films from other writers' novels or plays, he integrated several highly individual elements into "The Hitchcock Touch." One of the most obvious features of "The Hitchcock Touch" is the

| Reporter: | "What is the deepest logic of your films?" |
| **Alfred Hitchcock:** | "To put the audience through them." |

ordinariness of his central figures and their settings: audiences realize that the terrible things that happen to these characters can just as easily happen to them, and when they least expect it. Hitchcock said he wanted his typical hero to be "the average person to whom bizarre things happen, rather than the other way around" (quoted in Leitch xi), and in his hands those "bizarre things" struck audiences as unforgettably nightmarish. He began this technique very early, in *The Lodger* (1926), taken from Marie Belloc Lowndes's novel about a landlady who gradually realizes that her new renter is Jack the Ripper and shields him from the police until he leaves. Hitchcock himself called *The Lodger* "the first true Hitchcock film" (quoted in Leitch 185). He shifted emphasis from the landlady to her blonde daughter Daisy and cleared the lodger in the end, meshing domestic routine with melodrama. He also bookended an opening closeup of a screaming blonde victim and a cut to a flashing neon sign reading "To-night Golden Curls" with a closing shot of blonde Daisy in the lodger's arms and the same sign blinking outside the window (Leitch 185).

Hitchcock expanded the notion of ordinary people trapped in extraordinary circumstances in *The Man Who Knew Too Much* (1934), plunging a family vacationing in Switzerland beyond the help of authorities into international intrigue. In this nightmare world, the family's home, London, becomes just as lethal and full of unsettling shifts between comedy and menace as the

I suppose one has at one's finger-tips all the details of the famous [murder] cases of the past.

—Alfred Hitchcock

exotic Alps are. This film, like each of Hitchcock's 24 English films, was a technical and a psychological run-through for his thematically richer American movies. When Hitchcock remade this film starring James Stewart, who shared in the profits of both *The Man Who Knew Too Much* and *Rear Window,* and Doris Day in her first dramatic role, Hitchcock paired a "version of fifties domestic Americana" with his increasingly anti-Communist views on international politics. He replaced the Nazi kidnappers and killers of his earlier version with British Communists bent on assassinating a Communist-bloc leader with anti-Soviet nationalist policies and blaming the killing on the Americans, resulting in a film often inspiring political analysis (Leitch 198).

Hitchcock's villains also appeared as ordinary people, not recognizably criminal personalities. He once commented, "I always make my villains as charming as possible. The really frightening thing about villains is their surface likeableness; they use their charm to attract potential victims" (quoted in Leitch xi). An example is *Strangers on a Train,* adapted from Patricia Highsmith's chilling novel about two homicidal men. One, Charles Bruno, proposes to the other, Guy Haines, that they should trade murders—Bruno will kill Haines's wife if Haines will murder Bruno's father. Guilt gradually overwhelms Haines after Bruno, "a charming psychopath" who has already slain Haines's errant wife, drives Haines to kill Bruno's tyrannical father; Hitchcock, using Raymond Chandler's screenplay to maximum effect, successfully made Bruno, a charming killer, "perhaps the finest portrait" of any of his villains, propelling the film's irresistible momentum and made it the model for the combination of "suspense and gender politics" that typified his Cold War films (Leitch 320, 322).

Suspense is the hallmark of "The Hitchcock Touch." He insisted, "I believe in giving the audience all the facts as early as possible," so that he could as director "build up an almost unbearable tension" that crescendos throughout the movie (Martin 128). *Shadow of a Doubt,* often called Hitchcock's favorite among his films, though he claimed he gave that impression only because he knew it satisfied "plausibles and logicians" (Truffaut 151), "incontestably brings one of Hitchcock's major themes, the doubling of villain and victim, to its first full blossom" (Leitch 301) in one of the most suspenseful but outwardly the most ordinary of his films. It was the first of several that Hitchcock set near his northern California home with locals playing bit parts and extras. *Shadow of a Doubt,* one of only two films in which Hitchcock made his central figure a villain (the other was *Psycho*), traces young Charlie

Newton's psychological changes as her suspicion grows that her magnetic Uncle Charlie, with whom she shares a kind of telepathy, is a serial murderer who preys on wealthy widows. Hitchcock combined a recurring image of whirling dancers with a musical *leitmotif,* a scrap of the "Merry Widow" Viennese waltz which composer Dimitri Tiompkin distorted into a "sinister tone poem" (McGilligan 318), to build the audience's tension by constantly reminding them of the killer the press had dubbed "The Merry Widow Murderer." Eventually, while Uncle Charlie is trying to hurl her out of a train

> According to Hitchcock, the length of a film should be directly related to the endurance of the human bladder.

window, his niece Charlie manages to kill him instead, but like the landlady in *The Lodger* she keeps his secret afterward. Hitchcock also used technically challenging camera work, especially a demanding closeup of damning evidence, a ring on Charlie's hand taken from one of his victims and given to her by Uncle Charlie, to immerse "the audience in the tension, guiding them subjectively from 'the general to the particular,' in the words of screenwriter David Freeman, 'the farthest to the nearest'" (McGilligan 320).

The MacGuffin

Two men were traveling by train from London to Edinburgh. In the luggage rack overhead was a wrapped parcel.

"What have you there?" asked one of the men.
"Oh, that's a MacGuffin," replied the other.
"What's a MacGuffin?"
"It's a device for trapping lions in the Scottish Highlands."
"But there aren't any lions in the Scottish Highlands!"
"Well, then, that's no MacGuffin."

—An old anecdote, quoted in *The Art of Alfred Hitchcock,* xi

Hitchcock also almost always employed the "MacGuffin," a plot device that precipitates the film and keeps it moving. The main characters worry about it, but Hitchcock's audience does not; they instead worry about the safety of his hero and heroine. In a 1963 interview with Oriana Fallaci, Hitchcock explained, "... when I'm making a movie, the story isn't important to me. What's important is how I tell the story. ... Why should the character go to so much trouble? Is he looking for a bomb, a secret? This secret, this bomb, is for me the MacGuffin" (quoted in Gottlieb 62). When he was making *No-torious* in 1944, Hitchcock hit on a classic MacGuf-fin. He had to find a reason for the character Ingrid Bergman played to go to South America, and the notion struck him of having the Nazis building an atom bomb there. "Naturally," he said, "I didn't

> *Always make the audience suffer as much as possible.*
> —Alfred Hitchcock

even know what the atom bomb might be. But I knew that uranium existed, that since 1929 the atom had been split." Hitchcock then visited physicist Robert Milliken, director of the Manhattan Project, at the California Institute of Tech-nology. Milliken, horrified that classified information might have leaked out, sent him away and phoned the FBI, whose agents shadowed Hitchcock for the next six months (Gottlieb 62–64). David O. Selznick didn't care for the atom bomb MacGuffin, so he sold Hitchcock and stars Ingrid Bergman and Cary Grant to RKO for $800,000 and 50 percent of the profits. In spite of Selznick and the FBI, Hitchcock used his MacGuffin, the real atomic bomb exploded over Hiroshima less than two years later, and *Notorious,* released in 1946, made $8 million.

All of Hitchcock's mature films contain touches of black humor, sometimes carried to the point of audience queasiness, a quality Hitchcock also discussed with Fallaci. He insisted he could take no credit for this, because, he said, "For the English it's normal to mix humor with the macabre. You know the story about the two ladies at the fair watching a man eat the heads of live rats? Well, in horror one of them says, "Doesn't he ever eat bread with them?" (quoted in Gottlieb 64). Hitchcock believed that only a fine line exists between comedy and tragedy (Gottlieb 88), but he drew it, often in unforgettable one-liners, with his own brand of wit, combining "outrageous humor, audience manipula-tion, and blend of romantic melodrama and thriller" nowhere better illustrated than in his famous remark that he intended his films to "leave not a dry seat in the house" (quoted in Gottlieb xvii).

The Strengths of Hitchcock's Films

As Alfred Hitchcock's technical experimentation and expertise expanded, his vision of the thriller genre darkened. Throughout his creative life, Hitchcock's emotional stresses, which some observers call neuroses, increasingly affected his films. His filmmaking career includes his British period, 1926 to 1939; his American romantic thriller period, 1939 to 1960; and, primarily due to *Psycho* and the television series *Alfred Hitchcock Presents,* his international period of sinister psychological suspense, 1960 to 1972. In the 1960s, Hitchcock's repu-tation fell in America, although his European reputation, especially among progressive French critics, steadily burgeoned.

Hitchcock himself discussed the French theory of "Auteurism" with European journalists Nogueira and Zafetti in 1972, declaring, "I never think of the films I make as being *my* [italics in original] films" (quoted in Nogueira and Zafetti 119). One reason was that between the 1930s and *Topaz,* which he made in 1969, the studios he worked for mostly chose his films, so that unlike most artists, Hitchcock could not always pick his material, and, in fact, a clause in his contract with Universal Pictures expressly forbade him to make an adaptation of J.M. Barrie's *Mary Rose,* his greatest inspiration. Hitchcock observed to Nogueira and Zalaffi that the films he would make if he could would be very different from those he had done, "more dramatic, more realistic, possibly without humor," but he felt he had to satisfy his audiences, who had come to expect crime and his "trademarks: knives, slit throats, 'shivers.'" He also compared the genuine filmmaker's style to the style of a great painter: "We recognize at one glance a Rousseau, a Van Gogh, a Klee," and, like a painter, he felt it his artistic responsibility to create an emotion: "What attracts me is to discover what will provoke a strong emotion in the viewer and how to make the viewer feel it" (quoted in Gottlieb 120). Hitchcock's major filmmaking concern, therefore, was always his audience; he took pride "in his ability to gauge their interests and, thus, to control them" (Belton 17). Eventually Hitchcock's passion for control extended beyond his audiences' reactions to dominate his stars and his filmmaking teams.

While most film critics agree on the components Hitchcock integrated into "The Hitchcock Touch" and attribute his films' remarkable popularity to it, François Truffaut, the French New Wave filmmaker who developed the *politique des auteurs* in the mid-1950s, took a psychological approach in uncritically championing Hitchcock and his work. In a widely admired book-length series of chronological interviews with Hitchcock published in 1967, Truffaut declared that Hitchcock's "deep emotivity" impressed him most, tracing it to evidences in his films of Hitchcock's painful personal emotions due to his isolating bulky physique, his consequent withdrawal from the real world into the world of the cinema, and his frustrated Pygmalionship. Truffaut believed that Hitchcock as an *auteur* "achieved a real tour de force in inducing the public to identify with the attractive leading man, whereas Hitchcock himself almost always identified with the supporting role . . . the man who looks on without being able to participate," a role that Truffaut and others have attributed to Hitchcock's painfully isolated school days. Truffaut quotes an old Jesuit who had known Hitchcock at St. Ignatius and who described him as a boy: "alone, leaning against a wall, his hands already folded across his stomach, and an expression of disdain on his face as he watched his schoolmates playing ball" (Truffaut 347–348).

Hitchcock's Handicaps and Obstacles

From that lonely, disdainful little boy, Truffaut argued, came

> The man who was impelled by fear to relate the most terrifying stories; this man . . . who never had any woman except for his wife . . . this man was indeed the only one who was able to portray murder and adultery as scandals, the only man who knew how to do so—in fact, the only man who had the *right* to do so. (Truffaut 347; italics in original)

Hitchcock himself tried to keep as much as he could of that man a secret, which contributes to widely differing views of him and his work. At one extreme, British *Times* film critic John Russell Taylor published *Hitch: The Life and Times of Alfred Hitchcock,* the authorized biography, in 1978, a sympathetic treatment written with the cooperation of Hitchcock and his family. On the opposite end of the critical spectrum, shortly after Hitchcock's death, Donald Spoto's *Alfred Hitchcock: The Dark Side of Genius* (1982), relying heavily on gossip and containing many mistakes and inventions (Belton 19), painted Hitchcock as "a macabre joker, a frightened child, and a tyrannical artist," a view strongly protested by those who knew Hitchcock well. Patricia Hitchcock O'Connell has stated repeatedly that "Spoto took things and twisted them" (quoted in McGilligan 747), and he seems to be continuing to do so. Spoto's last three chapters of his third Hitchcock study, *Spellbound by Beauty: Alfred Hitchcock and His Leading Ladies*, delivers on the promise he makes in his preface, to relate "Hitchcock's sadistic behavior and his occasional public humiliations of actresses," but does so in "scornful language, inflated with innuendo" and "minimizes" fond recollections by actresses with whom Hitchcock worked (Gunz O11).

Was Hitchcock a tormented genius or a tormenting monster? A more balanced view indicates that "like many of his characters . . . Hitchcock was something of a split personality. . . . American critic Richard Schickel pointed out that "the director's *persona*—the jolly fat man with a macabre, punning sense of humor—was almost entirely fictional" (Gianetti and Eyman 313). One contemporary critical trend probes Hitchcock's fears about violence and sex by attempting to explain the development of his films in psychoanalytic terms. Robin Wood, a pioneering British film scholar, has produced four successive revisions (1969, 1977, 1989, and 2002) of his original Hitchcock study, *Hitchcock's Films* (1965). In his 1969 book, Wood defended Hitchcock's auteurism as "aesthetically rich and morally challenging," using suspense as a means of involving audiences in the characters' moral struggles as they work through their obsessions to a healing trust in love (quoted in Leitch 375). Wood's original reading of seven of Hitchcock's best known films (*Strangers on a Train, Rear Window, Vertigo, North by Northwest, Psycho, The Birds,* and *Marnie*) assumes a common thread, the value of human relationships in avoiding audiences' most profound fears, among them the dread of chaos, guilt, insanity, nightmare, the id. Hitchcock did not seem able to surmount those same fears through human relationships, and they escalated throughout his life. (By 2002, Wood had rethought auteurism, explored gender issues related to identification, and discussed Hitchcock's problematic relation to patriarchy.) Hitchcock's problems manifested themselves in tendencies some describe as borderline sadistic factors which seriously affected his filmmaking. Spoto goes so far in *Spellbound by Beauty* to describe Hitchcock as "a man so unhappy, so full of self-loathing, so lonely and friendless, that his satisfactions came as much from asserting power as from spinning fantasies and acquiring wealth. . . . Hitchcock may have felt he could get away with anything. Alas, in this case he was right" (*NYTBR* 42).

Already in the 1930s Hitchcock's filmmaking involved an "obsessive control of his artistic materials" (Wollaeger 337). "Materials" included his actors, the accepted view at that time, and to Hitchcock, infamously, actors were "cattle." The British film critic, writer, director, and producer Ivor Montagu, who worked on Hitchcock's English films, believed that "a good director must have something of a sadist in him. . . . his . . . telling characters to do this, undergo that, is necessarily akin to dominating them" (quoted in *Dark Side* 149). In all his Hitchcock studies, Spoto offers grisly anecdotes involving Hitchcock's cruel practical jokes on his filmmaking teams, actors and crew alike, like once chaining a crew member who was afraid of the dark to a camera and leaving him all night with a bottle of laxative-laced brandy. "Recognizing Hitchcock as sadistic *auteur* [sic] helps draw out the latent cruelty of his icy manipulations of character and viewer" (Wollaeger 338), especially in his 1963 to 1964 films centered on "extreme forms of psychological and social disturbance"—*Psycho, The Birds, Marnie*—a shift from the popular romantic thrillers of his American period that may be attributed to what Camille Paglia has called Hitchcock's "existential crisis."

That crisis began with declining health. In 1957, when a navel hernia he had neglected for years flared up with colitis and then gallstones, Hitchcock underwent two serious operations and was bedridden for four months. In 1958, Don Hartman, the Paramount producer who had allowed Hitchcock his greatest artistic freedom, died and Hitchcock's wife and closest adviser Alma was diagnosed with cervical cancer, then virtually a death sentence. She opted for a dangerous experimental radiation procedure and survived, but Hitchcock was badly shaken.

Hitchcock was also suffering profoundly from rejection by his professional peers. The New York Film Critics had frozen him out since *The Lady Vanishes* (1938), and between 1948 and 1960, he had received eight nominations but no wins as Best Director from the Directors Guild of America. After *Psycho,* his biggest box office hit, won him his last Best Director nomination, he lost the Oscar yet again, "a deep personal disappointment" that he tried to mask with levity, calling himself "always a bridesmaid" (McGilligan 606).

By 1964 Hitchcock was coping with even more personal grief, resentment, and shame. His gifted film editor George Tomasini died that November, and the U.S. Justice Department's 1964 breakup of movie studio monopolies had made Hitchcock's friend and agent Lew Wasserman the director's employer. Though Wasserman tried hard to keep the relationship amicable, Hitchcock resented their role reversal. In addition, he confessed to Jay Presson Allen, the screenwriter who had replaced Evan Hunter on *Marnie* and who became Hitchcock's trusted confidant, that he had become impotent; his "long-repressed sexuality was pushing its way violently to the surface of his personal life, and sexually based trauma became the dominant theme of his work," accompanied by his "increasingly urgent preoccupation with mortality" (McBride 24).

Hitchcock's use of the film industry's newly relaxed standards allowing previously forbidden subjects and imagery to incorporate so much graphic violence and misogyny into *Psycho, The Birds,* and *Marnie* revolted many audiences and critics. *The Birds* even required actors to smear their hands with anchovies and raw meat and endure savage avian assaults, and on especially bad days as many as 12 crew members would have to have hospital treatment for bites and slashes. After *Marnie* (1964), Hitchcock negotiated a new contract with Universal that made him "a bird in a gilded cage. . . . he would be worry-free financially, but creatively he had sacrificed his power and freedom" (McGilligan 654).

Marnie (1964), *Torn Curtain* (1966), and *Topaz* (1969) all did poorly at the U.S. box office. *Topaz,* virtually unknown except to Hitchcock scholars, lost more money than any other of Hitchcock's films and has never been re-released, probably because of "its quietly frightening view of the bankruptcy of all the values—family, romance, personal loyalty, political idealism," values that had made Hitchcock's earlier spy thrillers thrilling, morally uplifting, and "a strikingly prescient view of both cold-war politics and cultural analysis in general" (Leitch 339–340). Hitchcock's last major film, *Frenzy* (1972), combines rage at sexual impotence, disgusting food, and revolting sexual practices into "a brilliantly unpleasant stew": "If *Frenzy* is Hitchcock with the gloves off, it has made thousands of viewers thankful for gloves" (Leitch 115).

Hitchcock's Leading Ladies

As both a storyteller and a filmmaker, Alfred Hitchcock seemed fascinated by women, whom he made unusually and prominently both agents and objects in what are apparently stories of masculine desire and action. He overused the ingénue figure more than any other successful filmmaker has done, and some critics even feel he could not create convincing female characters. The ambivalence of Hitchcock's treatment of women characters in his films has given rise to interpretations of his work resting on psychoanalytic and/or feminist theories of sexuality.

> **To an Actress Asking Whether Her Right or Left Profile Was Better:**
> Hitchcock replied, "My dear, you're sitting on your best profile."

As early as 1935, Barbara J. Buchanan accused Alfred Hitchcock of conscious misogyny, disregarding "glamour, love-interest, sex-appeal and all the other feminine attributes which the American director considers indispensable" (quoted in Gottlieb 79). Hitchcock himself once cited the advice of 19th-century French dramatist Victorien Sardou, who attributed dramatic success to the formula "Torture the women" (Spoto 458), and the brutal damage inflicted on Hitchcock's female characters as catalogued by James McLaughlin seems to have carried out that advice: rape, poisoning, stabbing, beating, strangling, death by bird pecking, gassing, and above all psychological torment. Hitchcock also made some mothers, notably Norman Bates' invalid mother in *Psycho*, into monstrous ogres, responsible for warping their children into vicious criminals.

Casual observers attribute the appeal of Hitchcock's films to the mass audience's desire for sensational violence, especially the kind directed at women, but feminist critics "have [also] found themselves compelled, intrigued, infuriated, and inspired by Hitchcock's work." Ever since Laura Mulvey's 1981 essay "Visual Pleasure and Narrative Cinema," considered the "founding document of psychoanalytic feminist film theory," Hitchcock's films "have been central to the formulation of feminist film theory and to the practice of feminist film criticism" (Modleski 1), both of which tended initially to show that women in these films are portrayed as "passive objects of male voyeuristic and sadistic impulses" fulfilling male desires and expressing male anxieties, so that women filmgoers can relate to these films only masochistically (Mulvey 12). Some feminists also believe that Hitchcock needed "to convict and punish women for their sexuality" (Modleski 25). Other feminist commentators, however, see a conflict between Hitchcock's sympathetic identification with female characters and patriarchal claims made by his male voyeurs and by Hitchcock himself. Some of his films portray conflicts that are gender driven and resolved in a romantic couple, while others show conflicts driven by male anxiety, problems which seem encapsulated in "the best known fetish of his later career," Hitchcock's almost universal use of blonde actresses as his leading ladies (Leitch 36).

Hitchcock's first films starred dark-haired actresses, but he came to choose blonde actresses because he felt they photographed better in black and white than brunettes did. He also followed a long-standing literary tradition by linking the "sexual reticence" of the "cool blonde," usually British or Nordic, with concealed sexuality, as opposed to the southern European brunette's more obvious allure which Hitchcock told Truffaut prevented the element of surprise which gave romantic scenes their meaning (Truffaut 224). As Hitchcock

Hitchcock's Most Notable Cool Blonde Ladylike Stars

Madeleine Carroll
Carole Lombard
Grace Kelly
Janet Leigh
Tippi Hedren

himself repeatedly suggested, "Anything could happen to a [cool blonde] woman like that in the back of a taxi" (quoted in Leitch 37).

"Hitch always liked women who behaved like well-bred ladies," Hitchcock's designer Robert Boyle recalled (quoted in McGilligan 615), but he evidently had frequent and perseverant back-of-the-taxi fantasies, centered in his increasingly Svengali-like attachments to blonde actresses beginning with Madeleine Carroll, whom he described as "the first blond [sic] who was a real Hitchcock type" (quoted in Leitch 37) and directed, lavishly and lovingly lighted, in *The 39 Steps* and *Secret Agent*. When he arrived in Hollywood, he met the inexperienced and insecure Joan Fontaine, "the first blonde ingénue he could utterly dominate" (Leitch 37). He directed her in *Rebecca*, once slapping her to induce tears for a particularly emotional scene (Gunz O11). Fontaine suffered even more because Laurence Olivier, her dashing leading man, was reportedly so angry that Fontaine had taken that role away from his wife Vivien Leigh that he whispered obscenities in Fontaine's ear throughout the filming. Fontaine is said to have returned the favor to Cary Grant while making *Suspicion* (Leitch 108).

The blonde and strong-willed Carole Lombard responded to Hitchcock's well-known opinion that "Actors are cattle" by having three heifers labeled "Carole Lombard," "Robert Montgomery," and "Gene Raymond" (Truffaut 140) corralled on Hitchcock's set of *Mr. and Mrs. Smith*, Hitchcock's only comedy; Lombard did not last long with him. After successfully exploiting Ingrid

> **Ingrid Bergman:** "I don't think I can give you that kind of emotion."
> **Alfred Hitchcock:** "Ingrid—Fake it."

Bergman's understated sexuality in *Spellbound* and *Notorious*, Hitchcock attempted *Under Capricorn* with her in the lead, but Bergman rebelled against Hitchcock's tyrannical long takes, and the film became his second worst box office flop. Five years later, Hitchcock found his ultimate blonde, Grace Kelly, who starred in *Dial M for Murder, Rear Window*, and *To Catch a Thief*. Hitchcock described Kelly as "sensitive, disciplined, and very sexy . . . a volcano covered with snow" (quoted in Gottleib 65), but she left Hollywood to marry Monaco's Prince Rainier.

> Sarah, Hitchcock's West Highland Terrier, was perhaps the only Hollywood creature, male or female, who refused to take direction from the master.

Hitchcock spent the rest of his career trying to replace her as his "iconic heroine," using, with varying degrees of success, Shirley MacLaine, Doris Day, Kim Novak, Eva Marie Saint, Janet Leigh, and Vera Miles. Hitchcock became furious when Miles, his intended leading lady in *Vertigo,* became pregnant, commenting, ". . . she couldn't resist her Tarzan of a husband, Gordon Scott." When asked, "She [Miles] didn't know about the pill?" Hitchcock fired back, "She should have taken a 'Jungle Pill'!" (Gottlieb 123).

Finally, Hitchcock made his most notorious choice, Tippi Hedren, for *The Birds* and *Marnie.* He had spotted Hedren in a Pet Milk television commercial and cast her as Melanie in *The Birds,* presenting her at a Hollywood dinner with a pin with "three golden birds with seed pearls, in flight." Hedren, Hitchcock's wife Alma, and Lew Wasserman all cried. "It was a lovely moment," Hedren recalled (McGilligan 615), but it did not last. During the filming of *The Birds*, Hitchcock treated Hedren with unusual and obsessive cruelty, but most observers thought the part simply demanded scenes "calculated for their harshness and terror" (McGilligan 635).

Patrick McGilligan's *Alfred Hitchcock: A Life in Darkness and Light* (2003), evenhandedly treats the Hitchcock-Hedren *Marnie* debacle indicating the complexity of Hitchcock's attitudes toward women. *Marnie*, which Hitchcock had been contemplating for two years during his "existential crisis," was under way months before the premiere of *The Birds*. He had wanted Grace Kelly to resume her acting career with *Marnie,* but though Prince Rainier supported her return to film, circumstances in Monaco prevented her from taking the controversial role, so Hitchcock accepted Hedren instead.

Almost immediately scriptwriter Evan Hunter began to notice signs of dangerous artistic hubris in Hitchcock. Hunter refused to write the ferocious wedding-night rape scene Hitchcock wanted and quit the project, replaced by Jay Presson Allen. Hitchcock cast Sean Connery, anxious to change his James Bond image, as Marnie's husband, Mark Rutland, and for the first half of the filming at least, "Connery's professional amiability seemed to lighten the air" (McGilligan 645), but while Hitchcock had initially appeared infatuated with Hedren, showering her with gifts and trying to close her off from other people, he also was harboring hidden doubts about her acting abilities. As accomplished as Hitchcock was with filmmaking technique, human challenges—"the failures of an actor or actress to embody his vision sufficiently"—often stymied him. He panicked, trying to force Hedren "to *be* Marnie." An unthinkable flareup resulted at the end of January 1964 when Hedren reputedly called Hitchcock "a fat pig." He later commented, "She did what no one is permitted to do. She referred to my *weight*" (quoted in McGilligan 646, italics in original). When Hedren demanded to be released from her exclusive contract with him, Hitchcock declared he would destroy her career before he let her go. A month later, Hitchcock supposedly made "vulgar propositions" to Hedren which she has never revealed completely, though Spoto hypothesizes the situation luridly in *Spellbound by Beauty*. Although the nature and details of Hitchcock's action are unclear, it was clearly a personal error and failure for him. Ironically, many Hitchcock critics now feel *Marnie* was his "vital film," "a time capsule for gender representation and psychoanalytical ideas for key traumas and events" (Tony Moral, quoted in McGilligan 648).

This bitter episode left scars on both parties. Hitchcock continued to pay her $500 per week salary until she refused his request to appear in a Universal telefilm, dissolving her contract with him. Hitchcock also began losing team members with whom he had enjoyed what he called "a sort of telepathic communication that sets us right" (quoted in McGilligan 655) and his own health deteriorated. From that point, too, Hedren's career plummeted.

Hitchcock's Heroes

Although he notoriously manifested boredom on the set, probably to maintain as calm an atmosphere as possible and downplay personal engagement, Hitchcock made heavy physical and emotional demands on all his actors. His original technique of continuous filming, following characters in long takes, proved an arduous change for actors used to quick cutting, like Ingrid Bergman and her leading man Joseph Cotton who, when making *Notorious* in 1948, found themselves exhausted by the taxing combination of physical action and sustained emotional tension necessitated by the extremely long takes. Hitchcock's low opinion of actors also exacerbated movie-making tensions. In his 1963 interview with Oriana Fallaci, Hitchcock expanded his famous dismissal of actors as cattle:

> When they aren't cows, they're children. . . . The majority of actors . . . are stupid children. They're always quarreling, and they give themselves a lot of airs. The less I see of them, the happier I am. I had much less trouble directing fifteen hundred crows than one single actor. (Quoted in Gottlieb 64)

On the set, however, he bottled up his opinions, claiming, "I never have a row with an actor," but in 1973, responding to interviewer Arthur Knight's question, "If an actor is not playing the part the way you want him to, what would you say to him to get the performance you want?," Hitchcock flatly replied, "Go to the front office and pick up your check. Goodbye" (quoted in Gottlieb 172).

Before leaving England for the United States, Hitchcock's films had already revealed his absorption with power and impotence as two sides of the same coin, revealed in the male drive to dominate women. He had dreamed for a long time of adapting John Buchan's *The 39 Steps,* where accidental hero Richard Hannay, a cultured gentleman spy wrongly accused of murder, has to escape both enemy agents and the police. The considerable liberties Hitchcock took in this project involved adding "all of the film's prominent female characters who define Hannay's adventures" (Leitch 332), including a heterosexual romance and the filming of one of Hitchcock's eccentric practical jokes. On the first day of shooting, Hitchcock handcuffed star Madeleine Carroll to her leading man Robert Donat, whom she had just met, for a scene at a bridge, then "lost" the key for the rest of the day (Leitch 332), foreshadowing the film's climactic scene in which Hannay, handcuffed to a woman who thinks he is a killer, persuades a Scottish innkeeper and his wife that they are a honeymooning couple, "sexualizing the story's power relationships" (Leitch 333). Hitchcock's *The 39 Steps* presents the male hero as able to wander, gaze, and claim "temporary occupancy" of his locales, "a gendered privilege, usually denied to women." In escaping his various pursuers, Hannay also passes tests of intelligence, strength, and endurance, while women who overstep their boundaries are punished; women are thus limited to being "complementary and lesser partners to the hero" (Devas 45, 46).

When Hitchcock came to Hollywood to begin his "American period" he wanted to work with well-known male stars, although because American studios regarded thrillers at that time as second rate material, he often had to work with "next best" choices; Gary Cooper turned him down for *Foreign Correspondent* and he had to use the more relaxed Joel McCrea instead (Cooper later regretted that choice) (Truffaut 133). For the film version of *Rebecca*, Hitchcock had to make major compromises with producer David O. Selznick; the film received 11 Oscar nominations and won two, including Best Picture, but Laurence Olivier damned his association with Hitchcock with faint praise: "Happy with Hitchcock in *Rebecca*" (quoted in Leitch 242). In *The Paradine Case*, also for Selznick, Hitchcock had to accept American Gregory Peck as the English lawyer hero, although he felt Peck could not play the part convincingly (Hitchcock had wanted Olivier), and urbane Frenchman Louis Jourdan as the heroine's lover, a groom who Hitchcock felt instead should been "a manure-smelling stablehand" (quoted in Truffaut 173).

During his American romantic thriller period during World War II and the Cold War, Hitchcock began to integrate international and sexual politics. "For Hitchcock, politics [was] a male-dominated—indeed, exclusively male—world within which women . . . are pawns, to be manipulated, used, exploited, and often destroyed" (Wood 340). In addition, "To exercise his basically ironic artistic vision, Hitchcock frequently cast attractive [male] stars, and even though the characters they play are sometimes morally dubious, the good will they generate as cultural icons tends to smother our moral objections" (Giannetti and Eyman 314). Once away from Selznick, when Hitchcock had more liberty in his choice of leading men, he generally picked handsome, dark-haired "men's men" like Cary Grant and James Stewart, perhaps the best known male stars with whom Hitchcock worked, who alternated as Hitchcock's favorite actors, each appearing in four of his films during the 1950s. Before his "existential crisis" Hitchcock chose heroes who could convincingly portray romantic happy endings to the complicated issues he was presenting, though he could not resist hinting at "curious—and sometimes kinky—psychological quirks" beneath their pleasantly ordinary exteriors (Giannetti and Eyman 316).

The opinion that Hitchcock cast Cary Grant in roles that Hitchcock himself would have liked to have lived may not completely represent the complicated reasons behind the effective working relationship the two men enjoyed. Hitchcock had not been able to obtain Grant, an Anglo-American heartthrob best known for light comedic roles, for *Mr. and Mrs. Smith,* but he signed Grant for *Suspicion,* which in its novel version had had the hero killing his wife. Even though Grant's popular image prevented Hitchcock from portraying him as a murderer, *Suspicion* proved a box office hit, followed by *Notorious* with Ingrid Bergman and a deeper, more opaque role for Grant that demanded he prostitute the woman he loves because he is afraid of admitting he loves her. As a cat burglar in *To Catch a Thief,* Grant had to elude the marriage-minded Grace Kelly, and in *North by Northwest,* he struggled to escape a powerful maternal attachment that keeps him from a satisfying relationship with any other woman. Thomas Leitch notes that Hitchcock used Grant's "suave urbanity to defang male fears of romantic commitment in order to explore them more completely" (124).

Hitchcock had also wanted Grant for *Rope,* but he settled for all-American actor James Stewart instead, giving rise to the observation that Stewart represented Hitchcock as he really was: under Hitchcock's direction, Stewart's down-home charm overlay a complicated mixture of insecurity and simmering rage. In *Rope,* Stewart played a former headmaster who as a publisher fostered the lethal fantasies of former students. *Rear Window,* with Grace Kelly, demanded that Stewart combine the *persona* of a charming invalid with the unsettling compulsion of a *voyeur;* and in Hitchcock's remake of *The Man Who Knew Too Much,* Stewart again merged apparently contradictory traits, insecurity and professional authority, as Doris Day's physician husband and father of their kidnapped child. In *Vertigo,* one of Hitchcock's less financially successful films, Stewart portrayed an agoraphobic ex-policeman with all of the qualities that had made Stewart's aw-shucks American film *persona* so appealing—innocence, idealism, romantic diffidence—caught up in the sexual wiles of a ruthless heroine played by Kim Novak. Frequently taken as a scathing self-portrait of Hitchcock as Svengali, Stewart's role in *Vertigo,* torn between fear of falling and an unquenchable desire to do so, gave Hitchcock "the richest metaphor of his career, [linking] . . . love, death, and the perverse pleasures of film spectatorship" (Leitch 357). Overall, Hitchcock's 1950s heroes also reflect the American ideal of the patriarchal nuclear family, which feminists claim has always been based on the subordination of women.

Beginning in the 1960s, Hitchcock began to de-emphasize his heroes, a reflection of his own highly complex "existential crisis." In the shockers *Psycho, The Birds,* and *Marnie,* Hitchcock explored upsetting and even repugnant aberrant behavior, even shooting *Psycho*'s horrifying shower scene himself. Actor Anthony Perkins defined the rest of his career by playing apron-strings-strangled Norman Bates, who described his invalid mother as being as harmless as a stuffed bird, the parent being blamed for the child's aberrations. That sinister image led to Hitchcock's *The Birds,* his most expensive film ever, where he underplayed his male lead Australian Rod Taylor. Feminist critic Margaret Horwitz suggests psychoanalytically that "the bird attacks function primarily as extensions of Lydia's hysterical fear of losing her son" (quoted in Deutelbaum and Poague 279). Hitchcock turned his own avian phobia—he even refused to eat eggs—and his claustrophobic memories of World War II London bombings into filmic terror, culminating in a horrific scene that was the single most difficult shot of his entire career.

Marnie, about a frigid kleptomaniac blackmailed into marriage by a man she robbed, offered Hitchcock the chance to remake *Spellbound,* reversing the doctor-patient roles so that a man's unconditional love could cure the woman he adores. Sean Connery, forced to play a devoted husband who is also an implacable rapist, pleased Hitchcock, perhaps because Connery's character, in "trying to control, dominate and possess Marnie, expresses Hitchcock's own feelings as a frustrated Pygmalion" (Truffaut 346). The film failed to capitalize fully on either Connery's or Hitchcock's talents, possibly because its conclusion hints at female subjugation through marriage. It failed to reach the top 20 in movie profits in the United States, but due to Connery, then at the peak of his fame as James Bond, it became the twelfth most successful British film of 1964.

Hitchcock's Villains

One of Alfred Hitchcock's cardinal rules of filmmaking was, "All villains are not black and all heroes are not white. There are grays everywhere" (quoted in Gianetto and Eyman 316). Another was, "The more successful the villain, the more successful the picture" (Truffaut 191). As the strictures of the movie industry's Production Code loosened, Hitchcock turned away from the villain whose Byronic hero charm masked lethal intentions, like Uncle Charlie in *Shadow of a Doubt,* and from the suave, distinguished conspirator James Mason played in *North by Northwest.* Hitchcock experienced difficulty in modernizing melodrama by making a villain both smooth and threatening (Truffaut 107), so he developed a villain as antithesis of his "manly man" heroes, especially focusing on neurotic figures warped by domineering mothers, like *Psycho*'s pathological killer Norman Bates. Those late mother figures "constitute a grim gallery of ogres [and his filmic] mother-son relationships are generally neurotic, with sadomasochistic undertones" (Gianetti and Eyman 317).

In *Murder!* (1930), Hitchcock had presented a villain with accepted Hollywood visual hints at homosexuality, a device he continued with murderer Bruno Anthony in *Strangers on a Train* and with bisexual Philip Vandamm in *North by Northwest.* Hitchcock apparently was fascinated with the notion of homosexual behavior, which he had encountered in Europe in his youth. His portrayal of villains like *Rebecca*'s Mrs. Danvers and Bruno Anthony as gay generally contributed to his homophobic reputation, although feminist critics generally feel his work exemplifies "the patriarchal gaze" celebrating the subjugation of women in traditional family structures. Robert Corber has argued that Hitchcock's Cold War films link homosexuality to un-American activities, and recent Queer Theorists postulate that Hitchcock's male and female figures are both bisexual.

Hitchcock's Associates

In his 1950s heyday, Alfred Hitchcock worked with some of Hollywood's most illustrious craftspeople, such as costume designer Edith Head, with eight Oscars the most honored woman in movie history. As one of his most frequent collaborators, she worked on six of his films: *Rear Window, The Trouble with Harry, The Man Who Knew Too Much, Vertigo,* and *Marnie.* She also created the wardrobes for Tippi Hedren in *The Birds* and Julie Andrews in *Torn Curtain.* Composer Bernard Herrmann, almost as powerful a personality as Hitchcock, began working with him in 1955, producing some of the movies' most memorable scores for six Hitchcock films and becoming the staff composer for *Alfred Hitchcock Presents.* Herrmann claimed that "When Hitchcock finished a film, it's only 60% complete. I supply the other 40%" (quoted in Leitch 157). He wrote scores for *The Trouble with Harry, The Man Who Knew Too Much, The Wrong Man, Vertigo, North by Northwest, Psycho,* and *Marnie,* but around 1965 he broke with Hitchcock over the score for *Torn Curtain,* and they never spoke again. Losing Herrmann and George Tomasini, the film editor who had cut all of Hitchcock's films except *The Trouble with Harry* until Tomasini's death in 1964, dealt heavy blows to Hitchcock's personal and professional life, as did the deaths in 1966 of Hitchcock's first American producer David O. Selznick and Hitchcock's ghostwriter James Allerdyce, who composed the Hitchcock monologues opening and closing *Alfred Hitchcock Presents* and the subsequent *Alfred Hitchcock Hour.*

Of all Hitchcock's associates, the most important influence was his wife Alma Reville Hitchcock, who almost always worked on his films, frequently without screen credit. She had been an assistant director herself in England, and when they came to America, she actively participated in Hitchcock's filmmaking. British film historian Charles Barr declared that according to Hitchcock himself, "he constantly referred, and often deferred, to her judgment" (quoted in Leitch 276). After her bout with cancer in 1958, Alma suffered a severe undiagnosable illness in 1969 and a partially paralyzing stroke a year later while Hitchcock was filming *Topaz.* A more severe stroke in 1972 left her mostly bedridden; by 1978 her keen mind was badly affected, and Hitchcock made heroic efforts to care for her. She outlived Hitchcock by two years, dying in July 1982 without knowing he had preceded her.

THE ENDURING APPEAL OF ALFRED HITCHCOCK'S FILMS

The unique and enduring appeal of Alfred Hitchcock's films rests on three achievements. First, by developing "The Hitchcock Touch," a totally new and highly effective combination of creative techniques designed to appeal to audiences while cleverly directing their responses, he held up a creative ideal to filmmakers who followed him. Brian De Palma claimed that "dealing with Hitchcock is like dealing with Bach—he wrote every tune that was ever done" (quoted in Rebello 192). François Truffaut celebrated Hitchcock's technical legacy: "When a director undertakes to make a western, he is not necessarily thinking of John Ford, since there are equally fine movies in the genre by Howard Hawks and Raoul Walsh. Yet, if he sets out to make a thriller or suspense picture, you may be certain that in his heart of hearts he is hoping to live up to one of Hitchcock's masterpieces" (Truffaut 19).

Second, in an industry not usually commended for its ethical standards, Hitchcock for a long time maintained his integrity. In a 1950 interview, he appeared satisfied in serving his employers to the best of his ability because, he said, "I have too much conscience to take a million dollars and make a film that would please only me and the critics. . . . it is harder to make a film that has both integrity and wide audience appeal than it is to make one that merely satisfied one's own artistic conscience" (quoted in Gottlieb 37). The violence, horror, and unbridled sexuality of his last films testifies to the film industry's decline fully as much as it underscores the effects of the profound "existential crisis" Hitchcock experienced in the 1960s.

Finally, especially through *Psycho,* his most famous film, Hitchcock left a legacy of

> . . . a worldview and a cultural sensibility which has perhaps come to dominate the modern world. Detached, ironic, blackly humorous, stylish and self-aware, the sensibility . . . is aligned to modern metropolitan existence at the start of the twenty-first century. Hitchcock has transcended his status as a filmmaker to become a cultural phenomenon of the first order. (Haeffner 113)

THE HITCHCOCK SPINOFFS

In 1955, ever conscious of furthering his reputation, Hitchcock licensed his name to *The Alfred Hitchcock Mystery Magazine,* a monthly periodical, and many other anthologies like *Twelve Stories They Wouldn't Let Me Use on TV,* but he had no other connection with those publications. CBS' immensely popular Sunday evening television series *Alfred Hitchcock Presents* debuted on October 2, 1955, with "Revenge," labeled with his well-known profile self-portrait sketch, preceded by a clever monologue delivered by Hitchcock but written by James Allardice, and directed by Hitchcock himself. He directed only 16 more of the episodes, which moved to NBC in 1960. The program was nominated for several Emmys before it closed on June 26, 1962. That September it returned as CBS's *The Alfred Hitchcock Hour* and lasted until May 1965; Hitchcock directed

Television has brought murder back into the home— where it belongs.
—Alfred Hitchcock

only one of those episodes. Both *Alfred Hitchcock Presents* and *The Alfred Hitchcock Hour* used actors famous from Hitchcock's films, various writers, and virtually the same production crew, which worked out of Universal Studios' television unit. *The New Alfred Hitchcock Presents*, based on the original series, began in 1985, four years after Hitchcock's death, and lasted for 76 episodes, until the close of the 1988 to 1989 season. All series carefully preserved the public persona that Hitchcock had cultivated so carefully during his life—the Master of Suspense.

PARALLEL CHRONOLOGY

Major Events Related to Alfred Hitchcock	World Events
	1880s First motion pictures with single camera made by E.J. Marey
	1889 Thomas Edison develops kinetograph with rolls of celluloid film
	1894 Edison opens first Kinetoscope Parlor (films less than one minute shown to one viewer at a time)
	1895 Lumière brothers (France) develop Cinématographe
	1896 Projection machines first used in New York City
1899 Alfred Joseph Hitchcock born in Leytonstone (East London)	
	1905 First movie theatre ("nickelodeon") built in Pittsburgh, PA
	1908 By that year, U.S. movie crafts had separated, overseen by director
1910 Alfred sent to St. Ignatius College	1910 "Star system" becomes prevalent; 26 million Americans going to movies each week
	1913 Hollywood becomes American movie capital
1914 Alfred's father dies; financial crisis	1914–1918 World War I; U.S. dominates film industry
1915 Alfred goes to work for Henley Telegraph Company	1915 U.S. Supreme Court breaks Edison's Motion Picture Patents Co.'s stranglehold on films on anti-trust grounds; D.W. Griffith's epic

(Continued)

Major Events Related to Alfred Hitchcock	World Events
	The Birth of a Nation takes in $18 million
1920 Alfred takes menial job designing film titles for Famous Players-Lasky	
1922–1925 Alfred is assistant to director Graham Cutts and doing scenarios and set design on Cutts's films	
1923 Alfred proposes to Alma Reville	**1923** C.B. DeMille makes *The Ten Commandments*
1926 Alfred and Alma are married; Hitchcock debuts in thriller genre with *The Lodger* and first uses cameo appearance	
1927 Hitchcock joins BIP (British International Pictures) as highest paid British film director	**1927** Dialogue introduced in *The Jazz Singer*
1928 Patricia, the Hitchcocks' only child, born; Hitchcock begins cinematic experimentation	
	Late 1920s First sound films
1929 Hitchcock's *Blackmail* one of first British sound films	**Late 1920s–1948** "Big Five" studios dominate movie industry
1930 Hitchcock forms Hitchcock Baker Productions	
	1932 Technicolor process developed
1934 Hitchcock signs contract with Gaumont British Pictures; finds his suspense thriller niche	
1934–1938 The "thriller sextet" establishes Hitchcock's technical, aesthetic, and entrepreneurial strategies: including *The Man Who Knew Too Much* (1934), *The 39 Steps* (1935)	
1939 Hitchcock begins work for producer David O. Selznick in U.S.; makes three films for Selznick until 1948, including *Rebecca* and *Spellbound*	
1941 Hitchcock makes *Suspicion*, his first as both producer and director	
1942 Hitchcock's mother dies; brother apparently commits suicide; Hitchcock's weight problem begins;	

Major Events Related to Alfred Hitchcock	World Events
diets and makes *Lifeboat* and anti-fascist films	
1943 *Shadow of a Doubt*, reputedly Hitchcock's favorite of his films	
	1945 Explosion of the atomic bomb; end of World War II
1946 Lew Wasserman becomes Hitchcock's agent	**1946** U.S.-USSR relations deteriorating; Churchill's "Iron Curtain" speech
1948 *Rope*, Hitchcock's first color film	**1948** Anti-trust legislation dismantles virtual monopoly of movie industry by "Big Five" studios; USSR tests atomic bomb
1950 *Stage Fright*, filmed in the U.K.	**1950s** Television begins to erode movie profits, necessitating technological innovations; the Cold War causes widespread tension until the 1980s
	1950–1953 Korean conflict
1954 *Dial M for Murder*, first of Grace Kelly's three films with Hitchcock	**1954** U.S. tests hydrogen bomb
1955 Hitchcock launches *Alfred Hitchcock Presents*; with Paramount Pictures produces *Rear Window* and *To Catch a Thief*; *The Man Who Knew Too Much* (1956) and *Vertigo* (1958); assembles regular team, uses glamorous stars and exotic settings	
	1956 Studios producing made-for-TV films
	1957 USSR launches *Sputnik*, first space satellite
1958 Hitchcock undergoes surgery; Alma has cervical cancer	
1959 *North by Northwest*	
1960 *Psycho*; Hitchcock's career slips but his critical reputation rises	**1960s** Independent filmmakers make low-budget films
	1961–1975 Vietnam War
1962 *Alfred Hitchcock Presents* closes after 268 episodes; *The Alfred Hitchcock Hour* begins	**Oct. 1962** The Cuban Missile Crisis
1963 *The Birds*	**1963** President John F. Kennedy assassinated
1964–1969 *Marnie, Torn Curtain*, and *Topaz* fail at U.S. box office	

(Continued)

Major Events Related to Alfred Hitchcock	World Events
1965 *The Alfred Hitchcock Hour* closes after 93 presentations	
1967 Hitchcock receives Irving A. Thalberg Memorial Award from Academy of Motion Picture Arts and Sciences	
	1968 Assassinations of Robert F. Kennedy and Martin Luther King, Jr.
	1969 Astronaut Neil Armstrong walks on moon; Woodstock Music Festival; Manson "family" killings; widespread antiwar riots
1970 Hitchcock's health fails; Alma has stroke	
	1971 "Pentagon Papers" begin to be published
1972 *Frenzy,* Hitchcock's last major film; Alma suffers severe stroke	
	1973 Watergate trials
	1975 U.S. departure from Vietnam
1976 *Family Plot,* Hitchcock's last film, a comic thriller with Bruce Dern and Karen Black	
	Late 1970s Science fiction and horror films achieve immense popularity
Jan. 1980 Hitchcock made Knight Commander of the Order of the British Empire	
April 29, 1980 Hitchcock dies of heart, kidney, and liver failure in Los Angeles	
1982 Alma Reville Hitchcock dies on July 6	
1985–1989 *The New Alfred Hitchcock Presents* runs for 76 episodes	

ALFRED HITCHCOCK'S FILMS

Films below with (*) were directed by Graham Cutts, with Hitchcock writing, designing sets, and except for *The White Shadow,* functioning as assistant director. Dates of release are given. Titles in quotation marks are titles of Hitchcock-directed episodes of *Alfred Hitchcock Presents.*

Number 13 (not finished) (1922)

Always Tell your Wife (Seymour Hicks, codirector); *Woman to Woman** (1923)

The White Shadow,* The Prude's Fall,* The Passionate Adventure* (1924)

The Blackguard* (1925)

The Pleasure Garden, The Mountain Eagle, The Lodge (1926)

Downhill, Easy Virtue, The Ring (1927)

The Farmer's Wife, Champagne (1928)

Harmony Heaven (co-directed), *The Manxman, Blackmail* (1929)

Elstree Calling, Juno and the Paycock, Murder! (1930)

The Skin Game (1931)

Rich and Strange, Number Seventeen, Lord Chamber's Ladies (1932)

Waltzes from Vienna (1933)

The Man Who Knew Too Much (1934)

The 39 Steps (1935)

The Secret Agent, Sabotage (1936)

Young and Innocent (1937)

The Lady Vanishes (1938)

Jamaica Inn (1939)

Rebecca, Foreign Correspondent (1940)

Mr. and Mrs. Smith, Suspicion (1941)

Saboteur (1942)

Shadow of a Doubt (1943)

Lifeboat, Bon Voyage, Adventure Malgache (1944)

Spellbound (1945)

Notorious (1946)

The Paradine Case (1947)

Rope (1948)

Under Capricorn (1949)

Stage Fright (1950)

Strangers on a Train (1951)

I Confess (1953)

Dial "M" for Murder, Rear Window (1954)

To Catch a Thief, "Revenge," *The Trouble with Harry,* "Breakdown," "The Case of Mr. Pelham" (1955)

"Back for Christmas," "Wet Saturday," *The Man Who Knew Too Much, The Wrong Man,* "Mr. Blanchard's Secret" (1956)

"One More Mile to Go," "Four O'Clock," "The Perfect Crime" (1957)

"Lamb to the Slaughter," *Vertigo,* "Dip in the Pool," "Poison" (1958)

"Banquo's Chair," *North by Northwest*, "Arthur," "The Crystal Trench" (1959)

"Incident at a Corner," *Psycho*, "Mrs. Bixby's and the Colonel's Coat" (1960)

"The Horseplayer," "Bang! You're Dead!" (1961)

"I Saw the Whole Thing" (1962)

The Birds (1963)

Marnie (1964)

Torn Curtain (1966)

Topaz (1969)

Frenzy (1972)

Family Plot (1976)

MEDIA ADAPTATIONS

Short Story

"The Murder of Monty Woolley," short story Hitchcock wrote for *Look* magazine, 1943, and reprinted in *Games* magazine, November/December 1980.

Television

Alfred Hitchcock Presents, with Hitchcock as host and occasional director, 1955–1962; 268 episodes

The Alfred Hitchcock Hour, again with Hitchcock as host, 1962–1965, 93 episodes

The New Alfred Hitchcock Presents, using colorized introductions by Hitchcock, 1985–1989, 76 episodes

Books

Alfred Hitchcock and the Three Investigators, juvenile detective series with Hitchcock as a character; originally written by Robert Arthur

Hitchcock lent his name to a series of eight collections of short fiction, though he did not read, review, edit, or select the stories in them.

Magazine

Alfred Hitchcock's Mystery Magazine

Newsletters

The MacGuffin (Australian quarterly; founding editor Ken Mogg)

The Hitchcock Annual (only American periodical devoted entirely to Hitchcock's work)

Works Based on His Work/Life

High Anxiety (comedy spoof)

Hitchcock & Herrmann (play about Hitchcock's relationship with composer Bernard Herrmann)

Remakes of Hitchcock Films by Others

A Perfect Murder (1998) (remake of *Dial M for Murder*)

Psycho (1998) (remake by Gus Van Sant)

Rear Window (telefilm (1998) remake starring wheelchair-bound Christopher Reeve)

Board Game

Why? Milton Bradley board game presented by Alfred Hitchcock

Journal

The Hitchcock Annual, Richard Allen and Sidney Gottlieb, eds. Published yearly since 1994 as the journal of record for Hitchcock studies. London: Wallflower Press, 1994 and continuing.

WORKS CITED

Belton, John. "Can Hitchcock Be Saved from Hitchcock Studies?" *Cineaste* 28 (Fall 2003): 16–21.

Bogdanovich, Peter. *Who the Devil Made It.* New York: Knopf, 1997.

Deutelbaum, Marshall, and Leland Poague, eds. *A Hitchcock Reader.* Ames: Iowa State University Press, 1986.

Devas, Angela. "How to Be a Hero: Space, Place and Masculinity in *The 39 Steps.*" *Journal of Gender Studies* 14 (March 2005): 45–54.

Gianetti, Louis, and Scott Eyman. *Flashback: A Brief History of Film.* Englewood Cliffs, NJ: Prentice-Hall, 1986.

Gottlieb, Sidney. *Hitchcock on Hitchcock.* London: Faber & Faber, 1995.

Gunz, Jeff. "Digging the Dirt on Hitchcock Leaves the Author Vulnerable," Review of *Spellbound by Beauty*, by Donald Spoto. *The Sunday Oregonian,* November 2, 2008: O11.

Haeffner, Nicholas. *Alfred Hitchcock.* London: Longman, 2005.

Kenworthy, Christopher. *The World of Cinema.* London: Evans Brothers, 2001.

Leitch, Thomas, ed. *The Encyclopedia of Alfred Hitchcock.* New York: Checkmark Books, 2002.

McBride, Joseph. "Alfred Hitchcock's *Mary Rose.*" *Cineaste* 26 (2001): 24–28.

McGilligan, Patrick. *Alfred Hitchcock: A Life in Darkness and Light.* New York: Regan Books, 2003.

Martin, Pete. "I Call on Alfred Hitchcock." In *Filmmakers on Filmmaking,* edited by Harry Geduld. Bloomington: Indiana University Press, 1969.

Modleski, Tania. *The Women Who Knew Too Much.* New York and London: Methuen, 1988.

Mulvey, Laura. "Visual Pleasure and Narrative Cinema." *Screen* 16 (1975): 6–18.

Nogueira, Rui, and Nicoletta Zakaffi. "Hitch, Hitch, Hitch, Hurrah!" In *Alfred Hitchcock Interviews,* edited by Sidney Gottlieb. Jackson, MS: University of Mississippi Press, 2003, 119–128.

Rebello, Stephen. *Alfred Hitchcock and the Making of Psycho.* New York: St. Martin's Press, 1990.

Review of *Spellbound by Beauty* by Donald Spoto, *New York Times Book Review* 7 December 2008: 42. Cited in text as NYTBR 42.

Spoto, Donald. *The Dark Side of Genius.* New York: Ballantine, 1983.

Taylor, Alan. *Jacobean Visions: Webster, Hitchcock and the Google Culture.* Berne: Peter Lang Verlag, 2007.

Truffaut, François. *Hitchcock.* New York: Simon & Schuster, 1985.

Wollaeger, Mark A. "Killing Stevie: Modernity, Modernism, and Mastery in Conrad and Hitchcock." *Modern Language Quarterly* 58 (September 1997): 323–350.

Wood, Robin. *Hitchcock's Films Revisited.* 1989; 2nd ed. New York: Columbia University Press, 2002.

FURTHER READING

Allen, Richard. "*The Lodger* and Hitchcock's Aesthetic." *Hitchcock Annual* (2001): 36–78.

———, and Sam Ishii-Gonzales. *Hitchcock: Past and Future.* London: Routledge, 2004.

Auiler, Dan. *Hitchock's Notebooks.* New York: Avon, 1999.

Belleur, Raymond. *The Analysis of Film.* Bloomington: Indiana University Press, 2000 (originally published in French, 1979).

Barr, Charles. *English Hitchcock.* Cameron & Hollois, 1999.

Bouzereau, Laurent. *The Alfred Hitchcock Quote Book.* New York: Citadel, 1993.

Cameron, Ian, and V.F. Perkins. "Interview with Hitchcock." *Movie* 6 (1963): 4–6.

Cohen, Paula M. *Alfred Hitchcock: The Legacy of Victorianism.* Lexington, KY: University of Kentucky Press, 1995.

Conrad, Peter. *The Hitchcock Murders.* London: Faber & Faber, 2000.

Dellolio, Peter J. "Hitchcock and Kafka: Expressionist Themes in *Strangers on a Train. Midwest Quarterly* 45 (Spring 2004): 240–255.

DeRosa, Steven. *Writing with Hitchcock.* London: Faber & Faber, 2001.

Durgnat, Raymond. *The Strange Case of Alfred Hitchcock.* Cambridge, MA: MIT Press, 1974.

Fawell, John. *Hitchcock's Rear Window: The Well-Made Film.* Carbondale, IL: Southern Illinois Press, 2001.

Garrett, Greg. "Hitchcock's Women on Hitchcock: A Panel Discussion with Janet Leigh, Tippi Hedren, Karen Black, Suzanne Pleshette, and Eva Marie Saint." *Literature/Film Quarterly* 27 (1999): 79–89.

———. *Alfred Hitchcock: Interviews.* Jackson: University Press of Mississippi, 2003.

————, and Christopher Brookhouse, eds. *Framing Hitchcock*. Detroit, MI: Wayne State University Press, 2002.

Hitchcock O'Connell, Patricia, and Laurent Bouzereau. *Alma Hitchcock: The Woman behind the Man*. New York: Berkley, 2003.

Kapsis, Robert A. *Hitchcock: The Making of a Reputation*. Chicago: Umiversity of Chicago Press, 1992.

Kraft, Jeff, and Aaron Leventhal. *Footsteps in the Fog: Alfred Hitchcock's San Francisco*. Santa Monica, CA: Santa Monica Press, 2002.

Krohn, Bill. *Hitchcock at Work*. New York: Phaidon, 2000.

LaVallee, Andrew W.A. "'Can't You See?': Women and Aura in Hitchcock's *Vertigo*." http://hitchcock.tv/essays/aura.html, retrieved 11/20/2007.

LaValley, Albert J. *Focus on Alfred Hitchcock*. Englewood Cliffs, NJ: Prentice-Hall, 1972.

McArthur, Colin. "The Critics Who Knew Too Little: Hitchcock and the Absent Class Paradigm." *Film Studies* 2 (Spring 2000).

McDevitt, Jim, and Eric San Juan. *A Year of Hitchcock: 52 Weeks with the Master of Suspense*. New York: Scarecrow Press, 2009.

McLaughlin, James. "All in the Family: Alfred Hitchcock's *Shadow of a Doubt*." In *A Hitchcock Reader*, edited by Marshall Deutelbaum and Leland Poague. Ames: Iowa State University Press, 1986.

Mogg, Ken. *The Alfred Hitchcock Story*. London: Titan, 1999.

Price, Theodore. *Hitchcock and Homosexuality*. Metuchen, NJ: Scarecrow Press, 1992.

Rothman, William. *The Murderous Gaze*. Cambridge, MA: Harvard University Press, 1980.

Sloan, Jane. *Alfred Hitchcock: The Definitive Filmography*. Berkeley: University of California Press, 1995.

Smith, Susan. *Hitchcock: Suspense, Humour and Tone*. London: BFI, 2000.

Spoto, Donald. *The Art of Alfred Hitchcock*. Anchor ed. 1992. New York: Doubleday, 1976.

————. *Spellbound by Beauty: Alfred Hitchcock and His Leading Ladies*. New York: Random House, 2008.

WEB SITES

http://hitchcockpresentsdvd.com (Official Web site)

http://www.hitchcockonline.org (Contains online essay and links)

http://www.labyrinth.net.au/~muffin (Online extension of the Hitchcock journal, *The McGuffin*)

http://www.writingwithhitchcock.com (Companion site to Steven DeRosa's *Writing with Hitchcock*)

http://zalla/dk/euroscreenwriters/interviews/alfred_hitchcock.htm (Text and voice interviews with Hitchcock)

Illustration by Sidney Paget for "The Greek Interpreter."

Sherlock Holmes:
The Genius Detective

Come, Watson, come! The game is afoot.

—Sherlock Holmes

No other fictional detective has so firmly captured the world's attention as Sherlock Holmes, created by a young, impecunious, and imaginative physician, Arthur Conan Doyle. With Doyle's first collection of short stories (1891), Holmes, assisted by his confidant and chronicler Dr. John H. Watson, became and remains the most famous detective in history, renowned for his minute observation, deduction, eccentric personality and habits, and memorable utterances—the prototype of the "genius detective," inspiring thousands of fictional and nonfictional writings, and even convincing many fans that a real person lived and worked at 221B Baker Street, London.

HISTORICAL/CULTURAL CONTEXT

At the time of Sherlock Holmes's first case, "The Adventure of the 'Gloria Scott,'" set in 1873, late-Victorian Britain still seemed a peaceful nation of outstanding commercial success, quiet home-lovers, religion, order, hard work, and above all, morals—or morality. However, disruptive influences soon would push the nation to "the brink of a long slide-down from a position of true power and rare stability" (Keating 1979, 5–6). Except for the Crimean War, 1853 to 1856, Britain had not experienced major warfare since disposing of Napoleon, but its free trade policy contributed to colonial losses; Ireland's economic grievances were growing; imperial rivalries were stirring, especially Russian encroachments on British interests in India and border disputes with the Boers in South Africa; and the brash United States was competing strongly for British markets.

In response, the British Reform Bill of 1884 established universal male suffrage, encouraging voters to demand social democracy just when technology—automobiles, telephones, electric lighting—was exponentially increasing the pace of daily life and transforming society. Optimism and confidence began to erode, and "an emphasis on comfort and pleasure replaced the earnest, hardworking striving of the mid-Victorians" (Youngs et al. 342). The rich became richer and the affluent middle class enjoyed Britain's "cheap food" policy, abundant domestic help, the theater, and light reading.

That apparent well-being was only illusory, because though both classes deplored the evils of poverty, the poor "lived in appalling squalor . . . in the crammed rookeries of the great cities it was each man for himself" (Keating 1979, 11), a perfect breeding ground for crime. Life in urban streets was a threatening presence in constant motion and transition, so that "heightened anonymity, social insecurity, and urban poverty" furnished "fertilizer for criminals" (Murphy x). Crime-filled urban streets filled with strange, seemingly inexplicable, activity forced people to demand police protection and seek out consulting detectives "for help in shedding light on their life and to rescue them from menacing terror" (Harper 68) and encouraged writers to explore detective methods. Nervous middle-class readers longing for security immediately snapped up their stories.

France and the United States had pioneered detective literature. The enigmatic progenitor of all Western police detectives was Eugène François Vidocq, the first paid detective in the Sûreté, France's national police force. Vidocq, born in Arras in 1775, "left memoirs that inspired mainstream 'greats' like Victor Hugo, Balzac, and Dickens . . . and helped germinate the detective fiction of Edgar Allan Poe and Arthur Conan Doyle" (Brunsdale 2), and still fuels the imaginations of detective authors. As a poor boy Vidocq himself experienced crime and prison; later he became a police informer and then a paid-per-arrest supervisor of the Sureté's four unsalaried agents. After he resigned from the police in 1827, he opened the first European private investigation agency, dying in disgrace in 1857, framed for a crime he did not commit. His *Memoirs* reveal sympathy for the poor, an awareness of the vast range of human capacities from good to evil, and the often saving grace of humor.

American author Edgar Allan Poe, nearly Vidocq's contemporary, created the genre of detective fiction with *Murders in the Rue Morgue* (1841), which Dorothy L. Sayers called "almost a complete manual of detective theory and practice" (Sayers 1928, 81). It featured Chevalier C. August Dupin, the world's first "genius detective," an eccentric who lived behind closed shutters and emerged nocturnally to solve crimes through deduction. In "The Mystery of Marie Roget" (1842), Poe initiated the device of a mystery based on a real event, and in "The Purloined Letter" (1848), he made Dupin attempt to replicate in his own mind the criminal's mental processes. Poe's Dupin stories also introduced the "locked room" puzzle, the use of a comparatively dull associate as chronicler of the great detective's adventures, obvious clues usually overlooked by readers, and a Hegelian dialectic where the detective represents Good and Order and the murderer Evil and Chaos, "culminating in the solution-as-synthesis and a triumph of understanding" (Murphy 395).

Émile Gaboriau, 1832 to 1873, produced the first French *romans policiers* (police novels) and *romans judiciaries* (judicial novels), combining police procedure with popular sensational fiction topics and techniques. His hypersensitive and eccentric sleuth Ledoq, first an amateur detective, later joined the police, where he brilliantly solved crimes through deduction and intuition. Messieurs Dupin and Ledoq are often cited as Sherlock Holmes's literary ancestors.

Between 1887, Conan Doyle's first Sherlock Holmes story, *A Study in Scarlet,* and 1893, when Holmes and his archenemy Professor Moriarty vanished over the Reichenbach Falls, unsettling trends were percolating through British intellectual and social circles. Britain's 1870 Education Act mandating universal compulsory schooling by 1892 gave Britain "a large layer of society which could . . . read and had some grasp of scientific method" so that they "could tackle reasonably difficult material" (Keating 1987, 17), such as Darwin's *Descent of Man* and Renan's *La Vie de Jesus* portraying Christ not as God but strictly as Man, works irretrievably jolting intellectual opinions and religious sensibilities. Friedrich Nietzsche's theory of the evolutionary "Super-man," and his shocking announcement in 1886 that "God is dead," were considered "another manifestation of the rot that had set in with Darwin's overturning of the time-sealed order of things" (Keating 1979, 109–110).

In the 1890s, detective literature celebrating the "good old days" provided a temporary refuge from such disruptions, where Right and Good could prevail over Chaos and Evil because sleuths, like medieval knights-errant, pursued the wicked and brought them to justice. In the earlier Holmes stories, Conan Doyle vividly depicted a world of solid Victorian sureties, but after 1902, he looked back on, not into, the comfortingly stable world which had made his earlier stories so absorbing.

During the 1890s and 1900s, average Britons increasingly accepted the notion that poverty, unemployment, and ignorance and the crime they spawned were neither inevitable nor the fault of individual perpetrators, but the consequence of social arrangement for which government was responsible. The newspapers Conan Doyle constantly read featured sex, crime, and violence. Church attendance was dropping and "a significant number of Victorians were attracted by spiritualism—the attempt at séances to communicate with the dead—as a substitute or complementary religion" (Arnstein 187). Only the favored few enjoyed Edwardian prosperity from 1901 to 1910, when British wages were barely matching rising prices and working-family salaries stood still.

AUTHORSHIP

The eldest son and second child of Charles and Mary Doyle, Arthur Conan Doyle was born in Edinburgh on May 22, 1859. Both sides of his Roman Catholic Irish family boasted artistic and literary talent. His paternal grandfather John Doyle had been a London political cartoonist; his uncle Richard, an illustrator, was a friend of Dickens and Thackeray; and his father Charles was a British government architect and amateur painter. One side of Arthur's mother's family descended from the Plantagenets, while the other was connected to Sir Walter Scott. "Arthur Conan Doyle grew up in a stable society . . . [without] any reason to be a reformer. His great detective would one day uphold the values of this social order . . . a mainstay of the status quo" (Freeman 1, xiv).

Arthur began his demanding Jesuit boarding-school education at Stonyhurst in 1870, where he discovered the writings of Thomas Babington Macaulay (1800 to 1859,) a highly influential and conservative British historian with a rousing prose style and an unshakable belief in British superiority. Conan

Doyle carried Macaulay's essays with him throughout his life and claimed that Macaulay had influenced him more than anyone else. At Stonyhurst he excelled at cricket and read voraciously, preferring Sir Walter Scott's historical novels, tales of the American wilderness, and works by Oliver Wendell Holmes, and he regaled his schoolmates with his own tales of horror and adventure. When he visited his Uncle Richard in London at Christmas 1874, Arthur "indulged his fascination with the macabre" at Mme. Tussaud's Chamber of Horrors on Baker Street and "dallied over instruments of torture . . . at the Tower of London" (Riley and McAlister 20).

Arthur spent 1875 at an Austrian Jesuit school, studying German and reading detective stories by Poe and Gaboriau, and the next year, now a large, loud young man who liked boxing and playing a big bass tuba, he enrolled at Edinburgh University to study medicine, at that pre-anesthetic, pre-antiseptic, pre-antibiotic time a profession requiring considerable determination and a strong stomach. There he encountered Dr. Joseph Bell, a surgeon whose remarkable diagnostic gift was based on minute observation of a patient's appearance and behavior. Arthur became Bell's outpatient assistant, learning deductive techniques that later would be integral to Sherlock Holmes's success.

> Today, experts in such disparate fields as dermatology, forensics, educational psychology, accounting, and martial arts cite Sherlock Holmes as a model for their deductive methods.

At six, Arthur Conan Doyle had already demonstrated his narrative talent and his interest in gory violence by composing a story about a man eaten alive by a tiger. At 20, his first published story, "The Mystery of Sassasa Valley," appeared in an Edinburgh weekly, and in 1880 he spent seven months as ship's doctor in the Arctic, where he enthusiastically hacked up whales and butchered seals. In 1881 as a ship's doctor, he took a nightmarish trip to West Africa that included typhoid fever, a shark attack, and an onboard fire.

Conan Doyle then briefly joined the Plymouth practice of a former Edinburgh classmate, George Budd. An unscrupulous quack with a mercurial temperament ranging from brilliant conversation to moody silence, Budd may have contributed energy, bizarre behavior, a wide range of interests, and periods of depression to Sherlock Holmes, but he also viciously backstabbed his erstwhile partner, leaving Conan Doyle with a lifelong horror of deception and betrayal: "It was as though in the disguise and dress of a man I had caught a sudden glimpse of something subhuman—of something so outside my own range of thought that I was powerless against it" (*The Stark Munro Letters* 271).

Budd's betrayal coincided with the severe alcoholic decline of Conan Doyle's father. Conan Doyle at this point repudiated Catholicism and began reading spiritualistic tracts which claimed that contacts could be made with departed souls through "mediums" at séances. He set up his own practice at Southsea, a Plymouth suburb, in 1882, and married Louise ("Tooie") Hawkins, the sister of a patient, in August 1885. His sluggish practice left him time to attend séances and write stories, at first dishearteningly rejected. He sold all rights to his first Holmes tale, *A Study in Scarlet,* for 25 pounds to a "shilling shocker," *Beeton's Christmas Annual,* for 1887 publication. It appeared in book form in 1888, illustrated cartoonishly by Conan Doyle's father, now confined to an asylum.

> An 1887 *Beeton's Christmas Annual,* where Holmes's first adventure, *A Study in Scarlet,* first appeared, sold at auction in 2007 for $156,000.

Arthur Conan Doyle really wanted to write historical novels, not detective fiction. In 1888 he produced *The Mystery of Coomber,* a melodramatic story resembling Wilkie Collins's *The Moonstone,* with Indian assassins stalking through an English castle. Conan Doyle's novel of the 17th-century Monmouth rebellion, *Micah Clarke,* appeared in February 1889, just after his first child, Mary Louise Conan Doyle, was born. While writing *The White Company,* a medieval novel and his own favorite work, he and Oscar Wilde received invitations to dine with Joseph Stoddart of the American *Lippincott's Monthly Magazine,* with happy results: Wilde's *The Picture of Dorian Gray* and Conan Doyle's *The Sign of Four* were both published in *Lippincott's* in 1889.

Conan Doyle then studied ophthalmology in Vienna, but after relocating his family to London to practice as an eye specialist, he did not have one patient there. A tough bout with influenza helped him see "how foolish I was to waste my literary earnings to keep up an oculist's room in Wimpole Street, and I determined with a wild rush of joy to . . . trust for ever in my power of writing" where he could "be my own master" (quoted in Riley and McAlister 23). He closed his practice, the family moved to a suburban London villa, and in July 1891 "A Scandal in Bohemia" appeared in the tremendously popular new *Strand Magazine,* whose editor believed "that here was the greatest short story writer since Edgar Allan Poe" (quoted in Sutherland 197). The British public, conditioned by screaming newspaper headlines about Jack the Ripper and longing for "insight, competence, and cool, blade-sharp logic" (Riley and McAlister 22) went wild. Arthur Conan Doyle had invented the series story, and overnight Sherlock Holmes became a household name.

Despite that gigantic success, Conan Doyle felt that Holmes took "my mind from better things" (quoted in Sutherland 197). He continued writing historical fiction and eventually came to hate Holmes, even though Holmes made him one of Britain's wealthiest authors. After the phenomenally selling

The Adventures of Sherlock Holmes (1892) containing 12 stories, Conan Doyle was already thinking of winding Holmes "up for good and all" but his mother expressly forbade it. He continued with *The Memoirs of Sherlock Holmes* (1894) containing 11 stories, amid personal tragedies. After his son's birth in November 1892, Tooie was diagnosed with tuberculosis, virtually a death sentence. After visiting the Reichenbach Falls in Switzerland with Tooie, he declared to his mother that he was writing the last Sherlock Holmes story: "I am weary of his name" (quoted in Riley and McAlister 25).

When Holmes went over the Reichenbach Falls locked to the dastardly Professor Moriarty, "All of London exploded. . . . Women wept . . . and dressed in mourning clothes, and men donned black silk armbands . . . twenty thousand canceled their subscriptions to *The Strand*" and even Queen Victoria was "not amused" (Riley and McAlister 21). Conan Doyle had to resurrect the Great Detective for two more novels, *The Hound of the Baskervilles* (1902), set prior to Holmes's disappearance; and *The Valley of Fear* (1915); as well as three more story collections, *The Return of Sherlock Holmes* (1905), 13 stories; *His Last Bow* (1917), 8 stories; and *The Case Book of Sherlock Holmes* (1927), 12 stories.

Arthur Conan Doyle never took his Sherlock Holmes stories seriously. At first he churned them out "quickly, effortlessly, often while entertaining friends" (Riley and McAlister 23), which accounts for discrepancies and shifts in scenes, chronology, names, and other details that have provoked intense speculation ever since. After Holmes's "death," Conan Doyle spent about 10 years attending séances and investigating haunted houses, lecturing in America, and he also volunteered for medical work during the Boer War, which brought him a knighthood in 1902. He socialized with Britain's most glittering society, playing cricket, shooting, and motoring. He fell in love with Scottish opera singer Jean Leckie in 1897, though they maintained a proper platonic relationship until they were married a year after Tooie's death in 1896. He also wrote obsessively—horror stories, plays, political pamphlets, and of course historical novels.

In 1901, Conan Doyle's golfing partner Fletcher Robinson told him an eerie Dartmoor legend about a ghostly hound howling in the moonlight. After they toured the area "in a trap driven by a man named Baskerville" (Riley and McAlister 26), Sherlock Holmes's game was afoot again. The first installment of *The Hound of the Baskervilles* appeared in August 1901, just before acclaimed American actor William Gillette brought his famous play *Sherlock Holmes* to the London stage. The novel earned immense royalties for Conan Doyle, and he hurriedly produced more Holmes stories, even answering letters addressed to the Great Detective with cards signed "John H. Watson," some collected in *Letters to Sherlock Holmes* (1985). Nonetheless, after his return from the Reichenbach Falls, Holmes "was like an Old Man of the Sea to Conan Doyle" (Symons in Winks 209).

While Jean and Conan Doyle raised a daughter and two sons and he turned out new Holmes adventures, he also involved himself in social causes, including clearing innocent men of crimes and crusading for spiritualism, although his proclaimed belief in fairies detracted from his reputation as creator of the "reasoning and observing machine" Sherlock Holmes (quoted in Riley and McAlister 33). Conan Doyle wrote tirelessly, producing science fiction novels and plays which he occasionally financed and directed himself, including a dramatization of "The Speckled Band" which fell flat when the starring live boa constrictor refused to slither appropriately.

Politically, Conan Doyle never abandoned his staunch conservatism and patriotism, unsuccessfully standing for Parliament from Edinburgh in 1906, pamphleteering in defense of the Crown and opposing women's suffrage, though he supported divorce law reform. Already in 1911 he suspected Germany of invidious motives, and when World War I erupted, he raised funds and formed a local volunteer corps, even involving Holmes in capturing a German spy in "His Last Bow."

Britain's monstrous wartime losses intensified Conan Doyle's espousal of spiritualism, which in 1917 he said he approached "not in the spirit of a detective approaching a suspect, but in that of a humble religious soul, yearning for help and comfort" (quoted in Riley and McAlister 31). Jean's brother was killed in the war, and between October 1918 and February 1919, Conan Doyle lost both his son Kingsley and his beloved younger brother Innes, both wounded and succumbing to influenza. His grief drove him to fervently crusade for spiritualism in 13 books and many articles and worldwide lectures and Jean, who became a medium with a talent for "automatic writing" supposedly dictated by departed souls, supported his efforts enthusiastically.

Although suspicious neighbors railed against Conan Doyle's séances and some hecklers even called him the "Anti-Christ," he maintained his faith in spiritualism to the end—and perhaps beyond. A day after he died from heart disease on July 7, 1930, family members and his public began receiving his messages from "the other side," which continued, mostly channeled by Jean until her own death in 1940, a fascinating contradiction to Sherlock Holmes, "who reassures us that even the most baffling mysteries can be solved by reason, and who challenges us to use our powers of observation" (Freeman xx).

PROFILE OF THE GREAT DETECTIVE

Personal Background

A highly reliable source for biographical material regarding Sherlock Holmes, Dr. John H. Watson, and their major associates is Leslie S. Klinger's *The New Annotated Sherlock Holmes* (2004–2005), which includes speculations from William S. Baring-Gould's *Sherlock Holmes of Baker Street: A Life of the World's First Consulting Detective*, speculations which Klinger claims the Holmes Canon does not support. Klinger dates canonical cases from *The Date Being—?: A Compendium of Chronological Data*, by Andrew Jay Peck and Leslie S. Klinger.

Arthur Conan Doyle warned readers that "the doll and its maker are seldom identical" (quoted in Klinger 1979, 97). Not the date, nor the place, of Sherlock Holmes's birth, nor much about his ancestry is clear. Despite his dedication to the Victorian status quo, Holmes's few revelations about himself have a decidedly Darwinian flavor. In "The Mystery of the Greek Interpreter," set in 1888, Dr. Watson suggests that Holmes's deductive and observational capabilities were products of "systematic training." Holmes replies that his ancestors were country squires "who led much the same life as is natural to their class," insisting his talent for deduction came through nature, not nurture—that is, through his French grandmother, a sister of the French artist Horace Vernet, 1789–1863, whose orderly mind was said to resemble a well-stocked and well-organized bureau, and whose observation was so keen one glance at a model allowed him to "record the minutest details" (Keating 1979, 98). In the same story, Holmes mentions his brother Mycroft, even more deductively gifted, now in Government service, and his nemesis-to-be Professor James Moriarty, who had "hereditary tendencies of the most diabolical kind" (quoted in Keating 1979, 101). The accepted year of Moriarty's birth is 1846; Mycroft's, 1847; Watson's, 1852; and William Sherlock Scott Holmes's, probably 1853. According to Klinger, Sherlock had another older brother, Sherrinford, who was born in 1845 and went up to Oxford in 1864 (849, 851).

Speculations about Sherlock Holmes's Father

Sherlock Holmes, Sr.?

Mark Moriarty?

Captain Siger Holmes?

Robert Holmes?

David William Holmes?

The vampire Radu the Handsome, Dracula's brother?

The first cousin of John Wilkes Booth?

The great-grandson of Napoleon I?

Sherlock Holmes's European travels during his childhood at least partially explain his facility with languages. From 1855 to 1860, he traveled with his family to Bordeaux, then Montpellier, before briefly returning to England. In 1860 they sailed to Rotterdam and then stayed in Cologne before a Continental tour in 1861, returning to Kennington, England, in 1864, when Mycroft and Sherlock entered a boarding school. After being severely ill in 1865, Sherlock studied as a day boy at a Yorkshire grammar school and sailed in 1868 to St. Malo with his parents, from there traveling to Pau and entering a fencing salon.

The question of Sherlock Holmes's higher education has never been authoritatively settled. Professor Moriarty may have tutored him in mathematics before he entered Christ Church College, Oxford, in 1872, two years later matriculating at Gaius College, Cambridge. In the 1930s Dorothy L. Sayers persuasively argued that Holmes matriculated at Sidney Sussex College, a smaller and less expensive one of the 17 Cambridge colleges in October (Michaelmas) 1871, possibly as a scholarship boy aiming at an Honours degree in Natural Science concentrating on chemistry and comparative anatomy and physiology, and perhaps proceeding to his Tripos examinations in his tenth term, Michaelmas 1874. She suggested alternatively that he might have come up to Cambridge in Lent or Easter of 1872, taking Tripos in his eighth term, Michaelmas 1872. She also conjectured that Holmes might have taken a second Cambridge course, possibly medicine, or (according to Sayers, "exceedingly probable") he may have studied chemistry and languages at a German university in 1875, returning in December to England to take his B.A. ("Holmes's College Career" 167–183). Nick Rennison's fictionalized *Sherlock Holmes: The Unauthorized Biography* makes many plausible suggestions about Holmes's life, but these are usually not considered Holmesian "fact." Rennison does suggest that Holmes acted in plays while at Cambridge and afterward acted at the Lyceum theatre in London as "a method actor ahead of his time" (Rennison 158).

After his university studies, Holmes spent "months of inaction" in Montague Street, London, in 1877. An imposing presence, "rather over six feet, and so excessively lean that he seemed to be considerably taller" (Rennison 158), he visited America as an actor in 1879 with the Sasanoff Shakespeare Company, returning to England in 1880. He met Dr. John H. Watson the following year, and they took rooms at 221B Baker Street, as recounted in *A Study in Scarlet*. There the "Great Canon" begins.

Sherlock Holmes's Career

The physical appearance of Sherlock Holmes familiar today did not spring full blown from Conan Doyle's imagination. When chosen in 1891 by *The Strand Magazine* to illustrate the Sherlock Holmes stories, Sidney Paget used his handsome younger brother Walter as model for the Great Detective, making "Hundreds of thousands of young women yearn . . . as they might yearn for a stage actor." Conan Doyle noted that Paget's portrait was much more appealing than his own Holmes, who, he wrote, had "a thin razor-like face with a great hawks-bill of a nose, and two small eyes, set close together on either side of it" (quoted in Riley and McAlister 2). Paget gave Holmes his famous deerstalker hat, while the tall eccentric American actor William Gillette supplied the curved pipe which later became Holmes's trademark calabash.

These visual effects gradually melded into the unforgettable character whose career began with the "Gloria Scott" case, the earliest mentioned in the Canon, which occurred during Holmes's university days, probably in 1874. Holmes related them to Watson, who "published" them in 1893. *A Study in Scarlet,* published in 1887, takes place in 1881; "The Final Problem," during which Holmes and Moriarty went over the Reichenbach Falls, was published in 1893 but is set in 1891. Between 1874 and 1891, Sherlock Holmes solved 27 cases that Watson later chronicled, although Holmes solved many more. "It has become a good-humored convention for Holmes scholars to treat the stories as historical events and the protagonists as real figures," with Conan Doyle often referred to "as the literary agent for Dr. John H. Watson" (Freeman xix). When Conan Doyle returned to writing Holmes stories nearly a decade later, he set *The Hound of the Baskervilles* in 1889, prior to "The Final Problem."

After his disappearance, Holmes was not seen again until February 1894, a period known as "The Great Hiatus." Thirteen new Holmes stories began to appear in *The Strand* in 1903 and were collected into *The Return of Sherlock Holmes* (1905). "The Adventure of the Empty House," one of the earliest of these, is set in the spring of 1894. Watson, still grieving over the loss of Holmes, one evening bumps into a white-whiskered old book collector who snarls and disappears—only to return to Watson's Kensington home and miraculously shape-shift into Sherlock Holmes. After Watson recovers from the only faint he ever experienced, Holmes explains that he had been traveling in Tibet and the Mideast, carrying out secret British missions

Sherlock Holmes's Disguises

A sailor in *The Sign of Four*

A groom and a clergyman in "A Scandal in Bohemia"

An opium addict in "The Man with the Twisted Lip"

A common loafer in "The Adventure of the Beryl Coronet"

A bookseller in "The Adventure of the Empty House"

An old Italian priest in "The Adventure of the Final Problem"

A plumber in "The Adventure of Charles Augustus Milverton"

A dying man in "The Adventure of the Dying Detective"

An old sporting man in "The Adventure of the Mazarin Stone"

A woman in "The Adventure of the Mazarin Stone"

directed by his spymaster brother Mycroft in the "Great Game," the international intrigue then simmering between Britain and Imperial Russia over interests in India and Central Asia.

Another Sherlock Holmes novel-length adventure, *The Valley of Fear* (1915), is set in 1888, and two short story collections followed: *His Last Bow,* eight stories (1917), and *The Case Book of Sherlock Holmes* (1927) with 12 more stories. After the Great Hiatus, the Great Detective began exhibiting changes reflecting Conan Doyle's antipathy toward Holmes as well as disillusion with national and world events. In "The Adventure of the Norwood Builder" (1903), he mused, "London has become a singularly uninteresting city since the death of the late lamented Professor Moriarty," and that year, at 49, he made Holmes supposedly retire to potter around with his bees on the Sussex Downs. The cases Watson related thereafter, however, ranged farther afield than ever. Their plots involve stranger happenings, odder geographic locations, and increasingly peculiar murder weapons; Holmes even broke the law in "The Adventure of Charles Augustus Milverton" (1904), telling Inspector Lestrade, "My sympathies are with the criminals rather than with the victim, and I will not handle this case." Holmes obsessively needed opponents worthy of his mettle, and with Moriarty gone, he couldn't find them.

Sherlock Holmes's Retirement Income

Holmes's fee for solving "The Adventure of the Priory School" was £12,000. If he had divided it equally with Watson and invested his £6,000 ($30,000) at 3 percent per year, he could have lived comfortably at £180 ($900) per year "with his bees upon the Sussex downs."

In "The Adventure of Wisteria Lodge" (1908), Holmes complained that at home ". . . life is commonplace; the papers are sterile; audacity and romance seem to have passed forever from the criminal world." Between 1901 and 1910 Holmes may have "stepped back from the kind of criminal investigations in which he had made his name," and as international tension mounted, he engaged in "undertakings that are at best extralegal if not absolutely criminal" (Rennison 212). In "The Adventure of the Bruce-Partington Plans" (1908), Holmes apparently peered into the murky world of the "fledgling MI5 and MI6" (Rennison 214, 225). Holmes experienced physical ailments in "The Adventure of the Devil's Foot" (1910) and "The Adventure of the Dying Detective" (1913), where he suffered from a nasty contagious disease contracted from Chinese sailors. In "His Last Bow" (1917), told not by Watson but in the third person, Holmes, tracking a German spy, tried patriotically to buck up English morale during one of their darkest hours: "a cleaner, better, stronger land will lie in the sunshine when the storm has cleared."

Weapons Used in Sherlock Holmes's Cases

Air gun	Jellyfish
Blowgun	Poker
Hangman's noose	Revolver
Harpoon	Sheath knife
Horseshoe	Swamp adder

Conan Doyle's personal losses due to war and pandemic darkened the last Holmes stories. Mycroft died of influenza, too, and an exhausted Sherlock Holmes approached 66 in January 1920. In "The Adventure of the Creeping Man" (1923), he declared, "It's surely time that I disappeared into that little farm of my dreams," though he kept his Baker Street lodgings and saved an innocent man from hanging in the "Green Bicycle Case." Paradoxically, while Conan Doyle was proclaiming the reality of spirits and fairies, Holmes insisted in "The Adventure of the Sussex Vampire" (1924) that his "Agency stands flat-footed upon the ground. . . . No ghosts need apply." In retirement, Holmes himself wrote "The Adventure of the Lion's Mane" (1926), in the first person, describing his 1907 return from retirement to investigate a horrible death. Holmes's last activities are harder to trace than those of the Great Hiatus, for in the last two Holmes stories published, "The Veiled Lodger" and "Shoscombe Old Place" (both 1927), Holmes did little or no detecting. Watson had not seen him for three years when the Great Detective slipped off into rural oblivion and probably died on June 23, 1929 (Rennison 249). Watson, who himself died in 1929 (Klinger 871), could not record Sherlock Holmes's final exit, this time unchallenged by his public.

Two Possible Descendents of Sherlock Holmes

Nero Wolfe and Captain James T. Kirk

Sherlock Holmes's Strengths

Arthur Conan Doyle made Sherlock Holmes "a man of his time." Like Conan Doyle himself, Holmes wholeheartedly opposed the evils he felt the Industrial Revolution had engendered and Britain's decline from world leadership. "He was a knight-champion called forth by the hour to combat the dragon that about that year 1870, broke through the bars that had seemed so securely to constrain it" (Keating 1979, 18).

Holmes was a Victorian knight-champion, though hardly the rough-mounted early medieval soldier and landed vassal who rode to war and Crusade in pursuit of spoils; and still less the romantic 14th-century idealistic courtly lover sporting his lady's favor. From the late 18th century to World War I, a revival of the medieval chivalric code held sway in England, "creating ideals of behavior, by which all gentlemen were influenced, even if they did not consciously realize it" (Girouard, unpaginated Preface). Cricket-loving Arthur Conan Doyle, once described as "that paladin of lost causes," whose mother brought him up on chivalry and tales of his ancestors, liked to recall he was descended from Norman Doyles linked with the Dukes of Brittany, and he once slapped his son's face for calling a woman ugly. He would have liked to have been remembered most for his medieval novel *The White Company,* and he gave Holmes the Victorian chivalric virtues of unquestioned patriotism, conservatism, and personal honor, also paradoxically equipping Holmes with scientific and technological advancements that were destroying his cherished Victorian world.

Holmes told Watson that during "The Adventure of the 'Gloria Scott,'" when he learned that evil was stalking the cozy Victorian home of his friend Trevor's father, Holmes hurled himself into this first sally of his life-long battle against "devilry," armed with the very Victorian weapon of applied science (Keating 1979, 19–20). As Holmes's cases progressed, his applications of science and technology to detection burgeoned. In *A Study in Scarlet* he cited Darwin's evolutionary opinion that music had existed long before humanity achieved speech, but although Holmes championed order and many Darwinian concepts, he often "found himself locked in combat" with popular misinterpretations of Darwinism, like the notion that barriers of society were crumbling and "the long-fixed order of things was soon to tumble: . . . the beasts could be kept from roaming where they would only by the ceaseless exercise of reason coupled with that indefinable but powerful quality, decency. They were Holmes's weapons" (Keating 1979, 40), and he never put them down. Sherlock Holmes's popular championship of those ideals, shows that for a little while chivalric knights "influence[d] the lives and characters of officers, gentlemen, schoolboys, lovers, and Boy Scouts" in England and around the world (Girouard 14), until those ideals perished with the men who cherished them in the trenches of the First World War.

In the early Holmes stories, Dr. Watson built up the attractive and optimistic aspects of the Great Detective's character. Holmes "laughs, chuckles, smiles, and jokes" (Freeman xvii); he relished good cigars and researched tobacco; he enjoyed German opera, and he both composed and played difficult music on his Stradivarius. He read voraciously, even quoting the German master Goethe in the original; he had considerable knowledge about and affection for dogs; and he especially delighted in England's new "board schools" which he considered "beacons of the future," bringing enlightenment to the British masses.

Named and Unnamed Canines in Sherlock Holmes Stories

Carlo, a sick spaniel in "The Adventure of the Sussex Vampire"

Toby, a mongrel in *The Sign of Four*

Pompey, a "draghound" in "The Adventure of the Missing Three-Quarter"

Roy, a wolfhound in "The Adventure of the Creeping Man"

The Baskerville Hound in *The Hound of the Baskervilles*

A black spaniel in "The Adventure of Shoscombe Old Place"

A dying terrier in *A Study in Scarlet*

An Airedale in "The Adventure of the Lion's Mane"

A bull terrier in "The Adventure of the Gloria Scott"

Watson also portrayed a wide range of Holmes's eccentricities. Some of Holmes's habits, like his meditative violin-scraping and stabbing his correspondence onto the fireplace mantel with a pocket-knife, are humorous, but others, like his essentially solitary lifestyle, not only reflect a brilliant intellect, powerful deductive ability, and relentless logic, but they also hint at Holmes's darker side, one inextricably intertwined with his lifelong battle against "devilry." The basic puzzle of Holmes's character is why Conan Doyle, a "super-typical Victorian" created "an egocentric drug-taking hero so alien from his own beliefs." One answer lies in the influence of Nietzsche and Wagner, whose work Conan Doyle admired: "Part of Holmes's attraction was that, far more than any of his later rivals, he was so evidently a Nietzschean superior man. It was comforting to have such a man on one's side" (*Mortal Consequences* 65).

Sherlock Holmes's Nemeses

If Sherlock Holmes represents the late Victorian knight-errant, the dragon he pursued was pure Evil, as spawned by the Industrial Revolution's societal and cultural upheavals. It prowled both the world Holmes inhabited and found so wicked and the world of his inner self, shaped by his heredity and conditioned by his environment.

Conan Doyle had been "powerless to explain" his own betrayal at the hands of his unscrupulous partner Dr. Budd, and thereafter, "Whenever he depicts some descent into the abyss of vice, it is inevitably without any insight into how a soul makes such a journey. It is always taken as merely a fact of existence" (Freeman xvii). Holmes considered his most important work was identifying, tracking, and capturing evildoers, preferably causing them to wreak horrible justice on themselves through a process that he described in *A Study in Scarlet* as discerning "a chain of logical sequences without a break or flaw." Such a chain of sequences usually began from a human vicissitude like greed or pride or the desire for power, like the heinous polygamous Mormons of *A Study in Scarlet,* or abusive relatives who victimized helpless women like Mary Morstan, who would become Dr. John Watson's wife. Foiling such major villains sustained Holmes. "The work itself," he told Watson at the opening of *The Sign of Four,* "the pleasure of finding a field for my peculiar powers, is my highest reward" (90). Within Holmes himself, however, lurked a dark "fact of existence" that he struggled continuously to hold at bay. He would do anything to satisfy his real addiction, detective work. The cocaine-injecting scene which opens *The Sign of Four,* a routine Watson had been witnessing three times a day for many months, demonstrates Holmes's driving need for "mental exaltation." He abhorred stagnation, and if he could not find stimulating work, he was willing to pay for mind-altering drug use with "black reactions," periods of paralyzing depression (*Sign* 90). In Holmes's day, the use of such drugs as cocaine and opium was fairly widespread, since they were legally used in patent medicines. In the last half of the 19th century, a cocktail of alcohol and coca became a recreational drink praised in "testimonials from Thomas Edison, Jules Verne, Alexandre Dumas, and Pope Leo XIII, among others" (Riley and McAlister 88). Watson always categorically disapproved of Holmes's drug habit.

Holmes's addiction to ever more ingenious and dangerous cases led him to confront his ultimate adversary, Professor James Moriarty, whom Conan Doyle did not introduce until "The Final Problem." Watson described Holmes's view of Moriarty, an Irishman born in 1846 and possibly modeled on the real-life London crime organizer and fence Jonathan Wild, as "a man of good birth and excellent education, endowed by Nature with a phenomenal mathematical faculty. . . . But the man had hereditary tendencies of the most diabolical kind. A criminal strain ran in his blood" (quoted in Keating 1979, 101). Holmes also calls Moriarty's chief of staff, big game hunter Colonel Sebastian Moran, the "second most dangerous man in London"; as Moriarty's "muscle," Moran helps him with "high-class jobs" (Riley and McAlister 125). A description of Moriarty in "The Final Problem," as "a spider in the centre of its web . . . [with] a thousand radiations, and he knows well every quiver of each of them" parallels one in "The Adventure

---

Arthur Conan Doyle's Five Favorite Holmes Stories

1. "The Adventure of the Speckled Band"
2. "The Red-Headed League"
3. "The Adventure of the Dancing Men"
4. "The Adventure of the Final Problem"
5. "A Scandal in Bohemia"

of the Cardboard Box": "He loved to lie in the very centre of five millions of people, with his filaments stretching out . . . responsive to every little rumor or suspicion of unsolved crime"—a thumbnail portrait of Sherlock Holmes. Thus Moriarty is not only Holmes's worthy adversary, but his mirror image, both possibly modeled on Nietzsche's *Übermensch* (Super-man): tall, lean, intellectually gifted; perhaps Moriarty is even the fictionalization of the dark side of Holmes's personality. Their plunge over the Reichenbach Falls can be read symbolically: "Europe's greatest detective and its greatest criminal locked arm in arm, tumbling together into eternity over a vast abyss, form . . . [a] powerful . . . image of the mysterious duality of good and evil" (Freeman xxxi).

Sherlock Holmes's Associates

John H. Watson was born in 1852 and during his childhood lived briefly with his family in Australia before entering England's Wellington College in 1865. Dorothy L. Sayers postulated "Hamish" as Watson's middle name, theorizing that he had a Scottish mother. This would explain the apparent discrepancy in "The Man with the Twisted Lip" when Mary Morstan Watson refers affectionately to her husband as "James," the English form of the Scottish "Hamish" ("Dr. Watson's Christian Name" 186–188).

In 1872, Watson enrolled at the University of London and worked as a surgeon at St. Bartholomew's Hospital ("Bart's"); in 1878 he received his Doctor of Medicine degree and took a course in army surgery before sailing for India, where he was wounded in the Battle of Maiwand, 1880, and came down with enteric fever at Peshawar, returning to London on a slim pension of 11 shillings sixpence a day (about $20 per week). After becoming Holmes's assistant and chronicler, Watson fell in love with Mary Marston in *The Sign of Four*, and married her in 1888 when he established his practice at Paddington. He sold it three years later, around the time of Mary's death ca. 1892. In "Dr. Watson, Widower," Sayers suggested that Watson was staying with friends, not remarried as some commentators insisted, when he was temporarily absent from Baker Street in the 1890s. Sayers did not think Watson remarried until possibly 1902. William S. Baring-Gould, in *The Annotated Sherlock Holmes* (1967), postulated three marriages for Watson, the first in 1886 to a lady he had met in America, from ca. November 1, 1886, to late December 1887 or early January 1888; the second, to Mary Marston, about May 1, 1889; and the third in October 1902. Most commentators, however, agree with Leslie Klinger that Watson was married only twice. Watson moved to Queen Anne Street in 1902, remarried, and returned to successfully practicing medicine. He chronicled all but two of Holmes's adventures until his own death in 1929 "under circumstances unknown" (Klinger 848–872).

"Watson" has become the generic term for the well-meaning but slightly dull admiring friend who writes down and publishes the cases of a "genius detective," since that detective may himself seem stilted, arrogant, or blasé. The

My name is Sherlock Holmes. It is my business to know what other people don't know.

—Sherlock Holmes

original Dr. Watson, an "ordinary man," displays unsinkable courage, physical stamina, and unshakable loyalty to Holmes, making his narratives vivid and absorbing. Conan Doyle possibly put much of himself into Watson, another medical man who became a widower; "Holmes may be the greater character, but Watson is the better characterization" (Murphy 516).

As a private "consulting detective," Holmes had to strike a delicate balance in his relationships with the police. In Britain ordinary crime seemed to have decreased during the last half of the 19th century, due to street lighting, slum clearances, and the creation of the Metropolitan Police (later known as Scotland Yard) in 1829. Holmes preferred to take on extremely difficult cases, especially those allowing him to duel against a first-class criminal mind. He boasted, "I am not retained by the police to repair their deficiencies," but he held a certain respect for the unimaginative but tenacious Inspector Lestrade, who appears for comic relief in several stories beginning with *A Study in Scarlet*; Holmes called Lestrade "the best of a bad lot." Inspector Tobias Gregson and Inspector Bradstreet, less often mentioned, seem to be even less gifted than Lestrade, but by "The Adventure of the Three Garridebs" (1924), Holmes conceded that the Yard "leads the world in thoroughness and method"—effectiveness—in Holmes's mind at least—that they no doubt had learned from him.

Holmes also developed his own citywide network of informants and assistants, the Baker Street Irregulars, street "arabs," children who lived "at the very bottom of the great pyramid of late Victorian society" (Keating 1979, 42). Holmes hired them at a shilling each day as his invisible "eyes and ears" throughout London, then a teeming capital of 5 million.

Sherlock Holmes easily moved from the lowest ranks of late Victorian life to the highest circles of government, where he solved intricate cases involving the designs of his older brother Mycroft. Although Mycroft seems to have had considerably less ambition and energy than Sherlock, he rose to shadowy preeminence in the British government, perhaps as a precursor to Ian Fleming's "M." Sherlock famously remarked of Mycroft in "The Bruce-Partington Case," "Again and again his word has decided the national policy . . . occasionally he *is* the government . . . the most indispensable man in the country" [italics in original]. Mycroft had "the greatest capacity for storing facts of any man living," so he could coordinate diverse fields and quickly adopt effective policies (quoted in Keating 1979, 101). In "The Greek Interpreter," Sherlock described his brother as "absolutely incapable of working out the practical points which must be gone into before a case could be laid before a judge or jury." Since "practical points" were Sherlock's domain, Mycroft often employed his energetic and resourceful younger brother on ticklish international assignments involving important personages who could not afford publicity, like the leaders of Holland, Scandinavia, and Turkey, and even the Pope.

In 1881, about 15 percent of the British labor force made their scanty livings in domestic service. Sherlock Holmes's Scottish landlady Mrs. Hudson seems to have been his only personal servant. Horrified as she was at the filthy feet of the Baker Street Irregulars pattering up her clean staircase, Mrs. Hudson served, adored, fussed, and worried over Holmes faithfully for 28 years, providing food and comfort and minor detective services like moving his bust in a lamplit window to befuddle the wicked Colonel Moran. Even though he was "the very worst tenant in London," Mrs. Hudson "stood in the very deepest awe" of Holmes and provided "his most satisfying relationship with the opposite sex" (Riley and McAlister 189).

> *Watson, the fair sex is your department. . . . My brain has always governed my heart.*
> —Sherlock Holmes

The Woman for Sherlock Holmes

Sherlock Holmes, like Freud, declared himself incapable of understanding what women want. In "A Scandal in Bohemia" he complained, "Woman's heart and mind are insoluble puzzles to the male," and declared. "The motives of women are so inscrutable. . . . Their most trivial action may mean volumes, or their most extraordinary conduct may depend upon a hairpin or a curling-tongs." Holmes also liked to pretend total disinterest in women, maintaining that he thought of his female clients only as daughters or nieces, but two managed to capture his attention differently. Near the end of his career, when he was safely beyond physical temptation, Maud Bellamy's "perfect clear-cut face" made him realize "no young man would cross her path unscathed." The other, Irene Adler, an operatic diva, had earlier posed a much greater disruption to Holmes's bachelorhood; in "A Scandal in Bohemia" (1891), she, "the daintiest thing under a bonnet on this planet," actually outwitted the Great Detective. For Holmes, no matter how "dainty" Irene appeared, it was her mind that captivated him, and she became *the* woman in his life. Watson summed up Irene's allure and Holmes's reaction: "It was not that he felt any emotion akin to love for Irene Adler. All emotions, and that one particularly, were abhorrent to his cold, precise, but admirably balanced mind. . . . And yet there was but one woman to him."

Selected Sherlock Holmes Media Portrayals

Nearly 200 actors have appeared in various stage, radio, movie, and television roles related to the Great Detective's cases, with more than 70 actors playing Sherlock Holmes in over 200 films. The earliest actor to have portrayed Sherlock Holmes was the slim, haughtily handsome American William Gillette (1855 to 1937), whose startling blue eyes and aquiline nose helped overcome American puritanical hesitation about the theatre. A proponent of realism and naturalism best known for his title role in *Sherlock*

Holmes, his own 1899 dramatic adaptation, Gillette played Holmes regularly on stage until 1931 as well as in his only film appearance (1911), making the deerstalker cap, the cloak, the curved pipe, and the phrase, "Oh, this is elementary, my dear Watson" (which never appears in the Canon), Holmes's eternally distinguishing accoutrements.

The earliest Holmes film was *Sherlock Holmes Baffled* (1903), made in America, followed by three more American productions, and an Italian movie; and in Denmark the first two Holmes film series (non-Canonical) between 1909 and 1911, followed by several German Holmes films prior to 1920. The first actor to be identified with Holmes for his generation was Eille Norwood (1861 to 1948), who made over 35 1920s Holmes films, basing his performance on Sidney Paget's illustrations. The first British Holmes film with sound, *The Speckled Band* (1931), starred Raymond Massey and followed the story closely, but Massey's performance did not seem convincing, probably because the producers equipped his Holmes with glass flowers, modern-art furniture, and Dictaphones. In his second autobiography, *A Hundred Different Lives,* Massey called the film "a travesty of the classic."

Shakespearean actor Basil Rathbone (1892 to 1967), by birth South African but educated in England, came to Sherlock Holmes, his best known role, after acting first in London with Henry Baniell, who later played Moriarty in "The Woman in Green," and then moving to New York and beginning his film career. He worked with Errol Flynn in swashbuckling Hollywood roles before starring in *The Hound of the Baskervilles* in 1939, and with Nigel Bruce as Watson, he played Holmes in film and on radio for the next seven years. According to Rathbone's 1962 autobiography *In and Out of Character,* he grew annoyed with the Great Detective, whose stories he felt were old-fashioned and outdated. Rathbone resented Holmes's "perpetual seeming assumption of infallibility; his interminable success (could he not fail just once and prove himself a human being like the rest of us!)" (*In and Out* 182). Rathbone's Holmes occasionally misread clues and walked into traps and once actually had to be rescued by Watson.

In the 1970s, "The Great Detective became the focus of experimentation for writers and performers," like the BBC's bizarre Comedy Playhouse "Elementary, My Dear Watson" and *Saturday Night Live*'s comedic skit "The Case of the Scarlet Membrane" (Davies 100–101). Having starred in one of the most successful series in the history of Russian television, Vasily Livanov was awarded the British Order of the British Empire for portraying Sherlock Holmes between 1979 and 1986, accompanied by Vitali Solomin as Watson. On January 16, 2007, Livanov filmed NTV's "The First Person" at the Sherlock Holmes pub in London, playing the Great Detective as "the personification of gentlemanly behavior" ("Vasily Livanov and Vitaly Solomin").

A great revival of interest in Sherlock Holmes began in the 1980s. British Shakespearean actor Jeremy Brett (1933 to 1995) in the 1960s twice considered unsuccessfully for the role of James Bond, played Sherlock Holmes on stage and in 41 episodes of Granada Television's 1984 to 1994 series, adapted by John Hawkesworth and originally intended to include all of the Holmes stories but derailed by Brett's death from heart failure. While working on the series, Brett was suffering from bipolar disorder, grief over his wife's death, and heavy smoking, and during the later Holmes episodes his health was visibly deteriorating. He is considered the definitive Holmes of his era, accompanied first by David Burke and later Edward Hardwicke as Watson.

In the 1990s, the quietest decade for Sherlock Holmes's screen career, he did not appear in the cinema at all. Several British and American Holmes telefilms began to appear in 2000, including *The Hound of the Baskervilles* and *The Sign of Four* for Hallmark, starring Matt Frewer and Ian Richardson, who had portrayed Holmes in the acclaimed 1983 productions of *The Hound of the Baskervilles* and *The Sign of Four* and starred as Dr. Joseph Bell, Conan Doyle's mentor, in telefilms based on Doyle's life before Richardson's death on February 9, 2007. James D'Arcy and Roger Morlidge appeared as young Holmes and Watson in *Sherlock—Case of Evil* (2002); the BBC aired RDF Television's two-part production of *Sherlock Holmes and the Baker Street Irregulars* on March 18, 2007, with Jonathan Pryce as Holmes. To mark the 150th anniversary of Conan Doyle's birth, Guy Ritchie's martial arts-based film *Sherlock Holmes* (2009) starring Robert Downey, Jr., celebrated the young Holmes's use of fisticuffs and "baritsu" to defeat his dastardly opponents.

Conan Doyle's First Interest in Criminal Investigation

A fictionalized account of Conan Doyle's first interest in criminal investigation, *The Dark Origins of Sherlock Holmes,* appeared as a two-part Victorian telefilm thriller on BBC America March 5 and 12, 2000. Shot in Edinburgh and starring Robin Laing as young Doyle and Ian Richardson as Dr. Joseph Bell, Doyle's forensic pathologist mentor, it "exposes the dark underbelly of Victorian society with its rigid class system tainted by labyrinthine evil" (Mason 17).

Sherlock Holmes film adaptations currently available on DVD include 14 restored 1940s Basil Rathbone films; and the 1954 television series of 39 Holmes cases, starring Ronald Howard (son of Leslie Howard of *Gone with the Wind* fame). Peter Cook and Dudley Moore starred as Holmes and Watson in *The Hound of the Baskervilles* (1978), a spoof version from MGM. Jeremy Brett's several Holmes series include *The Adventures of Sherlock Holmes*, with 13 cases (1984–1985); *The Return of Sherlock Holmes*, with 11 cases (1986); *The Casebook of Sherlock Holmes,* with 6 cases (1991); *The Memoirs of Sherlock Holmes*, with 6 cases (1994); and a collection of 5 feature films, also starring Edward Hardwicke as Watson: *The Hound of the Baskervilles* (1983), *The Sign of Four* (1983), *The Master Blackmailer* (1992), *The Eligible*

Bachelor (1993), and *The Last Vampyre* (1993). Actor Christopher Lee as Holmes and Patrick MacNee as Watson starred in *Incident at Victoria Falls* (1991) and *The Leading Lady* (1992), and Jonathan Pryce starred in *Sherlock Holmes and the Baker Street Irregulars* (2007).

Warner Brothers' new cinema adaptation of Sherlock Holmes appeared at Christmas 2009, directed by Guy Ritchie and starring Robert Downey, Jr., as a young, patriotic, and bohemian Holmes, Jude Law as a capable and womanizing Dr. Watson, Rachel McAdams as the fiery Irene Adler, and Mark Strong as Holmes's new adversary, the mysterious cult leader Lord Blackwood, based on black magician Aleister Crowley. Apprehended and sent to the gallows by Holmes who is shown as capable with his fists as he is with intellectual deduction, Blackwood as he had promised returned from the dead to execute revenge on Holmes and Watson, and carried out a plot to destroy Britain itself. Producer Lionel Wigram wove several Holmes stories together to develop a portrayal of a youthful Holmes both more faithful to Doyle's original Great Detective and more appealing than his more cerebral cinematic predecessors to contemporary action-loving audiences.

SHERLOCK HOLMES'S ENDURING APPEAL AND PLACE IN POPULAR CULTURE

In "The Most Asked Question: Why Do People Read Detective Stories?" Gladys Mitchell suggested, "For full enjoyment of the [detective] story, the reader needs to use his brains. A problem has been set before him, and the true addict obtains pleasure from doing his best to solve it" (quoted in Winks 334). Sherlock Holmes not only stimulated the intellects of his puzzle-loving contemporary readers, he provided exciting vicarious adventure, comforting reassurance of the late Victorian love of the status quo, and satisfaction that justice could prevail and Good triumph over Evil. Even now with unparalleled access to computerized adventure, the Victorian status quo forgotten except by desperate graduate students, and justice as well as Good sprawled at the mercy of powerful bureaucracies, Big Business, and technology-crazed media, "It is the immortal pair [Holmes and Watson] we cherish" (Morley, "Preface"). Sherlock Holmes has become one of the most familiar figures in world literature.

Men find Holmes fascinating because he is self-contained; women see him as a challenge—they want to expose the emotion beneath that icy demeanor.

—Jeremy Brett

In her 2001 Afterword to the Signet Classic edition of *The Hound of the Baskervilles*, Anne Perry pays tribute to Arthur Conan Doyle's command of "all the elements of brilliant storytelling; mystery and the supernatural, suspense, evil and innocence, intellect, romance, human villainy, adventure, and the ultimate in terror." Holmes's eternal appeal is "a deeper symbolism of the elements of life that lie within the experience of all of us" (*Hound* 241), because he is a "true myth" who can release people

---

Ten Famous Sherlock Holmes Societies Worldwide

The Baker Street Irregulars (New York)

The Sherlock Holmes Society of London

The Japan Sherlock Holmes Club—the world's largest Holmes organization

The Sherlock Holmes Society of India

The Spence Munros, Nova Scotia

The Sherlock Holmes Society of Australia

L'Hotel du Dulong (France)

The Amateur Mendicant Society of Madrid

Sherlock Holmes around the World

The Adventuresses of Sherlock Holmes

---

from their own preconceptions" (Keating 1987, 18), "the Knight Errant who will ride in and do battle for us with superior knowledge, untiring energy, and ask from us in reward no more than we can give" (*Hound* 243) at times in history, when, like the late Victorians of his day, we seem to stand on the brink of disasters at home and abroad, without and within our own personalities. That fearsome hound personifying all the evil that stalks through the Holmes stories and through our lives "is inescapable vengeance for the past, a Hell that does not show mercy, repentance, or forgiveness—except with the intervention of Sherlock Holmes. A modern St. George for our personal dragons?" (*Hound* 245).

PARALLEL CHRONOLOGY

Major Events Related to Sherlock Holmes	World Events
1789–1863 Life of Horace Vernet, implied by brother Mycroff	
	1841 Poe introduces C. Auguste Dupin, first amateur genius detective
1844 Siger Holmes and Violet Sherrinford marry	
1846 Prof. Moriarty born	
1847 Mycroft Holmes born	**1847** Mormons settle at Great Salt Lake
1852 John H. Watson born	
1853? 1854? Sherlock Holmes born	**1856** Aniline dyes invented

(Continued)

Major Events Related to Sherlock Holmes	World Events
1859 Arthur Conan Doyle born May 22 in Edinburgh	**1859** Darwin's *Origin of Species*
	1860s Bessemer steel process implemented
1865 Arthur writes first story, about a man eaten by a tiger	
	1866 Kelvin: Theory of Thermodynamics; first transatlantic cable; Gaboriau introduces M. Lecoq and initiates first *roman policier*
	1867 Invention of typewriter; diamonds discovered in So. Africa
1868 Arthur attends Jesuit school in England; later rejects Catholicism	
	1870 Telegraph invented; British Education Act; start of Franco-Prussian War
1871 Holmes matriculates at Cambridge	**1871** Darwin's *Descent of Man*
	1872 New British policy to solidify Empire (Imperialism); Nietzsche's *The Birth of Tragedy* published
1874? Setting of Holmes's first case, at either Oxford or Cambridge (Sayers favors Sidney Sussex College, Cambridge)	
1874 Arthur visits his uncle in London and visits Chamber of Horrors	
1875 Arthur studies German at school in Austria	
	1876 Invention of telephone; Queen Victoria declared Empress of India
1877 Conan Doyle enrolls at U. of Edinburgh Medical School; Dr. Joseph Bell's outpatient assistant; serves as ship's doctor on Arctic voyage	**1877** Invention of gramophone
1878 Dr. Watson receives medical degree at the University of London	
1879 Conan Doyle publishes first story (non-Holmes)	**1879** Invention of the lightbulb
1880 Watson wounded in India	**1880s** Adoption of internal combustion engines

(*Continued*)

Major Events Related to Sherlock Holmes	World Events
1881 Conan Doyle qualifies as Bachelor of Medicine and Master of Surgery; serves as ship's doctor on voyage to West Africa; Dr. Watson meets Sherlock Holmes; they share lodgings at 221B Baker Street, London; year of *A Study in Scarlet*	
1882 Conan Doyle sets up practice in Southsea	
	1883 Nietzsche's *Thus Spake Zarathustra*
1885 Conan Doyle receives M.D.; marries Louise Hawkins, who is in ill health	
1886 Watson marries Lucy Ferrier	**1886** Nietzsche's *Beyond Good and Evil*
1887 *A Study in Scarlet,* first Holmes story is published; Holmes's reputation soars; Lucy Watson dies	**1887** British newspapers screaming about Jack the Ripper
1888 Time of "A Scandal in Bohemia"; time of *The Hound of the Baskervilles*"; Watson marries Mary Morstan	**1888** Exhibitions of Belgian "XX" art group in London
1889 Conan Doyle publishes short novel on the paranormal and *Micah Clarke,* a historical novel	
1890 *The Sign of Four* published as Watson meets his future wife, Mary Morstan, in this story	**1890** Oscar Wilde's fin de siècle work, *The Picture of Dorian Gray*; Baring's Bank (London) fails
1891 Conan Doyle closes medical practice to write; historical novel *The White Company* published; Holmes stories begin to appear in *The Strand Magazine*; Professor Moriarty begins to engage Holmes's attention; Holmes tells Watson on April 24 about Moriarty; Holmes involved in service of France, receives Legion of Honor	
1891–1893 Great Hiatus; Holmes appears to have perished at the Reichenbach Falls but later tells Watson he had been traveling in Tibet and the Mideast; Rennison	

(Continued)

Major Events Related to Sherlock Holmes	World Events
conjectures Holmes was spying on Mycroft's orders in *The Great Game*. Watson's wife Mary thought to have died between 1891 and 1894	
1892 *The Adventures of Sherlock Holmes* is published; Arthur and Louise visit Reichenbach Falls in Switzerland	**1892** Wagner's *Siegfried* at Covent Garden
1893 Conan Doyle's father dies; Louise diagnosed with tuberculosis; Conan Doyle joins Society for Psychical Research; *The Memoirs of Sherlock Holmes* published, containing "The Final Problem" which causes immense outcry in London over Holmes's "death"	
1894 Conan Doyle publishes medical short stories; makes first visit to the U.S.; Holmes visits Watson in Park Lane	
1894–1901 Holmes "very busy" during this period	
1895 Fictionalized Doyle autobiography, *The Stark Munro Letters,* published	
1896 Conan Doyle publishes historical novel	**1896** First modern Olympic Games
1897 Conan Doyle falls in love with Jean Leckie but the relationship is platonic until they marry in 1907; Watson, now a widower, rejoins Holmes at Baker Street	**1897** Queen Victoria's Diamond Jubilee, Kipling writes "Recessional"; Bram Stoker publishes *Dracula*
	1899–1902 Boer War (South African War)
1900 Conan Doyle works in Boer War as Army doctor; first Holmes film, *Sherlock Holmes Baffled*	**1900** Publication of Freud's *Interpretation of Dreams*
1901 First installment of *Hound* in *Strand*	**1901** Queen Victoria dies; Edwardian decade known for relaxed morals
1902 *The Hound of the Baskervilles* published; Conan Doyle works in field hospital in So. Africa; publishes *The Great Boer War,* which results	

(Continued)

Major Events Related to Sherlock Holmes	World Events
in his knighthood; Holmes refuses knighthood, retires to beekeeping; returns to unmask German spy; Sayers conjectures Watson remarries	
1903 New Holmes stories begin to appear in *The Strand Magazine*	
1905 *The Return of Sherlock Holmes* is published	
1906 Louise dies from tuberculosis at 49; Conan Doyle helps exonerate George Edalji	
1907 Conan Doyle marries Jean Leckie, moves to Sussex	
1909 *The Crime of the Congo* is published	
1910 Conan Doyle investigates Oscar Slater case	**1910** King Edward VII dies; E.M. Forster's *Howard's End* is published
1912 Conan Doyle's first Challenger science fiction novel is published	
1913 Second Challenger novel published	
1914 Conan Doyle visits New York; Holmes spends time in U.S. and Ireland to trap German spy	**1914** Outbreak of World War I; Joyce's *Dubliners* published
1915 Last Holmes novel, *The Valley of Fear*, published	
1916 Conan Doyle announces conversion to spiritualism	**1916** Joyce's *A Portrait of the Artist as a Young Man* published
1917 *His Last Bow* published; Watson declares Holmes still alive but rheumatic	**1917** The Russian Revolution
1918 Conan Doyle's eldest son dies; his first book on spiritualism is published; Mycroft Holmes dies in influenza pandemic	**1918** World War I ends; influenza; pandemic
1919 Conan Doyle's brother dies; second book on spiritualism published	
1920–1930 Conan Doyle acts as advocate for Spiritualism	**1920** U.S. adopts women's suffrage
1920 Holmes said to be "exhausted" by 66th birthday	
1921 Conan Doyle's mother dies; Jean produces "automatic writing"	

(Continued)

Major Events Related to Sherlock Holmes	World Events
1922 Conan Doyle tours America to promote spiritualism	**1922** Eliot's *The Wasteland* and Joyce's *Ulysses* published
1924 Conan Doyle publishes autobiography *Memories and Adventures*	
1927 Last Holmes collection, *The Case Book of Sherlock Holmes* published; Conan Doyle announces Holmes's retirement	**1927** First "talking picture"; collapse of German economy
1929 Death of Sherlock Holmes (Rennison)	**1929** U.S. stock market collapse; worldwide depression begins
July 7, 1930 Conan Doyle dies from heart attack	
1940 Jean, Lady Doyle, dies from cancer diagnosed by her husband in 1936 through a medium	

PRIMARY SOURCES

DeWaal, Ronald Burt, and George Vanderburgh. *The Universal Sherlock Holmes.* 5 vols. Toronto: Metropolitan Toronto Library, 1994.

Doyle, Sir Arthur Conan. *The Complete Sherlock Holmes.* New York: Barnes & Noble Books, 1992.

———. *Sherlock Holmes: The Complete Long Stories.* London: John Murray, 1929 (allegedly written by Dr. John H. Watson).

———. *Sherlock Holmes: The Complete Short Stories.* London: John Murray, 1928 (allegedly written by Dr. John H. Watson).

Short Novels

A Study in Scarlet (1888)

The Sign of the Four (1890)

The Hound of the Baskervilles (1902)

The Valley of Fear (1915)

Short Story Collections

The Adventures of Sherlock Holmes (1892):

"A Scandal in Bohemia"

"The Red-Headed League"

"A Case of Identity"

"The Boscombe Valley Mystery"

"The Five Orange Pips"

"The Man with the Twisted Lip"

"The Adventure of the Blue Carbuncle"

"The Adventure of the Speckled Band"

"The Adventure of the Engineer's Thumb"

"The Adventure of the Noble Bachelor"

"The Adventure of the Beryl Coronet"

"The Adventure of the Copper Beeches"

The Memoirs of Sherlock Holmes (1894):

"Silver Blaze"

"The Yellow Face"

"The Stock-broker's Clerk"

"The 'Gloria Scott'"

"The Musgrave Ritual"

"The Reigate Puzzle"

"The Greek Interpreter"

"The Naval Treaty"

"The Final Problem"

The Return of Sherlock Holmes (1905):

"The Adventure of the Empty House"

"The Adventure of the Norwood Builder"

"The Adventure of the Dancing Men"

"The Adventure of the Solitary Cyclist"

"The Adventure of the Priory School"

"The Adventure of Black Peter"

"The Adventure of Charles Augustus Milverton"

"The Adventure of the Six Napoleons"

"The Adventure of the Three Students"

"The Adventure of the Golden Pince Nez"

"The Adventure of the Missing Three-Quarter"

"The Adventure of the Abbey Grange"

"The Adventure of the Second Stain"

His Last Bow (1917):

"The Adventure of Wisteria Lodge"

"The Adventure of the Cardboard Box"

"The Adventure of the Red Circle"

"The Adventure of the Bruce-Partington Plans"

"The Adventure of the Dying Detective"

"The Disappearance of Lady Frances Carfax"

"The Adventure of the Devil's Foot"

"His Last Bow"

The Case Book of Sherlock Holmes (1927):

"The Adventure of the Illustrious Client"

"The Adventure of the Blanched Soldier"

"The Adventure of the Mazarin Stone"

"The Adventure of the Three Cables"

"The Adventure of the Sussex Vampire"

"The Adventure of the Three Garridebs"

"The Problem of Thor Bridge"

"The Adventure of the Creeping Man"

"The Adventure of the Lion's Mane"

"The Adventure of the Veiled Lodger"

"The Adventure of Shoscombe Old Place"

"The Adventure of the Retired Colourman"

The Uncollected Sherlock Holmes, ed. Richard Lancelyn Green. Harmondsworth: Penguin, 1983.

The New Annotated Sherlock Holmes, ed. Leslie S. Klinger. New York: Norton, 2004–2005.

Selected Other Novels by Arthur Conan Doyle

The Land of Mist (1926). Involves spiritualism.

The Lost World (1912). Features dinosaurs.

Micah Clarke (1889). Doyle's first historical novel.

The White Company (1891).

The Stark Munro Letters (1895). Autobiographical novel.

The Poison Belt (1913). Adventure fiction.

Autobiography

Doyle, Sir Arthur Conan Doyle. *Memories and Adventures.* London: Hodder and Stoughton, 1922.

Selected Nonfiction by Arthur Conan Doyle

The History of Spiritualism (1926).

Through the Magic Door (1907). Account of Doyle's collection of Western classics.

Scholarly Journal

ACD: The Journal of the Arthur Conan Doyle Society, ed. Christopher and Barbara Roden, Ashcroft, British Columbia.

Collections

Friends of the Arthur Conan Doyle Collection at Toronto Reference Library

Richard Lancelyn Green's Sherlock Holmes Collection at City Museum of Portsmouth, UK

Bibliographies

DeWaal, Ronald Burt. *The World Bibliography of Sherlock Holmes and Doctor Watson.* New York: Bramhall House, 1974.

Green, Richard Lancelyn, and John Michael Gibson. *A Bibliography of A. Conan Doyle.* Oxford: Clarendon Press, 1983.

Selected Holmes Pastiches

Biggle, Lloyd Jr. *The Glendower Conspiracy.* Tulsa: Council Oak, 1986.

Boucher, Anthony. *The Case of the Baker Street Irregulars.* New York: Simon and Schuster, 1940.

Boyer, Richard. *The Giant Rat of Sumatra.* New York: Warner, 1976.

Collins, Randall. *The Case of the Philosopher's Ring.* New York: Crown, 1978.

Douglas, Carole Nelson. The Irene Adler series, beginning with *Good Night, Mr. Holmes,* 1990, and continuing through 2006.

Doyle, Adrian Conan, and John Dickson Carr. *The New Exploits of Sherlock Holmes.* New York: Random House, 1954.

Estleman, Loren D. *Dr. Jekyll and Mr. Holmes.* New York: Doubleday, 1979.

———. *Sherlock Holmes vs. Dracula.* New York: Doubleday, 1978.

Fawcett, Quinn. *Against the Brotherhood.* New York: Forge, 1997 (features Mycroft Holmes).

———. *Embassy Row.* New York: Forge, 1998 (features Mycroft Holmes).

Gardner, John. *The Return of Moriarty.* New York: Putnam, 1974.

———. *The Revenge of Moriarty.* New York: Putnam, 1975.

Hall, Robert Lee. *Exit Sherlock Holmes.* New York: Scribner's, 1977.

Hardwick, Michael. *Prisoner of the Devil: Sherlock Holmes and the Dreyfus Case.* New York: Proteus, 1979.

———. *The Private Life of Dr. Watson.* New York: Dutton, 1983.

———. *Sherlock Holmes: My Life and Crimes.* New York: Doubleday, 1984.

Harrison, Michael. *I, Sherlock Holmes.* New York: Dutton, 1977.

Jeffers, H. Paul. *Murder Most Irregular.* New York: St. Martin's, 1983.

Keating, H.R.F. *Crime and Mystery: The 100 Best Books.* New York: Carroll & Graf, 1987.

King, Laurie R. The Mary Russell series, beginning with *The Beekeeper's Apprentice,* 1994, and continuing. Russell is Holmes's much younger wife.

Kurland, Michael, ed. *Sherlock Holmes: The Hidden Years.* New York: St. Martin's Minotaur, 2004.

Leppek, Christopher. *The Surrogate Assassin.* Aurora, CO: Write Way, 1998.

Mallory, Michael. *The Exploits of the Second Mrs. Watson.* London: Top Publications Ltd., 2008.

Meyer, Nicholas. *The Seven-Percent Solution.* New York: Dutton, 1974.

———. *The West End Horror.* New York: Dutton, 1976.

Millett, Larry. *Sherlock Holmes and the Ice Palace Murders.* New York: Viking, 1998.

Murphy, Bruce F. *The Encyclopedia of Murder and Mystery.* New York: St. Martin's Press, 1999.

Oliver, John P. "An Eyewitness Account of Holmes," in *Murder Ink,* edited by Winks, Robin, rev. ed. by Dilys Winn. New York: Workman Publishing, 1984.

Palmer, Stuart. *The Adventures of the Marked Man and One Other.* New York: Aspen, 1973.

Queen, Ellery, ed. *The Misadventures of Sherlock Holmes.* New York: Little, 1944.

Robertson, Michael. *The Baker Street Letters.* New York: Minotaur, 2009.

Rowland, Peter. *The Disappearance of Edwin Drood.* New York: St. Martin's, 1992.

Seitz, Stephen. *Sherlock Holmes and the Plague of Dracula.* Greensboro, VT: Mountainside Press, 2007.

Stashower, Dan. *The Adventures of the Ectoplasmic Man.* New York: Morrow, 1985.

Thomas, Donald. *The Execution of Sherlock Holmes.* New York: Pegasus, 2007.

Trow, M.J. *The Supreme Adventure of Inspector Lestrade.* New York: Stein and Day, 1985.

Utechin, Nicholas. *Sherlock Holmes at Oxford.* London: Dugdale, 1977.

Van Ash, Cay. *Ten Years Beyond Baker Street.* New York: Harper and Row, 1984.

Victor, Daniel D. *The Seventh Bullet.* New York: St. Martin's, 1992.

Walsh, Ray. *The Mycroft Memoranda.* New York: St. Martin's, 1985.

Wincor, Richard. *Sherlock Holmes in Tibet.* London: Weybright, 1968.

Selected Sherlock Holmes Games

Video Games

221B Baker Street

The Lost Cases of Sherlock Holmes

Sherlock Holmes vs. Jack the Ripper

Board Games

The Case of the Dead Duke
Sherlock Holmes: The Fenian Murders
The Hand of Moriarty
221B Baker Street

WORKS CITED

Arnstein, Walter. *Britain Yesterday and Today,* 5th ed. Lexington, MA: Heath, 1988.

Baring-Gould, W.S. *Sherlock Holmes: A Biography of the World's First Consulting Detective.* London: Rupert Hart-Davis, 1962.

———. *The Annotated Sherlock Holmes.* London: Rupert Hart-Davis, 1967.

Brunsdale, Mitzi. *Gumshoes: A Dictionary of Fictional Detectives.* Westport, CT: Greenwood Publishing, 2006.

Davies, David Stuart. *Starring Sherlock Holmes.* London: Titan Books, 2001.

Freeman, Kyle. Introduction to *The Complete Sherlock Holmes,* Vols. 1, 2. New York: Barnes and Noble, 2003.

Girouard, Mark. *The Return to Camelot.* New Haven: Yale University Press, 1981.

Harper, Lila Marz. "Clues in the Street: Sherlock Holmes, Martin Hewitt, and Mean Streets." *Journal of Popular Culture* 42 (February 2009): 67–89.

Keating, H.R.F. *Sherlock Holmes: The Man and His World.* London: Thames and Hudson, 1979.

———. *Crime and Mystery: The 100 Best Books.* New York: Carroll & Graf, 1987.

Klinger, Leslie S., ed. *The New Annotated Sherlock Holmes.* New York: W.W. Norton, 2004–2005.

Massey, Raymond. *A Hundred Different Lives.* Boston: Little, Brown, 1983.

Morley, Christopher. Unpaginated Preface to *The Complete Sherlock Holmes.* New York: Barnes and Noble, 1992.

Murphy, Bruce F. *The Encyclopedia of Murder and Mystery.* New York: St. Martin's Press, 1999.

Rathbone, Basil. *In and Out of Character.* New York: Limelight Editions, 1956; rpt. 2007.

Rennison, Nick. *Sherlock Holmes: The Unauthorized Biography.* New York: Atlantic Monthly Press, 2005.

Riley, Dick, and Pam McAlister. *Bedside, Bathtub and Armchair Companions to Sherlock Holmes.* London: Continuum International, 1998.

Sayers, Dorothy L. "The Dates in *The Red-Headed League,*" in *Unpopular Opinions.* New York: Harcourt Brace, 1947: 210–221 (written June 1934).

———. "Dr. Watson's Christian Name," in *Unpopular Opinions.* New York: Harcourt Brace, 1947: 184–189 (probably written ca. 1934).

———. "Dr. Watson, Widower," in *Unpopular Opinions.* New York: Harcourt Brace, 1947: 189–209 (probably written ca. 1934).

———. "Holmes' College Career," in *Unpopular Opinions.* New York: Harcourt Brace, 1947: 167–183 (probably written ca. 1934).

————. Introduction to *Great Short Stories of Detection, Mystery, and Horror,* edited by Howard Haycraft. London: Gollancz, 1928 (titled *The Omnibus of Crime* in the U.S. edition).

Sutherland, John. *The Stanford Companion to Victorian Fiction.* Palo Alto, CA: Stanford University Press, 1989.

Symons, Julian. *Mortal Consequences.* New York: Harper & Row, 1972.

"Vasily Livanov and Vitaly Solomin: The Russian Sherlock Holmes and Doctor Watson." http://www.bakerstreetdozen.com/russianholmes.html, accessed 6/20/2007.

Wilson, Edmund. *Classics and Commercials: A Literary Chronicle of the Forties.* New York: Farrar, Straus, 1950.

Winks, Robin, ed. *Murder Ink.* Rev. ed. by Dilys Winn. New York: Workman Publishing, 1984.

Youngs, Frederic A., Henry L. Snyder, and E.A. Reitan. *The English Heritage,* 2nd ed. Arlington Heights, IL: Forum Press, 1988.

FURTHER READING

A list of 100 "indispensable" references for Holmes studies appears in Otto Penzler's "A Few Million Words about My Friend Holmes," in Robin Winks, ed., *Murder Ink.* Rev. edited by Dilys Winn. New York: Workman Publishing, 1984, pp. 234–239. Also note that on any given day in 2009, approximately 150 new Web sites mentioned Sherlock Holmes; this frequency appears to continue.

Atkinson, Michael. *The Secret Marriage of Sherlock Holmes and Other Eccentric Readings.* Ann Arbor: University of Michigan Press, 1996.

Barnes, Alan. *Sherlock Holmes on Screen: The Complete Film and TV History* (rev. ed.). London: Reynolds and Hearn, 2004.

Bayard, Pierre. *Sherlock Holmes Was Wrong.* New York: Bloomsbury USA, 2008.

Bunson, Matthew. *Encyclopedia Sherlockiana,* reprint ed. New York: Macmillan, 1994.

Carr, John Dickson. *The Life of Sir Arthur Conan Doyle.* New York: Harper, 1949.

Dakin, D. Martin. *A Sherlock Holmes Commentary.* Newton Abbot, UK: David and Charles, 1972.

Davis, J. Madison. "Mr. Monk & the Pleasing Paradigm." *World Literature Today* 83 (May/June 2009): 11–13.

Dorn, Jennifer. "Streetlights of London: Marylebone and the Sherlock Holmes Museum." *British Heritage* 27 (November 2006): 11–12.

Duncan, Alistair. *Eliminate the Impossible: An Examination of the World of Sherlock Holmes on Page and Screen.* London: MX Publishing, 2008.

————. *Close to Holmes: A Look at the Connections between Historical London, London, Sherlock Holmes, and Sir Arthur Conan Doyle.* London: MX Publishing, 2009.

Edwards, Owen Dudley. *The Quest for Sherlock Holmes.* Edinburgh: Mainstream Publishing, 1983.

Frank, Lawrence. "Dreaming the Medusa: Imperialism, Primitivism, and Sexuality in Arthur Conan Doyle's *The Sign of Four.*" *Signs* 22 (Autumn 1996): 52–85.

Green, Richard Lancelyn, ed. *The Uncollected Sherlock Holmes.* Harmondsworth: Penguin, 1983.

————. *The Sherlock Holmes Letters.* Iowa City: University of Iowa Press, 1986.

Godfrey, Emelyne. "Sherlock Holmes and the Mystery Baritsu." *History Today* 59 (May 2009): 4–5.

Groves, Derham. "Better Holmes and Gardens: Sense of Place in the Sherlock Holmes Stories." *Better Homes and Gardens* (Australia) 36 (Winter 2003): 466–472.

Haining, Peter, ed. *A Sherlock Holmes Compendium*. London: W.H. Allen, 1980.

Hall, Trevor H. *The Late Mr. Sherlock Holmes*. London: Duckworth, 1971.

Hardwick, Michael. *The Complete Guide to Sherlock Holmes*. New York: St. Martin's Press, 1986.

Herbert, Rosemary. *Whodunit? A Who's Who in Crime and Mystery Writing*. New York: Oxford University Press, 1999.

Higham, Charles. *The Adventures of Conan Doyle: The Life of the Creator of Sherlock Holmes*. London: Hamish Hamilton, 1976.

Kabatchnik, Ammon. *Sherlock Holmes on the Stage*. New York: Scarecrow Press, 2006.

Key, Jack D., Marc A. Shampo, and Robert A. Kyle. "Doyle, Holmes, and Watson—A 'Special' Trinity." *Mayo Clinic Proceedings* 80 (June 2005): 722.

Lellenberg, Jon. *The Quest for Sir Arthur Conan Doyle*. Carbondale: Southern Illinois University Press, 1987.

Lellenberg, Jon, Daniel Stashower, and Charles Foley, eds. *Arthur Conan Doyle: A Life in Letters*. Harmondsworth: Penguin, 2007.

Liebow, Ely. *Dr. Joe Bell, Model for Sherlock Holmes*. Bowling Green, OH: Bowling Green University Popular Press, 1982.

Lycett, Andrew. *The Life and Times of Sir Arthur Conan Doyle*. New York: Free Press, 2007.

Macintyre, Ben. *The Napoleon of Crime: The Life and Times of Adam Worth, the Real Moriarty*. London: HarperCollins, 1997.

McQueen, Ian. *Sherlock Holmes Detected: The Problems of the Long Stories*. New York: Drake, 1974.

Mason, M.S. "Cracking the Case of Sherlock Holmes." *Christian Science Monitor* 92 (March 3, 2000): 17.

Misek, Maria. "Sherlock Holmes, Consulting Detective: A Study in DVD." *EMedia* 13 (March 2000): 26–28.

Paul, Robert S. *Whatever Happened to Sherlock Holmes?* Carbondale: Southern Illinois University Press, 1991.

Roden, Alvin E., and Jack D. Key. *Medical Casebook of Doctor Arthur Conan Doyle*. Malabar, FL: Robert E. Krieger, 1984.

Shreffler, P.A. *The Baker Street Reader*. Westport, CT: Greenwood, 1984.

Starrett, Vincent. *The Private Life of Sherlock Holmes* (rev. ed.). London: Allen and Unwin, 1961.

Stashower, Daniel. *Teller of Tales: The Life of Arthur Conan Doyle*. New York: Holt, 1999.

Tracy, Jack. *The Encyclopedia Sherlockiana*. London: New English Library, 1978; 1997 edition retitled *The Ultimate Sherlock Holmes Encyclopedia*.

Wagner, E.J. *The Science of Sherlock Holmes, From Baskerville Hall to the Valley of Fear, the Real Forensics behind the Great Detective's Greatest Cases*. Hoboken, NJ: John Wiley & Sons, 2006.

Watt, Peter Ridgway, and Joseph Green. *The Alternative Sherlock Holmes: Pastiches, Parodies and Copies*. New York: Ashgate, 2004.

WEB SITES

http://www.sherlockian.net (Extensive and comprehensive Holmes Web site.)

http://www.sherlock-holmes.org.uk (The Sherlock Holmes Society of London Web site)

http://www.sherlock-holmes.co.uk (Sherlock Holmes Museum (Baker Street) Web site)

http://www.siracd.com (Material about Sir Arthur Conan Doyle)

http://www.casebook.org (Material on Jack the Ripper)

http://www.victorianweb.org (Material on Victorian culture, politics, history)

Georges Simenon with statue of Inspector Maigret. (Photo by Keystone Features/Getty Images.)

Inspector Jules Maigret:
The Gallic Gumshoe

I will know the murderer when I know the victim well.

—Inspector Maigret

At 28, already prolific Belgian author Georges Simenon considered his "Maigrets"—"police novels" featuring Inspector Jules Maigret—only a phase bridging his popular pseudonymous potboilers and his goal of writing "a novel capable of capturing the interest of all audiences" (letter from Simenon to Charles Gouverneur Paulding, December 2, 1931, Assouline 111–112). As arguably the best-selling novelist of all time, Simenon, who wrote exclusively in French, eventually sold an incredible half-billion books, but his enormously popular "Maigrets," not his *romans durs* (serious novels), earned him his worldwide acclaim. In 2003, the centennial of Simenon's birth, Maigret was hailed as "the Sherlock Holmes of non-English detectives" (Murphy 320), and Simenon's 110 Maigret novels and short stories were praised for bringing "a crucial innovation to the detective novel," re-creating it and transforming it into a viable literary genre that expressed "many important themes in the twentieth century novel—guilt and innocence, solitude and alienation" (Becker 2003, 59; quoted in Assouline 111–112).

HISTORICAL/CULTURAL CONTEXT

Between 1914 and 1918, the "War to End All Wars" killed an estimated 10 million persons and wounded another 20 million, depriving Europe of a generation of future leaders and changing its culture forever. France's losses alone were staggering: 1,400,000 men dead, 10.5 percent of the entire active male population; 1.1 million French soldiers were permanently disabled; and over 1 million peasants were killed or seriously wounded, crippling French agriculture, which relied as much on draft horses in the 1930s as it had in 1850. Postwar inflation hit France hard as well; the franc in 1939 against the dollar was only one-seventh of its 1913 value, eroding savings and causing most French parents to limit their families to one child. By 1936, France had a larger proportion of citizens over 60 than any other country.

Marx, Einstein, and Freud already had produced an intellectual ferment that created a relativistic world view, forever demolishing the ideal of a "land of dreams" Victorians had envisioned. Einstein's Theory of Relativity (1905) demolished trust in the senses by proving that no definitive yardstick or "objective correlative" existed to measure values. By 1919, Marxism, as interpreted by Lenin, deceitfully promised a new, fairer society in fallacious core maxims like "He who does not work, neither shall he eat," and "From each according to his ability, to each according to his work." Freud's *Three Essays on the Theory of Sexuality* (1905), undermined "the highly developed sense of personal responsibility, and of duty towards a settled and objectively true moral code, which was at the centre of nineteenth-century European civilization" (Johnson 11).

Freud implied that the individual was not responsible for his behavior, that personality resulted from inherited characteristics and childhood influences, and that sex was exalted as the quintessence of the libido, "the vaguely understood 'life-force' and powerhouse of the individual" (Horton and Hopper 427). Writers like France's expressionist André Gide, who became a fervent admirer of Simenon's work, expressed their philosophical relativism in novels and plays, "exploring the subconscious mind, naturalistically recording a meaningless world, or building highly personalized fantasies" (Horton and Hopper 428). After the 1918 Armistice, a spurious optimism permeated the 1920s, but in reality Europe's traditional values were collapsing, a cultural upheaval mirrored in the development of detective fiction.

The detective genre developed in three distinct national directions in the 1920s and 1930s. In the British "Golden Age" of detective fiction, "genius detectives," often eccentric and/or aristocratic amateurs created mostly by female authors like Agatha Christie and Dorothy L. Sayers, dominated the form, using Msgr. Ronald Knox's "Ten Rules of Fair Play," subordinating character development to plot, and creating ingenious puzzles that during the shaky postwar years helped reassure readers that Right, as defended by White Knight detectives, could and would prevail. "British writers wrote as if World War I had never happened, about upper-class people insulated from the disastrous postwar recession" (Murphy 208).

America's "Golden Age" of detective fiction reacted against the more genteel British tradition. Inexpensive American "pulp" magazines, led by *Black Mask* writers such as Dashiell Hammett, Erle Stanley Gardner, and Raymond Chandler, developed the new and uniquely American "hardboiled" school of detective fiction, where "the common man entered . . . not as the victim, the villain, or the hired help, but as the protagonist." These tough and relentlessly honest private detectives held to strict personal codes of ethics and so passionately defended society's victims they occasionally operated outside the law in plots that reflected the disappearance of former social and individual values and mores, failed attempts at peace, modernism, and Socialist/Communist ideology (Murphy 208).

France's detective fiction developed in yet another direction, following two founding fathers of detective fiction who influenced Georges Simenon's work in the genre. Eugène Françoise Vidocq's *Mémoires de Vidocq* (1828 to 1829) contained exaggerated recollections by a former criminal who in 1811 had become the first chief of the Paris Sûreté and later formed the world's first detective agency.

Émile Gaboriau based *Monsieur Lecoq* (1869), the first *roman policier* ("police procedural") on Vidocq's model for a series in which criminals and police were nearly indistinguishable, a "kinship of the hunter and the hunted" that resurfaced in Simenon's Maigret novels (Murphy 195). For his sleuth Lecoq, Gaboriau adapted Poe's "ratiocinative method," an "ingenious and intuitive process by which the hero's mind leaps from the available facts to the hidden truths of the case" (Daniel Hoffman in Herbert 153), foreshadowing Maigret's intuitive process. Gaboriau's Lecoq, egotistical and on occasion arrogant, makes astonishing deductions from tiny scraps of physical evidence, and Gaboriau's plots also usually turn on some sexual scandal, a colorful feature of earlier popular French sensational novels that would become an essential element of Simenon's Maigrets.

French mystery author Maurice LeBlanc's *The Exploits of Arsène Lupin* (1909) chronicled the adventures of a fictional master thief who was also a Don Juan and a skilled detective, while LeBlanc's contemporary Gaston Leroux, creator of *The Phantom of the Opera* (1911), produced the first "locked room" mystery (1908) with its "least likely person" device, a combination British Golden Age authors often employed. Disrupted, like most of French life, by World War I, French popular mystery fiction began to recover by 1922, when 19-year-old Georges Simenon left his home in Liège, Belgium, and arrived in Paris. He encountered not a scintillating "City of Light" but the decadent French capital quaking at the prospect of a German revival, resenting what appeared to be Britain's indifference to it, and feeling even weaker nationally than it actually was, a "consciousness of debility, marked in the Twenties . . . [that] became obsessional in the Thirties" (Johnson 140)—a recipe for national paranoia and eventual disaster. Instead of facing this debilitation and attempting to combat it, France's capital took refuge in the kinds of pleasures that caused Mark Twain to place the French several notches below the Comanches on the ladder of civilization. Roaring Twenties Paris and its pleasures helped Simenon to express in his Maigrets reactions to thematic material he had absorbed in his youth.

AUTHORSHIP

Georges Simenon left 27 volumes of autobiographical writings and dictation, but he warned that some of his early accounts might prove unreliable. Simenon believed that "a man absorbs material until the age of about 18. What he has not taken in by then, he never will" (quoted in Marnham ix), so Simenon's early life offers important clues to the development of Inspector Jules Maigret, his most famous literary creation.

In a 1953 *New Yorker* interview, Simenon claimed, "I was born in the dark and in the rain, and I got away. The crimes I write about are the crimes I would have committed if I had not got away." Even his birth date is a mystery. His birth certificate indicates he was born on Thursday, February 12, 1903, at 11:30 p.m., but according to family tradition, he actually arrived at 12:10 a.m. on Friday, February 13, and his mother superstitiously insisted that his father register the earlier date. Simenon's birthplace, Liège, an important Belgian manufacturing center, was filled with "the stench of poverty, an odor not unpleasant when you have known it since childhood" (Assouline 3). Georges's mother,

Writing is not a profession but a vocation of unhappiness.
—Georges Simenon

whose family had gone bankrupt, so greatly feared becoming poor after her marriage to Désiré Simenon, a fire insurance agent, that it dominated her life and through her the lives of her children. Even though the Simenons belonged to the bourgeois middle class, Georges as a boy experienced both physical and emotional deprivation, exacerbated by a stiff, distant relationship with his father whom he deeply respected and continual conflicts with his mother who had no faith in him and treated him like a stranger. "My father lacked nothing, my mother lacked everything," Simenon wrote in *Je me souviens,* and he portrayed her in his novel *Pedigree* as a tormented individual who begrudged his father's happiness in his life and work. Georges's parents gave him a relentless Roman Catholic schooling, first with the Sisters of Notre Dame, then the Christian Brothers, and finally the Jesuits, an order renowned for harsh discipline and intellectual rigor. These repressive family and religious educational influences instilled in Georges powerful guilt feelings, an obsessive sense of time, and a profound spiritual malaise.

Georges's relationship with his mother deteriorated after the birth of his brother Christian in 1906, whom she adored while rejecting Georges, a blow which resonated throughout Georges's life, although he idealized the Simenons' orderly, comfortable domesticity by transforming it into Inspector Maigret's cozy casserole-scented home. At first Georges was an exemplary student, serving as an altar boy for the 5:45 a.m. Mass at a nearby hospital chapel and even considering a religious vocation, but in 1911, his mother began to take in foreign boarders, young Central European women later portrayed in Simenon's books. They boosted the family's income but disrupted their home life, even infiltrating their kitchen, and their presence humiliated Georges's father and inflamed Georges's revolt against authority.

In 1915, Désiré Simenon fell seriously ill with then-untreatable angina pectoris. Georges later wrote that his father's death in 1921 caused Georges to leave school, but other factors influenced that decision. Only 12 days after Belgium declared war, the first German unit occupied Liège, choking out the innocence of Georges Simenon and his generation. Georges already resented his low day-pupil status at school and he increasingly lost interest in his studies. His adolescent taste for women, sparked by a dramatic sexual initiation at age 12, also contributed to his total rejection of his Catholic faith at age 15-and-a-half, when he began his writing career.

The German occupation with its humiliations, atrocities, and food shortages gave Simenon his first contacts with the criminal world which fascinated him throughout his life. "Everyone cheated," Simenon recalled; his mother smuggled black-market vegetables, the Christian Brothers risked their lives to provide information to the Allies, and even children like Georges were pressed into forbidden activities. Hunger, fear, and the German soldiers billeted on Liège's citizens aggravated domestic tensions, and eventually Georges condemned his mother as a domestic tyrant, emotionally blackmailing him and his father. By the summer of 1918, Georges's adolescent rebellion—drinking and fornication—was out of control. Just as Georges's expulsion from the Jesuits'

Collège St. Servais was looming, his father suffered a heart attack. Georges quit school and his mother found him a job he hated as a pastry apprentice. He also worked in a book shop, but he soon lost both positions. However, a few weeks after the November 11 Armistice, he wangled himself "a perfect job" at the right-wing Roman Catholic *Gazette de Liège* (Marnham 56). His editor soon assigned him to crime reporting, where he stayed for the next four years, learning about human nature, discovering he could "read the secrets of life," and writing them up as "Georges Sim." He cherished this experience, the inspiration for his Maigrets, all his life: "One runs up, notebook in hand, to the corpse which is still warm, one chases police cars, one brushes shoulders with the handcuffed murderer in the corridors outside the court . . . [and] suddenly the world belonged to me" (Simenon, quoted in Marnham 57).

Although in the 1960s Simenon denied he had researched police methods before he began the Maigrets, he attended forensics lectures at the University of Liège held in 1920 to 1921 because of surging postwar unemployment and consequent crime. The lectures included fingerprinting, which had just been introduced in Belgium, and Simenon produced a newspaper feature about *la police scientifique*. Neither Simenon nor Inspector Maigret could afford to attend a university, so Simenon's refusal to admit his exposure to academic police training possibly stemmed from resentment, exclusion, and pride in his own success.

The *Gazette* paid Simenon fairly well, about the same salary with which his ailing father supported their household, paid for Christian's schooling, and provided Georges with loans after he had squandered his wages on Guinness, nightclubs, and women "with bare shoulders, who pulled their skirts up to straighten their stockings" (Simenon, quoted in Marnham 62). Still a teenager, Simenon interviewed important world figures like Crown Prince Hirohito of Japan and Marshal Foch of World War I fame; he covered the main trial of Liège's wartime collaborators; and he authored *"le péril juif"* ("the Jewish peril"), a 17-article series exhibiting contemporary intellectual anti-Semitism, identifying Judaism with Bolshevism. Simenon later claimed his superiors had instructed him to write these pre-Nazi articles.

Besides interviews and topical series, Simenon wrote a daily column—314 columns in 1920 alone—and fiction. His first published stories comically and autobiographically involved a husband with a domineering, nagging wife, and between May and November of that year he completed a humorous novel, *Au Pont des Arches,* partially set in a pharmacy specializing in laxatives for pigeons. Another, *Jehan Pinaguet,* featured two of Simenon's lifelong preoccupations, food and sex.

When nominated for the title of *De Grootste Belg* ("the Greatest Belgian"), Simenon ranked 10th in the Walloon version, 17th in the Flemish version.

For another periodical, Simenon wrote articles supporting Walloon bilingualism with standard French, Walloon being the French dialect spoken in Liège, but he suffered for those unpopular views.

While working for the *Gazette,* Simenon fell in with an anarchic bohemian group that called itself "La Caque" (after a barrel stuffed so full of herring that the fish could not move) and devoted itself to sex, "poetry, drink, and drugs" (Marnham 77). After Simenon's death, one of the group's *"filles sérieuses"* ("serious girls"), Andrée Piéteur, described him as "a big boy with wavy hair . . . [and] a lot of charm . . . [who] actually preferred whores." Though Simenon always savored the company of prostitutes, he "entered matrimony on my hands and knees" (quoted in Marnham 77). Thoroughly drunk on New Year's Eve of 1921, he met a friend's sister, Régine Renchon, a *fille très sérieuse,* and sobered up by discussing art and literature with her. Soon they were lovers; Simenon changed her name to "Tigy" and they began to plan moving to Paris.

Later that year, Simenon suffered two significant losses. His father, the person he loved most, died unexpectedly at age 43 at his office on November 28, 1921. Simenon's wealthy uncles refused to loan him money for the funeral, so Simenon had to borrow money from the *Gazette.* Around the same time, a scandal involving the suspicious death of one of its members forced the dissolution of La Caque, the organization that had given Simenon tantalizing brushes with criminality, and, like the bitter German occupation, left him ambivalent toward right and wrong, one of the Maigrets' major themes. Less than a month after his father's death, Simenon took the night train to Paris, escaping his shady involvements in Liège.

Artist Frederick Franck, whose drawings of Paris accompany excerpts of Simenon's fiction in *Simenon's Paris* (1970) declared that every one of Simenon's books "was, and still is, a love letter to . . . the characteristically European variant of life, above all the Paris variant . . . perceived with awe-inspiring awareness and . . . unmatched poignancy" (Franck 9). Simenon's love affair with Paris overcame his initial dismay at its seamy working-class suburbs and his first few weeks on cheap wine, Camembert sandwiches, and occasional cold cuts with his old La Caque guru Luc Lafnet. A recommendation from *La Gazette* snared him a job writing short stories and reviews as the Paris correspondent of *La Révue sincère* of Brussels and enabled him to live in a small flat on the Rue de Faubourg Saint-Honoré.

In March of 1923, briefly back in Liège, Simenon married Tigy, whose new mother-in-law declared, "My God, she's ugly" (quoted in Marnham 109). He and Tigy immediately returned to Paris, where they set up a private American-style bar in the Place des Vosges and threw extravagant parties. Tigy painted and Simenon supported them with what he called *romans alimentaires* (potboilers): articles, reviews, and numerous novels speedily written under at least 17 pen names including "Georges Sim." Simenon immediately spent his earnings and soon began to spend what he had not yet earned (Assouline 63), but like American hard-boiled detective authors, he maintained a prodigious output. In 1925 alone, mainly by dictation, he produced 60 pseudonymous 1,000-word short stories and three 20,000-word pieces per month, establishing a substantial reputation for popular fiction.

"Sim" was also frenetically pursuing his youthful motto, *"manger et faire l'amour"* ("to eat and make love"), with infidelities which he claimed eventually totaled 10,000 sexual conquests. During a summer vacation at a seashore in Normandy, Tigy acquired a pretty 18-year-old maid, Henriette Liberge, who returned to Paris with them; Simenon renamed her "Boule" and unknown to Tigy, Boule became his mistress for 15 years, longer than any other woman except for one other affair which was shorter but far more flamboyant.

In the 1920s black American exotic dancer Josephine Baker, "obscene and divine" (Marnham 123), performed at the Folies Bergère in a handful of pink ostrich feathers or a skirt made of bananas, offering audiences unprecedented escapist erotic fantasies. Baker and *"le petit Sim"* enjoyed an energetic affair that temporarily dampened his literary output—only 11 novels in 1927. Simenon wrote in his *Mémoires intimes*, "I would have married her if I had not been afraid, obscure figure that I was, of becoming known as Monsieur Josephine Baker" (quoted in Marnham 123).

In the summer of 1927, "Sim" realized that *l'affaire Baker* was threatening the literary career he had created so painstakingly, and another vacation in Normandy, his favorite part of France, helped break Paris' spell on him. When he returned there he avoided his former superficially artsy crowd and Baker; her diary for August 1928 states, "Georges disappeared one day, as suddenly as he arrived. He is married" (quoted in Markham 128). Instead, he prowled sordid districts, looking for prostitutes and ideas for his novels in "that side of life which he remembered as being testing and vivid, the criminal world" (Marnham 125). In a 1963 interview he declared, "Deep down the policeman understands the criminal because he could so easily have become one. They inhabit the same underworld" (quoted in Marnham 128).

In 1928, Simenon produced 44 novels, enough to have a Norman fishing cutter built, on which he, Tigy, Boule, and Olaf, their Great Dane, would spend the next three years. He also explored a new literary direction in a handful of English-style "whodunit" short stories and his last 34 *romans populaires*, three of which involved a police inspector he named "Maigret," the source of his enormous fame. Although during his frenetic worldwide wanderings before he ceased writing fiction in 1973 with *Maigret et Monsieur Charles*, Simenon produced 117 serious psychological novels, which had print runs of only about

In May 2003 Simenon joined Montaigne, Dostoevsky, Proust, and Hemingway with publication of 21 of his novels in two volumes of Gallimard's prestigious *Bibliothèque de la Pléiade* collection. Publisher Hamish Hamilton currently sells all of the one-volume English-language Maigrets for under 10 pounds each.

30,000 each. His 75 novels and 48 short stories starring Inspector Jules Amédée François Maigret vastly outsold his serious work and gave the world a new species of literary detective.

> *Dostoevsky . . . corsé, constructed, economized, and filled with the poetry of pity.*
> —Ford Madox Ford's description of the early Maigret

PROFILE OF COMMISSIONAIRE JULES MAIGRET

Simenon described Maigret's origin in two autobiographical statements. In *"La naissance de Maigret"* ("The Birth of Maigret"), 1966, he recalled sitting in a little café, replete with schnapps and bitters, as "the powerful and imposing bulk of a gentleman" emerged, soon equipped with pipe, bowler hat, a heavy overcoat with velvet collar, and eventually an office with an old cast-iron stove. By the next afternoon, Simenon said, he had written the first chapter of his first Maigret, *Pietr-le-Letton* (*The Case of Peter the Lett*), published in 1931 and long believed the first novel Simenon published under his own name. A more generally accepted version of Maigret's origin, quite different, appears in Simenon's *Je suis resté un enfant de choeur* (1979), where he said Maigret appeared to him on his boat *Ostrogoth,* anchored in the Dutch port of Delfzijl, as a "big man, who ate a lot, drank a lot, followed the suspects patiently and eventually uncovered the truth" (quoted in Marnham 130–131). Despite Maigret's recurrent activity, *"Il s'est mis à boire"* ("he set about drinking"), Maigret did not seem to become drunk, an indication of Simenon's denial of his own alcoholism. He developed his own wine drinking habit when he began his first Maigrets, commenting, "I was rarely drunk, but I needed a pick-me-up as early as the morning, especially to write" (*Quand j'étais vieux* 225), but not until arriving in the United States in 1945, the setting for about a dozen Maigrets, did he admit he had become an alcoholic. Recent scholarship has proved both Simenon's accounts of Inspector Maigret's origin inaccurate. Simenon's first accepted "Maigret" story appeared in *L'amant sans nom,* written by "Christian Brulls" in 1929 with a bulky detective called "No. 49." *Train de nuit,* written in Delfzuil in September 1929 featured "Commissaire Maigret" of Marseille, as did several other "pulp novels" under the name "Georges Sim." Simenon probably wrote *The Case of Peter the Lett,* his first published novel with both the character and the Maigret style, in April 1930, and it was first published as a serial from July to October 1930.

Publishers had at first turned down his experimental "pre-Maigrets," written under various pseudonyms, even a novel written in Friesia, not Holland, featuring a huge heavy-overcoated married Maigret living in the Boulevard Richard-Lenoir and working with Juge Coméliau. "My God [no comma in original] it was a battle to launch Maigret," Simenon later recalled (quoted in Marnham 133). Paris publishers knew he could produce lucrative potboilers, but they were reluctant to take a chance on a *commissaire de police* who did not pursue clues or demonstrate superhuman deduction or even dedicate himself wholeheartedly to crimefighting (Marnham 132–133). Simenon himself launched his first two Maigrets at his "Anthropometric Ball," a "night of madness" in a Montparnasse nightclub, where he had invited the 400 guests, including the Paris *prefet de police*, by police record cards and fingerprinted them at the door. They wore costumes evoking the criminal world and were joined by another 400 gatecrashers; "Who knows how many tuxedo-clad pimps and plainclothes policemen were among the horde of guests?" breathlessly reported *Paris-Midi*, February 21, 1931. The festivities cost Simenon most of his unearned royalties, but the resulting publicity made his name and Maigret's familiar throughout Continental Europe. In 1931, he sold the Maigrets' translation rights in the United States, Britain, Spain, Italy, Norway, and Portugal, and Janet Flanner, writing as "Genêt" in *The New Yorker*, gave his translatlantic reputation a substantial boost. After 19 Maigrets, Simenon, bored with the Inspector, retired him to turn to more serious works; his publisher called him "insane," insisted he would never succeed at anything but detective novels, and told him flatly, "No author of detective novels has ever succeeded in other domains. . . . You'll be back" (Assouline 131), and he was. In 1942 Inspector Maigret began reappearing in roughly two novels a year and eventually three volumes of short stories, with a complicated publication and translation history.

> Today the Maigrets appear in several omnibus English editions: one from Octopus, 6 from Hamish Hamilton, and 14 from Penguin; Maigret single-volume paperback editions include Ace, Aaron, Digit, Four Square, Pan, Panther, Peacock, WDL, and Penguin.

Simenon's creative process became ritualistic: after something triggered an inspiration, he would prepare his materials, search for names in a telephone directory, isolate himself for the duration, write for two early-morning hours, and spend the rest of the day with walks, children, television, and an early bedtime, producing eight or nine chapters in as many days. While writing he would be moody, feeling "an urge to flee" into a world of his imagination, hanging a "Do Not Disturb" sign on his office door and becoming so oblivious to the outside world he could even fail to recognize his own wife. He sometimes borrowed material from actual events, like a trial he had attended in Arizona which he incorporated into *Maigret and the Coroner* (1949). He also limited the length of the Maigrets because he felt a good detective story should be short, capable of being read in two or two and a half hours.

> *The artist is above all a sick person, in any case an unstable one . . . why see in this some form of superiority? I would do better to ask people's forgiveness.*
>
> –Georges Simenon

The Maigrets posed substantial difficulties for translators. Simenon took advantage of French linguistic characteristics to reinforce his explorations of psychology. He deliberately stripped his French vocabulary down to about 2,000 words, repeating many stock expressions and descriptions throughout the series, to suggest the savage restrictions placed by society on individuals, especially the poor, who feel alienated and thus turn to crime. In the Maigrets, as in his serious novels, Simenon relied systematically on the French *imparfait* (imperfect) tense, which conveys repeated action. This tense admirably expresses Simenon's characters who are "slaves of habit," unable to shake off their yokes. The imperfect tense "symbolizes the presence of a circle, a clan, all that weighs so heavily on the individual who has to find himself and break free," suggesting "a certain weariness of life and the temptation to desert" (Narcejac 167). Although Simenon had freed himself from criminal temptations when he moved to Paris, he understood how for the criminals in the Maigrets, "deserting" meant defying the restrictions of law and preying on the society that had alienated them. Simenon also frequently used leitmotifs, reconstruction of the past by stages, a confession from the main villain, interior monologues, and retrospective narration (Assouline 351).

Inspector Maigret's Background

The Inspector tells his own story in *Maigret's Memoirs* (1951), a novel whose real value is that it "serve[s] to establish the yardstick on which all Maigret's judgments, not only of men but of society also, are based" (Raymond 156). In this novel, around 1927 or 1928 (Maigret says he has an imperfect memory for dates), Maigret's Chief assigned him to show thin, long-haired, 24-year-old "Sim" around police headquarters. "Sim" wanted to experience not the "workings of the police machine" but the atmosphere in which police operations occurred (*Memoirs* 6). Maigret was astonished when he realized that the novel Sim produced was really about him, Maigret, and that "Sim" was actually Georges Simenon, who in the *Memoirs* spent hours drinking raspberry brandy and discussing life and literature with Maigret. According to Maigret, the fame that resulted from "Sim's novels" was "not disagreeable," because it not only flattered the inspector's vanity, but also had practical benefits, like getting a good seat in a train or restaurant (*Memoirs* 23).

In the *Memoirs*, Maigret claims he is only concerned with posing one character against another, "one truth against another truth" (*Memoirs* 23). He recalls his family's roots in central France, where his grandfather was a tenant farmer for a local aristocrat. Helped by the village priest, Maigret's father studied agriculture and became the estate manager, respected by the peasants and idolized by his son. Maigret's father, like Simenon's own parent, was content with his position, conscientious, and dependable, a role model who never judged others and never abandoned hope in people. When Maigret was eight, Maigret's mother died in childbirth, as did the new baby.

Maigret's Motto

Maigret lives and works by the motto, "Comprendre sans juger" ("Understand without judging").

Maigret's childhood and its memories endowed his adult character with directness and simplicity and sharpened his awareness of atmospheres and environments "however stale, however startling" (Raymond 157). Maigret attended the village school, then spent a few homesick months at a boarding school, and later worked at an uncle's bakery. His father died at 44 of pleurisy, and for financial reasons Maigret could not finish his medical studies at Nantes, so he went to Paris, where he joined the Sûreté, a step toward the modest and humane ideal of serving his fellow men that he had learned from his father's example.

Inspector Maigret's Career

Once in Paris, Maigret found a cheap Left Bank hotel and became acquainted with Inspector Jacquemain, who reminded him of his father, patiently listened to Maigret's problems, and taught him that criminals were misfits who had ruined their own lives and needed human understanding. Bent on becoming an Inspector like Jacquemain, Maigret began as a police bicycle messenger, and soon was promoted to a plainclothes position, Secretary of the Station Officer of St. Georges Quarter. He met and fell in love with Louise, the future Madame Maigret, studied hard to pass the new police examinations, and learned firsthand various facets of policing from the Public Highway Squad to the Vice Squad, unarmed, pounding the Paris pavement in plainclothes, spending hours in the rain, becoming familiar with all the street people, beggars, organ-grinders, flower girls, the *apaches*—"tough guys" [and] . . . little tarts in black pleated skirts and large chignons"—pickpockets, cardsharps, and prostitutes, and filling his head with indelibly engraved figures and faces (*Memoirs* 78) that inhabit Simenon's Maigrets. He met some of the most desperate human specimens in those lonely patrols, making some arrests with remorse rather than "professional satisfaction." Looking back in his *Memoirs*, Maigret felt he would rather go on that duty again than take a "more sumptuous station" on a sunny corner of the Côte d'Azur (*Memoirs* 91).

At age 30, Maigret left the Hotel Squad and moved to the Special Squad, where he developed his unique method of catching murderers. Although in English versions of the Maigrets he is generally called "Inspector," the original French term "Commissaire" is roughly equivalent to "superintendent," in charge of the homicide division of the *police judiciaire*. In *Maigret in Court* (1961), Maigret holds the rank of "Commissaire divisionnaire," or "divisional chief inspector." In many of the Maigrets he is referred to as "Chief Inspector," the highest ranking working policeman in France. Although occasionally

Maigret worked outside Paris for the "Rue des Saussaies," an entity directly responsible to France's Ministry of the Interior and charged with dealing with political problems, he worked mainly at the Quai des Orfèvres, headquarters of the Police Judiciare, a section of the Paris police which operates almost entirely within the city and infrequently in the Department of the Seine, not to be confused, as the fictional Maigret claimed Simenon had done, with the Sûreté Nationale. Maigret's bourgeois appearance and lifestyle are constant throughout the series.

> He did not resemble the ordinary policeman. . . . His clothes were well-cut, of fine wool. He also shaved every morning and his hands were well groomed. . . . He was enormous and bony. . . . He was like a solid block and everything had to break against it. . . . His pipe remained clenched in his jaw. (*Memoirs* 21–22)

The pipe was never filled with Sherlock Holmes's exotic Latakia but always with *gris*, the coarsest grade of French tobacco. No matter where he is, Maigret can stop and savor the moment; all kinds of weather delight him, from Paris' delicate spring rains to the fierce sun of the Côte d'Azur. When he is home with one of his frequent colds, he reads Dumas's swashbuckling novels. He enjoys good food and drinks quite a bit, especially beer ordered from the Brasserie Dauphine, but he never appears drunk. In Paris Maigret and his wife live on the Boulevard Richard-Lenoir, and because Maigret never learned to drive, Madame Maigret drives them to spend quiet weekends at their country house at Meung-sur-Loire where Simenon had Maigret compose his memoirs. Overall, Simenon created three Maigrets: the first a "rough-hewn and uncompleted Maigret . . . the harsh, red-faced, suitably bowler-hatted investigator," and in a few of the last Maigrets, an "Old Pretender," while in between is "the Maigret that we recognize and feel we know," "the repairer of destinies" (Raymond 154).

Inspector Maigret's Method

"Maigret's strength is that he has no method at all" (Raymond 159). Very early in his career, Maigret felt a bond between the policeman and his quarry, and, incurably optimistic, he agreed with his old religion teacher's maxim that "a little knowledge turns one away from man, a great deal of knowledge brings one back to man" (quoted in Rom 33). Simenon also gifted Maigret with Désiré Simenon's seemingly inexhaustible patience. Maigret believed that "Some investigations take months. And certain criminals are eventually arrested only after long years, and then sometimes by pure chance." He also believed the process was the same in all cases:

> You have to *know* [italics in original]. To know the milieu in which a crime has been committed, to know the way of life, the habits, morals, reactions of the people involved in it, whether victims, criminals, or merely witnesses. To enter into their world without surprise, easily, and to speak its language naturally. (*Memoirs* 123)

This was particularly true of Maigret's relationship with the poor: "Like the poor themselves, Maigret belongs to a silent race. 'The poor,' he reflects, 'are used not to express their hopelessness, because life, work, and the hourly, daily calls of life lie forever ahead of them'" (Raymond 156). Through his decades on the job, Maigret considered criminals "as a fact . . . as creatures who exist and for the well-being of society . . . have got to be kept, willy-nilly, within certain bounds and punished when they overstep them" (*Memoirs* 126). Maigret rarely carried a gun, engaged in physical violence, "step[ped] out with the dolls" or participated in wild American-style chases. Although other detectives try to create barriers between themselves and their criminal quarries, Maigret seeks to remove them, and "Only when he finally and thoroughly understands the reasons why the crime came to be committed does he arrest his suspect" (*CA Online*). Maigret himself described the climax of his intuitive "non-method" in *Maigret and the Old Lady* (1951): at some moment in every case, when he would have had a little too much to drink, "it all began to rumble." He began to see people from the inside, "groping, not sure of himself, with the feeling that it would only need another tiny effort for everything to be clear and for the truth to be revealed by itself" (quoted in Raymond 161).

Inspector Maigret's Strengths

Overall, Maigret is a "quiet, unexcitable man who detests hurry, a stolid, peaceable figure who inspires confidence" (Becker 1977, 52). His props—a pipe, a heavy overcoat, the pot-bellied stove in the Quai des Orfèvres—remain the same through all the novels. Maigret witnessed all kinds of human depravities, but he still realized that that "they were compensated by a great deal of simple courage, good will, or resignation" (*Memoirs* 126–127). Maigret is no superhuman chivalric detective figure but a quintessential bourgeois. Simenon claimed, "When I wanted to create a sympathetic person who understood everything, that is to say Maigret, I gave him without realizing it certain of my father's characteristics" (quoted in Becker 1999, 50), chiefly his empathy with all kinds of human beings, his greatest strength both as a policeman and as a private individual.

In *Maigret on the Defensive* (1964), Maigret observes that if he had been a judge or a jury member, he could not have judged another person, whatever the crime, because to him it was not the crime that counted but what had occurred or is occurring within the criminal, adding that what appears evil may be understandable when all the facts are known. In all of his cases, Maigret is more interested in understanding the criminal than in solving the crime, and he believes that a murderer is to be pitied, because "every man is capable of becoming a murderer if he has sufficient motivation" (*Maigret voyage* 100). Simenon himself declared that he had never met anyone, no matter how unattractive he may seem at first sight, whom I did not finally like after having studied him" (quoted in Becker 1977, 50). In the *Memoirs,* Maigret seemed to resent Simenon's excusing him for not having been a physician—as his best friend in Paris was and as a boy he had spontaneously decided he wanted to become—but he also had unhappy memories of the alcoholic village doctor who had not been able to save his mother. These taught him that many people become misfits, and so he began to ponder how he might become more than a physician: a "mender of destinies"; "the ability to guess correctly people's feelings and hidden goals is important for the physician . . . and does not also a detective clarify fateful situations and destinies?" (Rom 31). Paul Rom once called Maigret "a spiritual brother of Adler," because Maigret intuitively applied the "context psychology" of Austrian psychologist Alfred Adler, an associate of Freud, which allows one to identify a lifestyle and anticipate what an individual will do (quoted in Rom 34). Maigret depends on qualities supporting that empathy—his extraordinary patience, his profound intuition, and his deep compassion for both victim and killer—to catch the criminals he hunts. He sees himself as a "repairer of destinies," someone who can put himself within everybody's mind (Raymond 153).

Inspector Maigret's Weaknesses

Being wise and kind, Maigret sympathizes with both the victims and the murderers, so that he seems to have no real enemies. No dyed-in-the-wool criminals appear in his cases, either, since he is not interested in professional villains but in ordinary people who are driven to crime. He does not pity them, but instead shares their discomforts: "The prostitute of the Boulevard de Clichy and the inspector watching her are both wearing cheap shoes and both have sore feet from the kilometers of pavement they have walked" (*Memoirs* 111). Maigret never felt disgusted either by squalid slum conditions or the professional criminals with whom he had to spend so much time, even those who begged him to attend their executions and saved their last dying look for him: "They did their best," he felt, and sent on their last letters to relatives with his own covering notes, a telltale signal of his essential compassion for humanity (*Memoirs* 109). Maigret has far less sympathy for the judicial system. Simenon held severe opinions about the French magistrature, depicting both advocates and judges, which the French legal system keeps totally separate, with "the same skilful, though different and unequal malice," depicting barristers as shallow, grasping, callous, and "slow on psychology," while making his magistrates the worst kind of arrogant, self-serving functionaries (Raymond 113). Maigret often has to smother his anger at the formulaic French legal process and "its necessarily gross simplifications . . . when faced with a particularly hidebound magistrate he clenches his fists in impotence at the way the rigidities of procedure have prevented the full truth from appearing"—the full truth that to him is indispensable in judging human reactions" (Keating 121). From the start,

Maigret also dusts up with the obnoxious examining magistrate, Juge Caméliau, who never sympathizes with Maigret. He also clashed with the sarcastic Juge Amadieu, though Simenon made both Juge Urbain de Chezaud and Juge Ancelin agreeable characters.

Inspector Maigret's Associates

Inspector Maigret's supporting cast includes a wide variety of subordinate detective inspectors, especially his faithful Janvier, a devoted family man; Torrence, resurrected after the first Maigret for further service; boyish young Lapointe, always sent to interview women of uncertain age; Lucas, talented but unable to hide his policeman's calling; cranky and henpecked Lognon, who always messes up; and Moers, the ballistic expert. Dr. Pardon, one of Maigret's closest friends, fruitlessly warns Maigret against drinking too many aperitifs, and Scotland Yard's unflappable Chief Inspector Pyke plays off Maigret's bourgeois Gallic personality. With all of them, Maigret maintains a quiet, sympathetic professional relationship as a father figure who convinces them as well as his readers that "there is an order, a structure, and a meaning to life" (Becker 1977, 53). All of Maigret's professional colleagues, either allies or enemies, "fence Maigret in, curbing his imagination, limiting his absorbent nature, blanketing his rage to understand and willing him to see with other eyes" (Raymond 162).

The Women in Maigret's Life and Work

Nowhere is order, structure, and meaning more evident in the Maigrets than in the inspector's home life, where "savory smells of [his] carefully prepared dinner always await [him], where everything is simple and neat, clean and comfortable" (*Memoirs* 125). He and Louise deeply regret having no children, but otherwise she is Simenon's ideal wife, totally devoted to pampering her husband, producing exquisite broths and *crème de citron* while he is sick in bed and even making him undress and bathe after work while she inspects his clothes for fleas caught on the job. She is such a gifted French cook that Robert J. Courtine, a leading French food writer, published *Madame Maigret's Recipes* (New York: Harcourt Brace Jovanovich, 1975), derived from Louise Maigret's fictional kitchen. Simenon may have given Maigret a domestic tranquility that his continual wanderings and complicated marital situation prevented. He divorced Tigy and married his pregnant mistress, Denise Ouimet, on successive days in 1950 in the same Reno, Nevada, courthouse. Not long after Denise's

Mme. Maigret's nephew Philippe Lauer is also a member of the police force and is close to them.

new maid Teresa Sburelin became Simenon's mistress in 1961, Denise entered a psychiatric clinic and their daughter, Marie-Jo, committed suicide in 1978 in Paris. Simenon, who had declared, "If I should cease writing, I would die," died in Lausanne on September 4, 1989. His remaining three children learned of his death on the radio, after he had been cremated and Teresa had strewn his ashes under a cedar tree in their garden.

Maigret often came into contact with the "other kind" of Frenchwomen, the lowest-class prostitutes who plied their trade in squalid Parisian venues like Les Halles, either "gamines of sixteen" fought over by pimps or "ancient harpies" who as the last word in insults to the police would flip up their skirts to show their bare backsides. Maigret's first name, Jules, which he would never have chosen for himself because it recalls the great Julius Caesar, became a street joke among the *filles de joie*. Some policemen would have locked them up for a few days for insulting them, but Maigret refused to do so, not from any sense of justice or pity but because he considered them children who insist on working a joke to death.

THE MAIGRETS' LASTING APPEAL

For the last 40 years of his life, Simenon's global sales topped 3 million books a year, recording Maigret's career in more novels than the exploits of any other Continental detective and making Simenon the world's best-selling author (Jackson 10). Already in 1939 Simenon was the most widely translated contemporary French-language writer in the world. Contemporary critics attribute such enormous success to two factors: Simenon's central figure, a detective like none other, and Simenon's unique departure from the traditional mystery/detection form.

Julian Symons declared in *Mortal Consequences* that Simenon's mastery of the crime story rests primarily in the creation of Jules Maigret, who is a minimal hero with none of Sherlock Holmes's flamboyance, one egoless enough to repeatedly lament his own shortcomings. Jacques Barzun and W.H. Taylor in their *Catalogue of Crime* also observed that the Maigrets are "not detection" because Maigret exercises "the patience of a god" to get the criminal he intuitively knows is guilty, "and what his readers enjoy is his boredom, wet feet, and hunger" (quoted in *CA Online*)—in short, Maigret's common bourgeois humanity. The Maigrets also contain ordinary characters with whom anyone anywhere in the world can identify. These novels successfully employ a conventional chronological plot structure, beginning with a crisis, evoking the past through flashbacks, and moving directly to a sometimes ambiguous but always realistic conclusion.

Writing in the 1950s, French critic Thomas Narcejac believed Simenon created three different Jules Maigrets: the 40-year-old Maigret of 1931 to 1934; the somewhat younger Maigret of *Maigret and the Hotel Majestic* in 1942; and the later Maigret, who Narcejac felt was "'fading happily into a legend" (115). For Narcejac, the early Maigrets were "hard and sharp like a green apple," with sketchy descriptions, a tense, serious style, and a Maigret unable to impose his own calmness because Simenon was always too hurried to bring his characters completely to life. Narcejac noted that after being away from Maigret for several years and perfecting his literary technique, Simenon provided one central setting per each new Maigret novel, employing that unity of place so dear to French letters, "a simplification of the drama, a meticulous study of character and complete mastery of atmosphere" (Narcejac 118). In the later Maigrets, Narcejac finds that Simenon had gotten into Maigret's skin so that the inspector shed all the detective equipment, becoming "a connoisseur of souls, like Simenon" (Narcejac 119). With plot now reduced to a minimum, Simenon developed character more strongly, so that the late Maigret is more poet than policeman and his adventures acquire completely new meaning and form, even good humor and comedy.

Simenon's work, especially the Maigrets, both looks backward to the great French novelist Honoré de Balzac and forward to French existentialism. As a voraciously reading boy, Simenon had devoured Balzac's works in the Liège public library. Balzac, who also began his literary career writing potboilers, also wrote very rapidly, producing his great novel *Le père Goriot* in only three days. Even when Simenon was a young writer critics compared him to Balzac, a cliché that always irritated Simenon, perhaps because it contained more than one grain of truth. If Balzac's *Histoire de treize*, not Poe's "Murders in the Rue Morgue" is seen as the archetype of the detective novel, Balzac may have been the real precursor of the Maigrets (Becker 1977, 36). Balzac's masterpiece, *The Human Comedy*, a collection of novels and short stories recreating French society of the first half of the 19th century, portrays every class and profession through minutely detailed individual characters. Simenon did write a longer novel, *Le Testament Donadieu*, illustrating a well-to-do family's downward spiral into collapse, but where Balzac consistently asked his readers to join him in condemning societal abuses like political corruption, neither Simenon nor Maigret ever passes judgment because for them both "there are only problems, no answers" (Becker 1977, 136). Nevertheless, over the span of the Maigrets, Simenon, like Balzac, evoked a half-century of French history in a vast canvas of people, customs, cities, and provinces, "imbuing the characters with a universality that transcends time and geographical boundaries" (Becker 1977, 137).

In a revealing autobiographical treatment, Simenon wrote a 7,000-word biographical essay, *Portrait-souvenir de Balzac*, as a radio talk in 1960, concentrating on Balzac's life and virtually ignoring Balzac's writing, sharing Balzac's feeling of worthlessness and the shame that impelled him to accomplish great things, and taking every opportunity to lead an event in Balzac's life back to Simenon's own biography, such as his observation about Balzac's unloving mother: "A novelist is a man who does not like his mother, or who never received mother-love" (quoted in Marnham 277). Balzac, Simenon observed, preferred older women and married one—a "motherly" woman, "sweet, forgiving, capable, who would not only love him but admire him" (quoted in Marnham 277)—a thumbnail description of Madame Maigret. Simenon's Balzac script reveals Simenon's inability to engage the work of others and his egoistic tendency to defend and justify himself, but it also illuminates Simenon's basic insecurity, expressed in statements like "Why struggle to live the life of others if one is self-assured and if one has no need to rebel against oneself?" (quoted in Marnham 277). By making Inspector Jules Maigret the epitome of self-assurance, calm self-acceptance, and domestic security even while surrounded by misfits and the crimes they bring on themselves, Simenon seems to have found the perfect complement to what he considered his own frailties.

On the other hand, Simenon's compassion for the poor he had learned to know as a boy seems to have made the criminal characters in his Maigrets appear as sufferers from a disease brought on by society, not a manifestation of personal wickedness, and his portrayals of criminals as lone individuals alienated from society place him close to his existentialist French contemporaries. Shortly after World War II, French novelist and philosopher Jean-Paul Sartre popularized the theories of 19th-century philosopher Søren Kierkegaard, who believed that existence should be emphasized over essence and that human reason could not explain the enigma of the universe; hence human beings and things have no meaning except as they are acted on. Existentialists feel that such meaninglessness produces discomfort, anxiety, and loneliness; human beings are totally free, but also totally responsible for what they make of themselves. Existentialism, however, also can allow the possibility of improvement, if an action is taken in contradiction to accepted principles. Human nature and society can be improved, but only from within the individual. "Of all mystery writers, Simenon . . . most displays the view of crime as essentially a disease" caused by society, not the intrinsic "evil" of an individual alienated from society and driven by it to "neurotic or psychotic behavior," so that Simenon's interest lies in accurately portraying such an individual's psychological motivations (Murphy 452).

Although Simenon himself seemed always to have suffered from an ambivalence about his achievements that made him declare near the end of his life, "I would like to be able to be silent," his admirers, among them Nobel prizewinner André Gide, praised his achievements highly; Gide went so far as to hail Simenon as "the greatest French novelist of our time," and not the least of his achievements was the creation of Inspector Jules Maigret.

The popularity of Simenon's Maigrets rests on the Inspector's ability to solve his cases by one transcendent talent: understanding. Maigret is the quintessential "detective as author, . . . a

> *If I were to cease writing, I should die.*
> —Georges Simenon

Grand Master

Simenon was named a Grand Master of the Mystery Writers Association in 1966.

The Movie Maigrets (French except where noted)

Pierre Renoir	Kinya Aikawa (Japanese)
Harry Baur	Boris Tenin (Russian)
Albert Préjean	Gino Cervi (Italian)
Michel Simon	Charles Laughton (British)
Maurice Manson	Heinz Ruhmann (German)
Jean Gabin	Jan Teuling (Dutch)

Mender of Destinies, a putter-right of the injustices of an imperfect and hide-bound world . . . a high priest of detection" (Keating 122).

MEDIA ADAPTATIONS

Maigret in the Movies

Simenon's relationship with the movie industry was long and complicated. At his death, 55 of his works had been adapted as films, but only 15 were based on the Maigrets. Already as a boy in Liège, Simenon had moonlighted for the French film industry's official review, *La Cinématographie française*. From 1919 on, he had enjoyed German expressionistic films in small Left Bank Parisian theatres, but in 1931 the publication of his Maigrets inspired producers and directors and changed his relations with the film industry completely. About a year after its 1931 publication, Simenon's Maigret novel *Le Chien Jaune* (*A Face for a Clue*) was filmed, with Simenon insisting on being credited as co-adaptor. He refused to allow the moviemakers to tinker with Maigret and enforced his right to select actors, because he had no faith in the film industry's ethics. Simenon and the famous French film director Jean Renoir became close friends on the next Maigret film, *La Nuit du Carrefour* (*The Crossroad Murders*), which like *Le Chien Jaune* failed both with critics and at the box office, infuriating Simenon because he had not been able to control all the manifold details of film production. He did make his fictional Maigret admit that the first screen Maigret, Pierre Renoir, was "tolerably true to life" though he found the next, Abel Tarride, "obese and bland . . . like an inflated rubber animal," and his successor Harry Baur, two decades older, "flabby and tragic" (*Memoirs* 32–33).

Simenon then decided he would make his own movies, starting with *La Tête d'un homme* (*A Man's Head*), where Maigret vies with a young murderer, a medical student, whom Simenon based on his friend Ilya Ehrenbourg. For whatever reasons, either rubber checks from crooked producers or his own lack of filmmaking experience, Simenon had to withdraw from the project. Though he had made decent profits from these first three cinematic Maigrets—his second biggest source of income in 1931—Simenon had become so embittered he wanted nothing more to do with the film industry.

As early as 1936, however, Simenon backpedaled. When he abandoned writing Maigrets, the resulting decline in his book sales may have affected his "return to the screen."

In any case, he became the contemporary French-language author whose works were most often adapted for movies and television: between 1932 and 1993, 56 films were made from Simenon's novels and short stories. Simenon was also the writer most often brought to the screen during the Nazi Occupation of France—as opposed to seven of Balzac's, nine of Simenon's books were filmed by the German firm Continental at that time, with capital diverted from the Occupation budget. In 1941 alone Simenon realized half of his large income from such films, and in a 1942 contract specifying he was of Aryan descent, Simenon sold three-year rights to the Maigret character to Continental.

Shortly after the war, British actor Burgess Meredith and producer Irving Allen planned to remake *A Battle of Nerves* starring testy Charles Laughton, the most notable English-language film Maigret, and by 1948 Simenon himself was negotiating with Hollywood. Although after a few days' visit there, he considered it "the most artificial city in the world" (Simenon, *Memoires intimes* 216). Hollywood moguls regarded Simenon so highly that he became one of their most sought after writers. Three Simenon films—*The Man on the Eiffel Tower, Midnight Episode,* and *The Man Who Watched Trains Go By*—all proved highly successful. Later, Simenon chaired the 1958 Brussels Film Festival, and by 1960 about 50 of his works had been made into movies, three with French star Jean Gabin, Simenon's favorite big screen Maigret. A whole new generation of filmmakers, mostly French, began bringing new Maigrets to the big screen in the 1960s as well.

Radio

Between 1976 and 1977, BBC Radio 4's Maurice Denham starred in 19 Maigret episodes, with Michael Gough playing the narrator, Georges Simenon. Radio 4's *Saturday Night Theatre* feature "Maigret and the Millionaires" (1984) starred Maurice Denham as well, while the same show featured Bernard Hepton as Maigret in "Maigret's Special Murder" (1986) and Barry Foster as Maigret in "Maigret's Christmas" (1998).

Radio 4 presented a four-part Maigret series (December 2002), starring Nicolas LePrevost as Maigret and Julian Barnes as Simenon: *A Man's Head, The Bar on the Seine, My Friend Maigret,* and *Madame Maigret's Own Case.*

The Television Maigrets (French except where noted)

Jean Gabin	Rupert Davies (British)
Bruno Cremer	Richard Harris (British)
Gino Cervi (Italian)	Michael Gambon (British)
Jean Richard	

The BBC Radio Collection issues for BBC Audio, Spoken Word, include four episodes: *Maigret and the Minister* (1992, reissued 1998), *Maigret Hesitates* (2000), *Maigret Sets a Trap* (2001), and *Maigret: A Man's Head* (2002).

Television

On French television, Jean Richard played Maigret in a long-running series, though Simenon disliked Richard's work, reportedly because Richard would not remove his hat before entering a room. Bruno Cremer played Maigret in over 40 other adaptations.

In Britain, other small-screen Maigrets were Britain's Rupert Davies, whom Simenon liked best, in a BBC series of over 50 adaptations, and Richard Harris, in a briefer British series. In the 1990s ITV series for Granada Television, starred Michael Gambon. Italy's Gino Cervi portrayed Maigret in a series lasting from 1964 to 1972 which Simenon considered possibly the best Maigret television adaptation overall.

PARALLEL CHRONOLOGY

Note: According to Marnham, Simenon frequently contradicted himself in his 27 volumes of autobiographical writings, even warning readers about their unreliability (ix). Simenon's works are cited here by their English titles.

Major Events Related to Inspector Maigret	World Events
Feb. 12, 1903 Georges Simenon born in Liège, Belgium	
Sept. 21, 1906 Christian Simenon born; Georges begins preschool	
1907 Georges's mother Henriette begins to take in foreign boarders	
1908 Georges enters Christian Brothers' elementary school	
1914 Georges enters Jesuit College of St. Louis	**Aug. 1914** Outbreak of World War I; German army occupies Liège

Major Events Related to Inspector Maigret	World Events
Sept. 1915 Georges renounces vocation, moves to College of St. Servais	
1918 Georges's father suffers heart attack; Georges leaves school	**Nov. 1918** German army surrenders; Armistice is signed; Liège is liberated; start of influenza pandemic
1919 Georges has column in *Gazette de Liège*; writes first novel, *Au Pont des Arches*	**1919** Official origin of the Communist Party
1920 Simenon begins 18 months of military service near his home; also writes for *Gazette*	
1920–1921 Simenon attends forensics lectures at U. of Liège	
1921 Georges is engaged to Regine Renchon ("Tigy"); his father dies	
Dec. 1922 Simenon leaves for Paris	
1923 Simenon and Tigy are married; in September; Colette accepts one of his short stories; he writes over 1,000 stories in the next 10 years	
1924 Simenon settles in Paris	
Oct. 1925 Simenon smitten by Josephine Baker	
1925–1934 Simenon writes 214 potboilers under 17 pseudonyms; "Boule" becomes Tigy's maid in 1925	
Summer 1927 Simenon breaks off with Josephine Baker	
1929 Simenon writes short mystery stories for *Détective* magazine	
	1930 Worldwide economic depression; despair and loss of direction apparent in European fiction, especially "novels of society"; 50 percent rise in European unemployment
1931 Simenon launches first two "Maigrets"	
1931–1934 Publishes Maigrets	
1933 Simenon writes "last" "Maigret" and first "dark" (psychological) novel, *La maison du canal*	**1933** Destruction of the German Reichstag, blamed on the Communists by Nazis; Germany withdraws from League of Nations

(Continued)

Major Events Related to Inspector Maigret	World Events
1934 *Maigret Returns* published	**1934** Adolf Hitler becomes Chancellor and President of Germany **1936** Creation of Rome-Berlin Axis **1936–1939** Spanish Civil War
1938 Simenon called up to Belgian Army; begins writing Maigret short stories again **April 19, 1939** Birth of son Marc	**1938** Munich crisis
	Sept. 2, 1939 France and Great Britain declare war; Belgium remains neutral **May 1940** Germany occupies Holland and Belgium
June 1940 Simenon and family caught in German occupied zone **1940** Simenon incorrectly diagnosed as terminally ill; begins writing *Je souviens* (memoir later turned into novel *Pedigree*) **1940s** Writes 20 *romans durs*	**June 22, 1940** French army surrenders
	Dec. 7, 1941 Japanese attack on Pearl Harbor; America enters war
1942 Accused by Vichy authorities of being Jewish and threatened with deportation to concentration camp; new Maigret novel *Maigret and the Spinster* published **1942–1972** Writes Maigrets	
	1943 Jean-Paul Sartre publishes *Being and Nothingness*
Summer 1944 Tigy discovers 15-year liaison between Simenon and Boule; Simenon flees Resistance purge **1945** Simenon and family move to Canada; Simenon hires Denise Ouimet as secretary and she becomes his mistress	**1945** Surrender of Nazi Germany and Japan; end of World War II; Nuremberg Tribunal condemns Nazi leaders **1945–1947** American films feature hard-boiled detectives **1946** Truman Doctrine counters Communism in Europe; beginning of Cold War
1947 Simenon and family move to Arizona	

Major Events Related to Inspector Maigret	World Events
1948 Boule's return produces *ménage à quatre*	**1948** Berlin airlift; NATO established
1949 Simenon asks for divorce from Tigy; Denise gives birth to John Simenon	**1949** German Federal Republic set up at Bonn; United Nations headquarters set up in New York
1950 Simenon gets Reno divorce and marries Denise the next day	**1950** Korean War begins
1951 Simenon's sales reach $3 million per year	**1951** Deaths of Josef Stalin and André Gide
1952 Simenon returns briefly to Belgium; elected to Belgian Royal Academy of Language and Literature	
1953 Birth of Marie-Georges ("Marie-Jo") Simenon	**1953** Cease-fire of Korean War
	1954–1975 Vietnam War
	1956 Suez Crisis; Hungarian Revolution suppressed
1957 Simenon and family make permanent home in Switzerland	**1957** USSR launches *Sputnik*
1959 Birth of Pierre Simenon	
1961 Simenon's new secretary, Teresa Sburlin, becomes his mistress	**1961** Berlin Wall crisis
1963 Denise enters psychiatric hospital	
	1964 Khrushchev falls from power in USSR
1966 Marie-Jo has first psychiatric treatment; bronze statue of Maigret erected at Delfzijl, the Netherlands	
	1969 U.S. astronauts walk on moon
1970 Marie-Jo has nervous breakdown	
1972 Simenon finishes last "Maigret," *Maigret and Monsieur Charles* and last psychological novel, *The Innocents*	
1973 Simenon announces his retirement from writing; six days later begins dictating memoirs	**1973** U.S. involvement in Vietnam ends
1977 Simenon announces he has had sexual relations with 10,000 women	
May 20, 1978 Marie-Jo commits suicide in Paris	
1985 Tigy dies at Parquerolles	
Sept. 4, 1989 Simenon dies at Lausanne, Switzerland	

SIMENON'S BODY OF WORK

The Maigret Saga

From 1931 through 1972, Simenon produced an average of 2.5 new Maigret investigations per year, totaling 75 novels and 28 short stories. Some of the Maigret novels best known in English translation include the following, with dates given of French publication:

The Strange Case of Peter the Lett (1931)

The Death of Monsieur Gallet (1931)

Maigret and the Hundred Gibbets (1931)

The Madman of Bergerac (1932)

Maigret Mystified (1932)

Maigret and the Yellow Dog (1936)

Maigret and the Hotel Majestic (novelette) (originally published in French, 1942; 1978)

My Friend Maigret (1949)

Maigret's First Case (1949)

Maigret's Memoirs (1951)

Maigret Has Scruples (1958)

Maigret in Court (1960)

Maigret and Monsieur Charles (1972)

Short Fiction

The following are published by Hamish Hamilton, London:

The Short Cases of Inspector Maigret (1959)

Maigret's Christmas: Complete Short Stories, Volume I (1976)

Maigret's Pipe: Complete Short Stories, Volume II (1977)

Other Fiction

George Simenon wrote three volumes of juvenilia in 1921; he published four volumes of short fiction in French between 1932 and 1953; he published 117 psychological novels between 1931 and 1972. He also published many works under pseudonyms between 1921 and 1991.

Autobiographical Writings

Je me souviens ("I Remember") (1945)

Quand j'étais vieux ("When I Was Old") (1970)

Simenon's Paris, illustrated by Frederick Franck. New York: Dial Press, 1970

Lettre à ma mère ("Letter to My Mother") (1974)

Simenon also published 22 *Dictées* (volumes of dictated memoirs) between 1975 and 1981.

Other Writings

Simenon's Paris, by Georges Simenon, with drawings by Frederick Franck (New York: Dial Press, 1970), pairs excerpts of Simenon's fiction with Franck's sketches, made shortly after World War II, illustrating Franck's conviction, shared with Simenon, that "love makes for seeing"; according to Franck, both creators activated "one's own awareness of the multiplicity, the joy, the despair, the grace of being human (Franck 11).

Radio Productions

BBC Radio 4 Home Service, December 1957: adaptation of *Maigret and the Young Girl.*
BBC Radio 4: 1984, 1986 (Saturday Night Theatre): 2 episodes starring Maurice Denham.
BBC Radio 4: 2002: 4 episodes starring Nicolas Prevost and Bernard Hepton, respectively.
CBC Radio Theater: 1970–1971: 5-episode Maigret Series I, starring Budd Knapp.
CBC Radio Theater: 1975–1977: 7-episode Maigret Series II, starring Budd Knapp.
4-Part Series, December 2002, starring Nicolas LeProvost as Maigret and Julian Barnes

Archives

The Centre d'études Georges Simenon, Liège, Belgium

The Simenon Center, Drew University, Madison, NJ

WORKS CITED

Assouline, Pierre. *Simenon: A Biography.* New York: Knopf, 1977.
Baryun, Jacques, and W.H. Taylor. *A Catalogue of Crime.* New York: Garland, 1971, rev. ed. 1989.
Becker, Lucille F. *Georges Simenon.* New York: Twayne, 1977
———. *Georges Simenon Revisited.* New York: Twayne, 1999.
———. "Celebrating the Georges Simenon Centennial." *World Literature Today* 77 (Oct.–Dec. 2003): 59–61.

Courtine, Robert J. *Madame Maigret's Recipes*. New York: Harcourt Brace Jovanovich, 1975.

Franck, Frederick. *Simenon's Paris*. New York: Dial, 1970.

"George Simenon" *Contemporary Authors Online*. http://web2.infotrac.galegroup .com.

Herbert, Rosemary. *Whodunit? A Who's Who of Crime and Mystery Writing*. New York: Oxford University Press, 1999.

Horton, Rod W., and Vincent F. Hopper. *Backgrounds of European Literature*. Englewood Cliffs, NJ: Prentice-Hall, 1975.

Jackson, Crispin. "Georges Simenon and 'Maigret.'" *Book and Magazine Collector* 98 (May 1992): 4–12.

Johnson, Paul. *Modern Times*. New York: HarperCollins, 1991.

Keating, H.R.F. *Crime and Mystery: The 100 Best Books*. New York: Carroll & Graf, 1987.

Marnham, Patrick. *The Man Who Wasn't Maigret*. New York: Harcourt Brace, 1994.

Narjerac, Thomas. *The Art of Simenon*. London: Routledge & Kegan Paul, 1952.

Raymond, John. *Simenon in Court*. London: Hamish Hamilton, 1968.

Rom, Paul. "The Development of a Contributive Lifestyle: Simenon's Memoirs of Maigret." *Journal of Individual Psychology* 36 (May 1980): 30–35.

Symons, Lucian. *Mortal Consequences*. Harmondsworth: Penguin, 1972.

FURTHER READING

Anderson, Isaac. Review of *The Crime of Inspector Maigret* and *The Death of Monsieur Gallet*. *The New York Times Book Review*, February 5, 1933: 16.

———. Review of *The Shadow in the Courtyard* and *The Crime at Lock 14*. *The New York Times Book Review*, March 4, 1934: 11, 21.

Becker, Lucille F. Review of "Carissimo Simenon, mon cher Fellini." *World Literature Today* 74 (Winter 2000): 113.

———. ". . . sans trop de pudeur." Review of *Correspondence 1938–1950*. *World Literature Today* 74 (Summer 2000): 629–671.

Bishop, John Peale. "Georges Simenon." *The New Republic* 104 (10 March 1941): 345–346.

Bresler, Fenton. *The Mystery of Georges Simenon*. London: Heinemann, 1983.

Broyard, Anatole. "Classical vs. Romantic Crime." *The New York Times Book Review*, 4 August 1975: 17.

Cobb, Richard. "Simenon at 80." *The Listener* 109 (February 17, 1983): 8–10.

Eisinger, Erica M. "Maigret and Women: *La maman* and *la putain*." *Journal of Popular Culture* 12 (Summer 1978): 52–60.

Evenson, Brian. "Georges Simenon Revisited." *World Literature Today* 74 (Spring 2000): 396.

Fernandez, Dominique, pref. to *Georges Simenon et André Gide, Correspondence 1938–1950*. Paris: Omnibus, 1999.

Harris, Lis. "Books: 'Maigret le flâneur.'" *The New Yorker* 55 (2 April 1979): 122–124.

Holman, C. Hugh. *A Handbook to Literature*. 3rd ed. New York: The Odyssey Press, 1972.

Jacobs, Jay. "Simenon's Mosaic." *The Reporter* 32 (January 14, 1965): 38–40.

Occhiogrosso, Frank. "Current Reviews: 'Maigret and the Apparition.'" *Armchair Detective* 10 (October 1977): 310–311.

Partridge, Ralph. "Detection in France." *The New Statesman & Nation* 19 (February 10, 1940): 184, 186.

———. "The Progress of Simenon." *The New Stateman & Nation* 19 (May 25, 1940): 678, 680.

Penzler, Otto. *The Private Lives of Private Eyes, Spies, Crime Fighters and Other Good Guys,* pp. 106–115. New York: Grosset, 1977.

Rolo, Charles J. "Simenon and Spillane: The Metaphysics of Murder for the Millions." In *Mass Culture: The Popular Arts in America,* edited by Bernard Rosenberg and David Manning White. Glencoe, IL: The Free Press, 1957: 165–175.

Symons, Julian. "About Maigret and the Stolen Papers," in *Great Detectives: Seven Original Investigations.* New York: Harry N. Abrams, 1981.

———. "Compulsion." *The New York Review of Books* 25 (October 12, 1978): 34–37.

Theroux, Paul. "Colorful Crimes." *The New York Times Book Review,* July 1, 1979: 10, 19.

Watson, George. "Kafka's Father, Simenon's Mother." *Sewanee Reviews* 103 (Fall 1995): 597–605.

Weisz, Pierre. "Simenon and 'Le Commissaire,'" in *Art in Crime Writing: Essays on Detective Fiction,* ed. Bernard Benstock. New York: St. Martin's Press, 1983: 174–188.

Wolfe, Peter. "Current Reviews: 'Maigret and the Toy Village.'" *The Armchair Detective* 13 (Winter 1980): 62–63.

Young, Trudee. *Georges Simenon.* Metuchen, NJ: Scarecrow Press, 1976.

WEB SITES

http://www.trussel.com/f_maig.htm (Simenon's Maigret: bibliography, statistics, online texts, links; contains plots of all Maigret novels and checklist of English translations)

http://www.imdb.com/title/tt0107221/ (Maigret at the Internet Movie Database)

http://www.kirhasto.sci.fi/simenon.htm (Selected bibliography and selected Maigret films)

http://www.ulg.ac.be/libnet/simenon/htm (*Centre d'études Georges Simenon et Fonds Simenon de l'Université de Liège*)

Humphrey Bogart as Philip Marlowe in *The Big Sleep*. © John Springer Collection/CORBIS.

Philip Marlowe: The Detective as Knight Errant

. . . down these mean streets a man must go who is not himself mean, who is
neither tarnished nor afraid.

—Raymond Chandler, *The Simple Art of Murder*

Like Chaucer's pilgrim knight seeking to heal a spirit weary from battling
the heathen, Marlowe, a man of honor who is not mean, nor tarnished, nor
afraid, walked Southern California's 1930s–1940s mean streets in search of
hidden truth, first under various *noms de guerre* in 20 pulp magazine short
stories, then as himself through novels that translated and published in over
20 languages by Chandler's death had become "central to the birth of what
became known as *film noir*" (Hiney viii). As arguably the world's most
famous hard-boiled private eye and a romantic idealist with a self-evolved
moral code, Philip Marlowe, in many respects his creator's alter ego,
remains "one of the most persistently interesting detectives in the history of
mystery literature" (Herbert 124).

HISTORICAL/CULTURAL CONTEXT

During Britain's Golden Age of detective fiction, a growing interest in psychology made writers and readers demand to know more than just "whodunit." Many female detective story writers thus turned away from the
"pure puzzle" detective story to deepen characterizations, while some, like
Dorothy L. Sayers, even moved toward the novel of manners. In America,
Erle Stanley Gardner, whose Perry Mason legal mysteries "reproduced
Christie's arid certainty" about right and wrong, and Rex Stout, who
matched Sayers "in creating an intellectualized, languidly triumphant detective hero," maintained "the calm spell of the clue-puzzle mystery" (Knight
135), but responding to post–World War I stresses, other male American
writers began to develop an entirely new approach to detective fiction. After
they had "seen Paree," survived the trenches, and come home to the Roaring
Twenties' Prohibition and crime waves, American men faced the 1929 stock
market crash and the Great Depression. U.S. popular culture responded
with vicarious wish-fulfillments ranging from comic strip crime-busters like
Dick Tracy and comic book superheroes like Batman to the development of
a new serious literary form, the hard-boiled detective novel with "real blood
[and] actual corpses instead of mere excuses for yet another demonstration
of the detective's superhuman skills" (Most and Stowe 163).

*The usual detective hero . . .
is largely a creature of the
mass media who nourishes
the daydreams of his readers.*
—Edward Margolies

Black Mask, the leading popular "pulp" magazine, had already been cultivating the hard-boiled
style of the indigenous American detective story for
about a decade when Raymond Chandler began
publishing his short stories in 1933. From 1926 to
1936, *Black Mask*'s editor Joseph T. "Cap" Shaw

encouraged writers like Dashiell Hammett, whose
private eyes embodied U.S. postwar violence and
disillusionment and blended that *Angst* with qualities of the traditional Western "lone wolf" inspired
by James Fenimore Cooper's laconic frontiersman
Natty Bumppo, the hero who from Ishmael and

*Those were the good old days,
when a Spade was a spade.*
—William Van Wert

Huck Finn to Nick Adams abandoned corrupt civilization for the solace of the
wilderness (Madden 176). Such heroes usually brought vigilante justice to a dis-
ordered society and then rode off into the sunset to fight evil another day. "Cap"
Shaw insisted on realism, clarity, plausibility, and belief, and plenty of action,
but he felt "action is meaningless unless it involves recognizable human character
in three-dimensional form" (quoted in Nolan 26), principles Chandler thoroughly absorbed.

Hard-boiled detective fiction writers soon divided into two different
groups. Race Williams, Carroll John Daly's ultra-tough dark-haired, dark-
eyed first American hard-boiled PI, carried machismo into melodrama
considered almost unreadable today, killing often with his two .44s but
brooding little, and claiming that his victims always "deserved it" (Murphy
528). Race Williams and his followers, like Mickey Spillane's Mike
Hammer, often acted so brutally that some readers find them virtually indistinguishable from the villains they oppose.

Hammett and Chandler created more complex iconic detective figures.
Drawing on his acquaintance with real-life detectives, Ross Macdonald
observed, "Sadists and psychopaths don't last very long in this rather exact-
ing work. . . . self knowledge, and a matching knowledge of the world, are
what the serious private detective may be after" (quoted in Murphy 232).
After creating his nameless Continental Op for *Black Mask*, possibly the
most perfect hard-boiled character ever invented (Murphy 232), Hammett
gave the world Sam Spade, widely considered "the literary model of the
hard-boiled sleuth," adding significant dimension to the detective character
and the entire genre. Raymond Chandler raised both to the level of art with
Philip Marlowe, a knight-errant detective who hides his profound humanity
behind a cynical mask (Murphy 232).

Philip Marlowe's milieu was 1930s to 1940s Southern California, in
particular "Hollywood-Southland," Walter Wells's term for a region emerging in the 1920s. Los Angeles' population grew about 100,000 a year
between 1915 and 1945, and even faster after that (Ward and Silver 214),
swelling "from hick town to metropolis" with the movie industry's coming
of age. Hollywood-Southland lured seekers of fame, fortune, or salvation,
offering a languid sub-tropical climate and miles of shoreline; a rapidly
changing metropolitan environment and population; and a "sprawling
stucco and neon landscape." Its structures were "almost as tentative as
Hollywood sets" (Wells 10), subject to natural disasters like earthquakes,
despoiled by the 1892 southern basin oil discoveries and corrupted by local
political scandals.

These elements combined in "a consistent pattern of effects" that gave most fiction based there the overarching theme of dissolution. Hollywood-Southland replaced "The old, the traditional, the real and the substantive" with either deadly substitutes or nothing at all; the loss of innocence and motivation resulted in "cynicism, morbidity, . . . hollow jadedness" and the breakdown of traditional values; weary resignation replaced shattered dreams; and love yielded to perversion, callousness, and isolation (Wells 12). During the Depression, Hollywood-Southland represented the American Dream for countless depressed and despairing young Easterners, Midwesterners, and even native Californians seeking "the golden land of dross and stones" (from a miners' ditty quoted in Delano 349). When they abandoned their former lives to seize it, though, that alluring dream evanesced into toxic smog. "The life of the spirit dwindle[d] and die[d] . . . life itself [was] destroyed" (Wells 13).

Much of that spiritual devastation could be blamed on the movie industry. Only six years after America's first movie theatre opened in 1904, 26 million Americans a week were going to the movies, and East Coast filmmakers, gravitating to Hollywood's year-around filming climate and the more relaxed lifestyle of that former temperance colony, produced the first Hollywood movie in 1911. Only two years later Hollywood became America's film capital. Pre-eminent directors like Cecil B. DeMille stamped their films with their personalities and swelled box office returns, like the $18 million earned by D.W. Griffith's *The Birth of a Nation* (1912). The "star system" also produced huge salaries for actors like Charlie Chaplin, who moved in one year from $1,250 per week to $1 million for eight films (Ward 227).

Such sudden wealth inevitably corrupted the motion picture industry, and scandals plagued Hollywood. The "studio system" consolidated its power in the 1920s, and the "Big Five" studios—Warner Brothers, RKO, Twentieth Century Fox, Paramount, and MGM—controlled the industry until 1948, when anti-trust legislation broke their U.S. film monopoly and the advent of television reduced movie attendance and altered film production forever.

Other 1930s–1940s Hollywood exposé novels include Horace McCoy's *They Shoot Horses, Don't They?* (1935), with gullible young lovers perishing in a Hollywood marathon *danse macabre*. John O'Hara's *Hope of Heaven* (1938) depicts sexual corruption, "Southland fiction's typical manifestation of dissolution." Nathaniel West's *The Day of the Locusts* (1939) links sex with sadism and reveals the empty sordidness of Southland where Midwesterners come to die. Budd Schulberg's *What Makes Sammy Run?* (1941) illustrates the movie industry's cave-in to mass entertainment dominated by wheeler-dealers and profiteers (Wells 25, 39, 50, 58, 87).

During the studios' 1930s to 1940s heyday, however, Hollywood's seductive version of the American dream dominated the popular imagination, disguising sordid realities behind its glamorous veneer, which several American authors bitterly stripped away. In 17 *Esquire* stories about Pat Hobby, a hack screenwriter and boorish schemer, F. Scott Fitzgerald portrayed Hollywood as "a dump . . . a hideous town . . . full of human spirit at a new low of debasement" and suggests that the movies had made Hobby an "exercise in self-mockery and an emblem of the Hollywood milieu" (quoted in Wells 103, 105). Hoping it would be the definitive Hollywood novel, Fitzgerald gave his unfinished novel *The Last Tycoon* "the last of his real talent." The fate of protagonist Irving Thalberg—"successes, bitter struggles, and untimely death"—"symbolized the death of both art and individualism in America. . . . Hollywood's fate was America's" (Wells 104–105).

Raymond Chandler most fully recognized the complexity of Hollywood-Southland's perversion of the American Dream. A year before he died, he said he wanted to "write the Hollywood novel that has never been written, but it takes a more photographic memory than I have. The whole scene is too complex and all of it would have to be in" (MacShane and Hiney 230). "All of it" for Chandler meant both corruption and opportunity; he said, "Hollywood is poison to any writer, the graveyard to talent. . . . But perhaps I have lived too close to it" (MacShane and Hiney 17). Nonetheless, despite his own battles with what he called "a degraded community whose idealism even is largely fake" (MacShane 1981, 64), and well aware of Hollywood-Southland's ambiguities, Raymond Chandler created an unforgettable hero embodying his own ambivalences, a convincing knight-errant romantic hero armored with cynicism, indefatigably battling the hundred-headed monster of decadent Hollywood-Southland, for Chandler "a living, heterogenous entity . . . that helped to shape [his] aesthetic" (Wells 71).

AUTHORSHIP

Chandler considered Philip Marlowe both "at least an exaggeration of the possible" and a projection of himself (Gardiner and Walker 43). Chandler only began to write fiction when his life was more than half over, but his early circumstances and experiences inspired Philip Marlowe's essential ambivalence as "half saint and half headsman" (Ruehlmann xvi). Chandler said he himself "was conceived in Laramie, Wyoming, and . . . should have preferred to be born there." He was born on July 23, 1888, in Chicago, "not a place," according to Chandler, "where an Anglophile would choose to be born" (quoted in MacShane 3). Soon after his engineer father, an alcoholic, disappeared, Chandler's Protestant Irish mother took her seven-year-old son to live in London as her own mother and sister's poor relations; he was the only male in a household of women. His Irishness and his "exotic" birthplace set him apart at the excellent

> *Essential dualism of mind . . . which perpetually balanced an innate romanticism against a very self-conscious cynicism.*
> —Jerry Speir on Raymond Chandler's morality

Dulwich School, where from 1900 to 1905 he played rugby, studied languages, attended classical music recitals, and absorbed the English public school code: ". . . egotism, brashness, and immodesty were the devils of modern life. Manliness meant forgetfulness of self . . . a man of honor is one who is 'capable of understanding that which was good; capable of subordinating the poorer part of his nature to the higher part'" (MacShane and Hiney 9). This atmosphere of "high Victorian rectitude" gave Chandler both his "fuzzy Puritanism" and his "exaggerated attraction to things masculine and tough." Knowing Chandler in the wreckage of his last years, Natasha Spender observed that he vehemently denied he had any homosexual tendencies, but she also noted that she and others made the "facile conclusion" that he was indeed a repressed homosexual (quoted in Gross 131). At Dulwich, Chandler said, he also acquired a lifelong respect for language: "A classical education saves you from being fooled by pretentiousness, which is what most current fiction is too full of" (MacShane and Hiney 238).

In his teens Chandler already wanted to be a writer, but his mother's brother, who funded his education, decided the boy should go into the British civil service, so "Ray" briefly studied French in Paris and then German in Munich. He had to swear allegiance to Great Britain to take the Civil Service Exams, in which he scored first in classics and third overall of 600 candidates, but after a few months he "thoroughly detested the civil service" and its "suburban nobodies" (MacShane and Hiney 250) and enraged his whole family by quitting the civil service to write.

Despite his English upbringing, Chandler felt he "was not English." Although he did not identify with America, he "resented the kind of ignorant and snobbish criticism of Americans that was current at that time" (MacShane 1981, 250). Fired deservedly, he said, from his first newspaper job, he then reported for *The Westminster Gazette* and the *Academy* while writing derivative romantic poems celebrating moral egalitarianism, which Jacques Barzun called "in essence the root idea of all [Chandler's] later tales." According to Barzun, Chandler's early work expressed "a hostility to things English, resentment against both convention and corruption, and self-pity over the common lot, mixed with the illusion of self-reliance in the effort to drown surrounding evils" (Bruccoli 72, ix). Chandler repeated those opinions three decades later in his "aggressively American essay" "The Simple Art of Murder" (Marling 11).

Plausibility is largely a matter of style. . . . It takes an awful lot of technique to compensate for a dull style, although it has been done, especially in England.
— Raymond Chandler

With an English accent "you could cut with a baseball bat" (MacShane and Hiney 250), Chandler returned to the United States in 1912, financed by a loan from his uncle, which he scrupulously repaid at 6 percent interest. He "arrived in California with a beautiful wardrobe, a public school accent and no practical gifts for earning a living" (MacShane and Hiney 236), and after a few menial jobs he took up bookkeeping, completing a three-year night-school course in six weeks. He and his mother lived in Los Angeles until he and a friend joined the Canadian Army in 1917, and "over there" as a 20-year-old infantry officer Chandler several times led his platoon into direct machine gun fire; after that, he said, "nothing is ever the same again" (quoted in Straub). The only survivor of his unit, he then trained for the Royal Flying Corps but was never commissioned, and in 1919 he was discharged in Canada with the British war and victory medals. Now 31, he took an accounting job with the Dabney Oil Syndicate and eventually became the vice president in charge of its Los Angeles office, where he witnessed a $100 million fraud perpetrated by a rival company.

Before leaving for war, Chandler met and fell in love with "Cissy," a "full-figured, soft-haired beauty" who had studied to be a concert pianist. Cissy was 18 years older than Chandler and married to the ailing Julian Pascal. While Chandler was in the service his romance with Cissy simmered, and when he returned, Cissy filed for an amicable divorce. Shortly after the death of Chandler's mother, who had disapproved of the match, they were married in 1924, "a union that became the central fact in his life" (Marling 12, 14).

Although Chandler later described his oil-executive career positively, he proved "arrogant and very litigious." Sensitive about her age, Cissy stayed home while he attended oil conventions where, according to fellow Dabney executive John Abrams, Chandler was often "stinko drunk and hovering in the wings with a bevy of showgirls" (quoted in Marling 16). By 1932, after almost 13 years with the firm, Chandler was drinking heavily, missing work, and frequently threatening suicide, and Dabney fired him. Chandler woke up at 44 with a serious drinking problem and an ailing 62-year-old wife. This taught him, he later wrote, not to take anything for granted. His annual income plummeted from $10,000 per year to less than $2,000 a year from his fiction during the early 1930s (MacShane and Hiney 59).

Though heretofore he had read only three or four detective stories, Chandler took a writers' correspondence course and, writing four hours a day, taught himself to produce private-eye fiction that he thought would appeal to a wide audience: "I could so easily have become everything our world has no use for. So I wrote for the *Black Mask*. What a wry joke" (quoted in MacShane 1981, 64). He especially wanted to see what language could do when it remained on "the level of unintellectual thinking" but he also acquired "the power to say things" usually presented in "literary" fiction (quoted in Speir 118). Chandler already knew serious novels by Joseph Conrad, Dickens, Dumas, and even Henry James, but now he read all the 20th-century American hard-boiled detective fiction he could and believing it was "honest," taught himself to write it (Durham 3). He also learned a lean prose style and the virtues of masculine ethos from Hemingway and an appreciation for urban life's raw vigor from Theodore Dreiser and Ring Lardner. Proletarian fiction, like Hammett's *Red Harvest,* that combined a tough vocabulary with an abhorrence of capitalistic evils,

My theory was that readers just thought that they cared about nothing but the action; . . . the thing they really cared about, and that I cared about, was the creation of emotion through dialogue and description.

—Raymond Chandler

also contributed to the literary seedbed for the "more complex, more visionary fiction" Chandler would later produce (*CA Online*).

Chandler's first short story, "Blackmailers Don't Shoot," appeared in *Black Mask* in 1933, earning him 1 cent per word. Editor Shaw was promoting tough heroes cynical on the surface but ever ready to fight injustice in a dark criminal-infested world where the law, the business community, and even the clergy were corrupt; Chandler later noted that the pulp crime stories, "even at [their] most mannered and artificial made most of the fiction of [their] time taste like a cup of lukewarm consommé at a spinsterish tearoom" (quoted in Gross 22). Chandler's most noticeable stylistic device, stunning similes and metaphors that appear either in Marlowe's wisecracking tough-guy repartee or in Marlowe's thoughts, helps the reader understand a situation, often from a startlingly fresh angle. At first Chandler imitated Hammett's nightclub scenes with superficially sophisticated but stupid gangsters, cynical police, and an Elizabethan litter of dead bodies (Symons, in Gross 29), but soon he began to enrich the genre. His early pulp protagonists struggle to maintain their moral equilibrium, and by 1935 he adopted first-person narration to intensify their alienation, "illuminat[ing] the moral deviations of the criminal world" in "caustic wit and barbed asides" (*CA Online*) that combine underworld vernacular with poetic diction in shocking images and figures of speech.

Besides debunking the genteel Golden Age puzzle-whodunits as "middling dull, pooped-out piece[s] of utterly unreal and mechanical fiction," Chandler gradually abandoned the "escapism and mere problem-solving" of hard-boiled detective fiction and called for "a literature of unsparing realism" consistent with his vision of America as "a slew of capitalist vice" (quoted in *CA Online*). His Los Angeles "urban nightmare" settings convey places' "feel," not merely their physical appearance (Ward and Silver 2), like "little candy stores where you can buy even nastier things than their candy" (*The High Window* 19). Chandler's trademark combination of "beauty and tawdriness" (Kirsch 4) illustrates the two-edged capacity of wealth to beguile and corrupt American life (*CA Online*). Chandler said he "cannibalized" his short stories to create his novels, building his first, *The Big Sleep* (1939), out of four earlier short stories, with Philip Marlowe investigating a seemingly routine blackmail scheme that descends into a maelstrom of generational evil based on abuse of wealth and power.

The pulps shaped Chandler, but they soon began to restrict him; "the novels," on the other hand, "enabled him to burst the bonds and to express the essential Raymond Chandler" (Symons in Gross 25). With *Farewell, My Lovely* (1940), his second and personal favorite novel, set in fictional "Bay City," a reflection of Santa Monica, he initiated the theme dominating the rest of his work, that corruption is a "massive chain of crime and coverup," and his favorite plot pattern, unmasking "the secret alliances between wealth and the underworld" (Gavin Lambert, quoted in *CA Online*). *The High Window* (1942), set in Pasadena, traces a wealthy clan's self-inflicted dissolution, and *The Lady in the Lake* (1943), a book Chandler could never reread (Hiney 131), returns to *Farewell, My Lovely*'s motif of female duplicity. *The Little Sister* (1949), his "most roundly attacked work" (Wolfe 191), probes the hypocritical Hollywood "dream factory" Chandler by that time had painfully experienced.

Chandler used the simple hard-boiled plot formula: a client hires the PI for an apparently minor case, and then the murders start; the detective catalytically both provokes the murders and solves them, relentlessly exposing the truth and either proving the client's guilt or showing that the minor incident was really "a distant epiphenomenon of a deeply hidden, far more heinous crime" (Most and Stowe 347). Critics failed to acknowledge Chandler's literary worth until *The Long Goodbye* (1953) (MacShane and Hiney 21), which features yet another scheming femme fatale matched against a tired, frightened, and aging Marlowe. It moves further into autobiography as Chandler's "most personal work [and his] boldest attempt to exceed the confines of the detective mystery" (Speir 65), giving the American detective story new resonance and paving the way for Ross Macdonald's best work.

At the same time, Chandler was also writing screenplays. In 1943, Paramount hired him at $750 per week for 13 weeks (Marling 37) to collaborate with director Billy Wilder on a film version of hard-boiled pioneer James M. Cain's 1943 "perfect murder" novel *Double Indemnity,* illustrating Cain's perseverant theme that cynicism and manipulation underlie the pretense of love, and focusing on lower-class brutality to explore psychological and social tensions. Chandler detested Cain's writing, calling him "the offal of literature," "not because [these writers] write about dirty things, but because they do it in a dirty way" (quoted in MacShane and Hiney 23), but Chandler's work on the *Double Indemnity* script launched him into Hollywood's "big time." He recalled in 1951 that he had had "a lot of fun there," adding ruefully, "You meet a lot of bastards there but they usually have some saving grace" (quoted in MacShane and Hiney 172).

Screenwriters' status at that time was so low that Chandler was not invited to the press conference which announced his Academy Award nomination for *Double Indemnity.* Like other disillusioned Hollywood writers, Chandler worked in "the Iron Lung" building "resounding with the dull moans of cloistered hacks and bums" and located next to a mortuary (Wells 119). After scripting *Double Indemnity* Chandler had planned to leave Paramount and work on a new novel, but he found himself so "completely pooped" he couldn't even write a letter (quoted in MacShane and Hiney 27). He returned to the Iron Lung until September 1944, where "increasingly there was a bottle in his drawer and a young woman to help him."

Guilt-ridden after one weeks-long affair, he bought Cissy a Lincoln too big for either of them to drive, a sad beginning of the end of Chandler's writing career.

Chandler then produced his classic detective fiction theoretical essay "The Simple Art of Murder," originally published in *Atlantic Monthly* for December 1944. To answer critics like Edmund Wilson who had recently disparaged the genre, Chandler legitimized hard-boiled detective fiction, attacking Golden Age mysteries for their lack of realism and brilliantly analyzing Hammett's work: "Hammett took murder out of the Venetian vase and dropped it into the alley. . . . [he] gave murder back to the kind of people that commit it for reasons, not just to provide a corpse; and with the means at hand, not hand-wrought dueling pistols, curare and tropical fish" (Chandler, 14).

Wilson's Viewpoint

The title "Who Cares Who Killed Roger Ackroyd?" of Wilson's 1944 dismissal of mystery and suspense fiction sums up Wilson's viewpoint.

Besides perfecting the new American fiction style, "a combination of idiom, slang, wise-crack, hyperbole and tough talk that in the hands of a man of genius can be made to do anything" (Madden 171), Chandler also defined his new detective hero as "a complete man and a common man and yet an unusual man . . . a man of honor" (Chandler 15). The "restless expanding southern California community" of Chandler's fiction "interact[ed] with the sexual and success fantasies of the movies, creating a pre-Watergate movement toward profit and power as politicians and lawyers and police chiefs combine with gangsters in the organization of crime" (Lambert 267); and in this sordid milieu, Chandler insisted, "the story is this man's adventure in search of a hidden truth" (Chandler 18).

The brutal truth of Chandler's own life was that once he had succumbed to Hollywood's monetary allure, he could not turn away. His own novels became such popular films he paid $50,000 in income taxes in 1945. His feverish work on the script for *The Blue Dahlia* (1946) won him another Oscar nomination, but his health and Cissy's were breaking down and he believed that Hollywood was destroying his talent for fiction. Plagued by skin problems that necessitated the use of morphine and frantic over Cissy's debilitating pulmonary fibrosis, Chandler then attempted "a novel of

In Chandler's notes for *The Blue Dahlia*, he said homicide detectives could "be very pleasant or very unpleasant without change of expression."

character and atmosphere with on [sic] overtone of violence and fear" (MacShane and Hiney 170) and sent *The Long Goodbye* to his publishers in July 1952. The title paid an unconscious farewell to his writing; Cissy died the next December and Chandler, stricken, mourned "the light of my life" (quoted in MacShane and Hiney 205) deeply, sinking into guilt and depression so severe he drunkenly botched a suicide attempt on February 22, 1955. He briefly underwent psychiatric treatment and then left for England, drinking heavily and maintaining the façade of "a gallant and bon vivant" (Marling 48), intermittently drying out in sanatoriums. In 1958 he published *Playback*, a "universally condemned" (Knight 139) novelization of his unproduced 1947 screenplay with a new "soft-boiled" Philip Marlowe that his fans disliked. Very ill, he returned to America, re-adopted American citizenship, and in February 1959, proposed to agent Helga Greene (she accepted) and received the presidency of the Mystery Writers of America. A month later, he died of pneumonia and only 17 people attended his funeral. Chandler left a Marlowe short story, "Poodle Springs," made into a novel by Robert B. Parker and published in 1989. Chandler transformed the detective story "from formulaic puzzlement to cultural inquiry" (*CA Online*), primarily through his hero, ". . . the best man in his world and a good enough man for any world" (Chandler 18)— "everything that Raymond Chandler was, wished he was, and feared he might be" (Hiney viii).

> Chandler never won an award or traded one favor for another. When he agreed to become the president of the Mystery Writers of America, he threw out his ballot rather than vote for himself.

PROFILE OF PHILIP MARLOWE

Philip Marlowe's Arthurian Roots

"Chandler actually dissected his own character as objectively as possible in order to apply what was appropriate to Marlowe" (MacShane 69). Philip Marlowe was everything the Dulwich School had taught Chandler he ought to be, but couldn't. Marlowe's physical presence and insight, not logical deduction, uncovers the truth while he suffers and inflicts violence in surprise-ending plots told in terse colloquial dialogue. Chandler called one of Marlowe's short story ancestors "Mallory," the most important clue to Marlowe's character, since Sir Thomas Malory's 15th-century *Le Morte D'Arthur* had been popular in the literary London of Chandler's youth, coming out in Rhys's Everyman edition in 1908, shortly before Chandler joined the British Civil Service, most commentators believe Arthurian concepts anchor Chandler's description of Philip Marlowe as "a shop-soiled Galahad" (*The High Window* 483).

From the late 18th century until the First World War, "embarrassingly large quantities" of revived medieval chivalry shaped ideals of gentlemen's behavior "even if they did not consciously realise it," like the upper-class Americans who "died with such style on the *Titanic*" (Girouard, unpaginated preface). In England, public schools like Dulwich followed Eton in exalting patriotism into a religion, where the supreme sacrifice was dying for one's country, probably a factor in Chandler's wartime conduct.

Medieval romances with noble knights acting out of love, religious or moral conviction, or the desire for adventure, fulfilled a function like the modern novel's, featuring protagonists in quests for some high goal— rescuing a maiden, besting some monstrous evil, and typically proving their mettle in duels. In Victorian England, moralists like Tennyson considered Arthur and his knights as sources of contemporary moral instruction, and Malory's vivid stories deeply moved romantic spirits. Malory's *Morte D'Arthur* "completely knocked over" young English gentlemen of Radical or at least Christian Socialist leanings (Girouard 185). Around the time Chandler was at Dulwich it helped inspire Robert Baden-Powell's revival of chivalry, the Boy Scouts: "A knight (or Scout) is at all times a gentleman . . . who [regardless of money] carries out the rules of chivalry . . . well disciplined, loyal, polite, brave, good-tempered, and helpful to women and children" (Robert Baden-Powell, *Scouting for Boys*, quoted in Girouard 255). Gentlemen with links to the Christian Socialist movement, which aimed to bring social classes together, were the chief supporters of the Boy Scout movement: the "knightly" gentleman, "however tough with the tough" is "invariably gentle with the weak"; "ready to come to the help of others, especially those less fortunate than himself"; distrustful of most politicians and despising the worship of money, the placing of expediency before principle, and the corruption of urban life (Girouard 260). Philip Marlowe, an older, wearier, and wiser Scout, still clings to his ideals.

The name "Philip Marlowe" involves other important resonances. Chandler may have paid homage to Sir Philip Sidney, the Elizabethan diplomat, soldier, and courtier who epitomized Renaissance chivalry, and "Marlowe," besides its relation to "Malory" may evoke two other ambiguous historical figures. The major Elizabethan poet, playwright, and spy Christopher Marlowe created powerful heroes destroyed by overweening passions, like some of the criminals Chandler's hero exposes. Chandler gave other characters names which recall medieval allegorical romance, too: "Grayle," "Quest," "Sternwood," and "Steelgrave" (Knight 161). Joseph Conrad's enigmatic, disengaged narrator "Marlow" also may have inspired both Philip Marlowe's essential isolation and his obscure origin, which Chandler deliberately left as vague as his hero's physical appearance.

Philip Marlowe's Background

Chandler gave only minimal clues to Marlowe's private life. Marlowe just "needed a drink. I needed a lot of life insurance. I needed a home in the country. What I had was a coat, a hat and a gun." Born in Santa Rosa, California, Marlowe debuted in *The Big Sleep* as 33 and "large," about 6 feet tall and 190 pounds. His interview with General Sternwood in *The Big Sleep* contains almost everything known about his background:

> I'm thirty-three years old, went to college once and can still speak English if there's any demand for it. There isn't much in my trade. I worked for Mr. Wilde, the District Attorney, as an investigator once. His chief investigator, . . . Bernie Ohls . . . told me you wanted to see me. I'm unmarried because I don't like policemen's wives . . . I was fired. For insubordination. I test very high on insubordination. (*Big Sleep* 7–8)

Philip Marlowe's Career

Chandler observed in 1949 that Marlowe

> never really has any private life, except insofar as he must eat and sleep and have a place to keep his clothes. His moral and intellectual force is that he gets nothing but his fee, for which he will if he can protect the innocent, guard the helpless, and destroy the wicked, and the fact that he must do this while earning a meager living in a corrupt world is what makes him stand out. (Quoted in MacShane and Hiney 115)

Marlowe lives in Los Angeles' Hobart Arms, a bare-bones apartment building in a neighborhood "that didn't have the look of having been excited by anything in the immediate past" ("Finger Man"). His efficiency flat with kitchenette and a fold-up Murphy bed is all he has "in the way of a home. In it was everything that was mine, that had any association with me, any past, anything that took the place of a family. Not much; a few books, pictures, radio, chessmen, old letters, stuff like that" (*Big Sleep* 107–108, 143, 147). He likes to replay championship chess games and he can quote Flaubert, Browning, and T.S. Eliot; he's a dead shot and his otherwise unidentified convertible has a secret gun compartment and usually a bottle of rye. His office, "my dog house on the sixth floor of the Cahuenga Building" (*Long Goodbye* 5), is "not much of a front," either: this "room and a half on the seventh floor at the back . . . has my name on it and nothing else, and that only on the reception room." He always leaves this unlocked, in case he has a client to sit down on a "faded old settee" or one of "two odd semi-easy chairs," near "net curtains that needed laundering and the boy's size library table with the venerable magazines on it to give the place a professional touch" (*Big Sleep* 50–51). His inner office holds a rust-red carpet, five green filing cabinets, "three full of California climate," the "usual desk with the usual blotter . . . and the usual squeaky swivel chair behind it" (*Big Sleep* 56). Marlowe works for "twenty-five bucks a day" plus expenses (*Big Sleep* 228), but he knows how to dress to call on $4 million: "a powder-blue suit, with dark blue shirt, tie, and display handkerchief," and when he has to be, he can be "neat, clean, shaved and sober" (*Big Sleep* 3).

Marlowe's personality is as ambiguous as Chandler's was. In his first five novels, Marlowe becomes more "case-hardened with each new foray into evil" (*CA Online*), but in the sixth, *The Long Goodbye,* Marlowe is 42, and Chandler allows his hero's tough-guy shell to be more easily and deeply penetrated, revealing Marlowe's repressed yearnings for male friendship and romantic love. *The Long Goodbye* inspired critical praise as Chandler's "most ambitious attempt to fashion a work of genuine literature from the restrictive materials of detective fiction" (Nolan 229). In *Playback,* Marlowe and Linda Loring renew their affair and she proposes to him, though he declines, not wanting to be a "kept man" (Winks 164). Chandler hinted at their married life in "Poodle Springs."

Philip Marlowe and Women

Ambiguity pervades Marlowe's romantic affairs, too. One lover asked him how he, a hard man, could be so gentle, and he replied, "If I wasn't hard, I wouldn't be alive. If I wasn't gentle, I wouldn't deserve to be alive" (quoted in *CA Online*). Chandler declared Marlowe was "neither a eunuch nor a satyr; I think he might seduce a duchess and I am quite sure he would not spoil a virgin" (Chandler 18). Despite his indiscretions, Chandler kept Cissy on a pedestal, but his fictional women often prove villainous, like the dish Marlowe described as "A blonde to make a bishop kick a hole in a stained glass window." Such women frequently lust after Marlowe, "a big, dark, handsome brute" (*Big Sleep* 3, 19), but instinctively he responds chivalrously to a woman's moral character, whether she's a temptress or a "lady." Marlowe's chivalric respect for women like Anne Riordan in *Farewell, My Lovely,* the nicest girl he ever met, made him warn her to steer clear of him and find some true-blue cop who can "tell the difference between right and wrong from fifty paces" (Ward and Silver 130).

Philip Marlowe is "As susceptible to female charms as any all-American hero" (Thorpe 54). Michael Mason, in "Marlowe, Men and Women" argues that Marlowe's rejection of corrupt women reveals both Marlowe's and Chandler's repressed homosexuality (quoted in Gross 53). Simpson notes that Marlowe sees other men as physically attractive and concludes that Marlowe is "a man of mingled sexual impulses" (47), but most critics prefer the "chivalric" reading of Marlowe's treatment of women as revealing Marlowe's code of ethics (Benstock 79).

Marlowe can take prowling women or leave them with a wisecrack: as he reminds a randy client, "I don't go whoring around after every pair of legs

I see." A classy dame can make him feel "as erotic as a stallion" but he puts duty over sex, and when after a memorable one-night stand in *The Long Goodbye*, Linda Loring asks him to marry her, he tells her he has been "spoiled by independence." When she leaves him in the morning, though, Marlowe feels "a lump of lead at the pit of my stomach . . . to say goodbye is to die a little." He seizes a sexual opportunity in *Playback* (Thorpe 56), but at the end of the case he finds himself alone "in a meaningless room in a meaningless house," ripe for Linda's call offering him a plane ticket to Paris. He insists on sending her one instead, thinking, "The air was full of music," but Chandler, despite marrying them off in his unfinished *Poodle Springs*, had doubts about their relationship: "I am writing him married to a rich woman and swamped by money, but I don't think it will last" (Gardiner and Walker 156).

Philip Marlowe as a Lone Wolf PI

Marlowe always worked alone. His penchant for insubordination prevents him from being a cop himself, but he knows what makes good cops such as Bernie Ohls, the DA's chief investigator, tick: Marlowe "happens to know" Bernie had killed nine criminals (*Big Sleep* 44), and he and Ohls respect and understand one another. Marlowe generally gets along with LAPD personnel like Captain Gregory of Missing Persons in *The Big Sleep*, "a plain ordinary copper. . . . As honest as you could expect a man to be in a world where it's out of style" (*Big Sleep* 204). As soon as Marlowe realizes Gregory is "a very smart guy" trying to play "a middle-aged hack fed up with his job" (*Big Sleep* 212), he sees that Gregory had cannily led him to the solution to *The Big Sleep*.

Marlowe also understands the ambiguities that turn cops bad. He hates the rich and the way they pressure police for special privileges, so he deplores the brutality such corruption engenders, but, he also knows that police brutality results from "betrayed loyalties . . . in the cold half-lit world where always the wrong thing happens and never the right" (*The Little Sister* 89). Those cops display "the hard hollow meaningless stare, not quite cruel and a thousand miles from kind. . . . Civilization had no meaning for them. All they saw of it was the failures, the dirt, the dregs, the aberrations and the disgust" (*Little Sister* 196). In *Farewell, My Lovely*, Marlowe pins the responsibility squarely on the society that encourages immorality: as one crooked sergeant declares, "Cops don't go crooked for money . . . they get caught in the system. You know what's the matter with this country, baby?. . . A guy can't stay honest if he wants to. . . . You got to play the game dirty or you don't eat" (quoted in Benstock 81).

Philip Marlowe's Strength and Fallibility

Marlowe experiences despondency like Chandler's at the end of each story, the inevitable result of his struggle for heroism in the face of a harsh world and certain death. Marlowe plays his own game by his own moral code with "wry self-mockery" (Speir 19), and as "an outsider, a loner, a man who will not fit the pattern," without either personal history or family bonds, he is "the archetypal modern man," struggling "to cleanse the modern world of its venality," to play fair with his clients, and maintain his integrity in an amoral materialistic society where large-scale honesty is irretrievably doomed (E.M. Beekman, quoted in *CA Online*). Paradoxically, Marlowe's fallibility reinforces his appeal, because readers are always aware that "they are in the presence of a human being, no matter how idealized" (O'Brien 75).

Philip Marlowe's Antagonists

For Chandler and Marlowe the enemy was always the vicious rich. They made Marlowe sick because he felt that they had sickened the American psyche and he believed the Hollywood-Southland scene was one of its worst cesspools. Marlowe, one lonely decent man, pits himself against gigantic wickedness, lethal femmes fatales, and clients who often conceal the truth or deliberately lie behind a mask of sincerity. As a medieval romance hero did, undertaking a quest for an unobtainable Holy Grail, Marlowe tries "to find hints of redemption in the mean streets" where he lives and works (W.P. Kenney, quoted in *CA Online*). Not the impossible goal but the willingness to make the painful journey matters most to such heroes, and like Lancelot, vouchsafed a holy vision after years of penance, Marlowe anachronistically survives in the popular imagination, battered but unbowed, able to laugh at himself and his enemies, one "parfit gentil knight" eternally traveling toward a shrine whose price only he, of all the pilgrims around him, truly comprehends: a selfless combination of physical courage, incorruptible honor, and the ability to look at himself and wryly smile.

PHILIP MARLOWE'S LITERARY DESCENDANTS

The most significant of the many literary detectives who followed Philip Marlowe is Ross Macdonald's Lew Archer, "a man who risks everything" (Macdonald, quoted in Benstock 117). Archer first appeared, like Marlowe, in short pseudonymous stories, eventually collected as *My Name Is Archer* (1955), seven years after the first Archer novel, *The Moving Target*, had appeared. Just as hard-boiled as Marlowe but more credible because he is more ordinary, Archer, a former policeman, left the force over a question of conscience; he employs snappy dialogue and engages in fast-moving corrupt-California action while investigating divorce cases, but Macdonald concentrated far more on plot than Chandler had, and he fleshed out Archer's past with alcoholism and a broken marriage as the basis for his values, so that Archer develops far more over his career than Marlowe did. Macdonald called his most innovative Archer novel, *The Galton Case* (1959), "the modern Oedipal legend."

Although the fictional hard-boiled PIs after Marlowe and Archer usually relied on perfunctory violence, they usually shared the stubborn, noble pursuit of truth and the criticism of materialistic society that Chandler had pioneered in detective fiction. John D. MacDonald's Travis McGee, although less profound, exhibits the "Marlovian" knight-errant self-image, consistently rescuing maidens from dragons (T.J. Binyon, in Gross 78). Later American crime novelists also seem to model new heroes on Marlowe. Peter Israel experimented with an evil "anti-Marlowe" in two novels; Jack LeVine put his "balding, Jewish private eye" back into Chandler's times; and Robert B. Parker created "an affectionate imitation of Marlowe" in Spenser, his chivalric Boston private detective (T.J. Binyon, in Gross 182).

MEDIA ADAPTATIONS

Movies

Philip Marlowe has received six widely differing cinema incarnations reflecting their screenwriters' challenges in adapting Chandler's vivid characters, his complex plots, and his ambiguous attitudes and atmospherics to film. Prior to the first Marlowe film, two Chandler films were made in 1942: *The Falcon Takes Over*, an MGM adaptation of *Farewell, My Lovely*, replaces Marlowe with "The Falcon," and *Time to Kill*, a Twentieth Century Fox adaptation of *The High Window*. *Time to Kill* (1942) turns Marlowe into Brett Halliday's Michael Shayne, played by Lloyd Nolan. Frank Sinatra's 1967 *Tony Rome* has been considered "an unacknowledged remake" of *The Big Sleep* and Tony Rome's 1968 sequel *Lady in Cement* a version of *Farewell, My Lovely*. No actor played Marlowe more than once. Dick Powell, previously known for light musical comedy roles, starred in *Murder, My Sweet* (1945), retitled from *Farewell, My Lovely*, because Humphrey Bogart, RKO's first choice for Marlowe, was unavailable; Bogart was actually finishing the first version of *The Big Sleep*. Chandler himself liked *Murder, My Sweet*, and critics praised Powell's portrayal for combining Marlowe's spirit with his own boyish appeal. *Murder, My Sweet* began Hollywood's private eye film cycle, and it has been ranked among "the best private eye films ever made" (Pendo 24–25).

Overwhelmingly the best-known portrayer of Philip Marlowe, though, was charismatic Humphrey Bogart, fresh from his acclaimed role as Sam Spade in Hammett's *The Maltese Falcon*. Bogart and co-star Lauren Bacall were then Warner Brothers' most popular box office pair, and several writers, including director Howard Hawks and novelist William Faulkner, evolved a long and complicated script of *The Big Sleep* that made for a convoluted production history. Released in 1946, the film was criticized for its confused plot and its brutal violence, and its risqué Bogie-Bacall dialogue laced the film with suggestive sex. Although Chandler believed that Cary

> Chandler never could understand why Americans were unable to see the humor in his work.

Grant most resembled his mental image of Marlowe, he admitted that Bogart was "the genuine article . . . tough without a gun [and with] a sense of humor that contains that grating undertone of contempt" (Chandler, quoted in Hardison and Gelfman 138). Bogart himself felt a bond with Marlowe, who often skipped his meals with the aid of a bottle of bourbon. Bogart's portrayal of Marlowe earned him enormous status as a cult hero and ensured Chandler's international reputation. Though Chandler's work does not seem to have influenced English detective fiction directly, Bogart's Marlowe achieved cult status in Britain, and Julian Symons has drawn connections between Chandler's Marlowe novels and a few British 1950s detective novels. Ironically, however, Bogart's interpretations of Sam Spade and Philip Marlowe spawned "a hyper-tough guy icon bearing minimal relation to any individual film and even less so to the source novels . . . all but occlud[ing] attributes" Chandler gave Marlowe, like his humanizing vulnerability and isolation, in favor of "a confident, controlled, sexually potent hero: a man recalling an imagined time when 'men were men'" (Abbott 305).

Actor-director Robert Montgomery played Marlowe in *The Lady in the Lake* (1946), the only film adaptation of his work Chandler helped to create and one calling for a Marlowe "infinitely more depressed and disillusioned" than in the novel. The second version of *The High Window,* released in the United States as *The Brasher Doubloon* (1947), starred ex-boxer George Montgomery in a conventional and shallow performance (Gross 73). *Marlowe* the 1969 color updating of *The Little Sister* starred James Garner, now equipped with "a nubile mistress and on-going sex life," and Elliot Gould played Marlowe in Robert Altman's *The Long Goodbye* (1973), as a "nonchalant, nervously smiling" youngish man (French, in Gross 74–75). In the elegiac 1975 remake of *Farewell, My Lovely,* Robert Mitchum, at 58 the oldest actor to play Marlowe and "the prime survivor of Powell's and Bogart's generation," returned to their authentic Forties concept of Chandler's hero, "going down the mean streets of Los Angeles in the summer of 1941, a Camel between his lips and a wide-brimmed hat on his head" (French in Gross 75). Mitchum allowed Marlowe no self-pity, instead charging the role with "selfconscious [sic] melancholy," in a "warmly affectionate meditation" on the detective film's form (French, in Gross 79); he reprised the role in a remake of *The Big Sleep* (1978).

Imitative Marlowe films appeared in the early 1970s, including the black detective John Shaft series (1971 to 1973); the much-praised *Chinatown* (1974), sometimes compared to Chandler's *Night Moves;* and *The Drowning Pool* (1975), made from Ross Macdonald's novel of the same name. These examples reflected Chandler's powerful impact on film noir, with its emphasis on violence, psychosis, and sexual deviation in depicting a world gone bad. *Poodle Springs,* starring James Caan, became an HBO telefilm in 1998, and in 2007, graphic novelist turned director Frank Miller began reviving Philip Marlowe for the big screen in *Trouble Is My Business,* reputedly first of a series of Marlowe films noir to be adapted from various Chandler stories and starring British actor Clive Owen, who earlier worked with Miller in *Sin City.*

Radio

While *The Brasher Doubloon* was in production, Chandler was trying to have Philip Marlowe, as a commercial property, join the popular crowd of radio serial detectives, as Sam Spade and Perry Mason already had done. He had nothing to do with any of the radio scripts and thought Marlowe's first radio season (1947) was badly written and poorly acted by Van Heflin, but he found 1948's *The Adventures of Philip Marlowe,* voiced by Gerald Mohr, better; it ran for two years in 100 shows and returned in 1951 with Mohr for three more months. Chandler wrote none of them. He said that the radio Marlowe had "about as much relation to Marlowe as I have to Winnie the Pooh" (quoted in MacShane 1976, 163), though he admitted that Mohr's performance pleased him. The *BBC Presents: Philip Marlowe* series lasted from 1977 to 1988.

Television

Although he thought the medium lacked good camera work, good directing, and good scripts, Chandler was also angling after a Marlowe television program in the early 1950s, though he did not live to see one. Dick Powell starred in a telefilm version of *The Long Goodbye* in 1954, but no televised Marlowe series appeared until 1959, when ABC's 13-episode series starring Philip Carey flopped because it was virtually indistinguishable from "the other homogenized private operatives . . . then clogging the airwaves" (French, in Gross 74), like Peter Gunn and Johnny Staccato. The London Weekend Television HBO Television series *Philip Marlowe, Private Eye,* starring Powers Booth, was more successful, running for 16 episodes in 1983 and briefly revived in 1986.

PHILIP MARLOWE'S ENDURING APPEAL

Biographer Frank MacShane believed that Chandler's double vision—"half English, half-American"—gave him exceptional insight into his world and made him "a prophet of modern America," who "from the European literary tradition . . . wrote about a world that both repelled and delighted him." Although Chandler was long disparaged by mainstream critics like Ben Ray Redman, who in 1952 dismissed him as "a master of erotic prose" and

Marlowe as a vicious hero who made Sam Spade look almost like a sissy (quoted in MacShane 31–32), Chandler's literary reputation today has risen, resting primarily on his "poetry" of Southern California's streets. Critics now recognize Chandler as "the most literary, and so the most respectable of crime writers" (Knight 138); his collected works appear in the Library of America collection, his screenplays contributed significantly to the development of film noir, and his hero Philip Marlowe stands as a valiant crusader against social ills, inspiring a throng of outwardly tough, inwardly vulnerable and idealistic, wisecracking PIs in fiction, radio, film, and television.

When British intellectuals raved about Chandler, he commented, "I tried to explain to them that I was just a beat-up pulp writer and that in the USA I ranked slightly above the mulatto" (Letter to Hamish Hamilton, April 27, 1955). But Chandler thought of himself primarily as a stylist and developed a remarkably sharp and accurate first-person narrative voice with "musical cadence, purity of syntax and unobtrusive rightness of word order, a metaphorical richness often consciously self-parodic, internally consistent and true to itself over a great emotional range . . . unimaginably influential during his lifetime and continuing to be so now" (Straub). He turned detective fiction away from the pure-puzzle story toward a valid social criticism that in view of Western culture's exponential plunge into decadence seems increasingly important, and he led the U.S. movie industry toward film noir, one of its most innovative achievements. Chandler's most lasting memorial, though, remains his anachronistic, romantic, chivalric hero, a hero human beings always want to believe exists, even though he may appear condemned to futility. For all the bleak settings and soulless criminals, all the depravity wealth can bring, all the misery and heartbreak of this world, this hero demonstrates that something warm and compassionate, something self-deprecating yet celebrating humanity, still flickers through the darkness: one good man, a man of honor not made mean or tarnished by it all, crusading in "a nostalgic rear-guard action" (Benstock 116) against the world's wickedness: Raymond Chandler's Philip Marlowe.

PARALLEL CHRONOLOGY

Major Events Related to Philip Marlowe	World Events
	1887 "A Study in Scarlet," first Sherlock Holmes appearance
July 23, 1888 Raymond Chandler born in Chicago, IL	
1894 Chandler's father abandons family	1894 Thomas Edison opens first "Kaleidoscope" parlor

Major Events Related to Philip Marlowe	World Events
1895 Chandler moves to England with his mother; attends local Upper Norwood school	
1900 Chandler attends Dulwich College, London	
1905–1906 Chandler studies in France and Germany	**1905** First movie theatre, Philadelphia
1907 Chandler worked in Admiralty, London, for six months	
1908–1912 Chandler was reporter for *Daily Express,* London, and *Westminster Gazette,* Bristol	
	1910 26 million Americans attend movies each week; filmmakers begin gravitating to southern California
1912 Chandler settles in Los Angeles	
1912–1917 Chandler keeps books for sporting goods company in California	
1913 Philip Marlowe born in Santa Rosa, CA	
	1914 Hollywood becomes filmmaking capital
	1914–1918 World War I
	1915 *The Birth of a Nation* earns $18 million
1917–1918 Chandler serves in Canadian Army	
1918–1919 Chandler serves in Royal Air Force	
1919 Chandler works in San Francisco bank and as reporter for Los Angeles *Daily Express*	**1919** Hollywood stars form United Artists
	1920s Hollywood transforms "from hick town to metropolis"
	1920s–1930s Golden Age of Mystery Fiction (England)
	1920–1933 Prohibition era
	1920–1951 Publication of *Black Mask* magazine, which developed American hard-boiled detective fiction
	1920 Agatha Christie's first Hercule Poirot novel, *The Mysterious Affair*

(Continued)

Major Events Related to Philip Marlowe	World Events
	at Styles; first regularly scheduled U.S. radio broadcasts
1922–1932 Chandler worked as auditor for Dabney Oil Syndicate, Los Angeles; becomes oil executive	**1922** Fatty Arbuckle rape/murder scandal
	1923 Dorothy L. Sayers's first Wimsey novel, *Whose Body?*
1924 Chandler's mother dies and he marries Pearl Cicely Pascal ("Cissy"), née Hurlbut, 18 years his senior	
	Late 1920s–1948 "Big Five" Studios dominate American filmmaking
	1929 Dashiell Hammett's *Maltese Falcon* debuts Sam Spade; U.S. stock market crash
	1930–ca. 1938 The Great Depression
ca. 1931–1932 Marlowe attends a state university in Oregon	**1931** Debut of Georges Simenon's Inspector Maigret
1932 Chandler fired from oil company job	
1933–1959 Chandler's writing career	
ca. 1933–1935 Marlowe works as insurance investigator and for Los Angeles D.A.'s office	
1933 Chandler's first published short story, "Blackmailers Don't Shoot" in *Black Mask*	**1933** End of Prohibition
1934–1938 Chandler publishes 15 short stories	**1934** James M. Cain's *The Postman Always Rings Twice*; Horace McCoy's *They Shoot Horses, Don't They?*
	1934 Erle Stanley Gardner begins Perry Mason series; Rex Stout begins Nero Wolfe series
ca. 1936 Marlowe fired from D.A.'s office; thereafter works as PI	
	1938 John O'Hara's *Hope of Heaven*
1939 *The Big Sleep*, Chandler's first novel	**1939** Beginning of World War II; Nathaniel West's *The Day of the Locust*
1940 *Farewell, My Lovely*	**1940–1941** F. Scott Fitzgerald's "Pat Hobby" stories published
	1941 Budd Schulberg's *What Makes Sammy Run?*; Fitzgerald's *The Last Tycoon*

Major Events Related to Philip Marlowe	World Events
	Dec. 7, 1941 Japanese attack on Pearl Harbor; U.S. enters World War II
1942 *The High Window;* Chandler works on screenplay of *Double Indemnity*	
1943 *The Lady in the Lake*	
1944 Lux Radio Theatre airs *Murder My Sweet*; Chandler nominated for Oscar for *Double Indemnity* screenplay; "The Simple Art of Murder"	
1945 Chandler writes screenplay of *The Blue Dahlia* (Paramount)	**1945** End of World War II
1946 Chandler receives MWA Edgar Award and Oscar nomination for *The Blue Dahlia* original screenplay; film *The Big Sleep* with Humphrey Bogart; the Chandlers move to La Jolla	**ca. 1946** Beginning of Cold War period
1947 NBC Radio Theatre airs *The New Adventures of Philip Marlowe*	
1948–1951 CBS Radio series *The Adventures of Philip Marlowe*	**1948** Antitrust legislation dismantles Big Five studio filmmaking monopoly
1949 *The Little Sister*	**1949** Ross Macdonald's *The Moving Target* debuts Lew Archer
	1950 Beginning of Korean War; television leads popular entertainment media
1952 The Chandlers vacation in London	
1953–1954 *The Long Goodbye;* Marlowe meets Linda Loring	
1954 Chandler receives MWA Edgar Award for *The Long Goodbye;* his wife Cissy dies	
1955 Chandler attempts suicide; moves to London	
1956–1957 Chandler alternates between London and La Jolla	
	1957 USSR launches *Sputnik*, opening Space Race
1958 *Playback*	
1959 Chandler becomes President of the Mystery Writers League of America	

(Continued)

Major Events Related to Philip Marlowe	World Events
March 26, 1959 Chandler dies in La Jolla, CA	
1959 Posthumously published short story, "The Pencil," originally published under various titles, including "Philip Marlowe's Last Case"	
1959–1960 ABC television series *Philip Marlowe*	
	1962 Cuban Missile Crisis
	1963 Betty Friedan publishes *The Feminine Mystique*
	1964 U.S. Civil Rights Act
	1972–1974 Watergate scandal
1976 Chandler's "English Summer," a Gothic romance, published posthumously	
1977–1988 *The BBC Presents: Philip Marlowe* series (radio)	**1977** Marcia Muller introduces Sharon McCone as female PI
	1982 Sara Paretsky debuts V.I. Warshawski and Sue Grafton debuts Kinsey Malone as female PIs
1983–1986 *Philip Marlowe* HBO television series	
1989 *Poodle Springs* (by Robert B. Parker); Marlowe marries Linda Loring	
1998 *Poodle Springs* HBO telefilm	
2007 Producer Marc Abraham announces that Clive Owen will play Philip Marlowe in *Trouble Is My Business*, first of a planned Marlowe film series directed by graphic novel writer Frank Miller	

PHILIP MARLOWE IN FICTION

Novels

The Big Sleep. New York: Knopf, 1939; based on short stories "Killer in the Rain" (1935) and "The Curtain" (1936)

Farewell, My Lovely. New York: Knopf, 1940; based on short stories "The Man Who Liked Dogs" (1936), "Try the Girl" (1937), and "Mandarin's Jade" (1937).

The High Window. New York: Knopf, 1942.

The Lady in the Lake. New York: Knopf, 1943; based on short stories "Bay City Blues" (1938), "The Lady in the Lake" (1939), and "No Crime in the Mountains" (1941).

The Little Sister. Boston: Houghton, 1949.

The Long Goodbye. Boston: Houghton, 1954 (published by Hamish Hamilton, London, 1953, as *The Long Good-Bye*).

Playback. Boston: Houghton, 1958.

Poodle Springs (unfinished at Chandler's death and completed by Robert B. Parker, 1989).

Short Story Collections

Five Murders. New York: Avon, 1944.

Five Sinister Characters. New York: Avon, 1945.

Red Wind: A Collection of Short Stories. New York: World, 1946.

Spanish Blood. New York: World, 1946.

Finger Man and Other Stories. New York: Avon, 1947.

The Simple Art of Murder (includes stories "Trouble Is My Business" and "Pick-Up on Noon Street," and essay "The Simple Art of Murder"). Boston: Houghton, 1950.

Trouble Is My Business: Four Stories from "The Simple Art of Murder." New York: Pocket Books, 1951.

Pick-Up on Noon Street. New York: Pocket Books, 1952.

Pearls Are a Nuisance. London: Hamish Hamilton, 1953.

Killer in the Rain. Boston: Houghton, 1964.

The Smell of Fear. London: Hamish Hamilton, 1965.

Smart-Aleck Kill (stories from *The Simple Art of Murder*). Harmondsworth, UK: Penguin, 1976.

The Blue Dahlia (ed. by Matthew J. Bruccoli from Chandler's screenplay). Carbondale, IL: Southern Illinois University Press, 1976.

Essay

"The Simple Art of Murder," originally published in *Atlantic Monthly,* December 1944, and later as *The Simple Art of Murder,* New York: Pocket Books, 1953.

Screenplays

Double Indemnity, with Billy Wilder, Paramount (1944); adaptation from James M. Cain's novel of the same name; published with introduction by Jeffrey Meyers (Berkeley: University of California Press, 2000).

And Now Tomorrow, with Frank Partos, Paramount (1944); adaptation from Rachel Field's novel of the same name.

The Unseen, with Hagar Wilde, Paramount (1945); adaptation from Ethel Lina White's *Her Heart in Her Throat.*

The Blue Dahlia, Paramount (1946).

Strangers on a Train, with Czenzi Ormonde, Warner Bros. (1951); adaptation from Patricia Highsmith's novel of the same name.

Raymond Chandler's Unknown Thriller: The Screenplay of "Playback." New York: Mysterious Press, 1985.

Other Works

Bruccoli, Matthew J., ed. *Chandler Before Marlowe: Raymond Chandler's Early Prose and Poetry, 1908—1912.* Columbia, SC: University of South Carolina Press, 1973.

Gardiner, Dorothy, and Katharine Sorley Walker, eds. *Raymond Chandler Speaking.* Boston: Houghton, 1962; letters, criticism, and fiction.

Kahn, Joan, ed. *The Midnight Raymond Chandler.* Boston: Houghton, 1971; omnibus edition.

MacShane, Frank, and Tom Hiney, eds. *The Raymond Chandler Papers: Selected Letters and Non-Fiction,* eds. Frank MacShane and Tom Hiney. New York: Atlantic Monthly Press, 2001.

MacShane, Frank, ed. *Selected Letters of Raymond Chandler.* New York: Columbia University Press, 1981.

———, ed. *The Notebooks of Raymond Chandler,* and "English Summer: A Gothic Romance." New York: Ecco Press, 1976.

Raymond Chandler and James M. Fox: Letters, privately printed, 1976.

Raymond Chandler: Later Novels and Other Writings. New York: Library of America, 1995.

Raymond Chandler: Stories and Early Novels. New York: Library of America, 1995.

Raymond Chandler's Philip Marlowe: A Centennial Celebration, with Brian Preiss. New York: Perigee Books, 1990.

Film Adaptations

(Those featuring Philip Marlowe are in bold type.)

The Falcon Takes Over (1942), RKO, based on *Farewell, My Lovely,* starring George Sanders as Gay Lawrence, the Falcon.

Time to Kill (1942), Twentieth Century Fox, based on *The High Window,* starring Lloyd Nolan as Michael Shayne.

Farewell, My Lovely, filmed as *Murder, My Sweet* (1945), starring Dick Powell and directed by Edward Dmytryk.

The Big Sleep (1946), starring Humphrey Bogart and Lauren Bacall, directed by Howard Hawks from an adaptation by William Faulkner and others.

The Lady in the Lake (1946), starring and directed by Robert Montgomery.

The High Window, filmed as *The Brasher Doubloon* (1947), starring George Montgomery and directed by John Brahm, had also inspired the film *Time to Kill* (1942).

The Little Sister, filmed as *Marlowe* (1969), starring James Garner and directed by Paul Bogart.

The Long Goodbye (1973), starring Elliott Gould and directed by Robert Altman.

Farewell, My Lovely (1975, starring Robert Mitchum and directed by Dick Richards.

The Big Sleep (1978), starring Robert Mitchum and written and directed by Michael Winner.

Radio Adaptations

Murder, My Sweet (June 11, 1945), CBS Radio; adapted from the 1944 film and starring Dick Powell.

The New Adventures of Philip Marlowe (June 17, 1947–September 9, 1947), NBC Radio series, starring Van Heflin; 13 30-minute episodes.

Suspense (January 10, 1948), CBS Radio; cameo appearance by series host Robert Montgomery in *The Adventures of Sam Spade* crossover, "The Kandy Tooth."

Murder, My Sweet (June 8, 1948), CBS Radio *Hollywood Star Time* adaptation of 1944 film starring Dick Powell.

The Adventures of Philip Marlowe (September 26, 1948–September 15, 1951), CBS Radio series starring Gerald Mohr.

The BBC Presents: Philip Marlowe (September 26, 1977–September 23, 1988), BBC Radio series starring Ed Bishop.

Television Adaptations

The Long Goodbye (October 7, 1954), CBS Television, *Climax!,* starring Dick Powell.

Philip Marlowe (October 6, 1959–March 29, 1960), ABC Television series, starring Philip Carey; 26 30-minute episodes.

Philip Marlowe, Private Eye (April 16–May 18, 1983, and April 17–June 3, 1986), London Weekend Television/HBO Television series, starring Powers Booth; 5 60-minute episodes.

"I'll Be Waiting" (1993), Showtime television, episode of *Fallen Angels,* starring Danny Glover.

"Red Wind" (November 26, 1995), Showtime Television episode of *Fallen Angels*, starring Danny Glover.

Poodle Springs (July 25, 1998), telefilm adapted from novel completed by Robert B. Parker, HBO Television, starring James Caan.

Audio

Free Old-Time Radio: *The Adventures of Philip Marlowe,* 90 episodes

Old-Time Radio Network Library: *The Adventures of Philip Marlowe,* 63 episodes

Goldfish, 1995, 60-minute cassette, Lodestone Media/Otherworld Media, starring Harris Yulin

Comic and Graphic Novels

The Little Sister (1997), Fireside; adapted and illustrated by Michael Lark

Playback: A Graphic Novel (2004), Arcade (French); (2006), Arcade (English), adapted by Ted Benoit, art by François Ayrole

ARCHIVES AND BIBLIOGRAPHIES

Department of Special Collections, Research Library, University of California at Los Angeles: manuscripts, notebooks, translations, memorabilia, and Chandleriana

AUTHORS INFLUENCED BY RAYMOND CHANDLER

Ross Macdonald, Robert B. Parker, Michael Connolly, Timothy Harris, Arthur Lyons, Max Allan Collins, Robert Crais, Walter Mosley, Sara Paretsky, Paco Ignacia Taibo II, Loren D. Estleman

WORKS CITED

Abbott, Megan E. "'Nothing You Can't Fix': Screening Marlowe's Masculinity." *Studies in the Novel* 35 (Fall 2003): 305–324.

Benstock, Bernard, ed. *Art in Crime Writing.* New York: St. Martin's Press, 1983.

Bruccoli, Matthew J., ed. *Chandler before Marlowe: Raymond Chandler's Early Prose and Poetry, 1908–1912.* Columbia: University of South Carolina Press, 1973.

Chandler, Raymond. *The Simple Art of Murder.* Boston: Houghton, 1950.

Dehaven, Tom, and Jerome Charyn, eds. New York: ibooks, Inc., 2005.

Delano, Alonzo. *Life on the Plains and Among the Diggers.* Auburn and Buffalo: Miller, Orton, Mulligan, 1854.

Durham, Philip. *Down These Mean Streets a Man Must Go.* Chapel Hill: University of North Carolina Press, 1963.

Gardiner, Dorothy, and Katharine Sorley Walker, eds. *Raymond Chandler Speaking*. Boston: Houghton, 1962.

Girouard, Mark. *The Return to Camelot*. New Haven, CT: Yale University Press, 1981.

Gross, Miriam, ed. *The World of Raymond Chandler*. New York: A & W Publishers, 1978.

Hardison, George P., and Jane R. Gelfman, eds. *Film Scripts One*. New York: Meredith, 1971.

Herbert, Rosemary. *Whodunit? A Who's Who in Crime and Mystery Writing*. New York: Oxford University Press, 1999.

Hiney, Tom. *Raymond Chandler*. New York: Atlantic Monthly Press, 1997.

Kirsch, Robert. *Los Angeles Times Book Review,* June 27, 1976.

Knight, Stephen. *Form and Ideology in Crime Fiction*. New York: Macmillan, 1980.

Lambert, Gavin. *The Dangerous Edge*. New York: Grossman, 1976.

MacShane, Frank. *The Life of Raymond Chandler*. New York: Dutton, 1976.

———, ed. *Selected Letters of Raymond Chandler*. New York: Columbia University Press, 1981.

———, and Tom Hiney, eds. *The Raymond Chandler Papers: Selected Letters and Non fiction*. New York: Grove/Atlantic, 2001.

Madden, David. *Tough Guy Writers of the Thirties*. Carbondale, IL: Southern Illinois University Press, 1968.

Margolies, Edward. *Which Way Did He Go? The Private Eye in Dashiell Hammett, Raymond Chandler, Chester Himes, and Ross Macdonald*. New York: Holmes & Meier, 1982.

Marling, William. *Raymond Chandler*. New York: Twayne, 1986.

Meyers, Richard. *TV Detectives*. San Diego: A.S. Barnes, 1981.

Most, Glenn W., and William W. Stowe, eds. *The Poetics of Murder*. New York: Harcourt, 1983.

Murphy, Bruce F. *The Encyclopedia of Murder and Mystery*. New York: St. Martin's Press, 1999.

Nolan, William F. *The Black Mask Boys*. New York: Morrow, 1985.

O'Brien, Geoffrey. *Hardboiled America: The Lurid Years of Paperbacks*. New York: Van Nostrand Reinhold Co., 1981.

Pendo, Stephen. *Raymond Chandler on Screen*. Metuchen, NJ: Scarecrow Press, 1976.

"Raymond Chandler." Contemporary Authors Online. http://web2.infotrac.galegroup.com.

Ruehlmann, William. *Saint with a Gun: The Unlawful American Private Eye*. New York: New York University Press, 1974.

Simpson, Hassell A. "'A Butcher's Thumb': Oral-Digital Consciousness in *The Big Sleep* and Other Novels of Raymond Chandler." *Journal of Popular Culture* 25 (Summer 1991): 83–92.

Speir, Jerry. *Raymond Chandler*. New York: Ungar, 1981.

Straub, Peter. "45 Calibrations of Raymond Chandler." http://www/conjunctions.com/archives/c29-ps.htm, accessed 1/9/2009.

Thorpe, Edward. *Chandlertown: The Los Angeles of Philip Marlowe*. London: Vermilion, 1983.

Ward, Elizabeth, and Alain Silver. *Raymond Chandler's Los Angeles*. Woodstock, NY: Overlook Press, 1987.

Ward, Greg. *The Timeline History of the USA*. New York: Barnes & Noble, 2005.

Wells, Walter. *Tycoons and Locusts: A Regional Look at Hollywood Fiction of the Thirties*. Carbondale, IL: Southern Illinois University Press, 1973.

Winks, Robin W., ed. *Mystery and Suspense Writers*. New York: Scribner's, 1998.

Wolfe, Peter. *Something More Than Night: The Case of Raymond Chandler*. Bowling Green, OH: Bowling Green State University Press, 1985.

FURTHER READING

Asher, Marty, ed. *Philip Marlowe's Guide to Life*. New York: Knopf, 2005.

Athenasourelis, John Paul. "Film Adaptations and the Censors: 1940s Hollywood and Raymond Chandler." *Studies in the Novel* 35 (Fall 2003): 325–338.

Bayley, John, ed. *Raymond Chandler: Collected Stories*. New York: Random House, 2002.

Brewer, Gary. *A Detective in Distress: Philip Marlowe's Domestic Dream*. Madison, IN: Brownstone Books, 1989.

Briggs, Asa. *A Social History of England*. New York: Viking Press, 1983.

Bruccoli, Matthew J. *Raymond Chandler: A Descriptive Bibliography*. Pittsburgh, PA: University of Pittsburgh Press, 1979.

Bunyan, Scott. "No Order from Chaos: The Absence of Chandler's Extra-Legal Space in the Detective Fiction of Chester Himes and Walter Mosley." *Studies in The Novel* 35 (Fall 2003): 339–365.

Cawelti, John G. *Adventure, Mystery, and Romance*. Chicago: University of Chicago Press, 1976.

Clark, Al. *Raymond Chandler in Hollywood*. Los Angeles, CA: Silman-James Press, 1996.

Claussen, Nils. "The Simple Art of Stealing: The Case of Raymond Chandler's Purloined 'Rats behind the Wainscoting.'" *ANQ* 19 (Summer 2006): 32–34.

Close, Alan, and Deirdre Gartrell, eds. *The Australian Love Letters of Raymond Chandler*. Ringwood, Australia: McPhee Gribble Publishers, 1995.

Eburne, Jonathan P. "Chandler's Waste Land." *Studies in the Novel* 35 (Fall 2003): 366–382.

Everson, William K. *The Detective in Film*. Secaucus, NJ: Citadel Press, 1972.

Ferncase, Richard K. "Robert Altman's *The Long Goodbye*: Marlowe in the Me Decade." *Journal of Popular Culture* 25 (Fall 1991): 87–90.

Freeman, Judith. *The Long Embrace: Raymond Chandler and the Woman He Loved*. New York: Pantheon, 2007.

Goulart, Ron, ed. *The Hardboiled Dicks*. New York: Pocket Books, 1967.

Henken, Bill. "Who Is Philip Marlowe?" http://www.geocities.com/Hollywood/loy/8628/marlowe/html?20097, accessed 1/7/2009.

Hickman, Miranda B. "Introduction: The Complex History of a 'Simple Art.'" *Studies in the Novel* 35 (Fall 2003): 285–304.

Hill, Jonathan, and Joseph Ruddy. *Bogart: The Man and the Legend*. New York: Mayflower Bell, 1966.

Howe, Alexander N. "The Detective and the Analyst: Truth, Knowledge, and Psychoanalysis in the Hard-Boiled Fiction of Raymond Chandler. *CLUES: A Journal of Detection* 24 (Summer 2006): 15–29.

————. *It Didn't Mean Anything: A Psychoanalytic Reading of American Detective Fiction.* Jefferson, NC: McFarland, 2008.

Luhr, William. *Raymond Chandler and Film.* New York: Ungar, 1982; 2nd ed. Tallahassee, FL: Florida State University Press, 1991.

MacDonald, Susan Peck. "Chandler's American Style." *Style* 39 (Winter 2005): 448–468.

Marling, William. *The American Roman Noir.* New York: Doubleday, 1953.

Moss, Robert F. *Raymond Chandler: A Literary Reference.* New York: Carroll and Graf, 2003.

Nazare, Joe. "Marlowe in Mirrorshades: The Cyberpunk (Revision of Chandler." *Studies in the Novel* 35 (Fall 2003): 383–404.

Newlin, Keith. *Hardboiled Burlesque: Raymond Chandler's Comic Style.* Madison, IN: Brownstone, 1984.

Olson, Brian. *Tailing Philip Marlowe.* St. Paul, MN: Burlwrite LLC, 2003.

Phillips, Gene D. *Creatures of Darkness: Raymond Chandler, Detective Fiction, and Film Noir.* Kentucky: University Press of Kentucky, 2000.

Pierce, J. Kingston. "Authors and Creators: Raymond Chandler." http://www.thrilling detective.com/trivia/chandler.html, accessed 1/9/2009.

Porter, Dennis. *The Pursuit of Crime.* New Haven, CT: Yale University Press, 1981.

Routledge, Christopher. "A Matter of Disguise: Locating the Self in Raymond Chandler's *The Big Sleep* and *The Long Good bye.*" *Studies in the Novel* 29 (Spring 1997): 94–108.

Ruhm, Herbert. "Raymond Chandler: From Bloomsbury to the Jungle—and Beyond," In *Tough Guy Writers of the Twenties and Thirties,* David Madden, ed., Carbondale: Southern Illinois University Press, 1968, 171–185.

See, Carolyn. "The Hollywood Novel: The American Dream Cheat," in *Tough Guy Writers of the Twenties and Thirties,* by David Madden, ed., Carbondale: Southern Illinois University Press, 1968, 199–217.

Sharp, Michael D. "Plotting Chandler's Demise: Ross Macdonald and the Neo-Aristotelian Detective Novel." *Studies in the Novel* 35 (Fall 2003): 405–426.

Simpson, Hassell A. "'So Long, Beautiful Hunk': Ambiguous Gender and Songs of Parting in Raymond Chandler's Fictions." *Journal of Popular Culture* 28 (Fall 1994): 37–48.

Spinks, Leo. "Except for Law: Raymond Chandler, James Ellroy, and the Politics of Exception." *South Atlantic Quarterly* 107 (Winter 2008): 121–143.

Van Wert, William. "Philip Marlowe: Hardboiled to Softboiled to Poached." *Jump Cut: A Review of Contemporary Media* 1974: 10–13.

WEB SITES

http://www.classiccrimefiction.com (Entry on Chandler is satisfactory).
http://www.thrillingdetective.com/trivia/chandler.html (Entry on Chandler is minimal).
http://www.booksfactory.com (Entry on Chandler is helpful).

Raymond Burr as Perry Mason in "The Sardonic Sergeant." Courtesy of CBS/Landov.

Perry Mason:
The Legal Sleuth

I get my business because I fight for it and because I fight for my clients.

—Perry Mason

Perry Mason, the most famous fictional lawyer-sleuth of all time, achieved worldwide fame first in the novels of Erle Stanley Gardner, an attorney himself and later in two perennially popular television series, portrayed by Raymond Burr. Mason's cases made Gardner the most widely read author of the post–World War II period; in 1958 he sold 100 million books in English alone, and by the late 1970s, his worldwide sales exceeded 300 million books. Mason's fans today include lawyers and judges he influenced to enter their profession; President Harry Truman avidly read Perry Mason novels, and when Einstein died, "a Perry Mason book was at his bedside. And when Raymond Burr . . . had occasion to meet Pope John XXIII . . . the pontiff seemed to know all about Perry Mason." CBS's *Perry Mason* television series, 1957 to 1966, closely supervised by Gardner, made Burr the wealthiest star in television history, by 1965 "rich enough to have purchased one of the Fiji Islands" (Kelleher and Merrill 4, 6, 45). Through Gardner's fiction,

> ### *Perry Mason 50th Anniversary Edition* DVD
>
> The four-disc DVD (2008) includes 12 episodes from the original 1957–1963 series, displaying Robert Redford, Burt Reynolds, Leonard Nimoy, Ryan O'Neal, and other stars as young talents; includes new interviews and archival footage—Raymond Burr's screen test and his appearance on Edward R. Murrow's *Person to Person.*

the CBS series reruns, and 26 NBC telefilms (1985 to 1993), Perry Mason continues to reassure his public "that the nation's legal system, however threatening and aloof, [is] fair and accessible" (Leitch 98).

HISTORICAL/CULTURAL CONTEXT

The name and character of "Perry Mason" evolved from popular American literature. In 1995 Erle's nephew Kenneth D. Gardner, Jr. disclosed that an old family trunk "carried 3,000 miles and saved for 50 years" among the Gardner family's treasures (Senate iv) contained proof that "as a boy of 8 to 13 . . . more than 30 years before he christened his lawyer-detective, Erle was reading the name of Perry Mason on the front pages of a children's magazine," *The Youth's Companion* for March 25, 1897, and September 2, 1902, published by Perry Mason and Company of Boston. Young Gardner probably also read Melville Davisson Post's novels about Randolph Mason, "more rogue than detective," who nosed out legal loopholes to help his clients cheat the law (Jon L. Breen, in Herbert 114).

Adventure stories with rule-defying heroes must have fortified rambunc- tious young Gardner's rebellion against formal education. After being sus- pended from high school in 1909, he spent a few weeks at Valparaiso University, where he learned law "from firsthand experience which sent him escaping from town just one jump ahead of the sheriff" (Hughes 47). He also learned to box and worked on railroad construction before he read for the law in lawyers' offices and passed the California bar in 1911 at 21, sub- sequently practicing "with all the brash impetuosity of youth and virtually no inferiority complex" (Gardner, quoted in Hughes 57). He married Natalie Talbert in 1912, and their only child, Natalie Grace, was born the following year.

While Gardner was thus occupied, "the pulps" were being born. Named for their cheap paper, these popular weekly magazines with lurid covers began to take over from the earlier "dime novels," sensational novellas pop- ular in America since the 1860s. The dime novels had initiated the Western genre, but they also presented mysteries, true crime, fantastic tales, adven- ture, and horror, though not until the 1880s did they branch out into detec- tion with the private eye Nick Carter, featured in over 1,000 stories and later popular in radio and television. *Detective Story,* the first pulp devoted solely to crime and detection, appeared in 1915, leading off a genre which included courtroom cases and "hero-thieves" (Murphy 408).

The detective pulp *Black Mask,* famously edited by Captain Joseph T. ("Cap") Shaw, launched the American "hard-boiled" school of detective authors such as Raymond Chandler, who later became Gardner's lifelong friend. Today pulp fiction anthologies include Bill Pronzini's *The Arbor House Treasury of Detective and Mystery Stories from the Great Pulps,* (1983) and the *Black Mask* anthology, *The Hard-Boiled Detective* (1977). As the horrifying realities of World War I mounted, disillusion and cynicism gradually seeped into pulp detective fiction, led by hard-hitting tough-guy heroes like Chandler's Philip Marlowe and Dashiell Hammett's nameless Continental Op, but the hard- boiled detectives soon split into a group so vicious as to be virtually indistin- guishable from the crooks they killed, and a group of wounded knights-errant, outwardly tough but inwardly sensitive such as John McDonald's Lew Archer. Posing as a "callous cynic," the hard-boiled knight-errant uses simple sentence structure, American vernacular, wise- cracks, and ironic remarks to "hide his humanity behind a mask of cynicism" (Murphy 232), and essentially a romantic, practices "situational ethics. Relentlessly honest and consistently devoted to the victims in society, [he] . . . sets his own high stand- ards." "Descended from James Fenimore Cooper's archetypal Leatherstocking," the hard-boiled hero "chooses an instinctive code of justice over 'the of- ten tarnished justice of civilization' and 'replaces

If facts can be shuffled in such a way that it will confuse a witness who isn't absolutely certain of his story, and if the attorney doesn't suppress, conceal, or distort any of the actual evidence, I claim the attorney is within his rights.

—Perry Mason to Della Street

the subtleties of the deductive method with a sure knowledge of the world and a keen moral sense'" (John M. Reilly, in Herbert 93). Both in his law career and in his fiction Gardner exhibited a personal code of justice and moral sense, so unusual it shocked his colleagues and confounded his opponents.

When Gardner began practicing law there in 1916, Oxnard, California, was "the brawling, shocking, young town in the county [Ventura], a place of brothels, gambling, open saloons, and violence" (Hughes 52). A prosperous Chinatown dominated the gambling business, widely patronized by Oxnard's white American Beet Sugar Company factory population, about 2,000. In a clean-up campaign, a grand jury demanded that the Chinese restrict their gambling activities to lotteries and the Chinese agreed, but the county, responding to anti-Chinese sentiment, then unjustly arrested 21 Chinese lottery sellers. Gardner first assisted a senior lawyer in defending the Chinese; recalling the early days of his 20-year legal career, Gardner indicated that his clients

> wanted a lawyer . . . to explain to a court that what they had already done was legal. . . . I never suborned perjury, never put a witness on the stand when I knew he was lying, never permitted my clients to "cut corners". . . they were for the most part Chinese who were only guilty of a little gambling among themselves and were arrested for it. (Quoted in Hughes 57)

Gardner singlehandedly devised a wickedly effective legal trap and won the case on his own, thus earning Chinatown's gratitude and business and revealing important elements he would later give to Perry Mason: a legal knight-errant's instinctive code of justice, a keen moral desire to defend the falsely accused underdog, and the challenge of finding legal loopholes to do it.

Between 1918 and 1921, Gardner took a business fling in the Consolidated Sales Company of his old friend Joe Templeton, but the big economic boom just after World War I fizzled, and they ended up, Gardner said, "completely and entirely broke" (Hughes 65). Gardner stayed afloat with anonymous cash "donations" to his bank account by an unknown Chinese man, and in 1921 he returned to working days and nights in the Orr & Gardner law practice at Ventura. He later noted that the more successful he became as a lawyer, the more he had to stay in his office, answering telephones, drawing up routine legal documents, and being constantly available to his partners and clients, mostly poor immigrants or the unjustly accused. He defended "vagrants, peeping Toms and chicken thieves as if they were statesmen," but he told *Time* in 1949, "That wasn't what I wanted," (quoted in Hughes 57), and it wasn't very lucrative, either.

Gardner, however, excelled in the courtroom. His law partner Frank Orr claimed,

> His way with a hostile witness was plain wizardry. He could coax the fellow along, right into telling outright lies, or into confusion so complete the fellow

would end up babbling. . . . At the proper moment, he would spring the precedent on the judge and jury. No one who had known him as a lawyer ever had to look far . . . to find where Perry Mason came from. (Quoted in Hughes 63)

AUTHORSHIP

Around 1920, Gardner decided to try writing fiction, which seemed to promise a good income and enough leisure for the outdoor pursuits—riding, archery, hunting, fishing—he so vastly preferred to office work. In his 1959 autobiographical notes, he declared he had no natural aptitude for writing, though he minutely analyzed plots to understand what people wanted to read. He knew what he wanted to do, but at first for the life of him he simply couldn't do it, and he briefly abandoned fiction. Then Gardner's wife sold a story of her own to the *Los Angeles Times* and he tried again, aiming at the pulps, collecting a drawer full of rejection slips before selling some jokes for a dollar apiece and a humorous skit for $10. In 1921 he sold his first story, "Nettie's Naughty Nightie," for $10 to the pulp *Breezy Stories* and gave the check to his proper New England-born mother. That year his writing made $974, less than he made in a month from his law practice, so since this was hardly the big money he had hoped for, he briefly tried a mail order course in "salesmanship" for lawyers. In 1923 he still was writing "'the worst stories,'" he said, "that ever hit New York City" (quoted in Hughes 77) when by accident *Black Mask*'s editor sent him a joke critique with yet another rejection slip. Gardner didn't get angry, he said, because he had been used to "standing up in police courts and dishing it out and taking it on the chin" (quoted in Hughes 78). He stayed up three nights "hammering away on the blood-spattered keys" of his typewriter; the embarrassed editor took the story for $160, and "'That did it,' Gardner proclaimed. 'I was launched on a literary career'" (quoted from Hughes 77–79).

Gardner's literary apprenticeship in the pulps made him one of *Black Mask*'s most successful authors. Between his legal cases he wrote formulaic detective stories, fantasy fiction, and Westerns "for twenty or so magazines under about a dozen pen names"—about 400 stories from 1921 to 1932, with 25 series detectives, including Speed Dash, the Human Fly with a photographic memory; Sidney Zoom and his police dog; Black Barr the gunslinger; El Paisano who could see in the dark; and Lester Leith, confidence man. Collections of Gardner's pulp fiction include *Dead Men's Letters* (1989), which features the "phantom Crook" Ed Jenkins; *The Adventures of Paul Pry*; and *Honest Money*, featuring lawyer Ken Corning. The pulps paid off handsomely for Gardner. In 1926, his writing brought in $6,627, and by the early 1930s, the beginning of the Great Depression, his sales from writing had increased to $20,000 a year, roughly equivalent to $295,168 in 2006, according to the Consumer Price Index and http://www.measuringworth.com. His pulp output peaked at about 1 million words per year, or more than one story published each week.

Around 1930, Gardner began working on *Reasonable Doubt* and *Silent Verdict*, two hard-boiled mystery novels involving lawyers and a female character named "Della Street." Two years later, Gardner's agent at the time, Robert Hardy, presented Thayer Hobson, the new young president of William Morrow and Company, with these manuscripts, beginning a long friendship between Hobson and Gardner, a publisher-author team that proved "one of, if not the most successful in the annals of publishing" (Hughes 98). Hobson suggested that Gardner tone down the hard-boiled elements and the staccato dialogue technique like Dashiell Hammett's in *The Maltese Falcon* (1930) and make his lawyer protagonist more subtle. Gardner painfully reworked *Reasonable Doubt*, using a fast-moving style and a totally new leading character he now called "Perry Mason," drawing on his own boxing days to define attorney Mason as "a fighter who is possessed of infinite patience. He tries to jockey his enemies into a position where he can deliver one good knockout punch" (quoted in Hughes 103). *The Case of the Velvet Claws*, the first Perry Mason novel, appeared on March 1, 1933.

Even before Perry Mason, Gardner's enormous amount of fiction had proved impossible for either two fingers, however bloody, or even the new electric typewriter to produce. Gardner forced a dictating machine on his horrified legal secretaries to meet his self-imposed quota of 5,000 words a day, a man-killing rate he maintained for 10 years with after-hours help from Jean Walter, his office manager and executive secretary. In October 1932, he began to call himself the "Fiction Factory": "Rather than write his fiction, Gardner talked it" (Van Dover 24). A secretary typed his dictated stories, he edited and revised them before another typing, and then they would be proofread before the final typed version went to the publisher. Jean's sisters Peggy and Honey Walter eventually joined the Fiction Factory, and when he finally left his law practice, they stayed with him, working at his Rancho del Paisano near Temecula, California. The three sisters merged into Perry Mason's loyal secretary Della Street, one of Gardner's most popular characters. Jean made Gardner's work her life, and after Natalie's death in 1968, Jean and Gardner were married on August 7 of that year.

Gardner and Natalie had amicably separated in 1934. The breach had probably started between their 1931 trip to China and Gardner's decision to put the Fiction Factory on wheels in June 1933, bundling his secretaries, his German Shepherd Rip, and his writing paraphernalia into a primitive mobile camping outfit he called "Podunk." Gardner had proved a born bachelor who, Natalie knew, needed an outdoors life, so she settled in Oakland. According to Gardner, Rip in 1936 nosed out a 150-acre ranch for Gardner near Temecula, California, then a desert crossroads town of about 200 with a post office-general store and a gas station. His neighbors were the Pala

Indians and the 90,000-acre Vail Ranch, whose owners Gardner regularly joined at the poker table. His Rancho del Paisano, eventually 3,000 acres, was primarily Gardner's workplace, but he also generously entertained his friends there. Being a pushover for animals, too, he turned it into a haven for horses, stray dogs who occupied all the best furniture, and even a pet coyote.

Gardner evolved a simple, yet immensely successful formula for his Perry Mason books: Mason acquires a client enmeshed in suspicious circumstances, who appears guilty, and who then is charged with murder. The plot thickens until the client's conviction appears inevitable and Mason seems mired in a legal quicksand, just where he says he likes most to be (*The Case of the Screaming Woman,* in *Seven Complete Novels*). Then Mason confidently risks everything—his reputation, career, sometimes even his own life—on one last gambit, which pays off in a climactic courtroom-scene shocker, with last-minute evidence that saves the client and unmasks the real killer. His readers loved it, particularly from the 1930s to the early 1960s, when popular opinion still revered the American legal system. By the mid-1960s, Perry Mason novels were selling some 26,000 copies a day, chaining Gardner to his factory and keeping six secretaries busy typing from his recorded dictation. He worked on several books at the same time, and reportedly he was never sure which was most recently published.

Besides his 99 Perry Mason novels, Gardner published the 29-novel Donald Lam-Bertha Cool private detective series under the name "A.A. Fair" and under his own name the 9-novel D.A. Doug Selby series; 2 books each in the Terry Clane series and the Granpa Wiggins series; 7 volumes of short mystery stories and 1 science fiction collection; and 17 nonfiction works, most dealing with environmental issues in California and the American Southwest. His "Reference Drawer" reflected his copious and varied reading, from archaeology to his golf problems. "Gardner, more than any other writer, popularized the law profession for a mass-market audience, melding fact and fiction to achieve a unique blend; no one ever handled courtroom drama better than he did. . . . His books, however imaginative, were authentic" (Winks 422).

Through most of Gardner's career, the U.S. public generally regarded lawyers with respect if not affection, but he always believed that "'lawyers in general were treated unfairly. . . .' He wrote that there were 'two classes of persons who automatically enjoy poor public relations: the attorney *at* law and the mother *in* law'" (quoted in Kelleher and Merrill 5, italics in original). In 1948 he founded the Court of Last Resort, a lawyers' organization he intended to improve the administration of justice. Gardner devoted a considerable amount of his annual income to it, because it meant more to him than anything else in his career. In 1951, NBC televised 35 episodes of *The Court of Last Resort,* with actors playing lawyers and criminologists attempting to free framed victims of the judicial system. Convicted persons claiming their innocence gradually inundated the organization, and after 12 years Gardner withdrew from the group. When it was eventually dissolved, he arranged to convey its work to the American Polygraph Association.

Overwhelmingly successful as it had proved in print, Gardner's Perry Mason formula did not initially transfer happily to other media. In the mid-1930s, Warner Brothers bought the film rights to several Perry Mason novels and made six films, hoping to use Gardner's successful formula to capitalize on the "sophisticated murder-comedy" trend started by *The Thin Man.* Gardner detested Hollywood's treatment of his work so violently that he accused Warner Brothers of trying to ruin it. He commented about the first Perry Mason film, *The Case of the Howling Dog* (1935): ". . . [the Hollywood Mason] had about an acre of office and Della was so dazzling I couldn't see her for her diamonds. Everybody drank a lot" (quoted in Kelleher and Merrill, 8). Mason's admirers agreed the movie was awful, and after five more Mason movies bombed, Warner turned Gardner's *The Case of the Dangerous Dowager* into a Western called *Granny Get Your Gun,* writing Perry Mason out completely. Gardner swore off movie adaptations and "never forgave Hollywood" (Kelleher and Merrill 8).

Not long after the movie debacle, however, Gardner sold the Perry Mason radio rights to the giant soap company Procter & Gamble. Beginning in 1943, CBS aired the resulting "soap opera" five days a week nationwide. Gardner tried to write radio scripts for it, but he soon discovered "As a soaper, I stunk." For at least the first three years of its 12-year radio run he deplored its various pedestrian actors and its melodramatic treatment of his material, eventually allowing the show to serve as "a kind of continuing advertisement for his books" (Kelleher and Merrill, 9). In the mid-1950s, Gardner mustered "considerable business and creative savvy" (*TV Detectives* 45), separating the soap opera from the detective mystery, removing Mason entirely, and bringing the radio cast, crew, and the soap opera format to television as *The Edge of Night,* still running as a daytime staple.

By the time television sets had invaded almost all American homes, Gardner was planning to bring his hard-hitting lawyer hero to the small screen. In 1955 he reputedly turned down a million-dollar offer for total rights to a televised Perry Mason series and instead formed his own Paisano Productions, named for his Temecula ranch. Starting in 1957, Gardner packaged

The Original Cast of the CBS *Perry Mason* Series

Perry Mason—Raymond Burr

Della Street—Barbara Hale

Paul Drake—William Hopper

D.A. Hamilton Burger—William Talman

Lt. Arthur Tragg—Ray Collins

Perry Mason for CBS, personally approving every script, and retaining control for its nine-season prime-time run as the most popular legal series in television history, earning him about $15 million. Introduced by Fred Steiner's signature music "Park Avenue Beat," *Perry Mason* continues to be rerun across the United States; DVD releases of the original episodes began in 2006, and the show has been broadcast abroad in 16 different languages.

Much of the series' impact came from its Canadian star, Raymond Burr. Burr lost nearly 150 pounds to audition for the part of Mason's prime adversary, District Attorney Hamilton Burger, but when Burr arrived, Gardner allegedly exclaimed, "He's Perry Mason!" Raymond Burr later recounted Gardner's million-dollar remark, "He's Perry Mason," to David L. Stanley of Oakland, New Jersey, at dinner the night after the auditions (Hill 61). Gail Patrick Jackson, executive producer of *Perry Mason,* originally considered William Holden, Richard Egan, Mike Connors, and sci-fi movie actor Jack Carlson for the role. Gardner dismissed Efrem Zimbalist, Jr. from consideration because he felt Zimbalist was too much of a "pretty boy," and in March 1956 he told Jackson to cast Fred MacMurray as Mason, though that plan later evaporated. Over 50 actors were auditioning for the part when Gardner chose Burr.

Burr was then 39, a tall, heavyset, rugged actor previously best known for playing stage and film villains like the sinister wife-murderer umasked by Jimmy Stewart in Alfred Hitchcock's *Rear Window.* Burr fit Gardner's concept of Mason as an improved version of himself: tall and well if bulkily built, with long legs and wavy hair, rugged features that might have been "carved from granite," a "boyish grin," and steely blue "gimlet eyes," like Gardner's own. Gardner thought that all lawyers, including himself, were actors and that Perry Mason was "a helluvan actor" (quoted in Hughes 14). Jack King, current staff attorney of the National Association of Criminal Defense Lawyers, concurs with Gardner's opinion, declaring, "A good trial lawyer is always an actor" (quoted in Dribben 3). That professional association requires its members to participate in acting classes, which are consistently well attended.

Raymond Burr was "a helluvan actor," too, and even more luckily, "Gardner and Burr were kindred spirits; both were workaholics. Their combined chemistry took possible lead and turned it into television gold" (*TV Detectives* 45). Both were also extremely generous men. Contrary to his movie villain roles and his tough hero roles like Perry Mason and Robert Ironside, the wheelchair-bound police chief he played from 1967 to 1975, Burr was a compassionate man who had experienced several major tragedies. To conceal Burr's homosexuality, Hollywood publicists may have manufactured some biographical details, such as statements that Burr's first wife was killed in an airplane shot down by Germans during World War II; that their son died of leukemia at age 10; that Burr's marriage to Isabella Ward ended quickly in divorce, and that his third wife died of cancer soon after their marriage. Burr never came out, but his longtime partner and business manager did, sometime after Burr's death. Burr struggled with lifelong weight problems and a variety of serious illnesses; by age 50 he had undergone nine operations and at various times had contracted malaria, typhoid, and hepatitis.

Instead of becoming embittered by his own problems, Burr looked after his parents in their old age, educated his nieces and nephews, and directly supported 12 people, even paying hospital bills for insolvent acquaintances. He donated huge sums of money to charity, including his salaries from the 1985 to 1993 Perry Mason telefilms, made substantial gifts to the McGeorge School of Law in Sacramento, and sponsored over 30 needy children all over the world. He approached the role of Perry Mason with the utmost gravity, telling *TV Guide* in 1965 that he considered the program and its hero "a public trust" and himself its "chief executor" (quoted in Whitney 113); he memorized all his lines, never used a teleprompter, and practiced legal terms away from the set.

Burr became obsessed with his work on *Perry Mason* and sacrificed his personal life for it, rarely taking time off to socialize or vacation. "He got about four or five hours of sleep a night . . . and existed on coffee and cigarettes all day and one big meal at night" (Hill 70). Through major and minor illnesses and accidents, Burr tried never to interrupt the filming of the show's 271 episodes. While he compared his nine years of the *Perry Mason* series to "being in a plush concentration camp while living on the set," he never regretted them (quoted in Hall 162). Burr, Barbara Hale, who played Della Street, and the show as a whole won Emmy Awards in 1959, and beginning in 1985, when *The Return of Perry Mason* swept all ratings as the nation's number one telefilm, Burr reprised the role in 26 two-hour telefilms from 1985, until he died from cancer in 1993. He also taught drama at the University of Southern California, invested in real estate and other businesses, ran his California vineyard, imported and exported rare orchids from his farms around the world, maintained his various charitable activities, and indefatigably visited over 27,000 U.S. soldiers in the Far East.

The authorial function of the CBS *Perry Mason* series, all but one episode shot in black and white, gradually migrated from Gardner, its creator, to Burr, its star, apparently with Gardner's consent and approval. From the beginning . . . Gardner's television auteurship, "a term used in film studies to indicate the role of a director who despite the constraints of the production process and product conventions . . . is able to establish a particular style" (Bounds 11) was "a far cry from authorship . . . he never wrote or rewrote a line for the television series or took an active role in production" (Leitch 6, 62–63). In Gardner's fiction, Perry Mason usually tiptoed through legal land mines to frustrate Hamilton Burger, but the television series translated this action into courtroom confessions. Gardner did insist on Mason's defense of accused persons whom he invariably proved innocent by ingenious technical legal maneuvers.

Perry Mason's writers gradually incorporated plot devices Gardner had never considered. They showcased famous guest stars to contrast with

> ### *Perry Mason* **Series Trivia**
>
> - 1,904 actors appeared on the series between 1957 and 1966.
> - Episode 249 had its largest cast size, 25.
> - Episode 35 had its smallest cast, 8.

Mason's majestic imperturbability, like Bette Davis who appeared in 1963's "The Case of Constance Doyle," allowing maximum impact without threatening Mason's primacy. Exotic subcultures provided more novelty for the show, like the episodes involving one of Burr's personal pursuits, the study of art. The most celebrated variations to the *Perry Mason* formula put major members of the cast in jeopardy, like Mason's flamboyant detective associate Paul Drake, whom Mason extricated from a murder charge in "The Case of Paul Drake's Dilemma." In "The Case of the Dead Ringer" Burr even played an unusual double role, both Mason and "Grimes," an old sailor hired to impersonate and discredit Mason (Leitch 67–69). With Gardner's approval, these scripting developments allowed "Gardner's wily Mason [to yield] to television's avuncular Mason," cementing Burr as "America's lawyer" (Leitch 77) and even displacing Gardner as the original franchise's trademark.

Thomas Leitch notes that by 1960, Burr's photograph began to appear on the space usually reserved for the author's photograph on paperback reprint editions of Gardner's Perry Mason novels, and that on the same reprints the type for Burr's name also dwarfed Gardner's. According to Leitch, the most compelling evidence of Burr's ascendancy is the 1959 Transogram board game, "The Perry Mason Game: The Case of the Missing Suspect" (79–80), which features Burr's unsmiling photograph "on every surface capable of displaying an image" and "unites paternal reassurance with patriarchal authority," in contrast to the figure of the "corny, wishy-washy, do-nothing 'Pop'" prevailing in 1950s television sitcoms (Spigel 65).

After Gardner's death in 1971, CBS's attempt to revive *Perry Mason* with Monte Markham as its star turned into a 15-episode (1973 to 1974) resounding flop, largely due to Burr's absence, but the permissive authority-defying 1960s, followed by the Watergate scandal of the early 1970s, had also exploded what positive attitudes toward attorneys America still held. The scandal rapidly deposed Nixon administration officials and forced President Richard Nixon to resign, contributing to substantial changes in the U.S. legal profession's image and its reflection in the popular media when Raymond Burr, considerably older, much heavier, and far less mobile, returned in 1985 to play Perry Mason for NBC's two-hour *Perry Mason Mystery* telefilms. Lawyer jokes were proliferating around water coolers and cocktail tables and on late-night television, and public opinion polls placed attorneys among America's most distrusted professionals. "Once the progressive social engineers of the

1950s and 1960s, attorneys were reviled as hairsplitting shysters interested only in preserving the wealth of their corporate clients or augmenting their own by solicitous attention to their billable hours" (Leitch 85).

In this anti-attorney atmosphere, Viacom daringly bought the Perry Mason rights and presented the public with an anti-lawyer hero. Despite Burr's increasing physical problems, his dramatic expertise made Mason's new image as a vintage 1950s anachronism convincing. Scriptwriters incorporated abundant in-jokes based on the original series, downplayed mysteries, and de-emphasized courtroom procedure and conventions, while Burr modulated the role into an affirmation of faith in an idealized view of the American legal system, something viewers wanted badly to believe in, rather than the evidence of the nightly news to the contrary.

> After Burr died in 1993, NBC knew better than to recast Mason's role. Prior to his death, Burr had suggested that, in case of his absence, Perry should be out of town on business with a guest-star colleague covering for him at his office, which NBC implemented in the four telefilms aired after his death. Hal Holbrook played a canny country attorney in three of the non-Mason telefilms.

Everyone who knew Gardner felt he was always a lawyer at heart, and not long before his death from cancer on February 11, 1970, Gardner downplayed his purposes in creating Perry Mason: "I write to make money, and I write to give the reader sheer fun" (quoted in *CA Online*). He did both, but his lawyer-detective and Raymond Burr's acting prowess also embedded Perry Mason still more solidly in the national consciousness.

PROFILE OF PERRY MASON

Perry Mason's Personal Background

Erle Stanley Gardner believed that "The real definition of a character is one who stands out from the common run of mankind" (quoted in Kelleher and Merrill 4). He made Perry Mason, his most famous character, reflect his own qualities as a self-made man, with dashes of four attorneys he knew during his Oxnard practice. Gardner primarily gave Mason the thirst for excitement that he described in his unpublished autobiography, "The Color of Life": "I want adventure. I want variety. . . . If variety is the spice of life, I want cayenne pepper" (quoted in Fugate and Fugate 154), and he made Perry Mason insist, "The games I sit in on are always no-limit games" (*Screaming Woman*, in *Seven Complete Novels* 429).

Mr. Mason, . . . you seem to find yourself in predicaments from which you extricate yourself by unusual methods which invariably turn out to be legally sound.

—One of Gardner's fictional judges

> **Erle Stanley Gardner's Fried Filet Mignon**
>
> Heat skillet to medium-hot. Iron pan is good. Sprinkle with salt. Drop in thick filet mignon. Leave it—do not turn to seal juices. Cook until you are ready to turn it JUST ONCE. Turn and cook on second side. For rare: a few minutes on each side (Valerie J. Naso, Gardner's granddaughter, quoted in Senate 56).

Gardner and Mason both preferred rare filet mignon, baked potatoes, and fresh green salads, but Gardner deliberately steered clear of providing Perry Mason with a full-scale personal history. Probably born in 1891, Mason as a practicing lawyer first lived in a Los Angeles apartment and later for convenience moved to a luxury apartment hotel. He also had an expensive office suite at Broadway and Seventh Street, though he occasionally muttered about its cost. Even in the 1930s he commanded six-figure retainers, but he willingly lost money when clients didn't or couldn't pay up: "When a client asks him if he would defend a poor person against a millionaire, Mason replies, 'I'd fight for a client against the devil himself'" (Penzler 132), insisting that "an attorney's entitled to take advantage of every technicality in the law" (*Screaming Woman,* in *Seven Complete Novels* 423).

Perry Mason belonged to the Remuda Golf Club, an unspecified lodge and a private club where he stopped after work for an occasional drink. He first drove a Buick coupe, but soon he sported a convertible which Paul Drake accused him of driving "like Hell on wet roads," though by the mid-1950s Mason was promising Della Street he would drive his dark, medium-sized sedan carefully and limit himself to one light drink before doing so. Like Gardner, Mason enjoyed the good food he enthusiastically cooked himself on his hunting and fishing trips. His interests included skiing at Bear Valley, California; the plants and geology of the desert; and astronomy. He read voraciously—psychology in the 1930s, legal materials in the 1940s and 1950s, and mysteries in the 1970s—though in the 1960s he complained he was "too damn busy" to read (Penzler 134). His nerves often drove him to chain smoking his Raleighs, but he never lost his self-confidence, believing firmly in his ability "to swing any jury if the situation requires it," and he never asked a client whether he was guilty or not: "Either way," Mason insisted, "he's entitled to a day in court" (quoted in Penzler 135), convinced that "the practice of criminal law isn't slimy unless you make it slimy" (*Screaming Woman* 425). Mason's real, almost his only, life was his work, since Gardner refused to "recognize the environment as an effective accomplice in his moral dramas: a man is responsible for his own actions, and should not consider shifting blame onto his parents, his economic class, his diet, etc." (Van Dover 20). Neither the *Perry Mason* series nor the Perry Mason telefilms revealed many details about Mason's background or personal life, either.

"The [Perry Mason] stories are timeless," said 45-year-old Ron Dunevant, production manager for Portland, Oregon's KPTV, which has aired *Perry Mason* as the linchpin of its daytime programming since 1970; "even a kid could understand what was going on in *Perry*."

Perry Mason's Career

Gardner claimed that transforming Ed Stark, the hard-boiled lawyer hero of Gardner's early novel *Reasonable Doubt,* into Perry Mason as he first appeared in *The Case of the Velvet Claws* was "about the hardest job I have ever tackled" (quoted in Fugate and Fugate 179), but once achieved, it produced a mythic characterization celebrating simpler times and values. First, Gardner removed Stark's "bruiser" appearance and intellectualized Mason by comparing his impassive face to a chess player's when studying the board. Mason's office thus "held an atmosphere of plain, rugged efficiency, as though it had absorbed something of the personality of the man who occupied it" (all quotations from *Velvet Claws* appear in Fugate and Fugate 179–187). Instead of Stark's "big hands" scooping up money, Mason fingers a paperweight on his desk, with "long and tapering fingers" "filled with competent strength" suggesting first a masculine artist or a musician, though "the hand could have a grip of crushing force should the occasion require." Stark's face is "grim and determined," but Mason's face is "set in lines of patient concentration." While Stark lengthily outlines his pulpy qualifications, Mason cuts quickly to the chase: "If you look me up through some family lawyer or some corporation lawyer, he'll probably tell you that I'm a shyster. If you look me up through some chap in the District Attorney's office, he'll tell you that I'm a dangerous antagonist, but he doesn't know very much about me. If you look me up through a bank you won't find out a damned thing." Mason has social graces, too, that Stark would never possess or think necessary. Mason customarily dons his jacket to see clients, and he never engages in protracted physical conflict, preferring to patiently maneuver his opponents into an economically final "straight left" that drops them like "sack[s] of meal" (quotations from Fugate and Fugate 179 ff.). Mason's intellect and personality remained constant throughout Gardner's novels.

Gardner believed that "a writer in starting a story should first decide what lowest common denominator of public interest, or what combination of common denominators he is going to put into the story" (quoted in Van Dover 15). Once he had launched Perry Mason's career, Gardner never varied his "combination of common denominators." Describing them in a guide for his television scriptwriters, he said he felt that the "virtually indestructible" mythic characters of Cinderella and Robin Hood best exemplified his aims in Mason's formulaic cases, because Cinderella, "a soothing syrup to the unfortunate," gave Perry Mason "a fairy godmother touch . . . in which justice is brought to the unfortunate," while the story of Robin Hood satisfied people's "vast yearning . . . to be reassured that God is in His heaven, that all is right with the world and that justice will triumph over tyranny" (quoted in Van Dover 22). Gardner seldom fine-tuned Mason, but he did eliminate religious or racially prejudicial references and thoughtless clichés that had appeared in his 1930s novels; "the rest of Mason's cases confine themselves to the society of white, Anglo-Saxon Protestants" (*Murder in the Millions* 71). Gardner did consider abandoning Mason in 1937, when Della Street convinced Mason to vacation in China, but after only seven months, he brought Mason back in *The Case of the Substitute Face* (1938). Overall, Gardner's fictional "world is permanently sunlit; the only obscurity results from a single cloud which his penetrating intelligence regularly disperses. The reiteration is part of the reassurance" (Van Dover 23).

Gardner and Burr shared their workaholism and their generosity, an enormous respect for the law, support for human rights, and the desire to eliminate discrimination through education. Perhaps most important, they both passionately defended the underdog. Nazi propagandist Josef Goebbels banned Gardner's books in 1939 for that position, and in 1993 Burr received an Honorary Doctorate of Humane Letters from the University of Colorado for creating the School for the Arts in downtown urban-renewal Denver.

Like Gardner, Burr had a talent for practical joking. Gardner once "adorned his [legal] office with indiscreet art in order to horrify strait-laced visitors . . . snapping women at close range as they climbed on streetcars" and producing a "gallery of legoramas [that] was the talk of the town (Johnston 49). In a similar vein, Burr often relieved the tension on *Perry Mason* sets with practical jokes, like filling Barbara Hale's "bathtub, sink, ashtrays, glasses, cigarette boxes, pin trays, and any other receptacle he could find" with lime Jell-O (Hill 75). Burr also had a temper that made co-workers stay out of his way until he cooled down, though Burr, gifted with expertise in many areas Gardner did not share, made Mason far more profound than the man Gardner sketched in his novels.

Gardner apparently did not object to the new developments Raymond Burr gradually incorporated into Mason's characterization and career. Gardner realized that "a formula's success lay in its accommodation of variation," and while "riding herd" by insisting on fidelity to the novels' central pattern, he saw that "invention was necessary to complement and complete" the formula's conventions (quoted in Bounds 113). In contrast to the edgy, laconic Mason of Gardner's novels, Burr's Mason of the early television series seems much more easygoing and approachable. In an interview Burr humbly claimed, "Sometimes I wish I had taken time to study law more thoroughly!" but Burr's co-star Barbara Hale felt that Burr's knowledge of law was "amazing" (quoted in Hill 171). Burr gave nearly 60 speeches before bar associations and received honorary law degrees from McGeorge College of Law and the University of New Mexico. His long time friend actor Charles Macaulay believed, "Raymond Burr really *was* Perry Mason. The two were one and the same. He was complicated, Byzantine . . . the more Byzantine it was, the more he liked it" (quoted in Bounds 157, italics in original).

Burr developed the character still more when he starred in the two-hour NBC telefilms. "I would give anything in the world if Erle Stanley Gardner could see the two-hour version," Raymond Burr said in 1985. ". . . At least he could have seen the fullness of the character as it was done thirty years later" (quoted in Hill 171). Older and wiser, Mason as an appellate court judge took on and deflated the kind of unscrupulous attorney viewers had come to suspect and even revile. While making these telefilms, Burr was battling the kidney cancer that eventually killed him, but he nevertheless made those films, like the *Perry Mason* series, indisputably his own.

Perry Mason's Strengths

Raymond Burr accurately analyzed Gardner's refusal to describe Mason in detail as one of the character's greatest strengths: "Erle wanted to leave these characters up to the reading audience's imagination and [that is] why the Perry Mason character has worked after thirty years. The audience *can* visualize an older man still doing his job and even becoming a judge! What people were after in 'Perry Mason' was the dream becoming a reality; to the *allure* of nostalgia" (quoted in Hill 171, italics in original). The chief strength of Gardner's fictional Mason and Burr's two-television portrayals is their ability to create and reinforce a dream, not a suspension of disbelief but a wholehearted belief in the power of the law as wielded by a hard-boiled knight-errant hero who follows his own moral principles and code of justice rather than the values of his culture. As "an officer of the court with an institutional responsibility to the laws of the land" (Leitch 11), Gardner's fictional Perry Mason talks as fast as any hard-boiled pulp detective, but his mind flies as swiftly as his fists do when necessary. For Mason, every legal loophole is fair game, so he can lie to the police, conceal evidence or clients, and use narrowly legal grounds to outflank the district attorney—just what readers wanted in a defense attorney.

Perry Mason is widely said to have shaped American attitudes toward the law. Raymond Burr's first Perry Mason arrived when real-life lawyers were starting to gather headlines, like Boston attorney Joseph N. Welch who effectively defanged Senator Joseph McCarthy in the 1954 Army-McCarthy hearings and became so well known he was later chosen to play "Judge Weaver" in the 1958 film version of Robert Travers's *Anatomy of a Murder*. *Perry Mason* mostly takes place in "the most ritualized space in television," a courtroom, because the opposing attorneys, like boxers in a ring, must fight out their conflict with "the most severe decorum," even to the death, if the case involves a capital crime (Leitch 27–28). Mason takes control immediately and dominates every scene, and whether or not he is actually in court, he always has the last word. He heads an idealized "family"—his loyal secretary Della Street as a "quasi-wife," and his legman Paul Drake as a "quasi-son"—that balances the corrupt or weakened "family" group of villains responsible for the crime. This paterfamilias image becomes even more powerful when Mason is an appellate court judge in the later telefilms.

The earlier television Perry Mason embodied a popular wish-fulfillment: the legal champion who personifies everything that is good, true, and just in the law, "incarnating the irresistibly appealing myth that moral justice, truth, and the law are congruent" (Leitch 74), but by 1985, when the first two-hour telefilm *Perry Mason Returns* arrived, the world seemed infinitely more dangerous than in those relatively innocent 1930s when Gardner was gestating "Perry Mason." Race riots, anti-war protests, and drug problems rocked the country after Watergate had engendered widespread and profound suspicion of lawyers. The elderly Mason, played by Burr not as a discoverer of truth but as a courtly sage, a stabilizing hero with conventionally dramatic emotions, became "the pole star in a fallen world," satisfying the audience's nostalgia for "the good old days when lawyers were all as trustworthy as judges, or as Perry Mason" (Leitch 88–89, 96).

Perry Mason's Adversaries

Just as the character Perry Mason appears as three successive lawyer-heroes, Mason's chief adversary Hamilton Burger displays three successive views of functionaries in the American judicial system. In Gardner's 1935 fiction, the bear-like Hamilton Burger, a newly elected District Attorney, struck Mason as "a square shooter. He wants to get convictions when he's certain he's prosecuting guilty people, but he doesn't want to convict innocent ones" (quoted in Van Dover 72). By the 1950s, though, open warfare had broken out between Mason and Burger, and the very sight of Mason often drives Burger near apoplexy, probably because despite his reputation as a good DA, he never successfully prosecuted a case against Mason. (In *The Case of the Terrified Typist*, Burger did convince the jury to find Mason's client guilty, but Mason had the decision reversed before the story ended.)

In the *Perry Mason* series, William Talman, an actor with self-inflicted troubles in his private life, played Burger. Gardner described Talman as "a wonder," because he actually looked as if he expected to win a case. Talman himself felt he knew more about Burger than Gardner did, claiming Gardner had presented Burger "as the most loathsome of prosecutors . . . the prototype of the loud, blustering sorehead" while he, Talman, gave Burger added dimensions (quoted in Kelleher and Merrill 67–70), going beyond temper tantrums to refreshing chumminess with Mason in a hunting lodge during *The Case of the Prudent Prosecutor.* After Talman's death from cancer in 1968, David Ogden Stiers took over as Mason's courtroom adversary in the telefilm *The Case of the Notorious Nun* (1986).

Perry Mason's clients were usually arrested by the LAPD's impatient, nervous Lt. Arthur Tragg, a slim, sophisticated bachelor first appearing in the 1940 novel *The Case of the Silent Partner,* replacing the bribe-taking cop Sidney Drumm of *The Case of the Velvet Claws* and the stereotypically brutal Sgt. Holcomb who lasted through the 1930s. From 1948 on, Tragg headed the LAPD's Homicide Bureau; he and Mason opposed one another, but they avoided the emotional antagonism sparking the conflicts between Mason and the volatile Hamilton Burger, remaining friendly enemies for three decades. Mason respected Tragg as "a live wire" and "a clever, fast thinker," and Tragg reciprocated, declaring Mason "has done more to solve murders than any man on the force" (quoted in *Private Lives* 137). Veteran actor Ray Collins played Lt. Tragg as an all-business thorn in Mason's side in the *Perry Mason* series, "the only person who occasionally addressed Perry by his last name, spoken with a mixture of malice and respect" (Kelleher and Merrill 77). When emphysema forced Collins to leave the series in 1963, Wesley Lau played the easygoing introvert Lt. "Andy" Anderson in the 1964 to 1965 season, succeeded by Richard Anderson as Lt. Steve Drumm, "a cross between the hard-hitting Tragg and the affable Anderson" and "a perfect second banana to Tragg" (Kelleher and Merrill 79).

Perry Mason's Romantic Interest?

Gardner based Della Street, "the most famous secretary in fiction," about 15 years younger than Mason, on Gardner's faithful secretaries, the Walter sisters, especially Jean, whom he married in 1968. From a family who lost their fortune during the Depression, Della is unquestioningly loyal through all Mason's cases and deeply in love with him, but nonetheless she refused all five of Mason's separate marriage proposals because he wouldn't permit a wife to work. As a dedicated career woman, she once told him, "You're not the marrying kind. I don't think you need a wife, but I know damn well you need a secretary who's willing to go to jail occasionally to back your play" (quoted in Penzler 135). Gardner conceived of Della as "dependable" and "easy on the eyes" (*Screaming Woman,* in *Seven Complete Novels* 403), "'saucy, tough, independent, and forever 'straightening the seams of her stockings'" (quoted in Kelleher and Merrill 54), but the *Perry Mason* series never showed her dating, instead hinting at a romantic involvement with Mason that Raymond Burr, for one, denied: "Funny the ideas people get. . . . They [Mason and Della] have a normal man-woman relationship. And that is many things to many people." Gardner concurred: "If [Perry] married Della, he would lose his sex appeal. . . . Those who want Della to sleep with

Barbara Hale played Della Street through both the *Perry Mason* series and all
the telefilms except for the last, non-Mason one, where she made only a
brief cameo appearance.

Perry are the ones who are afraid she isn't [and] those who think she
shouldn't are the ones who are certain she is. . . . if Perry and Della ever
have a romance, I'd write about it" (quoted in Kelleher and Merrill 54–55).
The only kiss on the lips Della and Mason shared came in 1993, not long
before Raymond Burr's death. Barbara Hale, the only actress to play Della
Street, won an Emmy for Best Supporting Actress in a Dramatic Series for
1958, and Raymond Burr named a rare orchid he developed for her.

Perry Mason's Associates

If Della Street was Perry Mason's "quasi-wife," Paul Drake, whose detective
agency down the hall from Mason's owed about three-fourths of its business to
investigating Mason's cases, was the lawyer's "quasi-son." Based on Gardner's
friend and ranch manager lanky cowboy Sam Hicks, who was "everything Erle
would have liked to have been in his youth" and what Gardner would have
liked in a son (Hughes 183), young, good-looking Paul Drake constantly and
fruitlessly flirted with Della. Drake lived on gulped hamburgers and consequent stomach remedies because of the peculiar working conditions Mason's
cases demanded. Drake never replaced the girl who dumped him in his youth,
and he tended to be overly pessimistic and superstitious. William Hopper, the
son of Hollywood gossip columnist Hedda Hopper, took on a variety of street-
smart detective roles doing the dirty work on *Perry Mason*—"the careful investigator, the duke-it-out-tough guy, the ladies' man, and the hipster . . . the fall
guy, the strikeout artist, the 'eating machine,' and the 'big kid,'" giving the
show much of its comic relief (Kelleher and Merrill 61), always rushing into
court at the last moment to give Mason the crucial shred of evidence Mason
needed to save his client. Hopper's Paul Drake had an eye for the ladies, but
his sex life was as mysterious as Della's and Mason's, though he must have
found the right girl eventually, since in "Perry Mason Returns," Paul Drake,
Jr., played by William Katt, Barbara Hale's son, helped Mason save Della from
being framed for murder. In the telefilms, Katt was replaced by William R.
Moses, playing graduating law student Ken Malansky, meant to appeal to
younger audiences, but he appeared "too raffish, cublike, and transparently
sincere" (Leitch 90).

Since the Mason–Della–Drake combination carried both the novels and
the television versions, Mason did not need other supporting players, only
his long-lasting receptionist Gertrude ("Gertie") Lade, hired in 1939, and a
few short-duration law clerks.

PERRY MASON'S ENDURING APPEAL AND PLACE IN POPULAR CULTURE

Much of Perry Mason's appeal stems from the human love of puzzles, but on a deeper level, Erle Stanley Gardner and Raymond Burr successively developed images of "America's lawyer" that mirrored the evolution of what Americans wanted to believe about "liberty and justice for all." Into his fictional Perry Mason, Gardner incorporated his own concern for the underdog Chinese immigrants he defended in Oxnard and his "last resort" defense of clients he felt deserved their day in court, giving his readers, just emerging from the Depression, what they wished for and felt they deserved, a Robin Hood attorney who protected the weak and enjoyed skewering their wealthy and powerful oppressors—even if those belonged to the legal establishment. Through Perry Mason and the Court of Last Resort, Gardner fueled this idealistic vision of American law in America, which coincided with his public's generally favorable opinion of American law and lawyers throughout World War II and the early 1950s. After the tumult of the 1960s and the Watergate scandal, however, Raymond Burr's subtle deepening of Perry Mason's characterization responded to citizens' skepticism about unscrupulous lawyers by demolishing every single opponent he faced in his television courtroom. Returning two decades later in the two-hour telefilms after yet more disillusion toward the legal profession had set in, the elderly Perry Mason represented those nostalgic "good old days" Americans longed for but could never recapture.

Two Major Effects on U.S. State Jurisprudence

Perry Mason has had two major effects on U.S. state jurisprudence. In 1999 Colorado granted jurors the freedom to question lawyers during a civil trial, "to buck jurisprudence tradition and elevate jurors' role from passive observer to active participant" (Lloyd 3). That year, a National Center for the State Courts found that 58 percent of Americans believed they could represent themselves (pro se cases), making contact between the courts and individuals more direct, for better or worse (Chinni 1).

Law as Perry Mason practices it has never been seen outside of books and television. It rests on three assumptions: that his clients are invariably innocent; that the truth shall set us free; and that the law itself is "transcendental, immutable, and accountable to a power beyond the reach of politicians, advertisers and mischievous citizens" (Leitch 53–57). Today's attorneys as a group seem to feel that legal television shows have blurred fact and reality, making them feel pressured to live up to the images and expectations evoked by movies and television. The National Association of County and

Prosecuting Attorneys complained that Perry Mason and his imitators had prejudiced real-life juries against prosecutors and led them to expect dramatic courtroom confessions (Kelleher and Merrill 22). A decade after Burr's death, "law professors . . . still exhort their students not to adopt Perry Mason as their presumptive model for legal procedures and professional ethics" (Leitch 53), and Jack King, staff attorney for the National Association of Criminal Defense Lawyers, believes that "Since 'Perry Mason' we've been having to compare ourselves" to him (Dribben). Like most realities pitted against idealistic dream, the actual suffers by comparison.

Fictional Bows to Gardner

The most obvious recent fictional bow to Erle Stanley Gardner is Susan Kandel's *I Dreamed I Married Perry Mason* (New York: William Morrow, 2004), starring woman mystery author Cece Caruso. The Gardner Estate chose Thomas Chastain to write two new Perry Mason mysteries, *The Case of Too Many Murders* and *The Case of the Burning Bequest* (both 1989). Mike Ashley's *Mammoth Encyclopedia of Modern Crime Fiction* (2002) listed 37 authors writing legal-related crime fiction, including best-selling authors Michael Gilbert, John Grisham, Ed McBain, Richard North Patterson, and Scott Turow.

By the 1990s, legal crime novels had dramatically proliferated. Whether such novels "are used to attack the legal system, to defend it, or merely to depict it in all its bewildering variety, the inherent drama of adversarial give-and-take will keep the category vital for years to come" (Winks 11–14). In Gardner's novels, Mason used the law against the law, while in the television series, Mason "conflates not only the roles of tireless advocate and officer of the court but the roles of defender of the innocent and scourge of the guilty," so that Mason "as the legal champion who personifies everything that is good, true, and just in the law . . . ultimately vindicates the legal system itself, incarnating the irresistibly appealing myth that moral justice, truth and the law are congruent" (Leitch 74). One reason the Perry Mason myth has proved so indestructible is because, as contemporary lawyer-author Scott Turow points out, it offers "a childlike delight in the surprise and in a plot as a revelation of character . . . the significant turn of the plot ends up deepening your understanding of somebody and what they had at stake in the situation" (McCrum 16). Even more attractive, like every heroic archetype, the myth of lawyer-detective Perry Mason that compassionate Erle Stanley Gardner outlined and generous Raymond Burr fleshed out satisfies, comforts, and reassures us—even if we know it only rarely, if ever, can come true.

I have never stuck up for a criminal. I have merely asked for the orderly administration of an impartial justice.

—Perry Mason to Lt. Tragg

PARALLEL CHRONOLOGY

Major Events Related to Perry Mason	World Events
	1880s Detective stories became prevalent in American "dime novels" with early sleuth Nick Carter
	1882 Chinese Exclusion Act passed, suspending Chinese immigration
	1884 *A Study in Scarlet* published
July 27, 1889 Erle Stanley Gardner born in Malden, Massachusetts	
1896–1908 Three novels about unscrupulous lawyer Randolph Mason published by Melville Davisson Post	**1896** Beginning of "the pulps"
1899 Gardner family moves to California	
1902 The Gardners move to Oroville, CA	**1902** Chinese Exclusion Act made permanent
	1905 First purpose-built movie theater
1906 Erle is suspended from high school	
1909 Gardner attended Valparaiso (IN) University Law School for 3 or 4 weeks	
1911 Gardner admitted to California bar; joins I.W. Stewart's Law Office	
1911–1916 Gardner practices law at Oxnard	
1912 Gardner marries Natalie Talbert	
	ca. 1914 Decline of dime novels and rise of "the pulps"
1915 Gardner and Natalie move to Ventura	**1914–1918** World War I
1916 Gardner forms law firm, Orr & Gardner	
May 17, 1917 Raymond Burr born	
1918–1921 Gardner is President, Consolidated Sales Co.	
	1918–1939 Heyday of "the pulps"
	1920–1933 Prohibition under the Volstead Act
1921 Gardner's first fiction sale, "Nellie's Naughty Nightie" under pen name; rejoins Orr Firm; admitted to Ventura bar	

Major Events Related to Perry Mason	World Events
1921–1933 Gardner practiced law at Ventura, CA	
1924 Gardner's first appearance in *Black Mask* under his own name	**1924** Immigration Bill limits immigration
1926 *Black Mask* editor suggests Post's Randolph Mason as model to Gardner	
1926–1933 Gardner writes prolifically for pulps under various names	
	1927 Lindbergh flies Atlantic nonstop
	1928 Disney introduces Mickey Mouse
	1929 U.S. stock market crash
	1929–1939 Great Depression
1931 Gardner and wife study Chinese with daughter of a Canton Mandarin family; visit China	
1932 Gardner practicing law only part time	
1933 First Perry Mason novel published, *The Case of the Velvet Claws;* Gardner all but gives up law to write; sees Raymond Chandler's work in *Black Mask*	**1933** The "Hundred Days" gets New Deal working; Hitler becomes Chancellor of Germany
1934 Gardner and Chandler begin lifelong friendship	
1934–1937 Warner Bros. produces 6 Perry Mason films; Gardner hates them	
1934 Gardner's German Shepherd Rip finds 150-acre Temecula ranch site for Gardner; Natalie and Gardner begin amicable separation	
1937–1949 Gardner publishes 9 "Doug Selby" mysteries	
1939 Gardner adopts pseudonym "A. A. Fair" for 29 Donald Lam-Bertha Cool novels published 1939–1970; Gardner works at MGM	**1939–1945** World War II
1940 Gardner leaves law practice	
1941 Gardner begins 27-year association with agent Willis Wing	
1943–1955 CBS runs Perry Mason radio series	
1944 Gardner sells 1 million copies of *The Case of the Curious Bride*	

(Continued)

Major Events Related to Perry Mason	World Events
	1945 U.S. drops first atomic bombs on Hiroshima and Nagasaki
	1946 Churchill delivers "Iron Curtain" speech
	1946–1980s Cold War period
1947 Gardner proclaimed "most popular whoduniter of his time" by *Golden Multitude: The Story of Best Sellers in the United States*	
1948–1960 Gardner founds and works with Court of Last Resort	
	1950–1953 Korean conflict; in 1950s television reaches nearly every home in the U.S.
1951 American Bar Assn. appoints committee to work with Court of Last Resort	
1952 Gardner publishes *The Court of Last Resort*	**1952** U.S. Supreme Court limits presidential powers
1954 Gardner reaches $50 million total sales	**1954** Supreme Court declares racial segregation unconstitutional
	1955 Supreme Court decrees integration of all public schools; black teenager Emmett Till murdered in Mississippi; Rosa Parks refuses to give up seat on segregated Atlanta bus, begins Atlanta Bus Boycott
	1957 USSR launches *Sputnik;* announce ICBMs
1957–1966 Gardner is consultant and editor, *Perry Mason* television show	
	1960 "Sit-ins" spread across U.S. South; John F. Kennedy wins presidency
	1961 Bay of Pigs invasion of Cuba
	1962 Cuban Missile Crisis; U.S. use of Agent Orange in Vietnam
	1963 John F. Kennedy assassinated; major civil rights activities, including the March on Washington and Martin Luther King's "I Have a Dream" speech; Betty Friedan publishes *The Feminine Mystique*
	1964 Radical U.S. Civil Rights Bill; Berkeley Free Speech Movement galvanizes student protests
	1965 U.S. Voting Rights Bill; U.S. begins bombing of North Vietnam;

Major Events Related to Perry Mason	World Events
	Medicare Bill signed; Voting Rights Act signed; Immigration Act replaces quotas; Watts riots break out; oral contraceptives become widely available; birth of rock music; Vietnam protests increase dramatically
Feb. 26, 1968 Gardner's wife Natalie dies; Gardner marries Jean Walter on Aug. 7, 1968	**1968** Martin Luther King, Jr. and Robert Kennedy are assassinated
	1969 President Nixon announces first withdrawal from Vietnam; Gay Liberation Front created; Neil Armstrong is first man to walk on the moon
Feb. 11, 1970 Gardner dies in Temecula, California	
	1971 Twenty-sixth Amendment lowers voting age to 18
1972 Nicaragua issues postage stamp in honor of Perry Mason	
1973–1974 CBS airs *The New Adventures of Perry Mason*	**1973** Supreme Court ruling on *Roe v. Wade* allows first trimester abortion; U.S. Vietnam involvement ends; Watergate burglars convicted and scandal erupts
	1974 Richard Nixon resigns presidency; Freedom of Information Act passes
	1977 Supreme Court rules capital punishment permitted by Constitution
1979 Mason novels have sold 310,910,603 copies and have been translated into 23 languages including Tamil and Urdu, a still-standing Guinness World Record	
1985–1993 Perry Mason TV Movies by NBC	
1993–1995 Four NBC telefilms with Mason "absent," each called *A Perry Mason Mystery*	
1995 Gardner's law office building declared a historical point of interest by the city of Ventura, CA	
2006 Continuing DVD release of 1957–1966 *Perry Mason* episodes	
2008 DVD release of the *Perry Mason 50th Anniversary Collection*	

THE PERRY MASON MYSTERIES: A SAMPLING

Note: Except as specified, all were published by William Morrow, New York.

The Case of the Velvet Claws (1933)
The Case of the Counterfeit Eye (1935)
The Case of the Perjured Parrot (1939)
The Case of the Rolling Bones (1939)
The Case of the Buried Clock (1943)
The Case of the Half-Wakened Wife (1945)
The Case of the Borrowed Brunette (1946)
The Case of the Dubious Bridegroom (1949)
The Case of the Glamorous Ghost (1955)
The Case of the Terrified Typist (1956)
The Case of the Screaming Woman (1957)
The Case of the Foot-Loose Doll (1958)
The Case of the Shapely Shadow (1960)
The Case of the Step-Daughter's Secret (1963)
The Case of the Beautiful Beggar (1965)
The Case of the Worried Waitress (1966)
The Case of the Fenced-in Woman 1972)
The Case of the Postponed Murder (1973)

Perry Mason Short Stories

The Case of the Murderer's Bride and Other Stories (1969)
The Case of the Crimson Kiss (1971)
The Case of the Crying Swallow, and Other Stories (1971)
The Case of the Irate Witness (1972)

Autobiographical Notes

The Color of Life

MEDIA ADAPTATIONS

Film

The Case of the Howling Dog (1934), starring Warren William; Warner Brothers
The Case of the Curious Bride (1935), starring Warren William; Warner Brothers

The Case of the Lucky Legs (1935), starring Warren William; Warner Brothers

The Case of the Velvet Claws (1936), starring Warren William; Warner Brothers

The Case of the Black Cat (1936) (based on *The Case of the Caretaker's Cat*), starring Ricardo Cortez; Warner Brothers

The Case of the Stuttering Bishop (1937), starring Donald Woods; Warner Brothers

Granny Get Your Gun (1940), loosely based on *The Case of the Dangerous Dowager* and not containing Perry Mason

Radio

A Perry Mason radio series 1943–1955, Columbia Broadcasting System

Comic Strip

Perry Mason Comic Strip, syndicated in the U.S. and Canada from October 16, 1950, to June 21, 1952

Poetry

Perry Mason inspired *The Whole Truth* (1986) by James Cummins, a book-length sestina collection.

Television

Perry Mason series (1957–1966), starring Raymond Burr; CBS; this series is now distributed by CBS Paramount Domestic Television and is still widely shown in local markets.

The New Adventures of Perry Mason (1973–1974), starring Monte Markham; CBS

Television Movies

(All starred Raymond Burr and Barbara Hale through 1993. All except where noted, were produced by CBS.)

Perry Mason Returns (1985) NBC

The Case of the Notorious Nun (1986)

The Case of the Shooting Star (1986)

The Case of the Lost Love (1987)

The Case of the Sinister Spirit (1987)

The Case of the Murdered Madam (1987)

The Case of the Scandalous Scoundrel (1987)

The Case of the Avenging Ace (1988)

The Case of the Lady in the Lake (1988)

The Case of the Lethal Lesson (1989)

The Case of the Musical Murder (1989)

The Case of the All-Star Assassin (1989)

The Case of the Poisoned Pen (1990)

The Case of the Desperate Deception (1990)

The Case of the Silenced Singer (1990)

The Case of the Defiant Daughter (1990)

The Case of the Ruthless Reporter (1991)

The Case of the Maligned Mobster (1991)

The Case of the Glass Coffin (1991)

The Case of the Fatal Fashion (1991)

The Case of the Fatal Framing (1992)

The Case of the Reckless Romeo 1992)

The Case of the Heartbroken Bride (1992)

The Case of the Skin-Deep Scandal (1992)

The Case of the Telltale Talk Show Host (1993)

The Case of the Killer Kiss (1993)

After Burr's death in 1993, four more Perry Mason telefilms were released. Mason was supposedly out of town, and his "friends" starred in them: Paul Sorvino played attorney Anthony Caruso in *The Case of the Wicked Wives*, followed by Hal Holbrook as attorney "Wild Bill" McKenzie in *The Case of the Lethal Lifestyle*, *The Case of the Grimacing Governor*, and *The Case of the Jealous Jokester*.

DVD Releases

Paramount/CBS Home Video is releasing the *Perry Mason* television series on DVD. Each episode is 53 minutes long, compared to today's 43 minutes for a one-hour TV show. Season I, Volume I, was released in July 2006 (first 19 episodes); Season I, Volume 2, was released in November 2006 (remaining 20 episodes); and Season 2, Volume 1, was released on June 19, 2007 (15 episodes). *The Perry Mason 50th Anniversary Edition* (2008), containing 12 episodes from the television series' nine-year run, also offers new interviews and archival footage, the *Perry Mason Returns* telefilm, and an Erle Stanley Gardner featurette.

ARCHIVES

The University of Texas' Humanities Research Center houses the Erle Stanley Gardner Collection of more than 38 million items, including manuscripts, papers, charts, lists, notes, correspondence, notebooks, and unpublished speeches. In 1970 Gardner's study, where he wrote most of his books, was reassembled on the fourth floor of the University's Academic Center.

Raymond Burr donated some of his *Perry Mason* scripts to the McGeorge School of Law.

GARDNER'S COMMENTARIES ON WRITING

The following is a chronological selection:

"An Author Looks at Agents," *American Fiction Guild Bulletin*, February 15, 1935.

"The Coming Fiction Trend," *Writer's Digest*, September 1936.

"Erle Stanley Gardner Claims Mystery Readers Best Detectives," *The Pocket Bookseller*, September 1944.

"The Case of the Early Beginning." In *The Art of the Mystery Story*, edited by Howard Haycraft. New York: Simon and Schuster, 1946.

"How I Came to Create Perry Mason," *The Listener*, April 12, 1948.

"The Many Meanings an 'Escape' Novel Holds for Its Many Readers," *New York Herald Tribune*, January 18, 1959.

"Who Is Perry Mason?" *Chicago Daily News*, October 2, 1965.

WORKS CITED

Bounds, J. Dennis. *Perry Mason: The Authorship and Reproduction of a Popular Hero*. Westport, CT: Greenwood Press, 1996.

Chinni, Dante. "More Americans Want to Be Their Own Perry Mason." *Christian Science Monitor* 93 (August 20, 2001): 1.

Dribben, Melissa. "Jurors Influenced by TV Shows Demanding Prime-Time-Style Evidence," *Philadelphia Inquirer*, February 19, 2006.

Fugate, Francis L., and Roberta B. Fugate. *Secrets of the World's Best-Selling Writer: The Story-Telling Techniques of Erle Stanley Gardner*. New York: Morrow, 1980.

Gardner, Erle Stanley. *Perry Mason: Seven Complete Novellas of Erle Stanley Gardner*. New York: Avenel, 1979.

Herbert, Rosemary. *Whodunit? A Who's Who in Crime and Mystery Writing*. New York: Oxford University Press, 1999.

Hill, Ona L. *Raymond Burr*. Jefferson, NC: McFarland, 1999.

Hughes, Dorothy B. *Erle Stanley Gardner: The Case of the Real Perry Mason.* New York: Morrow, 1978.

Johnson, Alva. *The Case of Erle Stanley Gardner.* New York: Morrow, 1947.

Kelleher, Brian, and Diana Merrill. *The Perry Mason Show Book.* New York: St. Martin's Press, 1987.

Leitch, Thomas. *Perry Mason.* TV Milestones Series, 2005.

Lloyd, Jillian. "More States Let Jurors Play Perry Mason." *Christian Science Monitor* 91 (May 4, 1999): 3.

McCrum, Robert. "To Hell with Perry Mason" (Interview with author Scott Turow), *The Observer,* November 24, 2002.

Meyers, Richard. *TV Detectives.* San Diego: A.S. Barnes & Company., 1981.

Murphy, Bruce F. *The Encyclopedia of Murder and Mystery.* New York: St. Martin's Press, 1999.

Penzler, Otto. *The Private Lives of Private Eyes, Crimefighters, and Other Good Guys.* New York: Grosset & Dunlap, 1977.

Senate, Richard L. *Erle Stanley Gardner's Ventura: The Birthplace of Perry Mason.* Ventura, CA: Charon Press, 1996.

Spigel, Lynn. *Make Room for TV.* Chicago, IL: University of Chicago Press, 1992.

Van Dover, Kenneth. *Murder in the Millions.* New York: Continuum International, 1984.

Whitney, Dwight. "Pleading His Own Case." *TV Guide: The First 25 Years,* ed. Jay S. Harris. New York: Simon & Schuster, 1978.

Winks, Robin W., ed. *Mystery and Suspense Writers: The Literature of Crime, Detection, and Espionage.* New York: Scribner's, 1998.

FURTHER READING

Belleranti, Guy. "Perry Mason: King of the Courtroom. http://www/loti.com/fifties_TV/perry_mason.htm.

Gardner, Erle Stanley. *The Case of the Counterfeit Eye.* New York: Morrow, 1935.

———. *Host with the Big Hat.* New York: Morrow, 1869.

Kandel, Susan. *I Dreamed I Married Perry Mason.* New York: Morrow, 2004.

Martindale, David. *The Perry Mason Case Book.* New York: Pioneer, 1991.

Meyers, Richard. *TV Detectives.* San Diego: A.S. Barnes, 1981.

Mott, Frank L. *Golden Multitudes.* New York: Macmillan, 1947.

Mundell, E.H. *Erle Stanley Gardner: A Checklist.* Kent, OH: Kent State University Press, 1969.

NPR. "Present at the Creation: Perry Mason." http://www.npr.org/programs/morning/features/patc/perrymason/index.html.

WEB SITES

http://www.perrymasontvseries.com (Lists many links to Perry Mason sites)

http://www.mysterynet.com/tv/profiles/perrymason/

http://www.perrmasontvshowbook.com/

http://www.comics.org/series.lasso?seriesid=1631 (Perry Mason at the Museum of Broadcast Communications Encyclopedia of Television)

Edgar Allan Poe. Courtesy of the Library of Congress.

Edgar Allan Poe:
The Father of
Detective Fiction

I become insane, with long intervals of horrible sanity.

—Edgar Allan Poe

A half century after Edgar Allan Poe's death, Arthur Conan Doyle hailed Poe as "the father of the detective story" (quoted in Matthews 287). Today most mystery historians agree that Poe established "an astonishing number" of the genre's conventions that mystery writers are still successfully following and adapting (Daniel Hoffman, in Herbert 153). Only a handful of Poe's over 60 pieces of short fiction can be classified as "mystery stories," and only three of those feature a detective, but both Poe and later literary historians recognized that, as he himself put it in 1846, "These tales of

Conventions of Detective Fiction Established by Poe

The Genius Detective

Unnamed Prosaic Narrator to Highlight Genius Detective

The Locked Room Mystery

A Wronged Suspect

Inept and Bungling Policemen

Sleight-of-Hand Placement of Clues

Metropolitan Setting

Top 10 Books Inspired by Poe

According to Matthew Pearl, author of *The Poe Shadow* and editor of *The Murders in the Rue Morgue: The Dupin Tales* (http://www.books.guardian.co.uk), the top 10 are:

1. *Poe Poe Poe Poe* by poet Daniel Hoffman
2. *Labyrinths: Selected Stories* by Argentinian poet, critic, and short story author Jorge Luis Borges
3. The Sherlock Holmes stories by Arthur Conan Doyle
4. *Ghost Story* by Peter Straub
5. *An Antarctic Mystery* by Jules Verne
6. *The Afterlife of Poe* by Scott Peeples
7. *Portraits of Poe* by Michael Deas
8. *The Pale Blue Eye* by Louis Bayard and *The American Boy* by Andrew Taylor
9. *Portnoy's Complaint* by Philip Roth
10. *The Goldbug Variations* by Richard Powers

ratiocination [deduction used to solve a mystery] owe most of their popularity to being something in a new key" (quoted in Rachman 54). Although Poe's literary reputation rests largely on his development of the short story form, his often macabre poetry, and his critical theory, his innovations as the inventor of the modern detective story have influenced almost every practitioner of the genre, from Doyle through Chesterton and Christie to hard-boiled American private eyes, elegant British psychological analysts like P.D. James, and the Argentinian magical realist Jorge Luis Borges. From an intensely troubled personality torn between the haunted Poe and the rational Poe, those innovations sprang, producing the detective genre and ensuring its continuing popularity: "Poe's focus on the gruesome nature of crimes—and the intellectual triumph in their solution—opened a door for readers to approach their fears and fascinations about crime and death" ("Murder at Harvard").

HISTORICAL/CULTURAL CONTEXT

Poe's life (1809 to 1849), roughly the first half of the 19th century, followed the fledgling United States from the aftermath of the Revolution to the gathering clouds of the Civil War. During this period the United States experienced profound growing pains: wars with Great Britain and Mexico; floods of immigrants from Europe; settlement of vast new territories; and industrial, economic, and technological revolutions. The War of 1812 shook off British bullying and allowed Americans to drive Native Americans from the Northeast; American shipping brought home the benefits of increased international trade. Roads, canals, and railway systems began to unify the country and encouraged towns to spring up along their routes, which eventually extended throughout the vast 828-million-square-mile Louisiana Purchase acquired in 1803. At only 4 million in 1790, the U.S. population grew phenomenally, increasing by over 30 percent in each of the next six decades to reach 23 million in 1850, just after the 1848 Mexican War had increased U.S. territory by another 919 million square miles. Even before the 1840s Potato Famine, over a third of the new U.S. citizens had come from Ireland, but eventually German immigrants overtook the Irish.

Although today it seems tragically short, Poe's lifetime matched the early 19th century's 40-year American life expectancy. Besides the hazards of frontier life which accompanied westward expansion, crowding and poor sanitation in eastern cities fueled epidemics of cholera, smallpox, measles, diphtheria, and tuberculosis; even ordinary diarrhea could be lethal with about one out of four American babies dying in infancy. Crime festered in the cities, too. As recorded in the *Memoirs* of real-life French police detective Eugène François Vidocq who in 1812 modeled the Sûreté (the criminal investigation bureau of the Paris police) on Napoleon's political police, European criminals were generally traced through volunteer witnesses until the bloody aftermath of the French Revolution, when urban populations began to demand professional police forces to maintain law and order. Members of the Sûreté, originally mostly reformed criminals like Vidocq himself, worked undercover, and by 1820 had become a 30-member team of experts that decreased the Parisian crime rate by 40 percent. (As the ancestor of Paris's present *Direction centrale de la police judiciaire,* today's Sûreté functions as France's national command and control organization and no longer employs staff detectives.) In 1829, Britain created Scotland Yard, the world's first Metropolitan Police Criminal Investigation Division, and New York followed suit in 1844, a year after the first appearance of the word "detective" in the English language. Boston, where Poe was born, hired its first official police detectives in 1846, becoming "one of the first American cities to realize the value of hands-on 'detection' of criminal activity" ("Murder at Harvard").

Notable First Members of the Sûreté

Eugène François Vidocq, founder and first chief

Sergeant Rioux

Fouche, a powerful and fearless person

Goury, a former swindler

Aube, a former forger

Coco Lacour, a sneak thief

Mystery historians often link the rise of detective fiction to sociological stresses. Bruce Murphy has remarked that the detective novel's popularity parallels the industrial revolution, because "heightened anonymity, social insecurity, and urban poverty are fertilizer for criminality" (x). During the 19th century, the U.S. population growth, spurred by industrialization and immigration, increased the hazards of everyday life, and after law-abiding citizens began to demand police protection from increasing urban violence, writers began to produce stories about a detective who might offer such protection. Poe was the first, but soon he had a host of followers.

A deep-seated psychological reason for the 19th century's growing interest in crime and detective fiction also exists. In her 1928 Introduction to *The Omnibus of Crime,* often hailed as "the finest single piece of writing about the detective story" (Hone 56), Golden Age mystery writer Dorothy L. Sayers traced the development of the genre to the Aristotelian unity of beginning, middle, and end, arguing that "the art of self-tormenting" by any kind of mystery "made to be solved" was a basic human need that transcended the desire for simple amusement" (Sayers, *Omnibus* 72), a human emotional-psychological need for consolation that a solution could exist for even the most perplexing problem in the most uncertain world. More recent commentators observe that the mystery story, which reveals fundamental human weaknesses, can also be seen as archetypal, suggesting the myth of Oedipus and even the Fall of Mankind, making readers aware of their own "intimate knowledge of the archetypal tempter and . . . [their] horrified fascination with the fallen" (Murphy xi), as illustrated metaphorically by Leo Perutz in *Master of the Day of Judgment:* ". . . we have a terrible enemy inside us. He lies there motionless, asleep, as if he were dead. Woe if he comes back to life" (quoted in Murphy xi). Few authors have been as woefully afflicted by that "terrible enemy" as Edgar Allan Poe, for according to Ross Macdonald, Poe drew his inspiration from "his own tell-tale heart . . . [and] invented the detective story in order to grasp and objectify the nature of the evil, and somehow place the guilt" (quoted in Murphy 395).

> *All religion, my friend, is simply evolved out of fraud, fear, greed, imagination, or poetry.*
>
> —Poe

AUTHORSHIP

Edgar Poe was born January 19, 1809, to actress Elizabeth Arnold Poe and David Poe, a failed alcoholic actor who two years after Poe's birth abandoned his wife and three children. Shortly afterward, Elizabeth wasted away from tuberculosis in Richmond, Virginia, and merchant John Allan, at his childless wife Frances's urging, took Poe into their home but never adopted him. Poe went to England with the Allans and attended English boarding schools from 1815 to 1820. He took "Allan" as his middle name, and after they returned to America, Allan sent him to the University of Virginia in 1826 on a meager allowance, expecting Poe eventually to join his business, but Poe suffered several major disappointments there. The family of Sarah Elmira Royster, to whom Poe had become secretly engaged, bitterly opposed their romance, and as a relatively poor boy among wealthy classmates, Poe went badly into debt for tailoring and gambling; Allan refused to pay Poe's bills and withdrew Poe from the University to work in Allan's counting house. Allan had no respect or sympathy for Poe's literary ambitions, either, and in 1827 they parted so unpleasantly that Poe left for Boston and thereafter used only the middle initial "A" when signing his name. Rumors suggesting "the haunted" Poe began to circulate about Poe's drinking problem at this time, but recent scholarship suggests that he may have had an abnormal sensitivity to alcohol, especially wine. That May, Poe enlisted in the U.S. Army, just before his first poetry collection, *Tamerlane and Other Poems,* appeared anonymously in June.

On her deathbed in 1828, Frances Allan begged her husband to help Poe win his release from the army, which Allan did in 1829 on condition Poe attend West Point. Allan remarried in 1830 and after he and Poe had another serious disagreement, Allan disowned Poe, who then got himself expelled from West Point for neglect of duties in 1831. Poe went to live first in New York and then in Baltimore, with his aunt Maria Clemm, whom he deeply loved as his second mother; he called her "Muddie," and called her young daughter Virginia "Sissy." John Allan died in 1834, leaving Poe nothing. Although he was virtually penniless, Poe liked to play the southern gentleman. From 1835, Poe eked out a scant living at a series of magazines, writing stories, poems, and over 300 book reviews, but because of his drinking he never stayed for long at any one job. The U.S. magazine culture in the 1830s and 1840s was turbulent; writers were poorly paid, and imitation, piracy, and plagiarism were rife. "Poe frequently contrived to sell magazines by courting controversy" (Rachman 55–56). He also attacked other literary figures in print, causing petty quarrels that injured his reputation for the rest of his life. Poe married Virginia Clemm in 1836 when she was 13, but no assurance exists that the marriage was ever consummated.

After his drinking had caused his dismissal from William Burton's *Gentleman's Magazine* in 1940, Poe suffered a total collapse. In his subsequent sobered-up "morning-after" condition, he resolved to "forswear the world of emotion for the sedater [sic] climes of reason" (Haycraft 13), and between 1840 and 1842, his most creative and financially successful period, "the rational Poe" edited *Graham's Gentleman's Magazine* in Philadelphia. He controlled his drinking and boosted the magazine's circulation from a modest 5,000 readers to an "unprecedented" 40,000, principally due to Poe's own writings, "of a uniformly higher standard and greater number than at any other point in his career," where he turned from "bathing insanely in hideous crime" to logically hunting it down (Haycraft 13). Well known at this time for being "an energetic, incisive, and caustic editor and critic" known as "the tomahawk man" (Rachman 55), Poe combined his interest in crime and his analytic delight in solving puzzles by creating "The Murders in the Rue Morgue," the world's first real detective story, and followed it with a few others that established "once and for all the mold and pattern for the thousands and thousands" of detective stories to follow (Haycraft 14).

In 1842, though, Virginia contracted tuberculosis, and Muddie and Poe brought her back to New York. Despite Poe's experimentation with short mystery stories, he did not receive any significant literary recognition until the publication of *The Raven and Other Poems* (1845, which brought him considerable acclaim though little income. "One could publish the most famous poem in America, have it reprinted in every paper in every city, and scarcely earn a dime off it" (Rachman 55); Poe's "wife, his aunt, and he himself were often near starvation" (Hoffman, in Herbert 152). Haunted by Virginia's illness, their poverty, and his lack of recognition, Poe plunged toward self-destruction. He savagely attacked 38 New York authors in a series of articles that ended in a libel suit and ruined his own reputation. He carried on "romances" with several other women while he was married to Virginia, who died in 1847, and after enduring "prostrate grief," Poe proposed to three women within the next few months (*Annotated Tales* xi). His last years were "a nightmare of poverty, disease, drink, and delusion" (Haycraft 14); in his entire life, Poe earned only $6,200 from his writing.

> *All that we see or seem, is but a dream within a dream.*
> —Poe

During an illness Poe suffered in 1847, the famous physician Dr. Valentine Mott diagnosed a "brain lesion" which may have produced Poe's manic-depressive behavior and his low tolerance for alcohol (Peithman xiv). Poe was experiencing "periods of instability and hallucination" that led him to attempt suicide in 1848, and on October 3, 1849, after five days which despite the best efforts of scholars still remain a mystery, he was found delirious and semiconscious in a Baltimore street near a tavern. He died in Washington College Hospital on October 7, 1849, from causes as yet undetermined, exclaiming "Lord help my poor soul" (Frank and Magistrale xxi).

The Lord may have helped Poe's soul, but did not save Poe's reputation from the "champion editor and compiler of his time" (Symons 161), Rufus Wilmot Griswold, named by Poe as his literary executor, even though he and Griswold had had severe disagreements. Poe had met Griswold, a licensed Baptist clergyman and literary journalist, in 1841, when Griswold was beginning his notable career as an anthologist. At first their relations were genial, but they soon deteriorated because of Poe's jealousy and Griswold's unproven allegations about Poe's drunkenness and use of opium, all of which Griswold based on second- or third-hand information. By the summer of 1843, Poe and Griswold were no longer speaking, and after Poe's death, Griswold viciously "set about to destroy Poe's reputation once and for all." In Griswold's pseudonymous *New York Daily Tribune* obituary of Poe, "every chance of personal denigration was taken" (Symons 155). Griswold declared Poe had "no friends and no faith in humanity," that Poe had been expelled from the University of Virginia, that he had deserted from the Army, that he had carried on an affair with John Allan's second wife, that he had wantonly plagiarized, and that he had been addicted to alcohol and possibly opium. Griswold's 1850 to 1856 edition of Poe's works include "wholesale forgery" in passages Griswold added in correspondence to show Poe's fawning admiration for him and to stress his kindness to Poe, forgeries that were not revealed until 1941. Due to Griswold's unscrupulous enmity, "The Poe legend was born" (Peithman xv).

POE'S LITERARY PRECURSORS

A commonplace of literary history insists that Edgar Allan Poe made a major contribution of "something new" to the development of the short story, but the theory of that "something" remained largely unexamined until after World War II, when scholars of American literature began to adapt principles of Russian formalism and French structuralism to the study of the genre of short fiction. Before exploring Poe's shaping of the genre, Charles May in 1991 traced the "progressive displacement [of short fiction] from the supernatural toward the natural" prior to Poe. In the Middle Ages, short narratives had typically recounted "episodic encounters" between primitive consciousness and the "sacred," like miracles or visions, but in his 14th century *Decameron*, Boccaccio made the short story realistic, dealing with everyday life governed by irony. In the 17th century, Cervantes developed characters in his *Exemplary Tales* who exist as if they are real, while in English short fiction between 1660 and 1700 an interest in psychological analysis and in verisimilitude began to appear.

Two literary movements that affected Poe profoundly paralleled the French Revolution of 1789 and the ensuing Reign of Terror in 1793. The Romantic Period in literature, 1780 to 1830, furnished ideas and ideals which gave rise to the slogan *Liberté, Egalité, Fraternité* and sparked the storming of the Bastille. Early Romantic writers rebelled against the dominant scientific view of the physical world, the emphasis on the material, and the "common sense" which had dominated the preceding Age of Reason. Instead, Romantics like the youthful William Wordsworth and Samuel Taylor Coleridge desired what Wordsworth called "something far more deeply infused" than what could be derived from ordinary observation. At the beginning of the Romantic Period, the development of the short story seems to have reversed itself, moving away from the realistic and back toward the supernatural or metaphysical, just as the poetry of Wordsworth and Coleridge presented "ordinary things" in "extraordinary ways" (May 9).

Coleridge as a young man had been inspired by the German Romantics, who as a group were fascinated with the narrator's role in short fiction. Ludwig Tieck, the leading German Romantic theorist of short fiction, also felt that the short story should be "strange and unique," but "seem commonplace" and objective in presentation (May 9). Tieck also believed that the short story should have a *Wendepunkt* (turning point) "from which it takes unexpectedly a completely different direction, and develops consequences which are nevertheless natural and entirely in keeping with characters and circumstances" (Tieck, quoted in May 9). All of these factors eventually appeared in Poe's short fiction.

Another reaction against 18th-century rationalism, the English craze for the Gothic—"the ancient, the primitive, the magical"—stemmed from pre-novelistic medieval romances, incorporating ancient ruins, beleaguered heroines, and ghostly apparitions into novels which began appearing in the late 1700s, especially Horace Walpole's immensely influential *The Castle of Otranto* (1764). After the ideals of the French Revolution had degenerated into the bloody Reign of Terror which then contributed to the rise of Napoleon Bonaparte, Gothic novels like Ann Radcliffe's *The Mysteries of Udolpho* (1794) and Matthew Gregory Lewis's notorious *The Monk* (1796) spurred the Romantic interest in nonrational experience, leading inward "to the exploration of a personal and social underworld." Such novels, usually taking place in sinister cobwebby medieval settings like run-down castles or convents, "employ lurid emotions, atmospheres of terror, and abounding horrors" exerted by sadistic villains over helpless heroines (Holman 244). Later, as Gothic novels gradually abandoned their quasi-medieval settings and stressed irrational emotions more sensationally, the term "Gothic" began to be used to express wickedness and guilt in a realistic setting, reaching literary high-water marks in Charles Dickens's novels and in Edgar Allan Poe's short fiction.

Poe, by all accounts a great reader, was well acquainted with Romantic literary theories, especially Coleridge's famous declaration in his *Biographia Literaria* (1817) that the imagination is a "shaping and modifying power of the mind" that "struggles to idealize and unify." Poe took the concept of artistic unity that Coleridge had adapted from the German Romantics as the "single unifying factor" of literature and made it the fundamental "something new" in all of his, Poe's, own work (May 11). "Unity," for Poe meant "a condition in which every portion of the work is indispensable for the structural completeness, symmetry, 'proportion,' or 'harmony' of the composition," and he repeatedly stressed "unity as the major formal aim of the 'skilful artist' in prose or verse" (quoted in Moldenhauer 285). Poe's critical theory of unity in fiction appears clearly in his 1842 Hawthorne review, where he declared that "Form and meaning emerge from the unity of the motifs of the story" (quoted in May 15). In addition, in "The Philosophy of Composition" (1846), he insisted that a short story should be studied beginning with its end, since a story cannot be told until after its events have occurred. In "Eureka: An Essay on the Material and Spiritual Universe" (1848), Poe broadened his theory of unity in fiction to the cosmic dimension, arguing that only God could achieve absolute unity, so that the author who strives for the perfect plot is attempting "absolute truth" in "perfect consistency"—the quintessence of "the rational Poe" and the central theme of all Poe's work (May 16).

As demonstrated in Poe's short fiction, his basic principle of unity required that the writer should create one and only one total psychological/spiritual effect on the reader, subordinating the plot to the calculated construction of "a single, intense mood in the reader's or listener's mind, be it melancholy, suspense, or horror." Thus as Poe mingled Romantic and Gothic elements in his short stories, he excluded subplots, digressions, and minor Characters. Fisher contends that by holding others to his own standards of absolute integrity in his texts which stimulated his readers' mental, emotional, and spiritual faculties, Poe established the rules and methods of the New Criticism, the leading school of 20th-century literary analysis, which insists that a literary text must be interpreted as self-contained apart from the critic's opinions of its author or the suitability of its themes (137).

Poe in his detective fiction concentrated on his superanalytical central figure August Dupin, often inaccurately identified with the 18th-century Paris policeman Eugène François Vidocq. Poe knew Vidocq's work and memoirs well and probably used Vidocq as his model for "Prefect G—," the intellectually challenged policeman introduced in "The Murders in the Rue Morgue," "too cunning to be profound" (*Annotated Tales* 223). In Dupin, "Poe hammers ceaselessly to drive home his acutely personalized thesis of the superiority of the talented amateur mind—meaning of course, his own" (Haycraft 14).

Despite, or perhaps because of, his insistence on unity in his literary work, however, not only Poe's personal life was "a mass of paradoxes" resulting from the clash between "the haunted" Poe and his rational self; many strange contradictions appear in his literary career as well, as enumerated in Steven Peithman's Introduction to *The Annotated Tales of Edgar Allan Poe* (xi). Though American, Poe set most of his stories outside the United States, and they often "seem alien to the American spirit." In France, he is widely considered a major literary figure, but American critics are divided between those who consider Poe a great writer and those who dismiss him as "merely a competent hack." His stories appear simple, but they can be interpreted in multiple ways. They have been treated as either autobiographical reflections of his own tormented psyche or as fictional psychological case histories. They may be Freudian or Jungian; Christian or existential; obscure or straightforward; romantic or classic. "Even after his death, Poe continues to puzzle and perplex" (Peithman xi).

Around 1840, when his rational self seemed uppermost, Poe's only socially significant story, "The Man of the Crowd," appeared, in which he began to probe "the type and the genius of deep crime" (Peithman 194). His reputation as an author of mystery fiction rests principally on the four short stories which followed: his three detective stories featuring C. Auguste Dupin: "The Murders in the Rue Morgue," "The Purloined Letter" (both 1841), and "The Mystery of Marie Rogêt" (1841–1842); and Poe's most popular story during his lifetime, "The Gold-Bug" (1843), a story of "ratiocination." He also wrote two less well-known experimental tales involving ratiocination, "The Oblong Box" and "Thou Art the Man" (both 1844).

In his 1842 essay on Charles Dickens's *Barnaby Rudge*, Poe set down the central paradox of his own mystery fiction: "The design of *mystery* . . . being once determined by the author, it becomes imperative, first, that no undue or inartistical [sic] means be employed to conceal the secret of the plot; and secondly, that the secret be well kept" (*Essays and Reviews* 233–234, italics in original). As the first of his "mystery" stories, "The Man of the Crowd," an apparently simple tale, incorporates subtle and disturbing clues to Poe's creation of detective fiction, but it keeps one secret so well it is never solved.

"All through Poe's fiction runs his hero—himself" (Haycraft 13). In "The Man of the Crowd," a nameless narrator recovering from a serious illness watches and categorizes passersby through a London coffee house window. A peculiar old man with an expression of "absolute idiosyncrasy" catches the narrator's eye, and he follows the man through the night and the next day, attempting to "comprehend the waywardness of his actions" (Peithman 191) which vacillate between obsessive determination and aimless hesitation, but not even when the narrator finally stares the man in the face can he understand them.

Poe, contemplating the human wickedness which haunted him, began this story with a reference to "a German book" which does not permit itself to be read (Peithman 187), intertwining art and reality by comparing it to horrifying deathbed scenes:

> Men die nightly in their beds . . . with despair of heart . . . on account of the hideousness of mysteries which will not *suffer themselves* to be revealed. . . . Now and then, alas, the conscience of man takes up a burden so heavy in horror that it can be thrown only into the grave. And thus the essence of all crime is undivulged. (Peithman 187, italics in original)

Peithman suggests that Poe may have modeled this passage after a similar one in Dickens' "The Drunkard's Death" in *Sketches by Boz,* which Poe had reviewed in 1836. Perhaps like Poe himself when he was recuperating from his 1840 collapse, Poe's narrator in that fragile but heightened "resurrected" condition which often follows a grave illness follows the old man from a bustling well-lighted London street down into the bowels of the city's worst slums and back again, until the narrator, "wearied unto death," confronts the Man of the Crowd, acknowledging in him the unknowable "type and genius of deep crime . . . I shall learn no more of him, nor of his deeds . . . perhaps it is one of the great mercies of God that *er lasst sich nicht lesen*" (Peithman 194).

As he did in some of his other short stories, Poe opened "The Man of the Crowd" with an aesthetic essay, first presenting an artistic theory in the abstract and then modulating it into realistic terms through his narrator-detective whose process of observation "mirrors the transformation of the [rational] eighteenth-century essayist into the [haunted] nineteenth-century artist," moving systematically down London's social scale from gentlemen of leisure and business, to criminals, prostitutes, exhausted laborers, and finally to the old man who seems to incarnate humanity's whole "wild history . . . of vast mental power, of caution, of penuriousness, of avarice, of coolness, of malice, of blood-thirstiness, of triumph, of merriment, of excessive terror, of intense—of supreme despair" (Peithman 191), a panorama of the unfathomable, and for Poe, infinitely compelling, human condition. "The Man of the Crowd" can thus be read as one of Poe's "double stories," where "the narrator sees the secret side of himself—his perverse shadow—in the old man" (May 100).

Poe's next innovation separated the narrator figure from the detective, a device crucial to the modern detective story. His detective, C. Auguste

A strong argument for the religion of Christianity is this—that offences [sic] against charity are about the only ones which men on their deathbeds can be made—not to understand—but to feel—as crimes.

—Poe

Dupin, is titled "The Chevalier" ("Chevalier" in 1839 was a title given to younger sons of French noble families who chose to follow military careers) (Peithman 216). Howard Haycraft names two real French brothers named Dupin who were Poe's contemporaries of whom he may have heard. André Dupin was an adroit politician, France's Procurator-Général, and a prolific writer on French criminal procedure; Charles Dupin was a mathematician and poet. Poe may have fictionalized them together as the talented villain "Minister D—" in "The Purloined Letter" (Haycraft 14). Michael Harrison has shown that Poe based his detective character on a real Chevalier Dupin, who lived from 1794 to 1873.

Poe's three Dupin stories feature "the contrast with . . . [the narrator's] bland and obtuse normality which dramatizes the genius of the detective" (Hoffman, in Herbert 153). As Arthur Conan Doyle later remarked, the amateur detective "provided the best opportunity to create a vivid individual character" (www.icons.org.uk). In creating Auguste Dupin, Poe established the prototype, not always applauded, for legions of fictional private detectives who have followed. Shortly after their first meeting in *A Study in Scarlet*, Dr. Watson says to Sherlock Holmes, "You remind me of Edgar Poe's Dupin. I had no idea that such individuals did exist outside of the stories." Sherlock Holmes comments in the same novel, "Now, in my opinion, Dupin was a very inferior fellow. . . . He had some analytical genius, no doubt; but he was by no means such a phenomenon as Poe appeared to imagine." Holmes's condescending remark, very different from Conan Doyle's high praise of Poe, seems to reflect his own intellectual arrogance. Some commentators have observed that Dupin also presented "an image of Poe himself—aristocratic, arrogant, and apparently omniscient," solving crimes "by his capacity as a reasoning machine" (Symons 222).

Although Poe revised all of his detective stories carefully to make the details of the crimes more plausible, some flaws still appear, like the impossibility for the orangutan in "The Murders in the Rue Morgue" to climb out and fasten the window by its secret catch. Poe also had to make some small but important changes between serial installments of "The Mystery of Marie Rogêt" to accommodate new evidence in the real-life case he had used as a basis for the story, but it is well to recall that Poe was writing almost 100 years before Golden Age mystery writers formulated the "rules" of detective fiction, many of them based on Poe's work.

C. AUGUSTE DUPIN

His Background and Character

Auguste Dupin, a "Parisian polymath" (Rachman 54), chose to live in eccentric isolation. Because his noble family had lost their fortune, he was reduced to living, like Poe himself who liked to claim descent from a possibly fictitious "General Poe," on a tiny income that allowed only one luxury—books. Poe supplies few other facts about Dupin's personal life and never describes Dupin physically, probably because he wanted to base the detective's characterization exclusively on intellect—"the rational Poe." Dupin, a poet and a mathematician, embodies Poe's opinion that "The *truly* imaginative [is] never otherwise than analytic" (quoted in Peithman 198, italics in original).

> *The same appeal that haunted houses on Halloween have for people Poe's work has as well.*
>
> —David Kipen

The narrator, more secure financially than Dupin, meets young Dupin at the beginning of their first story, "The Murders in the Rue Morgue," March 1841, while they are both searching for the same rare book in an obscure library. They agree to take up residence together in a Gothic setting, a "time-eaten and grotesque" deserted mansion in Paris' Faubourg St. Germain, where they share "the rather fantastic gloom" of their "common temper" (Peithman 200) and "live like vampires" (Murphy 154). The narrator and Dupin both love darkness, so much so that Dupin chooses total dark for meditation, a conventional Romantic contrast between physical gloom and intellectual illumination. At dawn he shutters all their windows, using only perfumed candles for lighting. The two spend their days indoors reading, writing, and arguing, and they venture forth only at night "in search of 'that infinity of mental excitement which quiet observation can afford'" (Peithman 200). The gloomy Parisian setting intensifies the story's exotic Gothic atmosphere.

"The Murders in the Rue Morgue" begins with a long theoretical discussion on games, especially chess and card games, reflecting Poe's own interest in games both as a pastime for gentlemen and as a recreation for his readers, and his fascination with how games engage the mental faculties in their "pure" form (Murphy 154). Poe connects human reason with "intuition":

> The analyst [glories] . . . in that moral activity which *disentangles*. . . . He is fond of enigmas, of conundrums, of hieroglyphics; exhibiting in his solutions of each a degree of *acumen* which appears to the ordinary apprehension preternatural. His results, brought about by the very soul and essence of method, have, in truth, the whole air of intuition. (Peithman 197, italics in original)

Poe intentionally gave his own impressive analytic powers to Dupin, who interprets persons' thoughts by reading their body language, and solves crimes by reading accounts in newspapers, so that his "apparently miraculous knowledge [is] based upon rational deduction" (Symons 223). In an 1846 letter, Poe confirmed his identification of Dupin with himself: "the reader is made to confound the ingenuity of the supposititious Dupin with that of the writer of the story" (Ostrom 2: 328).

Besides separating the pedestrian narrator and the genius detective, "The Murders in the Rue Morgue" concentrates not on the solution but on the steps toward solving the mystery, the true focus of detective fiction (Peithman 195). In his germinal 1907 Poe study, Brander Matthews commented that by thus giving human interest to the "tale of wonder," Poe "transported the detective story from the group of tales of adventure to the group of portrayals of character" (Matthews 293).

Poe sets the stage for Dupin's superlative analytic talent by having him apparently read the narrator's mind as they stroll one night down a "long dirty street" near the Palais Royal (Peithman 201). Not telepathy, however, but minute observation and probabilities of association lead Dupin to his accurate conclusion, which initially confounds the narrator and then, when Dupin explains the intellectual process, leaves the narrator in a state of profound admiration. "Pretense is in fact a part of the game, for Dupin's entire method comes down not only to the tenuous reason he exhibits, but to his capacity to identify with the situation. He reads the narrator's mind by means of identification, or inner impersonation" (Cox 85).

Shortly afterward, Dupin and the narrator come across newspaper accounts of a brutal murder in the Rue Morgue, and, while having no personal feelings about it, Dupin becomes intrigued by this apparently insoluble crime. Dupin decides to "enter into some examination for ourselves . . . [to] afford us amusement," a statement revealing that he, like Poe, sees crime-solving as a game. His acquaintance with the Prefect of Police gains them entry to the scene of the inhuman crime, where the mutilated and near-decapitated body of Madame l'Espanaye was discovered in a small yard and her daughter's corpse, horrifically excoriated, was found firmly wedged in the chimney of their apartment. After minute examinations of the evidence and thorough study of the newspaper accounts, Dupin systematically deduces that the killer was indeed inhuman—an orangutan escaped from the sailor who had brought it from the far East, a deduction marking the brilliant first appearance of "the amateur sleuth who solves crimes from the comfort of his armchair" (May 87). Demonstrating Poe's broad range of reading, Peithman cites possible sources for the ape-as-killer: an article titled "New Mode of Thieving" in the *Annual Record for 1834*, where an ape had been trained as a cat burglar; an early 19th-century story of a monkey who had tried to shave a customer in imitation of his owner, a barber; David Humphrey's poem "The Monkey," where the animal cuts its own throat; and Walter Scott's *Count Robert of Paris* (1831) in which a character is strangled by an orangutan.

Poe claimed a scientific purpose for his detective stories as "the medium of truth." Entering into what he called "a very long and rigorous analysis of [a] New-York [sic] tragedy" (Allen 83), Poe based his sequel, "The Mystery of Marie Rogêt," to "The Murders in the Rue Morgue" on an actual New York homicide case, the 1841 murder of Mary Rogers, a young woman who worked in an upper-Broadway cigar shop. Mary Rogers first disappeared from her home for two weeks in 1838, leaving a suicide note, but she returned. Two and a half years later, she vanished again, and her body was found three days later floating in the Hudson River. The murder was initially attributed to a gang of ruffians then active in the city. A few weeks later the body of her fiancé Daniel Payne, an apparent suicide, was found near the site of her murder. Poe's fictionalization of the story, again set in a seedy Paris neighborhood, appeared serially in 1842, discounting the gang theory and, he claimed in a letter, indicating the real assassin. He reworked the story before its final installment appeared, but scholarship has since demonstrated that he ignored evidence indicating Mary Rogers had died from a botched abortion.

For his epigraph to "The Mystery of Marie Rogêt" (November–December 1842) in February 1843, Poe chose a quotation from the German Romantic poet Novalis and used the original German text, translated as "There are ideal series of events which run parallel with the real ones. They rarely coincide. Men and circumstances generally modify the ideal train of events, so that it seems imperfect, and its consequences are equally imperfect . . . " (Peithman 226). By juxtaposing his tale of "Marie Rogêt" with the fate of Mary Rogers, Poe insisted that what ordinarily is called coincidence is in fiction "the artistic calculation of putting things together in a unified, parallel fashion" (May 89). Poe's story presents his idealized and super-unified conception of the detective, personalized in Dupin who solves the crime in his home, totally from information furnished in the newspapers, a chilly technique that has given rise to opinions which rank this story the least popular and least critically discussed of the three Dupin mysteries because of its lack of characterization and action.

Several groundbreaking developments in Poe's detective fiction appear in "The Mystery of Marie Rogêt," as announced by Dupin's friend the narrator. First, Dupin's name had grown into a "household word," because his solution to the Rue Morgue murders had never been explained to anyone else, and thus appeared "little less than miraculous" (Peithman 229). Second, that solution had won him the admiration of the Paris police, whose ineffectual Prefect, having failed to solve the murder of the humble cigar-girl Marie Rogêt, begs Dupin to save his reputation. Finally, Dupin's wide-ranging scientific expertise allows him to expose the errors in the newspaper accounts, a process exactly opposite to what he had done in "The Murders of the Rue Morgue" (May 90).

Poe's third story featuring Dupin and his last detective story, "The Purloined Letter" (September 1844), is probably the most enjoyable of the three because of its lighter tone and absence of ghoulish details. It has also received the most critical attention of the three, exhibiting elements which make it one of Poe's most important detective story experiments. Poe does not seem to have used any outside sources in "The Purloined Letter."

This story involves no murder; Dupin's problem is to protect a well-known lady by finding a letter that incriminates her, stolen by the heinous Minister D—, which Dupin accomplishes by outwitting everyone—the narrator, the police, and the reader—and again confirming the superiority of his intellect.

"The Purloined Letter" recounts a game of wits, the kind Dupin most likes to play. A great deal of crucial information is known, and in fact, the letter's owner even knows who stole it, causing Dupin to remark that the criminal's blackmailing power results from "the robber's knowledge of the loser's knowledge of the robber" (Peithman 302). Dupin illustrates his method of intellectual investigation by telling the narrator about an eight-year-old boy who gained "universal admiration" with his success at playing "even and odd." The boy wins because he can identify his intellect with his opponent's, an ability which the narrator concludes depends on "the accuracy with which the opponent's intellect is admeasured." Dupin reasons that the failure of the Prefect of Police's heroic efforts to find the letter by tearing up Minister D—'s apartment is due first to his inability to identify with his opponent, and second, to "non-admeasurement" or lack of correct estimation, of the opponent's intellect (Peithman 307).

Dupin, of course, not only out-identifies his opponents but he never underestimates them. In "The Purloined Letter," he projects himself into the mind of Minister D— who has stolen it and realizes that the minister would use an extraordinary means of hiding the letter, which in this case turns out to be an ordinary one: "To hide the letter by putting it in plain sight is to make the ordinary into the extraordinary" (May 92). Although in Poe's first two detective stories, he made Dupin approach but never attain the concept that "the intellect creates its own light," in "The Purloined Letter" he provides Dupin with the only case "truly worthy of his deductive powers. With this one brilliant solution, Dupin takes his place beside the greatest of fictional detectives" (Richard Steiger, in Herbert 57)—indeed, Dupin's creator "the rational" Poe inspired the creation of most of them. "The Purloined Letter" has become "the rallying point" for poststructuralist critics discussing the methods of Jacques Lacan, who used this story as a pretext for discussing psychoanalytic subplots and Jacques Derrida's motivation for deconstructionist debate (May 90).

Dupin's Only Associate

The relationship between Dupin and the unnamed narrator-chronicler, evidently an American living in Paris, has also inspired the sleuth-and-sidekick pairing so common in subsequent detective fiction. The narrator always appreciates Dupin's intellectual gifts and even idolizes him, but the narrator can never "make head or tail" of the significance of the clues on which Dupin bases his astonishing deductions (Murphy 154). The narrator also represents the reader, who plays the "game" of detection along with Dupin, although the detective seems always to be one step ahead of them all.

The Deficient Police

Establishing the pattern for generations of fictional police officials, the vain and myopic Prefect of Police, Monsieur G—, whom Dupin calls "contemptible," cannot understand Dupin's "off idea" that physical darkness, by shutting off the sometimes misleading sense of sight, may assist the intellectual processes of crime solving. In "The Purloined Letter," Dupin correctly diagnoses the incapacity of "the Prefect and his cohort": they cannot identify with the mind of the criminal and so they underestimate it:

> They consider only their own ideas of ingenuity, and, in searching for anything hidden, advert only to the modes in which *they* would have hidden it. They are right in this much—that their own ingenuity is a faithful representative of that of *the mass;* but when the cunning of the individual felon is diverse in character from their own, the felon fails them, of course. This always happens when it is above their own, and very usually when it is below. (Peithman 307, italics in original)

Poe's Other Tales of Ratiocination

Besides his three detective stories featuring Auguste Dupin, Poe wrote three other stories of "ratiocination," the analytic solution of crime. The most famous, "The Gold-Bug" (June 1843), was Poe's most popular story during his lifetime, involving a pirate treasure buried long before the action of the story takes place on Sullivan's Island, South Carolina, where Poe himself had been stationed at Fort Moultrie from November 1827 to December 1828. To recover it, the "genius" protagonist William Legrand must decode a set of enciphered directions, but the crimes of the treasure's original theft and the murder of several accomplices are never solved. This story, based on Poe's own interest in cryptography, perfectly exemplified Poe's theory of artistic unity, with each detail indispensable to the overall effect. It also contains two of Poe's "obsessive motifs: cracking the code is a metaphor for discovering hidden truths, and the embodiment of the ratiocinative principle, separated from the emotions by Poe's facultative psychology" (Daniel Hoffman, in Herbert 153).

Although some critics wonder whether "The Gold-Bug" is really a detective story because it contains no sleuth and Legrand does hide things from the reader to preserve the mystery, certain resemblances exist between this story and the Dupin tales. A narrator and friend of Legrand tells the story, and Legrand is both rather eccentric and expert in an obscure intellectual pursuit, the solution of puzzles. The story's primary motif is misunderstanding or miscommunication, resolved through analytically interpreting a pattern based on following "certain conventions and rules" (May 86). Legrand breaks the secret code intellectually by developing the rules which govern it, another demonstration of the power of rational deduction.

"The Oblong Box" (September 1844) and "Thou Art the Man" (November 1844) are Poe's "minor experiments with the ratiocinative story" (May 83), hinging on the role of the narrator and incorporating elements of Gothic horror. In "The Man of the Crowd," Poe had combined the narrator and "detective" with an inconclusive result, because that figure did not arrive at a "solution" to the mysterious stranger's behavior. In the Dupin stories and "The Gold-Bug," the narrator stands between the reader and the genius detective, highlighting the detective's prowess. In "The Oblong Box" and "Thou Art the Man," Poe returned to the narrator-sleuth, in both cases a person lacking ratiocinative talents or professional expertise. In "The Oblong Box," the narrator is wrong in his conclusions, and in "Thou Art the Man," possibly the first comic detective story, the narrator does not allow the reader to share vital information until the end of the story. The narrator of "The Oblong Box," driven by curiosity, suspects that the box contains a copy of Da Vinci's *Last Supper,* when in one of Poe's Gothic plot twists it really contains the body of a beautiful young woman, possibly inspired by a real-life case in which a murderer shipped a body packed in salt to St. Louis via New Orleans. In "Thou Art the Man," Poe's narrator maintains a light tone throughout, keeping his readers unaware of the mystery until in the dénouement a dead body that he had ingeniously wired springs up out of a shipping carton and by a grisly use of ventriloquism unmasks its murderer.

> So many fellow crime writers offered to write about movies based on Poe's phantasmagoria for *In the Shadow of the Master* that its editor Michael Connolly "had to say, no more!" (Cole 53).

THE EFFECT OF POE'S DETECTIVE FICTION ON POPULAR CULTURE

"Poe always concerned himself with the ways literature was becoming a powerful molder and potential manipulator of mass culture in antebellum America," and in both the cryptographic magazine contests he ran and in his Dupin stories he "exploited the public's interest in puzzle-solving in order to reach a mass audience" (Rachman 56). Although he recognized that he had created "something new" with his detective stories and that they were enjoying "an unprecedented popularity with the reading public" (Rachman 54), Poe disparaged their ingenuity in an 1846 letter to his friend Philip P. Cooke:

> . . . people think them more ingenious than they are—on account of their method and *air* of method. In the "Murders in the Rue Morgue," for instance, where is the ingenuity of unraveling a web which you yourself (the author) have woven for the express purpose of unraveling? (Ostrom 2: 328, italics in original)

Poe also complained in several letters that the public seemed to prefer his ratiocinative tales to what he believed were his worthier efforts, although he traded on their popularity when he dealt with editors and publishers (Haycraft 14).

Recent critics have also observed that many elements of the detective story Poe "invented" were present in literature long before he used them— suspense appears in Sophocles's *Oedipus Rex;* bloodcurdling ghosts and bloodthirsty revenge stalk *Hamlet* and *Macbeth* via Seneca's Roman tragedies. Brigid Brophy suggests that the basic pattern of the detective story is mythic. The detective hero, like the hero of ancient Greek myth, is a democratic hero, a superman though not by divine right, and his apotheosis consists in his becoming famous; circumstances of his birth are omitted; by chance or by being called in he becomes involved in solving a crime, with a confidant to emphasize the detective's talents; he performs miracles through common sense used to an uncommon, heroic degree in a closed community where police are failing to find the real criminal and are accusing the wrong person; and finally the hero reconstructs the crime, making the murderer's guilt obvious to all—"the plot of thousands of detective novels" but exactly the plot Poe used in "The Murders in the Rue Morgue" (Brophy 19–20).

Early novels like Fielding's *Tom Jones* also involve "mysteries" of birth and inheritance; Gothic tales like Ann Radcliffe's *Mysteries of Udolpho* meticulously analyze empirical evidence, and Victorian novelists like Dickens "used puzzle-solving as a metaphor to critique their society" (Van Leer 65– 66). Poe, however, wrote the first stories to win popularity for ingenious puzzle-solving, and besides the eccentric "genius detective," his stolid narrator-chronicler, and the ineffectual Prefect of Police, he also invented the "locked room" mystery, the unjustly accused suspect, "analysis by psychological deduction," and "the complementary solutions of the least likely person and the most likely place" (Van Leer 65), all devices still successfully used in detective fiction.

With the exception of "The Gold-Bug," Poe's detective fiction was initially overshadowed by his poems and tales of horror, strengthened by Griswold's defamatory obituary which produced the widespread impression that Poe's character had been weak if not downright reprehensible, and that his writing revealed his obsession with "morbidly unwholesome themes and situations." This impression substantially contributed to an early moralistic reaction, especially prevalent in America, which created "a major obstacle" to a fair assessment of his work until World War I (Carlson viii).

A few early admirers did praise "the rational" Poe's detective stories. About 10 years after Poe's death, in a little-known 1860 campaign biography of Abraham Lincoln, the young William Dean Howells observed that "the bent of his [Lincoln's] mind is mathematical and metaphysical, and he is therefore pleased with the absolute and logical method of Poe's tales and sketches, in which the problem of mystery is given and wrought out into everyday facts by processes of cunning analysis," claiming that Lincoln read Poe's works diligently every year (quoted in Haycraft 15). Abroad, although the French poet Charles Baudelaire, one of the earliest defenders and translators of Poe's work, saw Poe as the tormented artist who defied every bourgeois convention, a precursor of artistic Decadence, the Russian novelist

In one of 20 vignettes included in *In the Shadow of the Master,* mystery author Lisa Scottoline compares high school exposure to Poe to broccoli for teenagers—as something forced on them because it's good for them, a testimony to the present generation's lack of English vocabulary.

Fyodor Dostoevsky, himself absorbed with crimes and punishment, praised Poe's insight into humanity's darkest motivations and his "power to persuade the reader to believe in the most extraordinary events through the use of ordinary details" (quoted in Frank and Magistrale 102).

Griswold's slanders gradually receded over the years, but by 1874 Americans like Walt Whitman and Henry James were still deploring "the haunted" Poe's preference for "the abstract," a position that George Bernard Shaw berated in 1909 as "smug indifference to art" (Carlson ix). The general view of Poe changed materially in the last half of the 19th-century, mainly through Englishman John Henry Ingram's biography, meticulously compiled since the late 1860s and finally published in 1880, "the first full and coherent defense of the writer" (Symons 164), giving impetus for renewed interest in Poe's poems and short stories. Later 19th-century biographies supporting Griswold's opinions enraged Ingram, and he maintained until his death in 1916 that Poe had not been given his due.

Not until after World War I did literary critics utilize systematic research methods resulting in outbursts of biographies and critical essays in the 1920s and 1930s (Carlson ix), but they concentrated on poetry and prose created by "the haunted" Poe. Some, like D.H. Lawrence in *Studies of Classic American Literature* (1923), sympathetically investigated hitherto unexplored aspects of Poe's "psychic dramas," but others, notably Yvor Winters in his "literal rationalist-moralist" 1937 essay "Edgar Allan Poe: A Crisis in the History of American Obscurantism" concluded that Poe's work was "wholly without truth, theme, and moral values" (quoted in Carlson x). In

In 1946 the Mystery Writers of America named their prestigious award for the best mystery novel of each year the "Edgar."

the existentialistic aftermath of World War II, however, with its interest in "the irrational, the grotesque, the fantastic, the psychotic, and the sadistic, 'the haunted' Poe was recognized as a "great forerunner exploring the real horrors and self-realization of modern man" (Carlson xi).

By the late 1970s, when mystery critic Julian Symons, dissatisfied with existing biographies of Poe that fused his life with his work, undertook his own Poe study, Poe's life had been chronicled with enormous thoroughness. Symons's brief discussion of Poe's detective stories praises these stories as "totally original," "a single proof . . . of Poe's astonishingly inventive and ingenious mind," an assessment that has held firm to date as "the extreme expression of Logical Poe" (Symons 221–222). By incorporating Poe's concept of the eccentric genius detective into his enormously successful Sherlock Holmes, Arthur Conan Doyle followed his own advice to future mystery authors: "On this narrow path the writer must walk, and he sees the footmarks of Poe always in front of him. He is happy if he ever finds the means of breaking away and striking out on some little sidetrack of his own" (quoted in Symons 222).

A century later, "the rational" Poe's creation of detective fiction, today arguably one of the most popular forms of imaginative literature, holds firm, whether by illustrating urban dilemmas through analyzing popular newspapers and magazines or as "the genre of an age dominated by science and technology, an age characterized by mental-work-as-analysis" (Irwin xvi). "Poe's ratiocinative writings, with their treatise-like openings and air of method allowed readers to enter into a fictional world of urban mystery and crime and through analysis, impose order and truth upon it" (Rachman 56). Analysis, however, may not be the only reason for the popularity of Poe's detective fiction. Poe's emphasis on "unity" in fiction meant that to successfully penetrate criminal plots, Dupin, like the little boy with "odds and evens," had to enter the mind of the villain. Crime-solving "requires an impeccable intellectual talent like Dupin's but with a sinister side, a special madness very much akin to that of criminals," so Poe balanced Dupin's triumph of the intellect with his "astonishing eccentricity and unpredictability, [his] deviations from the plane of the ordinary" (Conger 14), achieving a synthesis in art that Poe never could attain in his life. Today "the rational" Poe and "the haunted" Poe live on together, honored on Hungarian, Nicaraguan, and United States postage stamps and toasted each January 19, Poe's birthday, since 1949 with an enigmatic visitor who brings three red roses and a bottle of cognac to his Baltimore grave; and mystery authors and critics, whatever their individual sidetracks, agree that Poe's influence on the detective story has been overwhelming.

> As the ultimate popular homage to Poe, Baltimore's football team is called "The Ravens."

PARALLEL CHRONOLOGY

Major Events Related to Edgar Allan Poe	World Events
	1789 The French Revolution
	1792 September massacres (France)

(Continued)

Major Events Related to Edgar Allan Poe	World Events
	1793 The Reign of Terror
	1794 William Godwin's *Caleb Williams,* with an amateur investigator and a police spy; Ann Radcliffe, *The Mysteries of Udolpho*
	1795 Matthew Lewis, *The Monk*
	1798 Wordsworth and Coleridge: *Lyrical Ballads*
	1799 Napoleon Bonaparte becomes First Consul
	ca. 1800 Paris police force established
	1801 Friedrich Schlegel suggests importance of the short story's style
	1804 N. Bonaparte becomes Emperor of France
	ca. 1804 Ludwig Tieck's romantic theories of short fiction
Jan. 19, 1809 Edgar Allan Poe born	
	1811 François Vidocq, former criminal, becomes chief of Paris Sûreté and later establishes first detective agency
1811 Poe's mother dies; John and Frances Allan take him in but never adopt him	
	1812–1814 War of 1812
1815–1820 The Allans take Edgar to England	**1815** Battle of Waterloo
	1817 Coleridge's *Biographia Literaria*
	1818 T.L. Peacock, *Nightmare Abbey*; Mary Shelley, *Frankenstein*
1820 Poe returns to Richmond	
1826 Poe enters University of Virginia; is dismissed same year; engaged to Sarah Royster (later broken)	
1827 Poe enlists in Army; publishes *Tamerlane and Other Poems*	
1827–1831 Poe publishes three volumes of poetry	**1828–1829** Vidocq's *Memoirs;* first modern metropolitan police force set up by Sir Robert Peel in London as the Criminal Investigation Division (Scotland Yard)
1929 Poe leaves U.S. Army; Mrs. Allan dies	

Major Events Related to Edgar Allan Poe	World Events
1830–1831 Poe briefly attends West Point, then moves to New York	
1832 Poe publishes first short story, "Metzengerstein"	
1834 John Allan dies, leaving Poe nothing	
1835–1845 Poe works at various periodicals	
1836 Poe marries Virginia Clemm, his cousin	
	1837 Accession of Victoria to British throne
1841 "The Murders in the Rue Morgue"	
1842 "The Mystery of Marie Rogêt"	
1843 "The Gold-Bug" wins a contest; "The Tell-Tale Heart" and "The Black Cat" published	**1843** First appearance of the word "detective" in English (O.E.D.)
1844 "Thou Art the Man!" and "The Oblong Box"	**1844** New York City's police force established
1845 "The Purloined Letter," "The Raven"	**1845** Failure of Irish potato crop; famine ensues
1846 Poe publishes "The Philosophy of Composition" and "The Cask of Amontillado"	**1846** Boston places first police detectives on city payroll; the Parkman Murder Case
	1846–1848 The Mexican War
1847 Poe's wife Virginia dies; Poe diagnosed with a "brain lesion"; Poe sues publishers of *The Evening Mirror* for libel	
1848 Poe delivers lecture "The Poetic Principle"; attempts suicide in November	**1848** Revolutions in France, Germany, Poland, Hungary, and Italy; Second Republic in France
1849 Poe's health deteriorates severely	**1849–1850** Dickens publishes *David Copperfield*
Oct. 7, 1849 Poe dies in Baltimore	
1850–1856 *The Works of the Late Edgar Allan Poe* (R.W. Griswold, ed.)	**ca. 1850** Cheap books about detectives begin to appear
	1853 Dickens's *Bleak House* with working-class detective, Inspector Bucket
	1865 Charles Felix's *The Notting Hill Mystery*, an early first detective novel

(Continued)

Major Events Related to Edgar Allan Poe	World Events
	1866 Seeley Register's *The Dead Letter,* first detective novel by a woman
	1868 Wilkie Collins's *The Moonstone* with Sergeant Cuff; first full-length detective novel
	1869 Emile Gaboriau's *Monsieur Lecoq,* with police detective
	1878 Anna Katharine Green's *The Leavenworth Case,* first novel by the "Mother of the Detective Novel"
	1887 A. Conan Doyle publishes first Sherlock Holmes story, "A Study in Scarlet"
	1899 Conan Doyle's brother-in-law E.W. Hornung publishes first "Raffles" story with gentleman thief
	ca. 1920–ca. 1940 Golden Age of Detective Fiction

POE'S DETECTIVE AND MYSTERY FICTION

"The Man of the Crowd" (1840)—Story of ratiocination

"The Murders in the Rue Morgue" (1841)—Detective story, featuring C. Auguste Dupin

"The Mystery of Marie Rogêt" (1842)—Detective story, featuring C. Auguste Dupin

"The Gold-Bug" (1843)—Story of ratiocination

"The Oblong Box" (1844)—Mystery story

"The Purloined Letter" (1844)—Detective story, featuring C. Auguste Dupin

"Thou Art the Man" (1844)—Comic story of ratiocination

Collections

Poe's detective and mystery stories were first published in periodicals. Subsequent collections (listed in chronological order) include:

Tales by Edgar A. Poe. New York: Wiley and Putnam, 1845.

Griswold, Rufus Wilmot, ed. *The Works of the Late Edgar Allan Poe,* 4 vols. New York: Redfield, 1850–1856.

Harrison, James A., ed. *The Complete Works of Edgar Allan Poe,* 17 vols. New York: Thomas Y. Crowell, 1902.

The Complete Tales and Poems of Edgar Allan Poe. New York: Modern Library, 1938.

Mabbott, Thomas O., ed. *Collected Works of Edgar Allan Poe,* 3 vols. Cambridge, MA: Belknap Press of Harvard University Press, 1969–1978.

Levine, Stuart, and Susan Levine, eds. *The Short Fiction of Edgar Allan Poe: An Annotated Edition.* Indianapolis, IN: Bobbs-Merrill, 1976.

Pollin, Burton R., ed. *Imaginary Voyages,* vol. 1 of *The Collected Writings of Edgar Allan Poe.* Boston: Twayne, 1981; New York: Gordian Press, 1994.

Connolly, Michael, ed. *In the Shadow of the Master: Classic Tales by Edgar Allan Poe.* New York: William Morrow, 2009.

Other Works by Poe

Essays and Reviews, ed. G.R. Thompson. New York: Library of America, 1984.

The Letters of Edgar Allan Poe, ed. John Ward Ostrom. 2 vols. Cambridge: Harvard University Press, 1948; New York: Gordian Press, 1966.

Bibliographies

Carlson, Eric W. "Bibliographical Essay Poe I: New Editions" and "Bibliographical Essay Poe II: New Critical Studies." *ANQ, A Quarterly Journal of Short Articles, Notes, and Reviews* 1 (July 1988): 25–32 and 105–112.

Dameron, J. Lasley, and Irby B. Cauthen, Jr. *Edgar Allan Poe: A Bibliography of Criticism, 1827–1967.* Charlottesville: University Press of Virginia, 1974.

Hyneman, Esther F. *Edgar Allan Poe: An Annotated Bibliography of Books and Articles in English, 1827–1973.* Boston: G.K. Hall, 1974.

Audio Collection

The Edgar Allan Poe Audio Collection (New York: HarperCollins Caedmon), 6 hours of 20 stories and poems read by Vincent Price and Basil Rathbone.

ADAPTATIONS OF POE'S MYSTERY FICTION

"The Murders in the Rue Morgue"

Sherlock Holmes in the Great Murder Mystery, a Danish silent film, blends Doyle and Poe (1908).

The Raven, a silent film with parts taken from this story (1912).

The Murders in the Rue Morgue, a full-length feature starring Bela Lugosi and Arlene Francis (1932).

Phantom of the Rue Morgue, starring Karl Malden, Patricia Medina, and Merv Griffin; changed the orangutan to a mad human killer (1954).

The Murders in the Rue Morgue, a full-length feature starring Jason Robards, Christine Kaufmann, and Lilli Palmer (1971).

"The Mystery of Marie Rogêt"

The Mystery of Marie Rogêt (also called *Phantom of Paris*), a full-length Universal feature film starring Maria Montez and Patric Knowles (1942).

Poe Must Die, a novel by Marc Olden 1978.

"The Purloined Letter"

"The Stolen Letter," by Wilkie Collins (a fairly direct steal, according to Peithman) (1854).

"The Gold-Bug"

Jules Verne translated "The Gold-Bug" in the *Musée des Familles* (1864).

Robert Louis Stevenson noted his debt to this story in his foreword to *Treasure Island* (1883).

The Raven: some elements of this story appear in the film (1912). *Manfish,* a film about Caribbean treasure hunting, starring Victor Jory and Lon Cheney, Jr., also contains elements of "The Gold-Bug" (1956).

"The Key," by Isaac Asimov: a extraterrologist uses a series of logical propositions to solve a cryptogram (1966).

"The Oblong Box"

The Oblong Box, film starring Vincent Price and Christopher Lee (1969).

Pastiches

Michael Harrison, *The Exploits of the Chevalier Dupin.* Sauk City, WI: Mycroft & Moran, 1968. Originally published in *Ellery Queen's Mystery Magazine.* A 1972 British version contains five additional stories.

Interactive Site

Knowing Poe, http://knowingpoe.thinkport.org/default%5fflash.asp, with John Astin appearing as Poe, was developed by Maryland Public Television (MPT) as an electronic field trip for middle and high school students, teachers, and Poe fans.

WORKS CITED

Allen, Michael. *Poe and the British Magazine Tradition.* New York: Oxford: 1969.

Brophy, Brigid. "Detective Fiction: A Modern Myth of Violence." *Hudson Review* 18 (1965): 11–30.

Carlson, Eric, ed. *Critical Essays on Edgar Allan Poe.* Boston: G.K. Hall, 1987.

Conger, Syndy M. "Another Secret of the Rue Morgue." *Studies in Short Fiction* 24 (Winter 1987): 9–14.

Cox, James. "Edgar Allan Poe: Style as Pose." *Virginia Quarterly Review* 44 (Winter 1968): 67–89.

Fisher, Benjamin F. *The Cambridge Introduction to Edgar Allan Poe.* Cambridge: Cambridge University Press, 2008.

Frank, Frederick, and Anthony Magistrale. *The Poe Encyclopedia.* Westport, CT: Greenwood Press, 1998.

Haycraft, Howard. "Detective Story." *Saturday Review of Literature* 24 (August 1941): 12–15.

Herbert, Rosemary. *Whodunit? A Who's Who in Crime and Mystery Writing.* New York: Oxford University Press, 2003.

Holman, Hugh. *A Handbook to Literature.* New York: Odyssey Press, 1972.

Hone, Ralph E. *Dorothy L. Sayers: A Literary Biography.* Kent, OH: Kent State University Press, 1979.

Irwin, John. *The Mystery to a Solution: Poe, Borges, and the Analytical Detective Story.* Baltimore: Johns Hopkins University Press, 1994.

Kennedy, J. Gerald. "Edgar Allan Poe." *Mystery and Suspense Writers.* Matthews, Brander. "Poe and the Detective Story," *Scribner's Magazine* 42 (August 1907): 287–293.

May, Charles. *Edgar Allan Poe: A Study of the Short Fiction.* Boston: Twayne, 1991.

Moldenhauer, Joseph. "Murder as Fine Art." *PMLA* 83 (May 1968): 284–297.

"Murder at Harvard." In "People and Events: Edgar Allan Poe, Detective Fiction, and The Parkman Murder," *American Experience,* http://www.pbs.org.wgbh .amex/murder/peopleevents/e_novel.html, accessed 2/7/2008.

Murphy, Bruce F. *The Encyclopedia of Murder and Mystery.* New York: St. Martin's Press, 1999.

Ostrom, John Ward, ed. *The Letters of Edgar Allan Poe.* 2 vols. Cambridge, MA: Harvard University Press, 1948; rpt. New York: Gordian Press, 1966.

Peithman, Stephen. *The Annotated Tales of Edgar Allan Poe.* New York: Doubleday, 1981.

Poe, Edgar Allan. *Essays and Reviews.* Edited by G.R. Thompson. New York: Library of America, 1984.

Rachman, Steven. "Poe, Magazines, & the Origins of Mystery Fiction." *The Strand Magazine* 13 (2004): 54–56.

Sayers, Dorothy L. Introduction to *The Omnibus of Crime,* edited by Howard Haycraft. New York: Payson and Clark, 1929.

Symons, Julian. *The Tell-Tale Heart: The Life and Works of Edgar Allan Poe.* New York: Harper, 1978.

Van Leer, David. "Detecting Truth: The World of the Dupin Tales," in *New Essays on Poe's Major Tales,* edited by Kenneth Silverman. Cambridge, UK: Cambridge University Press, 1993.

FURTHER READING

Asselineau, Roger. *Edgar Allan Poe*. Minneapolis: University of Minnesota Press, 1970.

Bennett, Maurice J. "The Detective Fiction of Poe and Borges." *Comparative Literature* 35 (Summer 1983): 262–275.

Bloom, Harold, ed. *The Tales of Poe*. New York: Chelsea House, 1987.

Bonaparte, Marie. *The Life and Works of Edgar Allan Poe: A Psycho-analytic* [sic] *Interpretation*. Translated by John Rodker. Introduction by Sigmund Freud. London: Imago, 1949.

Brand, Dana. "Reconstructing the "Flâneur: Poe's Invention of the Detective Story," *Genre* 18 (Spring 1985): 35–56.

Byrd, Max. "The Detective Detected: From Sophocles to Ross Macdonald." *Yale Review* 64 (October 1974): 76.

Canada, Mark. "Edgar Allan Poe Chronology." *Canada's America*, http://www.uncp.edu/home/canada/work/allam/17841865/lit/poe/htm.

Carlson, Eric. *The Recognition of Edgar Allan Poe*. Ann Arbor: University of Michigan Press, 1966.

Cole, Diane. "Investigate Tales of Edgar Allan Poe." *U.S. News and World Report* (Special Year-End Issue 2009): 53–54.

Davidson, Edward. *Poe: A Critical Study*. Cambridge: Belknap Press of Harvard University Press. 1957.

Dayan, Joan. *Fables of Mind: An Inquiry into Poe's Fiction*. New York: Oxford University Press, 1987.

"Edgar Allan Poe: An Introduction." http://www/enotes.com/edgar-allan-poe-masters/edgar-allan-poe-an-introduction, accessed 2/7/2008.

"Edgar Allan Poe Immortalized Through Interactive Site." *T H E Journal* 30 (February 2003): 7.

Elmer, Jonathan. *Reading at the Social Limit: Affect, Mass Culture, and Edgar Allan Poe*. Palo Alto: Stanford University Press, 1995.

Grossvogel, David I. "'The Purloined Letter': The Mystery of the Text." In *Mystery and Its Fictions*, 93–107. Baltimore: Johns Hopkins University Press, 1979.

Freeland, Natalka. "One of an Infinite Series of Mistakes: Mystery, Influence, and Edgar Allan Poe." *ATQ* 10 (June 1996): 123–140.

Haycraft, Howard. *Murder for Pleasure*. New York: Appleton-Centurey, 1941.

Hayes, Kevin J., ed. *The Cambridge Companion to Edgar Allan Poe*. New York: Cambridge University Press, 2002.

Howarth, William L., ed. *Twentieth Century Interpretations of Poe's Tales*. Englewood Cliffs, NJ: Prentice-Hall, 1971.

Ingram, John Henry. *Edgar Allan Poe: His Life, Letters and Opinions*, 1874.

Keller, Mark. "Dupin in the 'Rue Morgue': Another Form of Madness." *Arizona Quarterly* 33 (Autumn 1977): 249–255.

Krutch, Joseph Wood. *Edgar Allan Poe: A Study in Greatness*. New York: Russell and Russell, 1965.

Lemay, J.L. Leo. "The Psychology of 'The Murders in the Rue Morgue.'" *American Literature* 54 (May 1983): 165–188.

Meyers, Jeffrey. *Edgar Allan Poe: His Life and Legacy*. New York: Scribner's, 1992.

Miller, John Carl. *Building Poe Biography.* Baton Rouge, LA: Louisiana State University Press, 1977.

Pollin, Burton R. "Poe's 'Murders [sic] in the Rue Morgue': The Ingenious Web Unravelled." *Studies in the American Renaissance,* ed. Joel Meyerson, 235–259. Boston: G.K. Hall, 1977.

Ramde, Dinesh. "Writers Honor Poe in New Compilation." *The Forum* 25 (January 2009): 14.

Silverman, Kenneth. *Edgar A. Poe: Mournful and Neverending Remembrance.* New York: HarperCollins, 1991.

———. *New Essays on Poe's Major Tales.* New York: Cambridge University Press, 1993.

Wagenknecht, Edward. *Edgar Allan Poe: The Man behind the Legend.* New York: Oxford University Press, 1963.

Walsh, John. *Poe the Detective.* New Brunswick, NJ: Rutgers University Press, 1968.

Ward, Greg. *The Timeline History of the USA.* New York: Barnes & Noble, 2005.

Williams, Valentine. "The Detective in Fiction." *Fortnightly Review* 128 (September 1930): 380–392.

WEB SITES

http://www.nps.gov/edal (Edgar Allan Poe National Historic Site)

http://www.eapoe.org (Edgar Allan Poe Society, Baltimore, Maryland)

http://www.poemuseum.org (Poe Museum, Richmond, Virginia)

http://www.houseofusher.net (The Edgar Allan Poe Virtual Library)

http://www.gutenberg.org/author/Edgar_Allan_Poe (Works by Edgar Allan Poe at Project Gutenberg)

Dorothy L. Sayers, 1926. Used by permission of the Marion E. Wade Center, Wheaton College, Wheaton, IL.

Dorothy L. Sayers: Creator of Lord Peter Wimsey, the Aristocratic Sleuth

Time and trouble will tame an advanced young woman, but an advanced old woman is uncontrollable by any earthly force.

—Dorothy L. Sayers

HISTORICAL/CULTURAL CONTEXT

At Dorothy Leigh Sayers's cradle on June 13, 1893, a fairy godmother with a wicked sense of humor gave her everything she would need to become a brilliant medievalist scholar—"first class brains, a gift for languages and music, an artistic scholar's temperament, the soul of a great lover, and a life-long involvement with God"—but she also made sure Sayers won her wealth "in a way that effectively prevented scholars from taking her seriously" (Mann 188): Sayers would be forever known as the popular author who combined the classic Golden Age murder mystery with effervescent comedy of manners. Novelist Connie Willis, one of Sayers's ardent fans, recalls herself

> on a walking tour of Oxford colleges once with a group of bored and unimpressible tourists. They yawned at Balliol's quad . . . and the blackboard Einstein wrote E=mc^2 on. Then the tour guide said, "And this is the Bridge of Sighs, where [Sayers's] Lord Peter proposed (in Latin) to Harriet," and everyone suddenly came to life and began snapping pictures. Such is the power of books.

Such is the power of Sayers's mystery fiction. She believed that ". . . mysteries made only to be solved . . . comfort [us] by subtly pretending that life is a mystery which death will solve, and whole horrors will pass away as a tale that is told" (*Omnibus of Crime* 1928, 72). She also answered "What do brainy women want?" by creating Lord Peter Wimsey, an aristocratic sleuth endowed with everything Sayers herself wanted and in her youth could not have, and gave him Harriet Vane,

> a wish-fulfillment, what every scholastic woman wants to be. Brim full of learning and of fame, yet able—and in her thirties too—to work havoc in an undergraduate heart and hold to herself firmly, through year after year of refusals, a rich and noble lover. . . . "Oh, these are the dreams that visit women's pillows!" (Hamilton 6)

Sayers largely drew the hero and heroine of those dreams and the immensely successful mystery novels they inspired from the rich traditions of medieval literature.

Dorothy L. Sayers believed that people were instinctively "either 'gothic' or 'classical,'" and everyone, most of all herself, knew where she stood (*Maker and Craftsman* 3). Her spiritual home always lay among Oxford's "dreaming spires," and "Her first and enduring literary love was poetic

romance, epitomized in the figure of the Christian knight nobly championing the cause of Good—and frequently, like Roland, losing against eternal
Evil. That hero, and his mortal conflict, dominated nearly everything she
wrote" (*Medieval Mystery Maker* 423). At Oxford's Somerville College, she
first encountered him in two great medieval literary works, *La Chanson de
Roland,* written at the end of the 11th century; and *Le Roman de Tristan,*
composed by the Anglo-Norman monk Thomas of Britain around 1160,
now extant only in fragments.

As contemporary historians do today, Sayers saw the 1,000 years between
the 5th and the 15th centuries not as an interruption between the Classical
Period and the Renaissance but as "a fertile and dynamic period that produced a distinctive and permanently valuable culture of its own" (Wilkie
and Hurt 1279). Three distinct cultural impulses—the Classical emphasizing
reason; the Judeo-Christian, conscience; and the Gothic or Germanic, ceaseless energy—gradually merged in Europe into social organization centered
on two pyramidal institutions, feudalism and the Roman Church, each
reflecting the organization of the vanished Roman Empire.

In the chaotic, lawless 6th century, feudalism grew from the human need
for mutual protection in "a *personal* bond of mutual service and protection
between a lord (*seigneur*) and his dependent . . . affirmed in the rite of
'homage'" (*Song of Roland* 31, italics in original), which required that the
vassal place his hands between his lord's, swear an oath binding "while their
lives should last" and exchange a kiss on the mouth, a simple ceremony that
eventually became an elaborate system of obligations and rewards. In her
Introduction to her translation of *The Song of Roland,* Sayers noted that
"The rite of homage, by the hands, is still performed at the Coronation of
an English sovereign" (*Song of Roland* 31).

While the medieval Roman Church taught that all human beings were
equal before God, it also insisted that "the visible scene of human life was a
perpetual conflict between the kingdom of God and the Kingdom of the
Devil," and that human beings could find salvation only through the
Church's sacraments (Wilkie and Hurt 1280). Pope and feudal lord each
ruled at the apex of his field of influence. Below the pope came the cardinals
and then successively the archbishops, the bishops, the priests, and finally
individual believers. Below the great feudal lord came the knights of his
household and his chief vassals, themselves followed by their own vassals,
attended by followers of lesser ranks, "down to the serfs and peasant-
proprietors who owed military service to the lords whose 'men' they were"
(*Song of Roland* 33). The Church and the feudal system each had only two
classes: for the Church, the clergy and the people; and for the laity, the
nobility and the people.

First to emerge as a relatively stable European entity after the fall of
Rome was the kingdom of the Franks under Clovis (465 to 511 CE), whose
descendent Charlemagne by 800 had forged a Holy Roman Empire by con-
quering Germanic Saxons and Bavarians, Moors in northeast Spain, and

Lombards in northern Italy. *La Chanson de Roland* was based on a minor military incident in 778 CE that solidly captured Sayers's imagination. While battling the Saxons, Charlemagne agreed to aid Moslem Saracen princes in Spain against their own Moslem enemies. While he was besieging Saragossa, a new Saxon outbreak caused him to abandon the Spanish campaign, and in crossing the Pyrenees at Roncevaux his rear guard under Duke Roland of Brittany was treacherously ambushed and annihilated. Some 200 years later the tale of Roncevaux had "swollen to a vast epic of heroic proportions and strong ideological significance" (*Song of Roland* 8).

An unknown Old French author composed *La Chanson de Roland* from earlier oral sources in the late 11th century, when the Saracens had been menacing Christendom for at least a century. The First Crusade had inflamed Christians to recapture the Holy Land from the Moslems, the feudal system and its code of chivalry were in full flower, and pilgrims were passing through Roncevaux on their way to St. James's shrine at Campostela. Sayers saw that as "the earliest, the most famous, and the greatest, of those Old French epics which are called 'Songs of Deeds'—*Chansons de Geste*'" *La Chanson de Roland* presents "a world full of blood and grief and death and naked brutality, but also of frank emotions, innocent simplicities, and abounding self-confidence" and a hero who is "the Young Age as that age saw itself" (*Song of Roland* 10, 17), refusing proudly to call for aid until hope was lost. Dorothy L. Sayers never lost her infatuation with him, and perhaps the world never has, either.

Of all historical military figures, "none has had a longer career than the knight of the European Middle Ages, and none has had an equal impact on history, social and cultural as well as political," as warrior, as economic cornerstone of feudalism, and through the Church's sponsorship, as foundation of the nobility's class consciousness (F. Gies 3). The word "chivalrous" appears for the first time in *La Chanson de Roland*, in "a spirit of rugged Christian naiveté." Preferring death to dishonor when the Saracens attack, Roland, alone on the corpse-strewn field, thinks last of his lords, Charlemagne and God, to whom he holds up his glove as he dies, championing Christian Good against Moslem Evil. This early chivalric ideal "embraced generosity, honor, the pursuit of glory, and contempt for hardship, fatigue, pain, and death" (J. and F. Gies 184).

Sayers's other early medieval hero, the lover Tristan as drawn by Thomas of Britain, fell victim to Evil under the allure of illicit passion, not only committing adultery with Iseut, a married woman, but like Lancelot in the Arthurian legends breaking his oath of fidelity to her husband who was also his king—acts of monstrous evil in the medieval world. Thomas's greatest strength was "his delicate and discerning psychological analysis of his characters. He was less interested in their actions than in the motives of their actions." Thomas also rationalized the lovers' behavior by making them act out of reason rather than emotion (Schach xv–xvi), a demonstration of the lethal pride that subordinates faith in divine providence to human intellect.

Sayers's *Tristan* translation reveals her fascination with the beauty and terror of overwhelming passion:

> [T]he exasperating behaviour of the lovers conforms to the ordinary, human developments of that exasperating passion [which has] . . . a kind of desperate beauty faithful through years of sin and unfaith [sic] on both sides, and careless of lies and shifts and incredible dishonour. (Sayers's unpaginated Introduction to *Tristan in Brittany*)

Later she would explore both faces of the "ordinary human developments" of passion. When intelligent, well-born modern women found themselves as trapped in conventional roles as their medieval predecessors had been, as pawns in men's political and economic games, one rare result might be modernized "courtly love," in which the knight faithfully serves his lady for years at a distance, as Lord Peter Wimsey did, waiting for Harriet Vane to decide to marry him. Sayers knew that far more often it would inspire mayhem and murder.

Sayers searched both artistically and personally for a knightly hero like Roland and Tristan. "Brimful of learning" but sadly disappointed herself in three love affairs, she created that hero in her mystery fiction, declaring that the modern detective was "the true successor of Roland and Lancelot," a knight-errant eternally battling for Good against Evil, defending the weak, and bringing the wicked to justice (Sayers, "Omnibus of Crime" 76).

AUTHORSHIP

As the only child of older-than-average parents, an Anglican clergyman and choirmaster and his spirited and intelligent wife, young Dorothy lived until she was four years old at Oxford. The family and their six servants then moved to a large drafty rectory at Bluntisham in the Cambridgeshire fens, an isolated swampy area that meant she spent most of her childhood among nurses, a butler, a cook, and maids, governesses, parents, a grandmother, and an attentive aunt, "cut off from those of her own age by the barrier of class and those of her own class by the barrier of age" (Brabazon 13), almost guaranteeing the development of an infant tyrant. She first amused herself by creating stories for her toy monkeys and later starred herself as "the heroine (or more often the hero) of countless dramatic situations" (Brabazon's comment à propos of Sayers's unpublished "My Edwardian Childhood," Brabazon 13). She loved reading about romantic adventures, especially the glorious defeats of Thermopylae and Roncevaux, and for several years she exchanged letters with her cousin Ivy Shrimpton, five years Dorothy's elder, in the gallant persona of the poignant Athos of Dumas's *Three Musketeers,* which Dorothy at 13 had already read in French.

Sayers's Scholarly Standards

Throughout her life, Sayers upheld her own stern scholarly standards, insisting, "A facility for quotation covers the absence of original thought."

Languages were Sayers's natural element. From the age of six, tutored by her father, Dorothy had delighted in Latin grammar and "hugged as a secret delight" the linguistic intricacies of the Athanasian Creed (*Maker and Craftsman* 3), and at the Godolphin School near Salisbury from 1909 to 1911, a miserable period in her life, she incurred her classmates' animosity by detesting sports and causing her French teacher "to reel under the shock of hearing the subjunctive placed properly for the first time in her life from the lower fifth form" (Sayers's unpublished fragment "Cat o' Mary," quoted in Brabazon 15). At Godolphin she resorted to "slyness, defiance, buffoonery" to survive (Brabazon 48), and Godolphin's emotional Low Church pietism nearly drove her completely away from Christianity. In 1911, the accumulated stress nearly killed her with measles, then pneumonia, and after that a possible nervous breakdown. She emerged as an 18-year-old misfit.

Despite a radical intellectual shift stirring in England while Sayers was at Godolphin, with Darwinism, Freudianism, and Ibsen's then-shocking realistic dramas shattering Victorian certitudes, Dorothy faced all the limitations those conventions placed on a well-bred girl. She had been taught that Bible study was the central preoccupation of educated persons; that service to one's fellow man was a standard of public activity; and that preaching and clarity of expression were the British middle class' supreme educational duties. She would also have been expected to demonstrate her faith by a suitable marriage, praying with the children and servants, and running jumble sales to fund the conversion of the heathen. With her analytical mind, an already apparent gift for dead-on satire, and her impatience with hidebound hypocrisy, however, Dorothy might well have sided with the heathen.

When Sayers entered Oxford's then women-only Somerville College in 1912 on a prestigious Gilchrist Scholarship, she found her abiding intellectual and emotional home, later claiming "There's something about this place . . . that alters all one's values" (*Gaudy Night* 382). Somerville was founded in 1879 as Oxford's first nonsectarian women's residence hall by Mary Fairfax Somerville, "The Queen of Nineteenth-Century Science." Countess Somerville had had to learn her Euclid and algebra from behind a curtain in deference to male sensibilities because British doctors feared that "the strain of intellectual work would injure women's supposedly inferior brains and drive girls mad," but Somerville College grew into an institution now known as "the college of prime ministers (Margaret Thatcher and Indira Gandhi)," novelists (Dorothy L. Sayers, Rose Macaulay, and Iris Murdoch), and scientists, including Nobel Prize-winning chemist Dorothy Hodgkin (Roberts 46). While Sayers was there, Somerville's stringent academic standards and dedication to its foundress' passionate belief in women's rights genteelly defied Oxford's "close corporation of jolly, untidy, lazy, good-for-nothing, humorous old men" accustomed to electing their own successors "since the world began" (C.S. Lewis, quoted in Morris 338–339). Even after British nurses survived World War I's horrors, Oxford's Vice-Chancellor Dr. Lewis Farrell waged a violent rearguard action against women's encroachment on his sacred precincts, urging his Proctors by quoting Antony's Enobarbus: "Under a compelling occasion, let women die" (quoted in Morris 359).

Somerville enabled Sayers to be herself. From 1912 to 1915, probably the happiest years of her life, she reveled in dramatic clothes, dangling earrings, arm-revealing sleeves and "extravagant indoor head-gear" (Brittain, quoted in Hone 17). With two good friends she founded "the Mutual Admiration Society," and wrote and starred in satiric skits and sang contralto in Oxford's illustrious Bach Choir. Women at that time could receive only Oxford "degree certificates," not authentic degrees, but even the certificates would open up improved employment opportunities. Sayers was enormously fortunate, too, in her tutor, the renowned medievalist Mildred Pope, who appears thinly disguised as the lovable and gifted Oxford don Miss Lydgate in Sayers's *Gaudy Night*. Sayers won First Class Honours in French Language and Literature in 1915, the basis for her verse translation *Tristan in Brittany*, published in 1929. At Oxford she also began translating *The Song of Roland* but did not complete and publish it until just before her death in 1957. Sayers's translation reveals her deep admiration and enthusiasm for "the old, brutal incidents of the original Tristan tradition," her appreciation of his psychological insights, and "elaborate analysis of feelings, motives and problems of morality" (*Tristan in Brittany* xxx) and her fascination with flawed heroes, the magnetic but unfaithful Tristan, and the courageous too-proud Roland.

Sayers later declared her first attempt at translating *La Chanson de Roland* had been "very bad" (DLS Letter of September 26, 1952) but she felt more satisfied with her final translation, 40 years later, of this "tale of virile action," which she summed up as "the triumph of good over evil, of Christian ethics 'as naïve and uncomplicated as might be found at any time in the simplest village church' (DLS Letter of March 28, 1946), of welling blood and gushing entrails" (Hannay 120–121)—a fitting description for the struggle of Good against Evil she portrayed in her detective fiction.

Midway through Sayers's university years a worldwide struggle of Good against Evil shook Oxford. Between August 1914 and January 1916, 2,467,000 British men volunteered to fight for King and country, though the life expectancy of an English subaltern at the front lasted only about three weeks. Before World War I bled to a halt in November 1918, 750,000 British men, more than a tenth of those mobilized, had perished, and 2 million more returned severely injured—wounded, gassed, blinded, shell-shocked. Over 2,700 Oxford men died in the "War to End All Wars" (Morris 335),

A continual atmosphere of hectic passion is very trying if you haven't got any of your own.

—Dorothy L. Sayers

depriving the nation of future leaders and many British women of fathers, brothers, lovers, and husbands.

Sayers's immediate post-Oxford life proved bitterly unhappy, both professionally and emotionally. From 1916 until early 1917, she taught Modern Languages at Hull High School for Girls, chafing under a tiny salary, a tough teaching schedule, and underprepared students, and learning that fear was "brutal, bestial, and utterly degrading" during zeppelin attacks on Hull's port facilities (quoted in Brabazon 60). She concluded later that ". . . nearly all school murder stories are good ones . . . probably because it is so easy to believe that murder could be committed in such a place," one that brought on "nervous tension and mutual irritation" and "the utter spiritual misery that a bad head can inflict upon his or her subordinates" (Sayers, quoted in Hone 24).

Her next position, at Basil Blackwell's Oxford publishing firm, was equally brief. She learned about practical publishing, edited three volumes of *Oxford Poetry*, and wrote vigorous Anglo-Catholic poems. In the summer of 1918 she fell hard for Eric Whelpton, an egotistical recuperating lieutenant whose Parisian background, military career, and cavalier attitude toward women likened him to the wounded young "love 'em and leave 'em" hero Tristan (Brunsdale 75). She left Blackwell's in 1919 to become Whelpton's bilingual secretary at L'École des Roches, a famous boys' preparatory school in Normandy, but her unrequited passion for him foundered in 1920 when he abruptly proposed to a gorgeous young woman in London whose last name he did not even know. Though she was among the first seven women to receive Oxford degrees in October 1920 (the year Agatha Christie published her first detective novel, *The Mysterious Affair at Styles*), Sayers was bitterly unhappy in the summer of 1921. She wrote to her mother, "I can't get the work I want, nor the money I want, nor consequently the clothes I want, nor the holiday I want, nor the man I want!" (quoted in Brabazon 1). That fall, though, she pulled herself together and took up an idea she had been flirting with for about six months. By October she had finished *Whose Body?*, her first detective novel and the first appearance of her aristocratic sleuth, Lord Peter Wimsey.

Sayers produced her first two Wimsey novels, *Whose Body?*, sold in 1922 after five rejections, and *Clouds of Witness*, completed in 1923, under trying personal circumstances. Pursuing a quasi-bohemian lifestyle in London, she became involved with John Cournos, an arrogant, handsome, pretentious Jewish-American "Artist with a capital A" who possessed "a self-pity of cosmic proportions" (Brabazon 89–90) (Brabazon, Sayers's official biographer, had access to unpublished letters of Sayers's which John Cournos had deposited under conditions of "great secrecy" in the Harvard University Library (Brabazon 89)). He believed in "free love" and contraception and told her he would never marry; she wanted marriage and believed that

fulfillment consisted in bearing a child, "not simply in sexual intercourse or orgasm" (Brabazon
94). The conflict proved insurmountable, and
after completing *Whose Body?* and starting a new
job as a copywriter at Benson's, London's largest
advertising agency, she gave up on Cournos, who
soon after married the author Sybil Norton.

*Those who prefer their
English sloppy have only
themselves to thank if the
advertisement writer uses his
mastery of vocabulary and
syntax to mislead their
minds.*

—Dorothy L. Sayers

Now 30 and thrown over for the second time
by an egotistically fickle "hero," Sayers wrote
her mother around Christmas of 1922, "I am
coming home . . . on Saturday with a man and a
motorcycle." She called him simply Bill, and
described him as "a poor devil" without a "red cent or a roof" whose "intellect isn't exactly his strong point" (quoted in Brabazon 96). Neither were
Bill's ethics. By the next April, Sayers was pregnant. Bill refused to accept
the child born in January 1904, and she told him off for good that spring.

Sayers had taken two months off from Benson's and had given birth to
John Anthony in Bournemouth, returning to work two weeks later after she
had arranged to board him with her cousin Ivy Shrimpton at Oxford. While
trying to dream up catchy ad slogans, she was working on her second Wimsey novel, *Clouds of Witness,* and a few short detective stories, but she was
deeply distressed. She feared Benson's would fire her, and she lamented, "I
haven't even the last resort of doing away with myself, because what would
Anthony do then, poor thing?" (quoted in Brabazon 105).

As she always did, she coped with pain by working. Sayers exorcised
many of her disappointments in *Clouds of Witness,* demonstrating how passion fatally befogs human intellect, as Tristan's had, while producing one of
Benson's most successful ad campaigns, the Mustard Club, which featured
Baron de Beef, Lord Bacon, and Cookham, Lady Hearty, and Miss Di Ges-
ter. She also took up the saxophone and *le jazz hot,* and in the fall of 1925
she met Oswald Atherton Fleming, a divorced Scottish Army veteran whom
she married quietly the next April while working on her third Wimsey
novel, *Unnatural Death,* drawing material from the popular Sunday *News
of the World,* where Mac was filing crime reports. In the eyes of her High
Anglican belief, she lived in sin with Mac until his death in 1950, according
to her longtime literary agent and friend David Higham, hoping at the start
she could cure his alcoholism, which never happened. Though at first their
relations were amicable, Mac increasingly envied Sayers's growing literary
and financial success and resented her writing. Although he gave John Anthony his name, he never adopted the boy (Dorothy pretended to do so) and
she could never bring her son into their home. Though Dorothy declared
Mac was "good in bed" (Brabazon 116), he had expensive tastes and a
backlog of bills—until she herself died, Dorothy paid Mac's alimony to his
previous wife—so she felt compelled to produce lucrative detective fiction
featuring the knight-errant she really wanted: Lord Peter Wimsey.

At that time, a craze for detective fiction was sweeping Britain. Despite artificial euphoria in the late Roaring Twenties, Britain was experiencing widespread inflation and 10 percent unemployment. The 1927 German economic collapse, brought on largely by the Versailles Treaty's extravagant war reparations, and the American 1929 Wall Street crash together demoralized British and American readers, and by the early 1930s they were clamoring for fantasies of "the good old days" and the never-never land of Fred Astaire and Ginger Rogers, to escape the dismal here and now. "In this context Victorian class privilege acquired a classical status, and developed into a collection of atavistic values depicted in the popular culture dominated by P.G. Wodehouse, Noel Coward, Dorothy Sayers, and Agatha Christie" (Bentley quoted in Haigh 328).

These British writers all used "comedy of manners" to satirize wealthy parasitic socialites. Noel Coward's sophisticated stage comedies like *Private Lives* (1930) wittily skewered the "beautiful people"; Agatha Christie's intricately plotted puzzlers exposed the amusing as well as the grisly motives of the British upper middle class; and Wodehouse's comic Edwardian fiction featured "Bertie Wooster," a two-dimensional parody of inane English aristocracy, and his unflappable butler Jeeves. Dorothy Sayers observed that "We read tales of domestic unhappiness because that happens to us; but when these things gall too close to the sore, we fly to mystery and adventure because they do not, as a rule, happen to us" (*Omnibus of Crime* 1928, 109). Christie concentrated on the "whodunit," but Sayers emphasized the "howdunit" (*CA Online*), combining the clever satiric streak she had exercised in her Oxford skits with plots less ingenious than Christie's but with far more intellectually and emotionally profound characterizations. Her hero Lord Peter Wimsey began in the 1920s as a comic Woosterish figure, but through the 1930s, she developed him into "a true successor of Roland and Lancelot," using the conventions her readers expected then:

> Those were not the days of the swift bash to the skull followed by 60,000 words of psychological insight. Readers . . . expected that the puzzle would be dominant and that the murderer would demonstrate . . . almost supernatural cunning and skill. (P.D. James, Foreword to Brabazon xiv)

THE EVOLUTION OF LORD PETER WIMSEY

In 1920, Dorothy Sayers and her friend Muriel Jaeger were voraciously reading what the British literary establishment thunderously denounced as "sensational and immoral rubbish" (quoted in Mann 27) and planning their own detective series, which never materialized. Dorothy easily sorted out useful nuggets from the "rubbish,' like Anna Katharine Green's nosy old maid figure and Arthur Conan Doyle's deductive-genius detective. She had long admired the theologically conservative work of G.K. Chesterton, who anchored his highly successful Father Brown detective series on his rock-solid conviction of the dualism of Good and Evil:

> . . . we live in an armed camp . . . and . . . the criminals, the children of chaos, are nothing but the traitors within our gates. . . . The agent of social justice [is] the original and poetic figure, while the burglars and footpads are . . . happy in the immemorial respectability of apes and wolves. (Quoted in Hannay 14)

Chesterton's rousing imagery must have hit Sayers's passion for knights and noble deeds broadside.

Sayers also knew the novels of Eric Bentley, who had invented a completely new detective, violating several of Msgr. Ronald Knox's "Rules of Fair Play." Those rules specify that all clues must be available to the reader, with no supernatural interventions; only one secret passage can be employed; no twins or doubles are allowed; the detective cannot be the criminal; no fortuitous accidents or intuitions can help him; the "Watson" cannot be much stupider than the average reader and cannot hide his thoughts from that reader; and no unheard of poisons or complex gadgetry can be introduced—nor any "Chinaman" (possibly a reaction to the previous overuse of exotic foreign villains) (Murphy 169). Knox's rules also barred "love interests" from detective fiction. As a founding member, the creator of its lugubrious initiation oath on

---

The Detection Club

The Detection Club published collaborative works, including *The Floating Admiral* (1932), a novel where each author, including Sayers, contributed a chapter, not knowing what solution the others intended; *Ask a Policeman* (1933), where Sayers and others each solved the same fictional murder case; and a true crime volume, *The Anatomy of Murder* (1936), where Sayers and others each covered a famous homicide case. Sayers also contributed to two 1930s Detection Club collaborative BBC radio detective plays, *Behind the Screen* and *The Scoop*.

---

a skull she named "Eric" for Whelpton and third president of Britain's Detection Club, Sayers initially espoused the "Fair Play" rules, but her theory of detective fiction increasingly diverged from the "pure puzzle" toward the comedy of manners which she accomplished by humanizing her sleuth.

Lord Peter Wimsey's Personal Background

In her first three mysteries, *Whose Body?*, *Clouds of Witness, Unnatural Death*, and *The Unpleasantness at the Bellona Club*, published between

1922 and 1929, Lord Peter Wimsey appeared to male critics as an immensely wealthy Woosterish "silly-ass" second son of the Duke of Denver, "a blond, chinless, burbling type . . . prominent in English culture between the wars" (Green 464). "Sayers may well have intended to parody the 'strong, silent, quietly intelligent, stern-faced Englishmen' popular as literary detectives prior to 1920. . . . her Wimsey is the antithesis of this stereotype: he is short, pampered, garrulous, and not particularly attractive" (Leroy Panek in *CA Online*). Michelle Slung, however, compared Wimsey to Fred Astaire:

> Fair, slender, well-groomed, and dapper, athletic without being brawny, graceful, dignified but able to behave with humor in bizarre situations, chivalrous, romantic . . . a gentleman-scholar and a bibliophile [with] . . . an electric intellectual curiosity . . . underpoweringly sensuous to women in ways that are inexplicable often to other men. (Quoted in *CA Online*)

Sayers gave Wimsey everything she craved and couldn't afford: exquisite clothing, an irreproachable valet, a black grand piano in his primrose and gold and flame-decorated Piccadilly flat, and a taste for rare vintages, rarefied cuisine, and costly rare books, but she could not resist also giving Lord Peter, for all his affectations, more than meets the eye. He had to be "leisured and rich," because, Sayers insisted, he had to be able to drop everything to investigate a crime (*CA Online*). He also could associate effectively with individuals from all social classes, like Mr. Rumm, a burglar turned locksmith, and not one of his stories takes place in a country house.

Early in her literary career, Sayers told a friend that writing a mystery was like creating a mosaic, placing each apparently meaningless separate piece until "one suddenly sees the thing as a consistent picture" (Strout 424). That was Lord Peter's crime-solving method in *Whose Body?*, where a naked obviously Jewish male is found dead in a bathtub. Only after Wimsey had arranged the facts of how the crime was accomplished into a synthesis that provided the criminal's motivation could he arrive at the truth, dueling like a medieval knight with the murderer and leaving the punishment to God by allowing the killer to trap himself.

Lord Peter Wimsey's Detecting Career

In *Clouds of Witness*, her second novel, shadowed by Sayers's pain over the Cournos affair, Lord Peter lost much of his giddy chatter, so that he is closer to the 1930s English aristocracy's self-image: "socially and intellectually subtle, sophisticated, ruthless" (Green 464). His emotional stability grows as he strives to clear his older brother Gerald, the stodgy present Duke, of a murder charge. Like many of his fellow Great War officers, Wimsey suffers from intermittently disabling shell-shock, having been buried alive in an artillery burst, with crushing guilt over the men who died under his command. To balance this darker view of Wimsey, Sayers unleashed her satiric gift on flawed individuals: Gerald's horrifying

Duchess, Helen (possibly patterned on Cournos's wife); the money-grubbing Socialist, like Cournos, that Peter's sister Lady Mary nearly marries; and Denis Cathcart, who like Eric Whelpton, fell foul of a glamorous *femme fatale*. Compared with them, Lord Peter, even with affected Oxford drawl, prestigious Daimler (called "Mrs. Merdle"), monocle, and his terrifying manservant Bunter, seems eminently rational.

> *Bring the offender to justice, but remember that if we all got justice, you and I wouldn't escape either.*
> —Rev. Tredgold to Peter Wimsey
> in *Unnatural Death*

In *Unnatural Death* (1927) and *The Unpleasantness at the Bellona Club* (1928), Sayers humanized Wimsey even more. In *Unnatural Death*, he unmasks a killer with a kiss, but he has to wrestle with a severe dilemma: his delight in the game of criminal investigation clashes with his guilt over sending a human being, albeit a murderer, to the gallows. A kindly country vicar, possibly modeled after Dorothy Sayers's father, hears Wimsey's informal confession and offers a kind of absolution, sending him back into his chivalric battle against Evil with the admonition, "Do what you think is right, according to the laws which we have been brought up to respect. Leave the consequences to God" (*Unnatural Death* 191). *The Unpleasantness at the Bellona Club* opens brilliantly: an aged club member is discovered to have been dead under his newspaper for two days, but it also presents an alcoholic husband furious with "'hard-mouthed cigarette-smoking females who pretend they're geniuses and business women" (*Bellona Club* 55). His wife not only endures the abuse but tries to cover up his vicissitudes until Lord Peter swoops in to save her, like a knight in the shining armor of rectitude. This novel instantly appealed to Sayers's public because, as Sayers put it, ". . . in a nerve-ridden age the study of crime stories provides a safety-valve for the bloodthirsty passions that might otherwise lead us to murder our spouses" (Sayers, "Aristotle on Detective Fiction" 25).

The Unpleasantness at the Bellona Club is Sayers's riff on an old *Punch* joke: "Waiter, take away Lord Whatsisname, he's been dead two days."

Lord Peter Wimsey's Associates

Sayers felt that "Death in particular seems to provide the minds of the Anglo-Saxon race with a greater fund of innocent amusement that any other single subject" [to which she appended the note, "Except Love: but many aspects of this popular subject may be included under Sin"], and "when it is occasioned or accelerated by Sin in its more repugnant shapes, the fun grows faster and more furious" (*Omnibus of Crime* 1934, 11). She utilized this notion in Lord Peter's

> *Don't talk like Jeeves. It irritates me.*
> —Wimsey to Bunter in *Strong Poison*

comedic supporting cast. She three-dimensionalized Wodehouse's unflappable Jeeves into Wimsey's redoubtable Mervyn Bunter, Wimsey's wartime batman and now the quintessential gentleman's gentleman, possessing every virtue and every grace in Great House-style management and cookery as well as technological expertise, especially in photography. Bunter's clever below-stairs interrogation techniques, too, often complement Wimsey's murder investigations.

Jill Paton Walsh managed to marry Mervyn Bunter off in *Thrones, Dominations.*

Wimsey has no Watson, but as a stalwart and practical Oliver of unshakable integrity to Wimsey's dashing Roland, Scotland Yard's solid Charles Parker, who eventually marries Wimsey's sister Lady Mary, allows Wimsey to shine while quietly supplying necessary foot-slogging. An inspired addition to Wimsey's retinue, Miss Alexandra Climpson, the "nosy spinster" Sayers adapted from Anna Katharine Green's detective novels, heads Wimsey's "Cattery," harmless-appearing "superfluous" single women with time on their hands and unquenchable curiosity about other people's affairs who can easily ferret out village secrets and closet skeletons.

Wimsey's family also provides comic relief from the serious business of tracking killers. Lord Peter's mother, Honoria Lucasta, the Dowager Duchess of Denver, flits graciously through several novels, supplying details about her son and his doings in hilarious letters to her friends. Sayers loved to write lively fictional letters, as her epistolary novel *The Documents in the Case* (1930) indicates. Linguistically her fictional letters strongly resemble Sayers's own correspondence from 1928 to 1935. The Dowager Duchess' brother Paul Delgardie also provides Gallic insights (the juicier ones in French) into Peter's amatory development, while Helen, the infinitely awful current Duchess of Denver, and her husband Gerald offer targets for many of Peter's—and Sayers's—sallies against the purposelessness and debilitation of Britain's landed aristocracy.

Lord Peter Wimsey's Developing Strengths and Weaknesses

"As he matures, Wimsey turns more and more to traditional English and Christian values" (*CA Online*). According to Sayers, "as the detective ceases to be impenetrable and infallible and becomes a man touched with the feeling of our infirmities, so the rigid technique of the art necessarily expands a little" (quoted in Strout 426). With her successive additions of colorful secondary characters and enriched backgrounds for her hero, Sayers as early as *Unnatural Death* began to consider shifting from the flat picture-puzzle concept of mystery fiction to a "round" story combining the appeal to the emotions with the appeal to the intellect. However, she did not fully execute the change and the concurrent developments in Lord Peter Wimsey to accommodate it until after she had worked out her own theory of detective fiction, presented in introductions to three anthologies of crime and

As I grow older and older,
And totter to the tomb,
I find that I care less and less
Who goes to bed with whom.
　　　　　　—Dorothy L. Sayers

horror fiction, *The Omnibus of Crime* (1928, 1931, and 1934). In the first, hailed as "the finest single piece of analytical writing about the detective story" (Hone 56), she established the theoretical basis for her combination of the traditional detective novel with the comedy of manners, declaring that the demise of prewar certitudes required that crime fiction achieve "both a higher level of writing and a more competent delineation of character than before" as well as a sleuth with "a tenderer human feeling" under his "frivolous or ruthlessly efficient exterior" (quoted in Brunsdale 109).

Sayers wrote a group of romance-less Wimsey mysteries in the early 1930s—*The Five Red Herrings* (1931), *Murder Must Advertise* (1933), and *The Nine Tailors* (1934)—because she was still operating under her 1928 assumption that "the love interest" was "a fettering convention from which detective fiction is only very slowly freeing itself," and she found "blameworthy" "the heroes who insist on fooling about after young women when they ought to be putting their minds on the job of detection" (*Omnibus of Crime* 1928, 103). These mysteries sold well, but their readers wanted less pure puzzle and more Wimsey. In *The Five Red Herrings,* Lord Peter elegantly proves his solution, but he apologizes when the crime turns out to have been an accident, and Sayers allowed both him and the villain more "good streaks" and convincing "human feelings" (*Omnibus of Crime* 1928, 103) than she had in earlier books. *Murder Must Advertise,* based on Sayers's years at Benson's, which she left in 1931 to write full time, parallels two "cardboard worlds," the false world of advertising and the real-world drug scene. By thrusting Lord Peter into Pym's Publicity to break a drug ring, Sayers gave him a social conscience, making him realize the "enormous commercial importance of the lower middle class's hunger for luxury and leisure, which allowed them to be bullied or wheedled into wasting hardearned money on momentary and illusory gratification.

Sayers set *The Nine Tailors* in England's fen country and built it on her conviction that human beings are incapable of understanding God's infinite Mind. The case taught Lord Peter humility, because for the first time his vaunted powers of deduction stalled; he sallied forth to rescue a damsel in distress and found himself an innocent participant in homicide, so that he questioned whether he is "doin' good that evil may come" (*Nine Tailors* 214). Sayers later addressed this moral dilemma in several theological essays.

By the time Sayers finished *The Nine Tailors* in 1933 she was physically and mentally exhausted and on the verge of leaving Mac. After a three-week holiday, she decided to stay with him and informally "adopted" John Anthony under the surname of Fleming. By now, too, like Agatha Christie with Hercule Poirot, Sayers had become totally bored with Lord Peter Wimsey, and she contemplated an "infanticidal intention"—killing him off by the time-honored device of matrimony (Sayers's "Gaudy Night" essay, quoted in Haycraft 209). To do it, she would have to incorporate a convincing "love interest" into the business of crime detection and find a suitable woman to match Lord Peter's talents. That woman, of course, was Sayers herself.

Lord Peter Wimsey's Great Romance

Sayers took a considerable risk by reshaping Lord Peter into a husband, because his enormous popularity enabled her to support Mac, Anthony, her aunt, and a houseful of rescued dogs and cats in a tough economic period, but she "knew it was useless to try and write with a view of what the public might like, so she wrote what she wanted to write and hoped for the best" ("Gaudy Night" quoted in Haycraft 217). It took her three more detective novels to accomplish it: *Strong Poison* (1930), *Have His Carcase* (1932), and *Gaudy Night* (1935), as well as a postlude, *Busman's Honeymoon*, first a 1936 play and then a 1937 novel. She also left material resulting in two posthumous works, *Thrones, Dominations* (1998) and *A Presumption of Death* (2003), completed and published by Jill Paton Walsh. "I laid him [Wimsey] firmly on the operating-table," Sayers wrote in 1937, "and chipped away at his internal mechanism through three longish books. . . . At the end of the process he was twelve years older than when he started" ("Gaudy Night" in Haycraft 211–212) and a wholly different man.

In her Harriet-and-Lord Peter novels, Dorothy Sayers's challenge was to make Peter "a complete human being, with a past and a future, with a consistent family and social history, with a complicated psychology and even the rudiments of a religious outlook" ("Gaudy Night" quoted in Haycraft 211). These novels follow the lovers through a Hell-Purgatory-Heaven sequence that probably Sayers used unconsciously, since she had not yet begun to study and translate Dante's *Divine Comedy*. In the first two novels, Harriet and Peter recognize in others the horrifying results of sin, particularly the fundamental sin of pride. In *Gaudy Night*, they purge themselves of pride, the "kingdom of hell within us" (*Omnibus of Crime* 31) in Oxford's restorative scholarly atmosphere. May believes Sayers belongs to the "mythical vein" termed "Oxford Romantic," viewing Oxford as "not just a city of the intellect but of the soul" and hence a source of spiritual healing (May 233). In *Busman's Honeymoon*, the dénouement of the Wimsey saga, they reach heavenly bliss together.

In *Strong Poison*, Wimsey first glimpses Harriet Vane, the woman he will marry, in the dock, on trial for murdering her former lover, an "Artist with a capital A." With his chivalric instincts aroused and his intellectual curiosity piqued, Peter's "heart turned to water" (*Strong Poison* 35), and in a few weeks of penitential Advent, he saves Harriet from the gallows and offers her his aristocratic hand in marriage, assuring her he makes love "rather nicely" (*Strong Poison* 38)—only to be rejected. Sayers later commented, "I could not marry Peter off to the young woman he had . . . rescued from death and infamy, because I could find no form of words in which she could accept him without loss of self-respect" ("Gaudy Night" 211).

In the gloomier *Have His Carcase*, Harriet stumbles on a bloody corpse and attempts an investigation, only to discover she needs Wimsey's help. Physically intrigued because "he strips better than I should have expected" and emotionally caught up in "modified rapture" when Peter masters a skittish mare (*Carcase* 286), horsemanship being the defining element of chivalry, Harriet's dangerous pride still prevents her from accepting him.

In *Gaudy Night*, widely considered Sayers's best novel, she successfully integrated a detective plot with comedy of manners. Since *The Documents in the Case* (1930), her non-Wimsey epistolary novel, Sayers believed, ". . . each successive book of mine worked gradually nearer to the sort of thing I had in view" ("Gaudy Night," quoted in Haycraft 209), with a strong "criticism of life" necessary to each plot. *Gaudy Night* grew out of autobiographical attempts she made between 1930 and 1934, but she was specifically inspired by an invitation to offer the university toast at a Somerville "Gaudy," an annual reunion she had hitherto ignored. Back in Oxford's healing atmosphere, she discovered that one had to thank a university education "before everything" for "the habit of intellectual integrity, which is at once the foundation and the result of scholarship," the theme of this rich novel, where she also provided an unforgettable image of tragic mismarriage, comparing a once-brilliant scholar wed to an indigent farmer to "a Derby winner making shift with a coal cart" (*Gaudy Night*, 212, 45).

Sayers set Harriet Vane among gently satirized "Shrewsbury College" members of the Senior Common Room and in the amorous sights of a bumptious undergraduate to investigate a nasty case of poison-penmanship. When Peter at last arrived in Oxford, he and Harriet purged themselves of pride; he found the perfect words to seal their commitment as intellectual equals that have thrilled readers down the years: "*Placetne, magistra?*" After five years, Harriet could reply, "*Placet*" (*Gaudy Night* 382). Sayers claimed that the plot of *Gaudy Night* "exhibits intellectual integrity as the one great permanent value in an emotionally unstable world . . . the thing . . . that I had been wanting to say all my life" ("Gaudy Night" quoted in Haycraft 213).

Sayers's biographical note to *Gaudy Night* provides a new motivating background for Wimsey and deepens his "religious rudiments," so much like her own. In Oxford, too, she let Wimsey show Harriet his weaknesses, instead of the strengths she had heretofore admired: his "physical conceit" and resentment of his small stature, his "regret at the debilitation of his caste" (Brunsdale 126), and his "cursed hankering" after the old values that had spurred the Spartans at Thermopylae and Roland at Roncevaux (*Gaudy Night* 238). At the close of every case Peter finds himself torn apart by "the old nightmares and shell shock again" (Hannay 45), and at the end of *Busman's Honeymoon* he breaks down in Harriet's arms, weeping for the criminal that he consigned to the gallows. Sayers brought "the love-problem into line with the detective-problem so that the same key should unlock both at once" (Strout 426): the detective as successor to Lancelot and Roland, healed of his flaws by accepting equality between lovers. Sayers called their symbiotic relationship "the two moods of the artistic spirit . . . in two distinct personalities," with Peter "the interpretative artist, the romantic soul at war with the realistic brain" and Harriet "his complement, the creative artist. . . . Their only hope of repose is in union" ("Gaudy Night," quoted in Haycraft 53). Dorothy Sayers gave them a gift she herself never would enjoy. A hilarious *Busman's Honeymoon* at Talboys, their country estate, rounds off the Wimsey saga when on their wedding night they discover the week-old corpse of the former owner in the cellar.

THE ENDURING APPEAL OF SAYERS'S MYSTERY NOVELS

As the storm clouds of World War II gathered, Dorothy L. Sayers's interest in pursuing Lord Peter's married life dwindled. She privately printed *Papers Relating to the Family of Wimsey* in 1937, and the BBC produced her detective novels for radio in 1938.

She spent a brief and mutually unsatisfactory stint with the British Ministry of Information (she submitted a plan for reorganizing the entire Ministry which they ignored), and she retaliated on the Ministry in print during the dark "Phony War" winter of 1939 to 1940. The "Wimsey Papers," 11 morale-boosting articles for *The Spectator*, gave "the Ministry of Instruction and Morale" Lord Peter's loathsome sister-in-law Helen, with three secretaries paid "by a grateful country to endure her" (Sayers, "Wimsey Papers" 672).

Sayers wrote her last Wimsey story, "Talboys," in 1942. During the war she turned to theologically oriented literary pursuits, several religious plays for cathedral festivals and major religious essays, among them *The Mind of the Maker* (1941), an ingenious exploration of the doctrine of the Trinity. She also wrote and helped produce *The Man Born to Be King*, her 12-part radio play on the life of Christ, to bolster British morale during the Battle of Britain and the Blitz. During a 1944 Nazi rocket raid, she snatched up a copy of Dante's *Divine Comedy* for bomb-shelter reading. Dante instantly smote her with "a devouring passion": "What a writer! God's body and bones, what a writer!" (quoted in Brabazon 229). With the exception of one interruption in 1956 with her translation of *The Song of Roland*, she spent the rest of her life learning medieval Italian and translating the *Comedy* into English *terza rima*. When she died suddenly on December 17, 1957, her friend Barbara Reynolds seamlessly completed her translation of Dante's *Paradise*. Since then, Sayers's comprehensive Dante introductions and notes have won widespread praise. The Dorothy L. Sayers Society, founded in

1976, preserves Sayers-related materials and artifacts, holds conventions, and publishes essays, articles, and books.

SCREEN ADAPTATIONS

About 20 years after Sayers's death, British actor Edward Petherbridge—blond, monocled, impeccably tailored, and a member of Laurence Olivier's National Theatre Company—starred with his wife Emily Richard in screen adaptations of the Wimsey-Harriet Vane mysteries. Around the same time, dark-haired comic star Ian Carmichael who had played Bertie Wooster in the television series *The World of Wooster,* acted in five BBC drama series based on Sayers's earlier novels that proved popular even though most Wimsey fans envisioned their hero as either Leslie Howard or Peter O'Toole. Petherbridge and Carmichael also made audio versions of the Sayers novels in which they starred. The difference between the two portrayals illustrates the enormous gulf between the amusing silly-ass detective and the flawed but unforgettably chivalric human hero of Sayers's mature fiction.

SAYERS'S PLACE IN POPULAR CULTURE

During her lifetime, Sayers's later detective novels met with some critical disparagement. J.R.R. Tolkien, who liked Dorothy herself, ". . . could not stand *Gaudy Night.* I followed P. Wimsey so far, by which time I conceived a loathing for him not surpassed by any other character in literature known to me, unless by his Harriet" (quoted in Carpenter 109). Q.D. Leavis dismissed *Gaudy Night* as "a best-selling bundle of old clothes," denouncing Sayers's "literary glibness and spiritual illiteracy," and insisting that only D.H. Lawrence . . . could have reviewed [*Gaudy Night* and *Busman's Honeymoon*] adequately" (Q.D. Leavis 335). Symons in 1972 thought Wimsey had not changed at all in *Gaudy Night,* which he declared was a "women's novel," full of "tedious pseudo-serious chat," and declared that all of Sayers's mysteries, excepting *Murder Must Advertise,* display "an increasing pretentiousness, a dismal sentimentality, and a slackening of the close plotting that had been her chief virtue" (Symons 129). Today Sayers's detective novels and her theory of mystery fiction inspire respect for their erudition, wit, conservative Christianity, and their evolution of the "silly-ass" hero into a convincingly complex human being in the context of a detective story combined with the comedy of manners. Sayers

In respect for Sayers's theological achievements, six robed bishops took part in Sayers's memorial service in January 1958 in St. Margaret's Church, Westminster.

would surely be pleased by the great advances women have made since then [their first Oxford degrees in 1920], but she would detest the jargon-choked, muddy blandness of contemporary academic prose. And she would surely be dismayed at find how influential the idea has become that a woman academic had better take "the woman's point of view," or else be deemed guilty of complicity in sexism. (Haack 4)

Feminists generally see Sayers's mystery novels involving Harriet Vane as questioning "underlying hierarchies and binaries of our western culture: gender roles, work ethics, intellectual equality" (McClellan 321). From that perspective, *Gaudy Night* even "utilizes a genre with mass cultural appeal . . . to enact a potent critique of patriarchal culture and its attendant policing of gender and sexual identity" (McFadden 355).

A 2006 Chicago stage adaptation of *Gaudy Night* seemed to take a more measured approach, stressing that "the intersection between love and equality" illustrates "all of Sayers's doubts and confidence about her era: Can a smart woman still love? Does any man really believe in equality?" (Jones 2). Seeing *Gaudy Night* as Sayers's examination of "What do women want?" from several angles and her conclusion, "To be equal and individual" (Haack 2), Sayers's women readers—and perhaps some men—overall respond with a heartfelt or wishful "Amen."

Dorothy L. Sayers's fairy godmother allowed her to move the detective story from pure puzzle to "a book in which a whole social milieu could be examined and chronicled": no mean achievement, though it pales besides her grandest creation: Lord Peter Wimsey, "a character to be adored, or derided, and clearly one of the élite of Great Detectives" (Keating 53).

PARALLEL CHRONOLOGY

Major Events Related to Dorothy L. Sayers	World Events
	1841–1844 Poe's detective stories
	1863 LeFanu's stories become popular
	1867 Earliest detective novel, *The Dead Letter,* by Seeley Register (U.S.)
	1868 First English detective novel, *The Moonstone,* by Wilkie Collins
	1875 Oxford's first examinations for women
	1879 Opening of Somerville Hall, Oxford
	1881 Somerville Hall, Oxford, became Somerville College

Major Events Related to Dorothy L. Sayers	World Events
	1887 First Sherlock Holmes story, *A Study in Scarlet*
June 13, 1893 Dorothy L. Sayers born at Oxford	
	1894 All Oxford BA examinations open to women
	1897 Queen Victoria's Diamond Jubilee
1900 At Bluntisham she studies Latin with her father	
	1901 Queen Victoria dies; Edward VII becomes king
	1905–1909 Baroness Orczy writes popular detective stories
1906 Sayers meets her cousin Ivy Shrimpton	
	1908 G.K. Chesterton writes *The Man Who Was Thursday*
1909 She enters Godolphin School	
1911 Sayers leaves Godolphin due to illness	
1912 Sayers wins Gilchrist Scholarship to Oxford; Eric Whelpton begins at Oxford; John Cournos arrives in England from U.S.	1912 *Trent's Last Case,* by E.C. Bentley
1913 She acts, writes, debates at Somerville	1913 Suffragette demonstrations, London
1914 She takes summer trip to Continent	Aug. 1914 Outbreak of World War I
1915 She takes First Class Honours; begins reading detective fiction	1915 Margaret Sanger jailed for *Family Limitation*
1916 She teaches at Hull; *Op. 1* published; Whelpton invalided to England	1916 Battle of Verdun
1917 Sayers takes job at Blackwell's, Oxford; translates *Tristan*	1917 Bobbed hair becomes craze
1918 Whelpton appears in Oxford; "Mac" Fleming leaves army and wife	1918 Flu pandemic; British women over 30 receive vote; Armistice Nov. 11
1919 Sayers takes job in France with Whelpton	1919 Treaty of Versailles
1920 First mention of Lord Peter; Dorothy receives Oxford BA and MA	1920 *The Mysterious Affair at Styles,* Agatha Christie's first novel
	1921 BBC founded

(Continued)

Major Events Related to Dorothy L. Sayers	World Events
1921 *Whose Body?* completed; Cournos arrives in Oxford	
1922 Sayers works at Benson's; *Whose Body?* sold; begins *Clouds of Witness*; relationship with Cournos ends	**1922** Mercedes-Daimler dominates racing; Marie Stopes opens first British birth control clinic
Dec. 1922 Dorothy brings home "Bill"	
1923 *Whose Body?* published	
1924 John Anthony born Jan. 4; Jan. 28 Ivy takes over his care; Dorothy breaks off with "Bill"	
1925 Fleming's divorce is finalized	
1926 *Clouds of Witness* published; Dorothy marries Fleming on April 13	**1926** Princess Elizabeth of York born
1927 *Unnatural Death* published	**1927** German economy collapses
1928 Dorothy helps found Detection Club; *Lord Peter Views the Body* published	**1928** British women can vote at 21
1929 Dorothy buys house at Witham; *Tristan in Brittany* published	**1929** U.S. stock market collapse
1930 *The Documents in the Case* and *Strong Poison* published	**1930** Maginot Line begun
1931 *Five Red Herrings* published	
1932 *Have His Carcase* published	**1932** British depression and wide unemployment
1933 Crisis year for Sayers	**1933** Hitler elected chancellor; concentration camps begun
1934 *Nine Tailors* published; Sayers "adopts" Anthony; attends Oxford Gaudy	
1935 Sayers works on *Busman's Honeymoon*	**1935** Italy invades Ethiopia; purges in USSR
1936 Sayers works on "Thrones, Dominations"	**1936** George V dies; Spanish Civil War begins; Edward VIII abdicates
1937 Sayers begins writing religious festival plays	**1937** Chamberlain becomes Prime Minister
1938 Sayers begins work on Wilkie Collins project	
1939 Sayers writes patriotic essay *Begin Here*	**1939** Sept. 3, World War II begins
1940 *The Man Born to Be King* starts	**1940** Churchill becomes Prime Minister; Dunkirk evacuation begins May 25; Battle of Britain; The Blitz

Major Events Related to Dorothy L. Sayers	World Events
	1941 Japan attacks Pearl Harbor; U.S. enters war
1942 "Talboys," last Wimsey story, written	1942 Turning point of World War II; U.S. Pacific victories and British victory at El Alamein
Aug. 1944 Sayers comments on *Divine Comedy*	1944 June: Normandy invasion begins
Dec. 1944 She begins translating *Hell*	
	1945 Atomic bombing of Japan ends war
1946 Anthony discovers parentage	1946 Severe fuel crisis in Britain; Churchill's "Iron Curtain" speech
1947 Mac's health declining	1947 Nationalization of key British industries
1948 Translation of *Hell* published	
	1949 Berlin airlift
June 9, 1950 Mac dies	1950 Korean War begins
	1952 First U.S. hydrogen bomb tested
1955 *Purgatory* translation published	
1956 Sayers begins translation of *The Song of Roland*	1956 Suez crisis; Britain loses prestige
1957 Sayers dies at home at Witham	
1962 *Paradise* translation completed by Barbara Reynolds and published	
1971 First Wimsey television serial adaptation, *Clouds of Witness*, starring Ian Carmichael on Masterpiece Theater	
1973 Anthony's parentage discovered and published by Janet Hitchman; televised version of *The Unpleasantness at the Bellona Club* (Carmichael)	
1974 *Murder Must Advertise* televised (Carmichael)	
1975 *The Nine Tailors* televised (Carmichael)	
1976 The Dorothy L. Sayers Society is founded	
1977 *Five Red Herrings* televised (Carmichael)	
1979 *Dorothy L. Sayers,* by Ralph Hone published	

(Continued)

Major Events Related to Dorothy L. Sayers	World Events
1981 *Dorothy L. Sayers,* by James Brabazon published **1998** *Thrones, Dominations* completed and published by Jill Paton Walsh **2003** *The Presumption of Death,* shaped by Walsh from Sayers's notes, is published	

PRIMARY SOURCES

Mystery Fiction

Whose Body? London: Unwin, 1923.

Clouds of Witness. London: Unwin, 1925.

Unnatural Death. London: Benn, 1927.

The Unpleasantness at the Bellona Club. London: Benn, 1928.

Lord Peter Views the Body. London: Gollancz, 1928 (collection of short fiction).

The Documents in the Case (with Robert Eustace). London: Benn, 1930 (a non-Wimsey novel).

Strong Poison. New York: Brewer & Warren, 1930.

The Five Red Herrings. London: Gollancz, 1931.

The Floating Admiral. London: Hodder and Staunton, 1931 (collaborative novel with members of The Detection Club; Sayers contributed the Introduction, Chapter VII, and the Solution).

Have His Carcase. London: Gollancz, 1932.

Murder Must Advertise. London: Gollancz, 1933.

Ask a Policeman. London: A. Barker, 1933 (collaborative novel, with members of The Detection Club. Sayers contributed "The Conclusions of Mr. Roger Sheringham").

Hangman's Holiday. London: Gollancz, 1933 (collection of short fiction).

The Nine Tailors. London: Gollancz, 1934.

Gaudy Night. London: Gollancz, 1936.

Six against the Yard. London: Selwyn and Blount, 1936 (collaboration with members of The Detection Club).

Busman's Honeymoon. London: Gollancz, 1937 (novel adaptation of play).

Double Death. London: Gollancz, 1939 (collaborative novel with members of The Detection Club).

No Flowers by Request. Published as a serial in *The Daily Sketch,* 1953 (collaborative novel with members of The Detection Club; Sayers contributed Chapter 1).

Striding Folly, Including Three Final Lord Peter Wimsey Stories,. London: New English Library, 1972 (collection of short fiction, including "Talboys," written in 1942).

Lord Peter. New York: Avon, 1972 (collection of all twenty-one Wimsey short stories, plus Carolyn Heilbrun's article "Sayers, Lord Peter and God" and E.C. Bentley's parody "Greedy Night."

Thrones, Dominations (completed by Jill Paton Walsh from material in articles, notes, and unpublished manuscripts by Dorothy L. Sayers). New York: St. Martin's Press, 1998.

A Presumption of Death (a novel shaped by Jill Paton Walsh out of material left by Sayers). New York: St. Martin's Press, 2003.

Mystery Drama

Busman's Honeymoon (with Muriel St. Clare Byrne). London: Gollancz, 1937.

Romantic Comedy

Love All, posthumously published with *Busman's Honeymoon.* Kent, OH: Kent State University Press, 1984.

Religious Drama

Four Sacred Plays. London: Gollancz, 1948; includes *The Zeal of Thy House* (1937), *The Devil to Pay* (1939), *He That Should Come* (radio Nativity play) (1939), *The Just Vengeance* (1946).

The Man Born to Be King (12-part radio play cycle on the life of Christ, first presented by the BBC (December 1941 to October 1942); London; Gollancz, 1943.

The Emperor Constantine. London: Gollancz, 1951.

Translations

Tristan in Brittany. London: Benn, 1929.

The Heart of Stone, Being the Four Canzoni of the "Pietra" Group by Dante. Witham: Clarke, 1946.

The Comedy of Dante Alighieri, the Florentine. Harmondsworth, UK: Penguin, 1949–1964. (*Paradise* completed by Barbara Reynolds, 1962).

The Song of Roland. Harmondsworth, UK: Penguin, 1957.

Essays

Introduction to *Great Short Stories of Detection, Mystery, and Horror.* London: Gollancz, 1928 (U.S. title *The Omnibus of Crime*).

"The Present Status of the Mystery Story," *London Mercury,* November 1930.

Introduction to *Great Short Stories of Detection, Mystery, and Horror, Second Series.* London: Gollancz, 1931 (U.S. title *The Second Omnibus of Crime*).

Introduction to *Great Short Stories of Detection, Mystery, and Horror, Third Series.* London: Gollancz, 1934 (U.S. title *The Third Omnibus of Crime*).

"Aristotle on Detective Fiction." *English* 1 (1936): 23–25.

"Wimsey Papers." *The Spectator,* November 1939–January 1940.

Begin Here. London: Gollancz, 1940.

The Mind of the Maker. London: Methuen, 1941.

The Other Six Deadly Sins. London: Methuen, 1943.

"Gaudy Night" in *The Art of the Mystery Story,* ed. Howard Haycroft. New York: Simon and Schuster, 1946: 208–221 (essay originally published in 1937).

Unpopular Opinions. London: Gollancz, 1946.

Creed or Chaos? London: Methuen, 1947.

The Lost Tools of Learning. London: Methuen, 1948.

Introductory Papers on Dante. London: Methuen, 1954.

Further Papers on Dante. London: Methuen, 1957.

The Poetry of Search and the Poetry of Statement. London: Gollancz, 1963.

Are Women Human? Grand Rapids, MI: Eerdmans, 1971.

A Matter of Eternity. Grand Rapids, MI: Eerdmans, 1973.

Wilkie Collins: A Critical and Biographical Study. Edited by E.R. Gregory. Toledo, OH: Friends of the Toledo Public Library, 1977.

The Whimsical Christian. New York: Macmillan, 1978.

Sayers on Holmes. Altadena, CA: Mythopoeic Press, 2001.

Principal Unpublished Works

"My Edwardian Childhood" (autobiographical fragment) ca. 1932.

"Cat o' Mary" (autobiographical fragment) ca. 1934.

Other Works Related to Detection

Papers Relating to the Family of Wimsey, privately printed, 1936.

An Account of Lord Mortimer Wimsey, the Hermit of the Wash, privately printed, 1937.

The Wimsey Family: A Fragmentary History Compiled from Correspondence with Dorothy L. Sayers, compiled by C.W. Scott-Giles. New York: Harper, 1977.

Letters

(All edited by Barbara Reynolds. New York: St. Martin's Press.)

The Letters of Dorothy L. Sayers, 1899–1936: The Making of a Detective Novelist, 1996.

The Letters of Dorothy L. Sayers, 1937–1944: From Novelist to Playwright, 1997.

The Letters of Dorothy L. Sayers, 1945–1950: A Noble Daring, 1999.

The Letters of Dorothy L. Sayers, 1951–1957: In the Midst of Life, 2000.

The Letters of Dorothy L. Sayers: Child and Woman of Her Time, 2002.

Miscellaneous Other Works

Dorothy L. Sayers also wrote children's books, contributed essays, stories, and articles to books and periodicals, and reviewed books for the *London Sunday Times*.

Manuscript Collections

The Humanities Research Center, University of Texas, Austin, Texas.

The Marion E. Wade Collection, Wheaton College, Wheaton, Illinois.

Media Adaptations

(All available through Acorn Media unless otherwise specified.)

Busman's Honeymoon, an MGM movie (1940), a BBC television production (1947), and a BBC radio production (1949) (N/A).

Whose Body?, six-episode BBC radio production (Dec. 2, 1947, to Jan. 6, 1948) (N/A).

Murder Must Advertise, BBC radio production, 1957; BBC-TV Masterpiece Theatre production (1973), starring Ian Carmichael; VHS; DVD.

Strong Poison, BBC radio production (1963); video version starring Edward Petherbridge; VHS, DVD.

Have His Carcase, video version starring Edward Petherbridge; VHS, DVD.

Gaudy Night, video version starring Edward Petherbridge; VHS, DVD.

"Lord Peter Wimsey Stories," BBC radio series (April 6, 1970, to June 1, 1970) (N/A).

Unnatural Death, BBC radio production (1972) (N/A).

Clouds of Witness, BBC-TV Masterpiece Theatre production (1972) (also aired by PBS); starring Ian Carmichael; VHS, DVD.

The Unpleasantness at the Bellona Club, BBC-TV Masterpiece Theatre (1974), starring Ian Carmichael; VHS, DVD.

Murder Must Advertise, BBC-TV Masterpiece Theatre (1974), starring Ian Carmichael; VHS, DVD.

The Five Red Herrings, BBC-TV Masterpiece Theatre (1975), starring Ian Carmichael; VHS, DVD.

The Nine Tailors, BBC-TV Masterpiece Theatre (1976), starring Ian Carmichael; VHS/DVD.

Audio Tapes

(All unabridged and published by Chivers Audio Books.)

Busman's Honeymoon—Ian Carmichael

Clouds of Witness—Ian Carmichael

Documents in the Case—Ian Carmichael

Five Red Herrings—Nigel Anthony

Gaudy Night—Patrick Malahide

Hangman's Holiday—Ian Carmichael

In the Teeth of the Evidence—Ian Carmichael

Lord Peter Views the Body—Ian Carmichael

Murder Must Advertise—Ian Carmichael

The Nine Tailors—Ian Carmichael

Striding Folly—Ian Carmichael

Strong Poison—Ian Carmichael

Unnatural Death—Ian Carmichael

The Unpleasantness at the Bellona Club—Ian Carmichael

Whose Body?—Ian Carmichael

Thrones, Dominations—Edward Petherbridge

A Presumption of Death—Edward Petherbridge

Stage Adaptation

Gaudy Night, stage adaptation by Frances Limoncelli, Lifeline Theatre, Chicago, June–July 2006.

WORKS CITED

Brabazon, James. *Dorothy L. Sayers: The Life of a Courageous Woman.* New York: Scribner's, 1981.

Brunsdale, Mitzi. *Dorothy L. Sayers: Solving the Mystery of Wickedness.* Oxford: Berg, 1989.

————. "Dorothy L. Sayers: Medieval Mystery Maker." *Women Medievalists and the Academy,* edited by Jane Chance. Madison: University of Wisconsin Press, 2005: 423–439.

Carpenter, Humphrey. *The Inklings.* Boston: Houghton Mifflin, 1979.

"Dorothy L[eigh] Sayers." Contemporary Authors Online. http://web2.infotrac .galegroup.com, accessed 2/27/2007. Cited as *CA Online.*

Gies, Frances. *The Knight in History.* New York: Harper & Row, 1984.

Gies, Joseph and Frances. *Life in a Medieval Castle.* New York: Harper & Row, 1974.

Green, Martin. "The Detection of a Snob." *Listener* March 14, 1963: 464.

Haack, Susan. "After My Own Heart: Dorothy L. Sayers' Feminism." *New Criterion* 19 (May 2001): 23–33.

Haigh, Christopher, ed. *The Cambridge Historical Encyclopedia of Great Britain and Ireland.* Cambridge, UK: Cambridge University Press, 1985.

Hamilton, Edith. "*Gaudeamus Igitur.*" Review of *Gaudy Night. Saturday Review of Literature* 13 (February 22, 1936): 6.

Hannay, Margaret P., ed. *As Her Whimsey Took Her.* Kent, OH: Kent State University Press, 1979.

Harmon, Robert B. *An Annotated Guide to the Works of Dorothy L. Sayers.* New York: Garland, 1977.

Haycraft, Howard, ed. *The Art of the Mystery Story.* New York: Simon & Schuster, 1942.

————, ed. *The Omnibus of Crime,* originally published as *Great Short Stories of Detection, Mystery, and Horror.* London: Gollancz, 1928; cited as *Omnibus of Crime* (U.S. title).

Hone, Ralph E. *Dorothy L. Sayers: A Literary Biography.* Kent, OH; Kent State University Press, 1979.

Jones, Chris. "'Gaudy Night' is Feminist Thriller with Touch of Wimsey." *Chicago Tribune,* June 5, 2006.

Keating, H.R.F. *Crime and Mystery: The 100 Best Books.* New York: Carroll & Graf, 1987.

Leavis, Q.D., "The Case of Miss Dorothy Sayers." *Scrutiny* 6 (December 1937).

McClellan, Ann. "Alma Mater: Women, the Academy, and Mothering in Dorothy L. Sayers' *Gaudy Night.*" *LIT: Literature Interpretation Theory* 15 (October–December 2004): 321–346.

McFadden, Marya. "Queerness at Shrewsbury: Homoerotic Desire in *Gaudy Night.*" *Modern Fiction Studies* 46 (Summer 2000): 355–379.

Mann, Jessica. *Deadlier Than the Male.* New York: Macmillan, 1981.

May, Radmila. "Murder Most Oxford." *Contemporary Review* 277 (October 2000): 232–240.

Morris, Jan. *The Oxford Book of Oxford.* Oxford, UK: Oxford University Press, 1978.

Murphy, Bruce. *The Encyclopedia of Murder and Mystery.* New York: St. Martin's Press, 1999.

Roberts, Beth Ellen. "Mary Somerville and the College She Inspired." *British Heritage* (July 2007): 46–49.

Strout, Cushing. "Romance and the Literary Detective: The Legacy of Dorothy Sayers." *Sewanee Review* 109 (Summer 2001): 423–436.

Symons, Julian. *Mortal Consequences.* New York: Harper & Row, 1972.

Wilkie, Brian, and James Hurt. *Literature of the Western World.* 2 vols. Upper Saddle River, NJ: 2001.

Willis, Connie. *The Winds of Marble Arch and Other Stories.* Burton, MI: Subterranean Press, 2007.

FURTHER READING

Auden, W.H. *The Dyer's Hand and Other Essays.* New York: Random House, 1962.

Bargainnier, Earl F. *Ten Women of Mystery.* Bowling Green, OH: Bowling Green State University Press, 1981.

Briggs, Asa. *A Social History of England.* New York: Viking Press, 1983.

Brown, Janice. *The Seven Deadly Sins in the Work of Dorothy L. Sayers.* Kent, OH: Kent State University Press, 1998.

Byrne, Muriel St. Clare, and Catherine Hope Mansfield. *Somerville College, 1879–1921.* Oxford, UK: Oxford University Press, 1927.

Cawelti, John. *Adventure, Mystery, and Romance: Formula Stories as Art and Popular Culture.* Chicago: U. of Chicago Press, 1976.

Clarke, Stephan P., ed. *The Lord Peter Wimsey Companion,* rev. ed. London: The Dorothy L. Sayers Society, 2002.

Coomes, David. *Dorothy L. Sayers: A Careless Rage for Life.* Oxford: Lion, 1992.

Dale, Alzina Stone, ed. *Dorothy L. Sayers: The Centenary Celebration.* New York: Walker, 1993.

———. *Maker and Craftsman: The Story of Dorothy L. Sayers.* Grand Rapids, MI: Eerdmans, 1978.

Gaillard, Dawson. *Dorothy L. Sayers.* New York: Ungar, 1981.

Gilbert, Colleen. *A Bibliography of the Works of Dorothy L. Sayers.* Hamden, CT: Shoe String Press, 1978.

Girouard, Mark. *The Return to Camelot.* New Haven, CT: Yale University Press, 1981.

Hall, Trevor H. *Dorothy L. Sayers: Nine Literary Studies.* London: Duckworth, 1980.

Heilbrun, Carolyn. *Writing Women's Lives.* New York: Norton, 1988.

Higham, David. *Literary Gent.* New York: Coward, McCann and Geoghegan, 1978.

Hitchman, Janet. *Such a Strange Lady: An Introduction to Dorothy L. Sayers.* New York: Harper, 1975.

Hurst, Isobel. "Maenads Dancing before the Martyrs' Memorial: Oxford Women Writers and the Classical Tradition." *International Journal of the Classical Tradition* 12 (Fall 2005): 163–182.

Joshi, S.T. "Dorothy L. Sayers: The Highbrown Detective Story." *Million* 14 (March–June 1993): 14–15.

Kenney, Catherine. *The Remarkable Case of Dorothy L. Sayers.* Kent, OH: Kent State University Press, 1990.

La Grand, Virginia, and Craig E. Mattson. "Peter Wimsey and Precious Ramotswe: Castaway Detectives and Companionate Marriage." *Christianity and Literature* 56 (Summer 2007): 633–634.

Larsen, Gaylord. *Dorothy and Agatha.* New York: Dutton, 1990 (a novel).

Lewis, Terrence L. *Dorothy L. Sayers; Wimsey and Interwar British Society.* Lewiston, NY: Mellen, 1994.

McCarthy, Mary. "Highbrow Shockers." *The Nation* 142 (1936): 458–459.

Nott, Kathleen. "Lord Peter Views the Soul." *The Emperor's Clothes.* London: Heinemann, 1954.

Nurmi, Arja. "A Jolly Kind of Letter: *The Documents in the Case* and Dorothy L. Sayers' Correspondence on Trial." *European Journal of English Studies* 9 (April 2005): 53–59.

Panek, Leroy Lad. *Watteau's Shepherds: The Detective Novel in Britain, 1914–1940.* New York: Popular Press, 1979.

Plain, Gill. "'From the Purest Literature We Have' to 'A Spirit Grown Corrupt.'" *Critical Survey* 20 (2008): 3–16.

Reynolds, Barbara. *Dorothy L. Sayers: Her Life and Soul.* New York: St. Martin's Press, 1993.

———. *The Passionate Intellect: Dorothy L. Sayer's Encounter with Dante.* Kent, OH: Kent State University Press, 1989.

Reynolds, William. "Collaborative Detective Publications in Britain, 1931–1939." *Clues* 9 (1988): 49–70.

———. "The Detection Club on the Air: 'Behind the Screen' and 'The Scoop.'" *Clues* 1983: 1–20.

Schach, Paul, trans. *The Saga of Tristram and Isönd.* Lincoln: University of Nebraska Press, 1973.

Swinson, Chris. "There's More to Life Than Numbers." *Accountancy* 131 (January 2003): 81.

Symons, Julian. *The Detective Story in Britain,* rev. ed. London: Longmans, Green, 1969.

Tischler, Nancy. *Dorothy L. Sayers: A Pilgrim Soul.* Atlanta, GA: John Knox, 1980.

Whelpton, Eric. *The Making of a European.* London: Johnson, 1974.

Willis, Chris. "Dorothy L. Sayers' Sources in *the News of the World.*" *Newspaper Library News* 29 (Winter 2000–2001): 2–4.

Youngberg, Ruth T. *Dorothy L. Sayers: A Reference Guide.* Boston: G.K. Hall, 1982.

WEB SITES

http://www.sayers/org.uk (The Dorothy L. Sayers Society)

http://www.mysterynet.com/sayers/ (General Reference)

http://www.fantasticfiction.co/ek/s/dorothy-l-sayers/ (Bibliography of Sayers's books)

http://www.dorothyl.com/ (The Official Web site)

Humphrey Bogart as Sam Spade in *The Maltese Falcon.* Courtesy of Reisfeld/DBA/Landov.

Sam Spade:
The Hard-Boiled
Private Eye

Don't be so sure I'm as crooked as I'm supposed to be.

—Sam Spade

Appearing in only three short stories and one novel, *The Maltese Falcon*, and "enshrined in cinema history" by Humphrey Bogart, Dashiell Hammett's Sam Spade has become "a folk hero for his times, and perhaps still for ours" (Keating 41). *The Maltese Falcon* today stands as "the archetypal private-

> Sam Spade has appeared on the postage stamps of four countries besides the United States: Nicaragua, Guyana, Guinea, and Dominica.

eye novel, America's distinctive contribution to mystery fiction" (Keating 41), and critics have hailed Hammett as "one of the finest mystery writers of all time" (Layman 1981, 239), who in only a decade of creative activity "influenced and changed the detective story more radically than any other single author since Doyle" (Haycraft 417).

HISTORICAL/CULTURAL CONTEXT

Sam Spade debuted in 1930 as "a new man for new times" (Keating 42)—some of the most trying times in America's history. During the Roaring Twenties, the United States produced over half the world's output of manufactured goods, but a tumultuously prosperous veneer only temporarily veiled post-World War I omens of a mammoth economic and moral breakdown: the October 1917 Bolshevik Revolution, the 1918 influenza pandemic, the failure of the League of Nations, and the 1919 Treaty of Versailles.

Insisting that "the world must be made safe for democracy," President Woodrow Wilson attempted to counter fears of anarchy fueled by the Bolshevik Revolution with his 1918 "Fourteen Points" (war aims), promising that the Allies would not seize major German territories and promoting a vision of a future world without arms or trade barriers, with freedom of the seas and a "league of nations." Americans rejected Wilson's idealism; Theodore Roosevelt labeled the Fourteen Points "a product of men who want everyone to float to heaven on a sloppy sea of universal mush" (quoted in Ward 228), and Wilson had to sacrifice most of them to establish the League of Nations, which the United States never joined. The punitive Treaty of Versailles forced Germany to disarm, to relinquish substantial territory, and to pay such heavy reparations that observers from John Maynard Keynes to Adolf Hitler predicted that these conditions would inevitably produce another world war.

In the wake of widespread postwar disillusion, U.S. women's suffrage and Prohibition became law in 1920, with far-reaching effects on American culture. The world's first Woman's Rights Commission in 1848 proclaimed that "woman is man's equal," but it took a world war to demonstrate that American women who had nursed "dying young men in . . . sixteen-hour days of septic wounds and pus-soaked bandages" (King 35–36) could never return to prewar hobble skirts and corsets or the subservience to men those items symbolized. U.S. flappers bobbed their hair, hoisted their hemlines above the knee, learned the Charleston, and paid close attention to Margaret Sanger, who had opened the first U.S. birth control clinic in 1916. The roles of American women had changed forever.

Congress agreed to Prohibition in late 1917 largely because of animosity toward German-Americans who controlled the liquor industry and because of conservation policies limiting the use of grain for liquor. Long-standing American quasi-religious temperance movements also insisted all-male saloons fostered political corruption, prostitution, diseases, and absenteeism. Lasting from 1920 to 1933, the "noble experiment" prohibiting "the manufacture, sale, or transportation of intoxicating liquors" proved a disastrous attempt at social re-shaping that shattered the remnants of late-Victorian propriety and enabled an unprecedented era of American gangsterism.

In the 1920s, an American cultural fissure was widening between East Coast intellectuals and Midwest anti-intellectual populists. Eastern critic Van Wyck Brooks argued in 1917 that America had thus far taken the "best" of other cultures, and now it had to create its own, so that it could "cease to be a blind, selfish, disorderly people" (Brooks, quoted in P. Johnson 210). Many urbanites agreed with H.L. Mencken that Prohibition had been created by "ignorant bumpkins of the cow states who resented the fact that they had to swill raw corn liquor while city slickers got good wine and whiskey" (Fecher 159). However, what later would be called "middle America" or "the silent majority" which formed America's indigenous culture fiercely resisted the "aggressive dictatorship of a self-appointed scholastic elite" and backed the 18th Amendment (Prohibition), whose supporters were trying to preserve the concept of America's founding as a utopian society. "The Utopianism inherent in Prohibition . . . came up against the equally strongly rooted and active American principle of unrestricted freedom of enterprise" (P. Johnson 209–210).

Prohibition also lacked enforcement teeth to combat the bootleggers' free enterprise, much of it run by non-Anglo-Saxon minorities. In one example of national hypocrisy, San Francisco's mayor supplied free first-class bootlegged whiskey to the entire 1920 Democratic Convention. Thirteen more years of Prohibition "created the greatest criminal bonanza in American history" (Ward 237). It produced universal corruption and lost the nation an estimated $11 billion in tax revenue. It also established enormously powerful crime "families" which dramatically prospered while law-abiding Americans suffered, especially after the 1929 stock market crash. Prohibition substantially contributed to the Great Depression, along with American over-involvement with Europe's floundering postwar economy, high import tariffs precluding European recovery, and the Twenties' quasi-superstitious faith in the American stock market. The 1930s coupled crime and economic hardship to inflict unprecedented misery on ordinary U.S. citizens, setting the stage for the emergence of a totally new, totally American popular folk hero: the hard-boiled private eye.

AUTHORSHIP

As opposed to "slicks" like the *Atlantic Monthly* which featured works by and about the East Coast intelligentsia, the popular American "pulps" lured average readers to action mystery stories with cheap paper and lurid colored covers. After the first pulp, *The Argosy,* appeared in 1889 and Street & Smith's *Detective Story* came out in 1915, the pulps grew from about two dozen in 1918 to 200 in the mid-1930s, and were killed off by television in the early 1950s. *Black Mask,* from 1920 (about six months before Prohibition began) to 1951, was one of the best known pulps. It shaped and perfected the hard-boiled style, relying heavily on the work of Dashiell Hammett, Erle Stanley Gardner, and Raymond Chandler and enjoying a readership ranging from Presidents Woodrow Wilson and Harry Truman to arch-gangster Al Capone.

"The hard-boiled detective novel was born against a backdrop of prohibition and gangsterism and came of age around the time the bubble of American bliss burst" (Lehman 136). Britain's between-wars Golden Age of mystery fiction drew on the "genius detective" tradition established by Arthur Conan Doyle's Sherlock Holmes stories, depicting talented, well-to-do, and usually eccentric amateur sleuths cracking homicidal puzzles set in posh country estates or cozy villages. This still-popular mystery form, like crossword puzzles, bridge, and jigsaws, offers comforting respite from economic and social woes with a clear-cut eternal battle of Good against Evil, where the white-knight detective rescues threatened maidens and skewers vile criminal dragons. In 1920s America, however, the grisly detective novel Poe initiated modulated into the hard-boiled school of detective fiction, influenced by the gritty literary naturalism of Theodore Dreiser and Stephen Crane, who applied scientific determinism and Darwinism to social structure. Others, like Jack London, accepted Nietzsche's doctrine of the Super-man, in which a "will to power" set special individuals above ordinary human beings. Literary naturalists show human beings at the mercy of their environment, heredity, and internal stresses and drives they cannot fully understand or control; these writers present the results of these struggles in an objective, even documentary, style. Amoral in their view of human activity, naturalistic authors neither condemn nor praise human beings for uncontrollable actions; they are pessimistic regarding human capabilities and "frank and almost clinically direct" in portraying humans as animals driven by fundamental urges—fear, hunger, and sex. Naturalistic writers see human actions as deterministically explicable in cause-and-effect relationships, and frequently they choose primitive characters and simple acts of violence, features characteristic of most hard-boiled PI heroes who debuted in the pulps.

Responding to America's between-wars cultural ambivalence, hard-boiled detectives also merged naturalism and the Nietzschean concept of supermen with the peculiarly American romantic hero, the idealized strong and silent literary frontiersman. From Natty Bumppo to the Lone Ranger, these men rejected the norms of their hypocritical societies and operated under their own strict codes of honor and conduct. By the early 20th century, they had settled into popular mythology via the stories of Zane Grey and Owen Wister, exhibiting "courage, physical strength, indestructibility, indifference to danger and death, a knightly attitude, celibacy, a measure of violence, and a sense of justice" (Nolan 1969, 6). In the 1920s and 1930s, an era of "open criminal warfare, poverty, and festering political corruption," America accepted the detective as a modern frontiersman, "battling social and economic evils, trusting no one but himself . . . and seeing corruption on a daily level with an unflinching eye," upholding his ideals of justice and truth against his violent environment (Nolan 1983, 67, 37).

> The year 1922 was also Modernism's watershed year, with the appearance of "The Waste Land" and *Ulysses* as well as D.H. Lawrence's *Aaron's Rod*; Virginia Woolf's *Jacob's Room*; Katherine Mansfield's *The Garden Party*; Bertolt Brecht's first play, *Baal*, Sinclair Lewis's *Babbitt*, and Eugene O Neill's *Anna Christie*. F. Scott Fitzgerald set *The Great Gatsby* in 1922, since he believed that year defined the Jazz Age.

America's first hard-boiled detective, Carroll John Daly's Race Williams, appeared in the December 1922 *Black Mask,* boosting magazine sales a tidy 15 percent. Entirely devoid of chivalry, Williams killed often and without scruples, assuming his victims always deserved it, and claiming, "You can't make hamburger without grinding up a little meat" (quoted in Goulart xi). Philip Cody, *Black Mask*'s editor in 1923, advanced hard-boiled detective stories by favoring Dashiell Hammett's more complex and somewhat less vicious Continental Op, who had debuted in the same issue as Race Williams. When Joseph "Cap" Shaw took over in 1926, *Black Mask* turned hard-boiled detective fiction into "a distinct literary departure from the older school of writing" (Gardner, quoted in Haycraft 204), fostering Hammett's *The Maltese Falcon* (1930) with Sam Spade as the ultimate hard-boiled private eye. Hammett melded literary naturalism and the uniquely American Western hero, but he also introduced elements that became standard to hard-boiled detective fiction, like corrupt tinsel-town settings, scenes of disorder and violence, tough vernacular dialogue, and cynicism about wealth and authority, turning American hard-boiled detective fiction into "searing social criticism" (Mellen 18).

"There are mysteries about Hammett that neither the Op nor Sam Spade would have been able to solve" (Margolies 31), for he deliberately left very few clues to himself, covering his tracks by knowing "the concealment operation root and branch" (Wolfe 1). Samuel Dashiell Hammett began writing for *Black Mask* in 1922, under the pen name "Peter Collinson," chosen, Hammett later revealed, because "Peter Collins" was underworld slang for "nobody"—hence he authored his first three stories as "nobody's son" (Nolan 23), a hint at his personal demons.

At age 28 Hammett already knew grinding poverty and postwar disillusion. Born in 1894 in St. Mary, Maryland, he grew into a "fiercely independent, fiercely proud" (Mellen 21), and intellectually gifted child who at a very young age developed a lifelong passion for privacy and secrecy. Around 13, he left school to help support a brutally dysfunctional family—an overworked tubercular mother he adored and an alcoholic, womanizing father who abused her. Hammett later described his teenage self as "the unsatisfactory and unsatisfied employee of various railroads, stock brokers, machine manufacturers, canners. . . . Usually I was fired" (quoted in Nolan 11). A listing of his insatiable reading at public libraries includes over 150 books, most of them new publications when he read them. He also developed—and wallowed in—"working class habits," drinking, smoking, gambling, and catching his first case of gonorrhea at 19, internalizing "his father's behavior as that appropriate to a man even as he developed . . . a self-loathing for becoming what he despised. The rejection of his father which characterized his youth became rejection of himself." Alcohol helped him forget, but only temporarily (Mellen 22), an affliction throughout most of a life probably as enigmatic to him as his behavior was to others.

From 1914 until 1918, Hammett worked for the Pinkerton National Detective Agency, a private police force often hired by corporations to break strikes, a job suited to his nonconformity and his proclivity for secrecy. He found it challenging, demanding "wit, patience, adaptability and nerve"; he often assumed false identities (he favored posing as the secretary of the Civic Purity League) and capably used the gun he carried (Nolan 1983, 12). In 1918, prematurely white-haired like his father, Hammett enlisted in the U.S. Army, scoring the second highest IQ of all interviewees that year. He became a medical sergeant, but his military experience embittered and nearly killed him. After a tragic ambulance accident that kept him from ever driving again, he contracted influenza and his latent tuberculosis flared up, but he had to fight the government to receive his disability pay and his war pension.

Back at Pinkerton's, Hammett worked on cases that haunted him for years. He helped break the IWW (International Workers of the World) strike against Anaconda, and in 1921 he investigated the notorious rape case of popular comedian Fatty Arbuckle. When Hammett's tuberculosis recurred, he had to enter a sanatorium near Tacoma, Washington, as a disabled veteran.

Hammett's emotional problems were mounting as well. Like his father, "he was addicted to drink and to chippies." His "silence, his aloofness, his air of inaccessibility, [and] his startling intelligence and extraordinary good looks" made him irresistible to women, and while he was hospitalized he and his young nurse, Josephine Dolan ("Jose"), enjoyed a brief fling. He chivalrously married her on July 7, 1921, only because she was pregnant— by another man—and needed his help. "Neither of us," Hammett observed later, "ever said anything about seriously loving the other" (Mellen 24–25). They moved to San Francisco and he accepted Mary Jane, born in 1921, as his daughter; she died without knowing that he was not her biological father. In 1926 he and Jose had another daughter, Josephine. Hammett cherished both girls, but he was incapable of fidelity and came and went as he pleased.

By 1921 Hammett had also lost interest in detective work. He left Pinkerton's and took a job writing advertising copy for Albert S. Samuels's jewelry shop on Market Street. Samuels recalled, "He'd write copy for me all day, then go home to his apartment and drink most of the night. . . . Yet he was a man of honor . . . [and] his 'romantic approach' . . . was ideal for us" (quoted in Nolan 1983, 19). Hammett rented a cheap San Francisco hotel room, and, spitting blood, set about teaching himself to turn his adventurous life into fiction.

Starting in October 1923, Hammett wrote at a penny a word under his own name, dropping "Samuel." Drawing on his Pinkerton experience, he patterned the "Continental Op," a nameless agent of Hammett's fictional San Francisco's Continental Detective Agency, after Assistant Superintendent James Wright, Hammett's boss at Pinkerton's Baltimore office. By early 1924, Hammett had become one of *Black Mask*'s most popular writers, depicting his San Francisco setting, then seething with criminal activity, both realistically and dramatically, and revealing character in terms of action.

In April 1924, *Black Mask*'s editor, Phil Cody, published Hammett's first two-part serial, "The House on Turk Street" and "The Girl with the Silver Eyes," a Continental Op tale foreshadowing *The Maltese Falcon*. A few weeks later Cody rejected two new Op stories. Hammett needed cash; he was fighting tuberculosis, living on cheap food, coffee, soup, and cigarettes, and typing stories all night in San Francisco's raw foggy chill (Nolan 33), but he told *Black Mask* he understood: "The trouble is, this sleuth of mine has degenerated into a meal ticket . . . when I try to grind out a yarn because I think there's a market for it, then I flop . . . thank you . . . for jolting me into wakefulness" (*Letters* 26).

By 1924 mobsters had turned San Francisco into a jungle where graft dominated both politics and business, and Hammett's new Continental Op fiction mercilessly reflected it all. In "The Gutting of Couffignal" (1925), the Op tells deceitful Princess Zhekovsky, "Catching crooks is the only kind of sport I know anything about," before he shoots her in the leg. That year, Hammett's tuberculosis was declared cured and Jose and Mary Jane rejoined him in San Francisco, but his writing time fell away and bills multiplied; only three of his stories appeared in 1926 and for nearly a year he

*[Hammett] took murder out
of the Venetian vase and
dropped it into the alley.*
—Raymond Chandler

published nothing else, doing layout as well as
ad copy for Samuels and working with an assistant, Peggy O'Toole, who never realized that she
was probably Hammett's model for *The Maltese
Falcon*'s leading lady Brigid O'Shaughnessy.

When Joseph "Cap" Shaw, a World War I
bayonet instructor, took over *Black Mask* in 1926,
Hammett was already working toward an entirely new detective approach,
announcing in 1928 that he intended to "create literary art in the mystery
genre" (quoted in Brower 198). Shaw later acknowledged, "Hammett was the

> Hammett could not have failed to see that technology was revolutionizing
> modern life with innovations like the automobile, telephone, film, steel and
> concrete, oil, petroleum, and electricity.

leader in the thought that finally brought the magazine to its distinctive form
. . . [with] his rare ability of observation and his gift to analyze character
beneath a surface appearance . . . a new life of compulsion and authenticity"
(quoted in Nolan 1983, 42) first seen in Hammett's serialized Continental Op
novel *Red Harvest,* which rocked the reading world in 1928. André Gide called
this novel "the last word in atrocity, cynicism, and horror," and many observers
compared its "crisp, hard-boiled language of the underground" (quoted in
Nolan 1983, 48) to Ernest Hemingway's highly praised realistic dialogue. No
definitive proof exists of mutual influence between Hammett and Hemingway,
although Hemingway praised Hammett's work in his bullfighting book, *Death
in the Afternoon.* Hemingway owned copies of *The Thin Man* and *Blood
Money,* and he had his wife read him *The Dain Curse* when his eyes were both-
ering him.

Both *Red Harvest* and *The Dain Curse* (1929), the latter sometimes
accused of racism and often dismissed as Hammett's worst novel, brought
Hammett fame and plenty of money, which he threw away on booze, gambling, and women. After Hammett and Jose had separated permanently in
1927, he moved to a pricy Nob Hill apartment overlooking San Francisco
where, conscientiously sober while writing, he produced *The Maltese
Falcon.* When he sent it to Alfred A. Knopf in June 1929, he described it as
"the best thing" he had done so far (*Letters* 49). It appeared serially in
Black Mask between September 1929 and the next February, revolutionizing
American detective fiction, going through 24 hard-cover printings in three
separate editions during its first 15 years. Warner Brothers purchased its
film rights almost immediately for $8,500, a relatively small sum that none-
theless gave Hammett his critical and financial breakthrough.

Hammett borrowed $1,000 from Albert Samuels and moved to New
York in 1930, where he finished the novel *The Glass Key,* his personal

favorite. That year, after recurrences of tuberculosis and gonorrhea, he earned the most money he ever would, more than $100,000, and he started and abandoned a new San Francisco detective novel, later using a 65-page fragment of it in his last novel, *The Thin Man* (1933).

The putative gulf between popular and literary novels was being breached by Hammett and other mystery writers in the 1930s.

—Russel Gray

Lured to Hollywood in 1930 by the promise of screenwriting work, Hammett plunged into the Depression era's Sodom and Gomorrah. Hollywood reveled in flagrant debauchery while it churned out escapist film fare to temporarily drown its audiences' economic woes. Screenwriter Ben Hecht, who became Hammett's close friend, recorded "vivid people . . . nights of gaiety and gambling . . . wild hearts and the poetry of unrest" with "the mingled sounds of plotting and sexual moans" constantly drifting through transoms, and drinking, drinking, drinking. Hammett himself admitted, "I drank a lot in those days—partly because I was confused by the fact that people's feelings and talk and actions didn't have much to do with one another" (quoted in Nolan 1983, 78–79). In November 1930, coming off a five-day binge at a lavish party hosted by Darryl Zanuck, who had bought the movie rights to *The Maltese Falcon* for Warner Brothers, Hammett instantly caught Lillian Hellman's calculating eye, and she became his companion for the rest of his life. Hammett had completed his best work before they met, and Hammett's daughter Jo suggests that he would have been "irked and embarrassed" by Hellman's "myth of the Great Romance which she dramatized and exploited after his death" (*Letters* x). His relationship with Hellman profoundly affected both Hammett's personal life and his literary output.

After that fateful meeting with Hellman, Hammett's creative energy was nearly spent. He reviewed mysteries for newspapers and magazines, he created and wrote a comic strip, *Secret Agent X-9*, between 1934 and 1939, and he worked on various screenplays, but he had nothing to do with the first movie version of *The Maltese Falcon* (1931), a semi-comedy starring Ricardo Cortez. Three Sam Spade short stories appeared in the slick *American Magazine* in 1932, but all lacked Hammett's "depth and spark" (Nolan 1969, 83). He intended *The Thin Man* (1933) to be his last detective novel but it proved the last gasp of his literary talent. Hellman recalled that Hammett, dismally hard up for cash, wrote it cold sober in a rundown New York hotel with astonishing concentration and "care for every word" (quoted in Nolan 1983, 84). *The Thin Man* inspired six successful films starring William Powell and Myrna Loy from 1934 to 1947 (Hammett contributed only polishing touches to the first of these), a popular radio series, and eventually a television series, so that harddrinking, wise-cracking amateur detectives Nick and Nora Charles took their place in the American way of life.

. . . [Hammett] kept his work, and his plans for work, in angry privacy . . .

—Lillian Hellman

Notable Hard-Boiled PIs after Sam Spade

Philip Marlowe, created by Raymond Chandler

Lew Archer, created by Ross Macdonald

Travis McGee, created by John D. MacDonald

Joe Puma and Brock Callahan, created by William Campbell Gault

Parker, created by Richard Stark (Donald Westlake)

Also see James M. Cain's various protagonists and the protagonists of Cornell Woolrich's "black" novels

Radio and film adaptations of his fiction as well as "patch jobs" on other movies supported Hammett's increasingly profligate Hollywood lifestyle through the 1930s. Paramount made two versions of *The Glass Key*, and Warner Brothers produced another unremarkable version of *The Maltese Falcon* titled *Satan Met a Lady,* starring Bette Davis, in 1936. Hammett claimed he made $800 a week in 1930, twice as much in a month as the average American worker's yearly earnings, but "he spent it all, on starlets and hotel suites and limousines and chauffeurs and bootleg liquor and speakeasy nights. When he had money left over, he gave handouts to his friends" (Preface to *Letters* 7). Cruel as he could be while drinking, he nonetheless told Jose when they divorced in 1937, "Take care of the girls and I'll take care of you." His daughter Jo said he did, as long as he could (*Letters* x).

That year Hammett, intensely anti-fascist, took up left-wing political causes, failing to recognize what George Orwell had learned in the Spanish Civil War and exposed to a world that tragically refused to listen—that the Soviet Communists who supported the Spanish Loyalist cause Hammett so ardently defended were actually bent on totalitarian world domination. In 1939, Hammett and Hellman publicly denied what he inaccurately called the "fantastic falsehood that the U.S.S.R. and the totalitarian states [like Nazi Germany] are basically alike" (quoted in Mellen 112), and they approved Stalin's show trials and executions of Bolshevik leaders. Hellman thought Hammett was a Marxist, as he called himself, but a very critical one who often found fault with both the Soviet Union and the American Communist Party (Nolan 1983, 99). Hammett's daughter Jo believed, "All labels aside, he thought of himself as an American" (*Letters* x). Whatever his political views actually were, Hammett paid dearly for them.

In 1941, untested writer-turned-film director John Huston convinced Jack Warner to let him remake *The Maltese Falcon*. This film adaptation was nearly a word-for-word recopying of the novel, broken into dialogue and scenes; as film critic Allen Eyles observed, Hammett remained its real author "without ever having worked on it" (quoted in Nolan 1983, 102). With a cast led by Humphrey Bogart as Sam Spade, the film made cinema history as "possibly the most successful screen realization of a novel ever achieved" (Nolan 1983, 105). Hammett made no additional money from it, but it must have given him immense satisfaction.

Although his physical condition was rapidly deteriorating in 1942, Hammett at age 48 volunteered for the Army Signal Corps. He spent the next three years as "Pop" to his much younger comrades in the stormy far north Aleutian Islands, editing an Army newspaper. In 1948, stricken with emphysema, he followed his doctor's severe advice and quit drinking, but the same year his participation in the Civil Rights Congress, a Communist front group, brought him before the U.S. House Un-American Activities Committee. Hammett refused to supply names that in fact he did not know, and convicted of contempt of Congress, he served five months in a federal penitentiary. Released in December 1951, thin and sick, Hammett found himself blacklisted. His books were out of print, Hollywood rejected him as an ex-convict, and all his radio shows were off the air; he had sold all dramatic rights to *The Thin Man* television show; and the government sued him for back taxes he could not pay. At 58 Hammett attempted but could not complete an autobiographical novel, *Tulip*, and on January 10, 1961, two months after being diagnosed with inoperable lung cancer, he died in a New York hospital. He was buried as he wished, in Arlington National Cemetery.

TRACKING SAM SPADE

The Maltese Falcon's plot is simple, but its social, moral, and psychological ramifications are enormously complex. While hired by "Miss Wonderly" to pursue a possible killer, PI Sam Spade's partner Miles Archer is killed. Spade, duty-bound to "do something" about Archer's murder, becomes involved with her, and she is soon revealed as beautiful duplicitous Brigid O'Shaughnessy, who is plotting with and against a vicious international gang seeking a jewel-encrusted statue, the "Maltese falcon." Before the plot unravels, Spade faces two more murders, physical violence, and a "brutally realistic romance" with Brigid, finally turning her over to the justice she, a murderess, has earned (Hyams 75). Some years after *The Maltese Falcon*

> Two of the reasons Spade gave Brigid for refusing to let her escape reveal edgy motivations: revenge, because he has to "do something" about his partner Archer's death, and self-preservation, because he, Spade, is in danger of being hanged for Archer's murder.

was published, Hammett told James Thurber that he had been influenced by Henry James's *The Wings of the Dove,* which also involves a search for an exotic treasure and a beautiful amoral heroine.

Hammett's unflinching exposé of Sam Spade's foggy noir "Baghdad-by-the-Bay" was demonstrated in a 1992 Dashiell Hammett Walking Tour beginning at the Public Library he frequented, three blocks down Larkin Street from his and Jose's modest Eddy Street apartment. Then the tour moved to the nearby city hall where Spade told off the DA, not far from the Charing Cross Apartments where Hammett conceived Sam Spade; up Nob Hill, past Spade's office at 111 Sutter Street, to Spade's seedy efficiency apartment, Hammett's own, 891 Post Street, number 410, which still contains Hammett-vintage old mission-style furniture and dated fixtures, floorboards, and most appliances, with the bend in the passageway where Brigid O'Shaughnessy stood holding Cairo's pistol at her side. Close to Samuels Jewelers is the James Flood Building, where Hammett set his fictional Continental Detective Agency. A bronze plaque today marks where Spade's partner Miles Archer was killed, the opening of *The Maltese Falcon*.

Hammett deliberately made Sam Spade's world dark and claustrophobic to emphasize its urban pressures. *The Maltese Falcon* takes place within five days in December 1928 and within 10 square blocks of downtown San Francisco, with the exceptions of the burning ship *La Paloma* at the dock and the car chase to Burlingame. Most of the novel's action occurs in interiors, like Spade's seamy office, all he can afford, on the fifth floor of an imposing 1926 building with a marble hall and walls and a beamed, painted ceiling; other interiors are Spade's apartment, Brigid's suite, and various rooms of still-existing hotels bearing names Hammett changed only slightly for the novel.

Spade often ate at John's Grill on Ellis Street, now a National Literary Landmark and the only restaurant mentioned in *The Maltese Falcon* that still exists with the same name and location. John's now sports memorabilia from the films made from Hammett's books: rich leather booths, hard liquor, a menu listing "Sam Spade's chow of choice, chops, sliced tomato, and a baked potato" (Montagne) currently priced at $29 (Griffiths), and a special drink called the "Bloody Brigid" (Freeman 79). The entrance to John's upstairs dining room houses Hammett's books and a replica Maltese Falcon in a glass case at the entrance.

SAM SPADE'S LITERARY ANCESTRY

Hammett could probably not have developed Sam Spade had he not created the Continental Op first, a short, fat, merciless PI who lives for his work, "going forward day after day through mud and blood and death and

> Hammett often used the mythic figure of Sisyphus, forever laboring but getting nowhere, as a springboard for his protagonists.

deceit—as callous and brutal and cynical as necessary—toward a dim goal, with nothing to push or pull him to it except he's been hired to reach it" (Hammett, quoted in Nolan ix). The Op's ethical code lacks sentiment, but it insists on loyalty to his organization and fellow detectives, and since the agency forbids agents from receiving money for solving their cases, the Op is above "the greed and corruption of the Prohibition society in which he works" (Kelley in Herbert 39). In *Red Harvest* he stirs things up in "Personville" (aka "Poisonville"), a city full of crooked police and gangsters, by brutally setting them at each other's throats. The Op tells his own stories in a flat, stripped-down style sprinkled with criminal slang and solves his cases with "graphic violence and mayhem" (Kelley in Herbert 39). He "feels queer" about shooting a woman, but he does so anyhow. Capable of wry humor and even an occasional chivalrous act, he's impervious to sexual overtures: "You think I'm a man and you're a woman. That's wrong. I'm a manhunter and you're something that has been running in front of me. There's nothing human about it" (http://www.thrillingdetective.com/trivia/triv244.htm). The Continental Op may be the most perfect hard-boiled character[s] ever invented, or maybe it is "The Old Man," the boss he reveres and emulates, with "his gentle eyes behind gold spectacles and his mild smile, hiding the fact that fifty years of sleuthing had left him without any feelings at all on any subject" (quoted from Hammett in Murphy 110). Both characters prefigure Sam Spade, whose work and self-preservation are synonymous and all he lives for: "He has no church, no lodge, no hobbies, no affective ties, no neighbors" (Marling 140).

PROFILE OF SAM SPADE

Sam Spade's Personality

In his introduction to the 1934 edition of *The Maltese Falcon,* Hammett called Spade

> a dream man . . . what most of the private detectives I worked with would like to have been and in their cockier moments thought they approached. For your private detective does not . . . want to be an erudite solver of riddles in the Sherlock Holmes manner; he wants to be a hard and shifty fellow, able to take care of himself in any situation, able to get the best of anybody . . . whether criminal, innocent by-stander [sic] or client. (xi)

Although Hammett disclaimed any autobiographical connection to Spade, he is the first protagonist Hammett gave a name—his own first name and a surname suggesting the old-time private eye's tedious "spadework." In his introduction to the novel's 1930 edition, he traced the genesis of his characters Gutman, Cairo, Dundy, Effie, and Brigid to actual persons he had known.

Hammett's *leitmotif* for Spade, the phrase "a blond satan," reflects the essential ambiguity of both his character and the times that helped shape it. "Blond" conventionally indicates a morally upright hero/heroine, like the cowboy in the white hat, symbol of the moral righteousness middle America wanted to believe it possessed; but "satan" (Hammett used the lowercase "s") dramatically indicates its opposite, the nightmare of lawlessness that stalked the entire nation. Spade has wolf-like features: a long, bony jaw, a chin jutting in a "v" below the smaller "v" of his mouth, yellowish-grey eyes, and v-shaped heavy brows below a point of pale brown hair (*Falcon* 3), but Hammett surprisingly calls the effect "rather pleasant." Spade's body contrasts with that vulpine face: thickened in his thirties by those heavy restaurant meals, he resembles "a shaved bear" with hairless chest and "childishly soft and pink" skin (*Falcon* 12). Spade's blond coloring might suggest a "golden bear," California's state symbol (Marling 131).

The ambivalence of Spade's physique and physiognomy intrigues women but puzzles men, especially his opponents: are they confronting a wolf or a bear? The predatory wolf possesses lethal intelligence, speed, and slashing jaws; the bear, stubborn power, a crushing grip, near-indomitable will. Together, these attributes make Spade a highly dangerous enigma, allowing him to "get the best of anybody" and survive, even excel, in a world full of political, economic, and romantic snares. Since Hammett for the first time made most of the violence in *The Maltese Falcon* occur offstage, Spade relies most on his cunning intellect to overcome his enemies.

The character of Sam Spade, not the location of the Maltese Falcon or Spade's search for his partner's killer, is the real mystery of this novel. Alfred Hitchcock called Hammett's Falcon a "MacGuffin," an object or device which precipitates the central action and is assumed to be the characters' goal, yet which turns out only to distract from the detective's true goal. (William Marling also suggests that Hammett's classic MacGuffin, the search for the bejeweled bird statue, derives from the pursuit of lost Indian treasure in Conan Doyle's "The Sign of Four.") The most telling clue to Spade's personality is the "Flitcraft parable" he tells to Brigid, in which an ordinary man, nearly killed in a freak accident, abandons his entire life and makes a new one, only to discover both lives are identical: character is immutable. Julian Symons felt that Spade's Flitcraft Parable may have been Hammett's comment on his own life to that point, but other critics believe the parable signifies Spade's rejection of all morality and emotions. Hammett's much-discussed objective point of view both reveals and conceals the enigmatic workings of Spade's mind. "If we knew the detective's thoughts, we would understand why he acts the way he does, and there would be no mystery" (Marling 128). Patiently and methodically rolling a cigarette, Spade's reaction to learning that his partner Miles Archer has been killed is one of the most famous passages of the novel. It "represents Spade's interior state through elision . . . but what does Spade feel? We don't know" (Marling 128–129). Hammett's skill compels readers to try to find out. Hammett may have perfected the technique of intriguing understatement, leaving readers to fill in the blanks he left, through his work in advertising, and while many commentators praise that method, James Guetti in 1982 concluded that Hammett's descriptions of characters were "'provoking, even irritating,' because the descriptions are a 'collection of visual fragments'" (quoted in Marling 131).

Sam Spade's Love Life

In *The Maltese Falcon,* "romance . . . is blown to bits by bitter realism" (D. Johnson 82). Women easily succumbed to Sam Spade, but he knew them for what they were; the prime liars in Hammett's fiction were always women. Dorothy Parker described Spade as "so hard-boiled you could roll him on the White House lawn . . . with his clear eye for the ways of hard women" (quoted in Mellen 24), but his toughness is leavened by tenderness and subtlety (Wolfe 111). Critic William Marling sees the three women in *The Maltese Falcon* as the mythic three Fates, asking questions, representing mysteries, and possessing occult powers: Spade refers to Effie Perine's intuition; Iva can implicate or exonerate Spade in Archer's death; and Brigid (whose name recalls both a Celtic goddess and a Christian saint) can solve the mystery of the falcon (141). The way Spade treats these "Three Women"— "Brigid, Iva Archer, and Effie: murderer, bitch, and nice girl respectively" (Madden 89)—reflects both his milieu and his personality. Effie Perine, Spade's "lanky sunburned" and "boyish" secretary and the one decent woman in the novel, represents the spunky new working women who began to appear in the workplace and popular fiction during World War I, often raising male suspicions and resentment, especially among union men: "Nonsexual fraternization and nonpatriarchal structure were novel . . . and were often equated with communism" (Fearon 65). Spade's relationship with Effie is ambiguous. He relies on her professional capabilities, especially her efficiency and her discretion, as when he stashes Brigid with her for safekeeping, but his rejection of Brigid, whom Effie had supported, quenches the sexual spark between himself and Effie at least temporarily. At first Spade calls Effie "sweetheart," but after turning Brigid over to the authorities, when he lays his hand on Effie's hip (*Falcon* 3, 216), Effie, who recognizes Spade's uncompromising moral position but cannot fully grasp it, shrinks away from him: "You're right. But don't touch me now—not now" (*Falcon* 217), turning Spade "pale as his collar" because he "feels for the first time his existential loneliness" (Thompson 128).

Iva Archer, the widow of Spade's murdered partner, clings to the ashes of Spade's unabashed and now finished affair with her. Hammett and Spade both basically recognized only two kinds of women, the pure mother figure familiar from Roman Catholic adoration of the Virgin Mary, and the kind men casually took to bed. Iva controlled essential information, her whereabouts when her husband was killed, but her tawdry physical allure for

Spade has petered out, and he shudders when he realizes she is all he has left.

The several false names lovely lying Brigid O'Shaughnessy uses may suggest her "dispersed, variable personality" (Marling 133). She first appears to Spade as "Miss Wonderly," then calls herself "Miss LeBlanc," smooth on the surface as a new aerodynamic automobile, stringing Spade one fictitious line after another and shedding "aliases and stories much as a beautiful snake sheds its skin" (Sperber and Lax 153). Critics agree that Spade knows from the start that Brigid killed Archer (Marling 1982, 73), and when she begs Spade, "Help me," Spade replies cynically and memorably, "You won't need much of anybody's help. You're good. You're very good" (*Falcon* 35). Spade also knows Brigid is lying, but as a professional, he'll work for her—for a fee. For Spade, "emotional vulnerability is a far greater menace than physical vulnerability," so that sexual desire offers possibly the greatest threat to his invulnerability.

Spade sleeps with Brigid between chapters 10 and 11, but he gets up early to search her apartment; emotion and sex might tempt him to believe her, but he finally realizes, "'I should trust you? . . . You who've never played square with me for half an hour at a stretch since I've known you? . . . I wouldn't do it even if I could. Why should I?'" (*Falcon* 212). The totally amoral "black widow" character who exploits, betrays, and devours the men she uses quickly became stereotyped in fiction, film, and television, but when *The Maltese Falcon* first appeared, critics hardly knew how to deal with such a figure (Luhr 10) as Brigid, who cannot offer Spade more than a romantic and/or sexual appeal—"You didn't—don't love me—?"—that can never be enough for him. He brutally replies, "I think I do . . . What of it?" (*Falcon* 212). He cannot sacrifice his code of honor, even though rejecting Brigid leaves him as empty as the black leaden shell of a bird the jeweled Maltese Falcon turns out to be.

Sam Spade and the Police

In tracking his partner's killer, Spade deals with the San Francisco police mainly through Detective Tom Polhaus, sympathetic to Spade but basically handcuffed because he must function in a corrupt police system. Tom, discomfited, links Spade with Lieutenant Dundy and District Attorney Bryan, both illustrating the moral turpitude of 1920s public servants. Dundy, enraged at being outmaneuvered by Spade in the chapter "Horse Feathers" to keep himself, Brigid, and Cairo out of jail, slugs Spade, giving Spade, who can control his emotions, the upper hand in their confrontation (Thompson 115). Bryan's attempt to intimidate Spade with his position as District Attorney fails because Spade knows his own code and capabilities are superior to theirs: "I've had trouble with both of you before . . . my best chance of clearing myself . . . is by bringing in the murderers . . . and keeping away from you and the police because neither of you show any signs of knowing what in hell it's all about" (*Falcon* 149).

Sam Spade's Criminal Opponents

Like Brigid O'Shaughnessy, the major criminals pursuing the Maltese Falcon are outwardly smooth and inwardly rotten, all of them corrupted by lust for the jeweled bird. Levantine and effeminate, plump and glossy Joel Cairo, scented with *chypre,* wilts almost immediately in Spade's presence. The "fat man" Casper Gutman, a stylized version of Fatty Arbuckle, "flabbily fat with bulbous pink cheeks and lips and chins and neck" (*Falcon* 104), speaks in a throaty, ominously over-refined purr and abuses his daughter. In 1920s gangster slang, "gunsel" indicated not a minor hitman but a homosexual, as James Sandoe first pointed out. Ellery Queen noted that Hammett "virtually deceived the whole world" by using "gunsel" to describe Wilmer, because ever since detective writers have used the term to mean "gunman" (Queen 7–8). Gutman's gunsel Wilmer is homosexual, runty, and profane. In contrast to them all, Spade is at ease and confident he can outwit them, even balancing on the borders of the law himself (Luhr 11). United in pursuit of the Falcon treasure, all these villains are doomed anachronistic luxury-loving "saps," while Spade, maintaining a bare-bones lifestyle, limiting his contacts to useful and professional ones, sacrificing his emotional needs, and morally superior to deception and graft, can and does survive.

> *Wilmer Cook's sexuality may be ambiguous, which [would] create a text so rich we are only beginning to appreciate it 70 years later.*
>
> —Daniel Linder

Humphrey Bogart's Sam Spade

The third time Warner Brothers filmed *The Maltese Falcon* (1941), "they got it right" (Sperber and Lax 149), producing "the best private-eye melodrama ever made" (James Agee, quoted in Madden 81). As he had done earlier in *High Sierra,* fledgling director John Huston defied then-current movie industry practice and declared he would "follow the book rather than depart from it" (quoted in Sperber and Lax 149). The studio's first choice for Spade, George Raft, wanted nothing to do with either Huston or the film, so Humphrey Bogart took the part and the studio settled on former silent film star Mary Astor to play Brigid O'Shaughnessy. Astor called the script a "humdinger" and became Huston's perfect "enchanting murderess" (Sperber and Lax 153, 156). "Hammett's odd assortment of double-crossers, con artists, and killers in greedy pursuit of a jewel-encrusted statue," a reflection of American distrust of foreigners in the 1940s (Luhr 11), then came together, led by 357-pound English actor Sidney Greenstreet, shot from a low camera angle as the "Everest of menace" Casper Gutman (Sperber and Lax 158), and Peter Lorre, undersized and baby-faced and whispery-voiced, underplaying Joel Cairo's homosexuality (Sperber and Lax 156). Inspired choices of key supporting roles included Ward Bond as gravelly Tom Polhaus and Huston's father Walter in a cameo role as the dying captain of *La Paloma.*

Playing Sam Spade proved the watershed of Humphrey Bogart's career. Having recently portrayed gangster "heavies," Bogart at 42 projected maturity and depth, toughness and humor, connecting Spade to his earlier roles and adding to "his aura of moral ambiguity" (Sperber and Lax 155). Huston found Bogart "just *excellent* [italics in original]" and able to sustain the role flawlessly (quoted in Sperber and Lax 159). He photographed Bogart to suggest "a dark, inner turbulence" regarding the implications of his activities (Luhr 11), and he allowed Bogart to dominate almost every scene in a "chilling but somehow engaging characterization" with an "offhanded nonchalance" conveying both his sex appeal and his disillusion with love (Hyams 75). Mary Astor recalled that Bogart's acting ability made up for his dislike of love scenes: "Bogie didn't have to kiss the girl. . . . You knew by the way he looked at her" (quoted in Sperber and Lax 160).

Huston's film departed from Hammett's novel by replacing the "unsavory poetic justice" and the amorality of the original ending with "romantic closing images." As Astor, in police custody but not handcuffed, leaves them, Bogart and Bond remain with the statue, voicing the lines Bogart himself suggested:

Polhaus   "Um [it's]—heavy. What is it?"
Spade   "The stuff that dreams are made of."

Hammett made the jeweled raven a tribute paid by Crusaders to Charles V for Malta—"a distinct whiff" of the religious order—priceless artifact MacGuffin of the *DaVinci Code* and its many imitators.

Bogart then follows Astor, "a condemned soul en route to justice," to the elevator, where its folding gate throws bar-like shadows across her face. He passes out of the picture, holding the small black bird and the remnants of his own broken dream. The film's closing, far removed from the bitter isolation Hammett gave Spade, thus stresses honor over personal fulfillment: "Be true to your code even if it means breaking your heart" (Sperber and Lax 163).

Sam Spade's Radio Appearances

Sam Spade enjoyed several radio incarnations. Bogart, Astor, and Greenstreet appeared in 30-minute CBS versions of *The Maltese Falcon* in 1943 and 1946, and CBS featured a one-hour rendition with Edward G. Robinson as Spade (1943). Though Hammett was not entirely happy with Howard Duff as Sam Spade, Duff played Spade, his favorite role, in CBS's *The Adventures of Sam Spade* from 1946 to 1949, with several scripts contributed by

Hammett himself, who also created the less popular radio series *The Fat Man*, broadcast in the 1940s. Duff did 51 episodes of *The Adventures of Sam Spade* for NBC (1949 to 1950), but blacklisted like Hammett for suspected membership in the Communist Party, Duff was replaced by Steve Dunne for 24 episodes in 1950 and 1951, before NBC cancelled the series. Duff made a guest appearance as Spade in the only broadcast of *Charlie Wild, Private Eye* (September 24, 1950).

Sam Spade on Television

In 1966, Duff played Detective Sam Stone, patterned after radio's Sam Spade, in television's *The Felony Squad*. BBC Radio 4 presented *The Maltese Falcon* in 2001, starring Tom Wilkinson, Jane Lapotaire, and Nickolas Grace.

Sam Spade in Other Media

Rodlow Willard drew *The Maltese Falcon* in comics and manga in 1946 for David McKay Publications; the 1950s Wildroot Hair Tonic ads (single-page comic strips featured Spade, drawn by Lou Fine); and the manga (Japanese comics and print cartoons) *Detective Conan*, volume 21, contains a profile summary of Sam Spade for Gosho Aoyama Mystery Library.

SAM SPADE RESURRECTED

Like Hammett, three-Edgar-winning author Joe Gores put his own private eye experience into fiction, notably his DKA ("Dan Kearney Associates") series and several television detective series, including *Columbo, Kojak, Magnum P.I.,* and *Mickey Spillane's Mike Hammer*. Gores also paid affectionate tribute to Sam Spade's creator in *Hammett*, a fictionalized recreation of Dashiell Hammett as detective and author, filmed in 1982. Faithfully drawing on San Francisco's politically corrupt past, Gores postulated Hammett returning to PI work after becoming a famous novelist. More recently, Gore's prequel to *The Maltese Falcon, Spade & Archer,* sanctioned by Hammett's daughter Jo, appeared in 2009 as "a noble attempt to do the near-impossible . . . breathing new life into an iconic character created by a long-dead author" (Desilva B1). Gores intended to find out who Spade was when he started out, filling in details of Spade's background as a World War I sharpshooter and then setting him to investigate several different cases. Although Gores attempted to recreate Hammett's elaborate descriptions with meticulous research into the 1920s Bay Area, he did not achieve the crackle of Hammett's staccato dialogue. Though Gores's literary Lazarus project raises a few nostalgic smiles, his Spade, like Hammett's, remains enigmatic.

SAM SPADE'S LEGACY

Sam Spade's literary descendents abound, most reflecting more recent cultural developments. Closest to Hammett chronologically and literarily, Raymond Chandler (1888 to 1959), who acknowledged Hammett as his master, also initially wrote for the pulps, but he enlarged the concept of the hard-boiled private investigator into the sophisticated and complex figure of Philip Marlowe, introduced in *The Big Sleep* (1939), to evolve the detective story into a vehicle for serious exploration of profound themes (Murphy 93). Chandler faithfully portrayed southern California in the 1930s and 1940s, and like Hammett, kept crime in its conventional locales, big city alleys and streets, showing individuals corrupted by money and power.

Ross Macdonald (pen name of Kenneth Millar) (1915 to 1983) brought his hard-boiled detective Lew Archer out of short fiction, too. Beginning with his 1948 novel *The Moving Target,* Macdonald sought "a middle ground . . . between cultural change and the requirements of social order" (Margolies 14). Archer draws his values from his past and evolves into "the prototypic figure of the Vietnam and Watergate years," recognizing and exposing "self-deception and the plastic morality of the marketplace." Because of Macdonald's refining stress on the roots and results of social chaos, Archer indulges less in action than in talk, allowing "every witness . . . his own way of creeping up on the truth" (Larry Landrum, quoting Macdonald in Herbert 10). Later still, John D. MacDonald's Florida PI Travis McGee, more optimistic than his predecessors, adjusts nicely to social and cultural ambiguities.

Hammett's Sam Spade has inspired some strange spinoffs, including an FBI agent, Samantha ("Sam") Spade, played by Poppy Montgomery; "Sam Diamond," played by Peter Falk in the 1976 comic parody *Murder by Death*; "Sam Spud," an anthropomorphic potato in the educational children's show *Between the Lions*; "Sam Spayed," played by Garfield the Cat in *Garfield: His 9 Lives* and its accompanying animated television special; and "Sam Spade," an integrated network query tool for Windows 95, 98, NT, and Windows 2000, and a freeware tool for tracking down spam.

More recent detectives carry on Spade's hard-boiled tradition with solitary PIs, exotic backgrounds, and MacGuffins. In *Sons of Sam Spade: The Private-Eye Novel in the 70s,* David Geherin finds that Robert B. Parker's Spenser; Roger L. Simon's Moses Vine; and Andrew Bergman's Jack LeVine all comment on the deterioration of American life. In *Gorky Park* (1981), Martin Cruz Smith's Russian detective Arkady Renko follows Spade's premise: "When a man's partner is killed, he's supposed to do something about it." Marcia Muller's Sharon McCone, Sue Grafton's Kinsey Millhone, and

Sara Paretsky's V.I. Warshawski led off a growing parade of tough female shamuses in the early 1980s. Andrew Kleven's *Dynamite Road* (2003) positions a 1950s PI tale in modern San Francisco, and Lawrence Block's PI Matt Scudder has been probing "the dark side of human experience" for 20 years, most recently in *All the Flowers Are Dying* (2005) (Graff 16).

SAM SPADE'S ENDURING APPEAL

> *The Maltese Falcon* has endured because . . . it is a sophisticated detective story, a drama, a morality tale, a history lesson, and a study in cultural geography. It is a novel about honor, duty, professionalism, the philosophy of perception, the nature of authority, the power of lust, greed, betrayal, and the falsity of the American dream. . . . It transcends facile classification. (Layman 2005, 44)

So does Sam Spade, the remarkable protagonist to whom Dashiell Hammett gave so much of his tormented self. No literary character can be equated with the author who shaped him, but Dashiell Hammett put nearly everything he had—his eight years as a Pinkerton detective, his idiosyncratic rock-solid ethical code, his disgust with big business and big government, his saturnine humor, his ambivalent feelings toward women, his disillusion, his privacy, and his pain—into Sam Spade.

Spade shared Hammett's detective experience, his dedication to an individual moral code, his attitudes toward social and governmental institutions, his fears, his needs, his dreams and his cynicism, all in the context of a searing criticism of the corrupt, hypocritical, and crime-ridden American society of the 1920s and 1930s.

For all his own mistakes, his disillusion, and his pain, the ethical code Dashiell Hammett gave Spade in the novel saves Spade, because he behaves morally, with clearly stated reasons, at the conclusion, while the others prepare to continue their life of crime. William Ruehlman has commented that *The Maltese Falcon* does not praise that code, it examines the consequences for a man who has nothing else (paraphrased from *Saint with a Gun* in Metress 73). In the more extreme view of the present reconstructive era of American literary history, Spade seems to represent "the possibility of redirecting the insalubrious elements of an inherited frontier ethic into a more socially responsible new individualism" (Metress 91), a view consonant with Hammett's political positions.

Sam Spade today may most effectively be seen in the combined context of Hammett's novel and Huston's film. Whether Hammett approved or not and even though it shared "widespread isolationist American prejudices on the eve of World War II," the film establishes Spade's Americanism, while flawed, as the desirable norm (Luhr 11). The "blond satan" who tormented Dashiell Hammett gave to American detective literature had to walk those mean San Francisco streets, in Raymond Chandler's famous image, but he could not himself be mean. In turning Brigid over to justice, his choice of honor over emotion makes him "triumphantly moral . . . somehow human dignity and integrity have survived" in an inimical world (Thompson 131), blond satanic Sam Spade's saving grace.

PARALLEL CHRONOLOGY

Major Events Related to Sam Spade	World Events
	1887 First Sherlock Holmes story, "A Study in Scarlet" published
May 27, 1894 Samuel Dashiell Hammett born in St. Mary, MD	
	1903 Josef Stalin sides with Lenin in Bolshevik Party
	1905 First movie theater opens
1905 Lillian Hellman born in New Orleans	
ca. Late 1908 Hammett quits to work at various menial jobs	**1908** Establishment of FBI
1914–1918 Hammett works for Pinkerton National Detective Service	**1914–1918** World War I
	1915 U.S. movie industry booming; *The Birth of a Nation* rakes in $18 million; Street & Smith brings out *Detective Story Magazine*
	1917 Communist Revolution in Russia
1918–1919 Hammett served as driver in U.S. Army Ambulance Corps; beginning of his tuberculosis	**1918** U.S. socialist Eugene Debs imprisoned under Sedition Act
	1918–1922 Civil War in Russia
1919–1921 Hammett worked again for Pinkerton Agency	
Nov. 1920 Hammett's TB again active and he is hospitalized; meets Josephine Dolan, a nurse	**1920** Agatha Christie published her first Poirot novel, *The Mysterious Affair at Styles*
	1920s–1930s "Golden Age" of detective fiction
	1920 *Black Mask* magazine begins publication in U.S.; Prohibition begins; women's suffrage becomes law; pulp magazines firmly entrenched

Major Events Related to Sam Spade	World Events
June 1921 Hammett moves to San Francisco	
July 7, 1921 Hammett marries Josephine Dolan; daughter Mary born in October	
1921 Hammett involved as Pinkerton agent with Arbuckle case	
Dec. 1921 Hammett leaves Pinkerton though he may have worked part time until 1922	
1922 Hammett begins writing fiction; leaves Pinkerton	**1922** Stalin becomes General Secretary of USSR's Communist Party
Oct. 1922 George W. Sutton, Jr. becomes *Black Mask* editor; prints Hammett's first story in Dec. under pseudonym "Peter Collinson"	
1923–1927 Hammett publishes 32 stories in *Black Mask*	
October 1923 Debut of the Continental Op	
	1924 Lenin dies
	1924–1972 J. Edgar Hoover is FBI Director
1925 Lillian Hellman marries Arthur Kober	**1925** The Scopes "Monkey" Trial
1926 Hammett begins work for Samuels Jewelry in March; daughter Josephine born in May	**Nov. 1926** Joseph T. "Cap" Shaw becomes editor of *Black Mask*
1927 Hammett and Dolan separate; Hammett's *Red Harvest* begins serialization in Nov.	**1927** The first "talking picture," *The Jazz Singer*
Dec. 5 to Dec. 10, 1928 Time frame for action of *The Maltese Falcon; Red Harvest* published as book	**1928** Stalin consolidates supreme power in USSR; collectivizes agriculture, revives nationalism; promotes industrialism
1929 Hammett's *The Dain Curse* published	**1929** Hemingway's *A Farewell to Arms;* Faulkner's *The Sound and the Fury*
Sept. 1929–Jan. 1930 *The Maltese Falcon* serialized in *Black Mask*	**Feb. 1929** Valentine's Day Massacre
	Oct. 1929 U.S. stock market crash
1930 *The Maltese Falcon* published in book form; Hammett meets Lillian Hellman; their relationship lasts	**1930s** The Great Depression; the FBI operates against gangsters; violent purges in USSR

(Continued)

Major Events Related to Sam Spade	World Events
until Hammett's death; *The Glass Key* serialized in *Black Mask*	
ca. 1930–ca. 1946 Hammett works for various U.S. movie studios sporadically as screenwriter/script doctor	
Late 1930 Hammett moves from New York to Hollywood	
1931 *The Glass Key* published; first movie version of *The Maltese Falcon*; Hammett edits horror anthology *Creeps by Night*	
1932 Three Hammett short stories appear in "slicks"	
1933 Hammett completes last published novel, *The Thin Man*, in rundown New York hotel	**1933** Prohibition ends; Adolf Hitler becomes Chancellor of Germany
1934 *The Thin Man* published; Hammett writes only comic strip, *Secret Agent X-9*, and his last three short stories	**1934** Erle Stanley Gardner's first Perry Mason mystery; Rex Stout's first Nero Wolfe mystery; John Dillinger is shot by FBI
1934–1939 Hammett helps with 1934, 1936, and 1939 *Thin Man* films	
1934 *The Thin Man* (film)	
1936 Second film adaptation of *The Maltese Falcon, Satan Met a Lady*; *After the Thin Man* (film)	**1936–1939** Spanish Civil War
1937 Hammett and Dolan divorced; Hammett involved with left-wing organizations, probably joins the U.S. Communist Party; works with Hellman on *The Little Foxes*	**1937** Hemingway's film *The Spanish Earth*
1939 *Another Thin Man* (film)	**1939–1945** World War II
	1939 Russo-German nonaggression pact; Raymond Chandler's *The Big Sleep*
	1940s The FBI battles saboteurs
1941 *The Maltese Falcon* (movie) appears, starring Humphrey Bogart; Hammett adapts Hellman's *Watch on the Rhine* as movie	**June 1941** Germany attacks USSR; by 1945, 20 million Soviets are dead

Major Events Related to Sam Spade	World Events
	Dec. 7, 1941 Japanese attack on Pearl Harbor; U.S. enters World War II
1942–1945 Hammett serves in U.S. Army Signal Corps in the Aleutian Islands	
1943 Two radio play versions of *The Maltese Falcon*	
1944 Hammett writes *The Battle of the Aleutians* for U.S. Army	
1945–1966 Various reprints of Hammett's stories	**1945** U.S. drops atomic bombs on Japan
Sept. 1945 Hammett leaves Army with emphysema	
1946 Hammett elected president of New York Civil Rights Congress	**1946** Winston Churchill's "Iron Curtain" speech; U.S.–USSR relations deteriorate
	ca. 1946–ca. 1986 Cold War period
1946–1947 Hammett teaches creative writing at Jefferson School of Social Sciences	
1946–1951 Various radio series *Adventures of Sam Spade*	**1947** Anti-Communist Truman Doctrine; CIA established
1948 Hammett is national vice-chair of Civil Rights Congress; quits drinking; Hammett named to Jefferson School of Social Sciences board of trustees	**Aug. 1948** Anti-Communist scare stories proliferate and polarize the U.S.
1949–1956 Hammett serves again on Jefferson School of Social Sciences faculty	
	1949 Ross Macdonald introduces hard-boiled detective Lew Archer
1950s Sam Spade Wildroot Hair Tonic comic ads	**1950s** Hoover's FBI operates against "left-wingers"
	1950 Korean Conflict begins; McCarran Internal Security Act bars Communists from various functions; McCarthy begins anti-Communist witch hunts
1951 Hammett is New York state chair of Civil Rights Congress;	**1951** Alger Hiss jailed for perjury; the Rosenbergs are sentenced to death

(Continued)

Major Events Related to Sam Spade	World Events
convicted and imprisoned from July to December in federal prison for contempt of U.S. Congress and blacklisted thereafter; after release begins work on *Tulip*	for delivering nuclear secrets to the USSR
1953 Hammett testifies before McCarthy Committee	**1953** The Rosenbergs are executed; McCarthy heads Senate Sub-Committee on Investigations; Soviet dictator Stalin dies
	1954 Army-McCarthy hearings end; McCarthy censured by Senate
1956 Hammett sued by U.S. government for back taxes	
1957 IRS makes default judgment against Hammett and attaches his income for the rest of his life	**1957** McCarthy dies a broken man at 48; Eisenhower Doctrine promises arms to any Mideast country requesting aid against Communism; U.S.–USSR Space Race begins with Soviet launch of *Sputnik*
	1959 Fidel Castro assumes dictatorship in Cuba
1960 Hammett diagnosed with lung cancer	
Jan. 10, 1961 Hammett dies	
	1962 Cuban Missile Crisis
1963 Hellman and A.W.A. Cowan purchase Hammett's copyrights	
1965 *The Novels of Dashiell Hammett* published	
1966 *The Big Knockover* published, with unfinished Hammett novel *Tulip*	
	1969 Elmore Leonard publishes *The Big Bounce*
1975 *The Black Bird,* film spoof of *The Maltese Falcon*	
	1977 Marcia Muller publishes first mystery with female private eye (Sharon McCone)
	1982 Female PIs Sara Paretsky's V.I. Warshawski and Sue Grafton's Kinsey Millhone make first appearances
1984 Lillian Hellman dies	

Major Events Related to Sam Spade	World Events
	1987 Pres. Reagan challenges USSR to tear down Berlin Wall
	1989 Pres. George Bush and Mikhail Gorbachev announce end of Cold War; disintegration of USSR
1998 Huston's *Maltese Falcon* named one of 100 Greatest American Movies; *The Maltese Falcon* (novel) named one of 100 best novels in English of the 20th century	
2005 891 Post Street, Hammett's residence while writing *The Maltese Falcon*, named a National Literary Landmark	

DASHIELL HAMMETT'S WORKS

Novels

Red Harvest (1929), novel; serialized in *Black Mask* (1927); rpt. 1983.

The Dain Curse (1929), novel, based on short story "The Scorched Face"; rpt. 1983.

The Maltese Falcon (1930), novel (five-part serial in *Black Mask*, Sept. 1929–Jan. 1930); rpt. 1984.

The Glass Key (1931), novel; rpt. 1972.

The Thin Man (1934), novel; rpt. 1972.

Complete Novels, edited by Steven Marcus (1999).

Short Fiction

$106,000 Blood Money (1943), short fiction; published as *Blood Money* (1944) and as *The Big Knockover* (1948)

The Adventures of Sam Spade and Other Stories (1944), edited by Ellery Queen; published as *They Can Only Hang You Once* (1949); contains three Spade stories, "A Man Called Spade," "Too Many Have Lived," and "They Can Only Hang You Once"; all first published in *The American Magazine* (1932)

The Continental Op (1945); collection of Op stories

The Return of the Continental Op (1945); collection of Op stories

Hammett Homicides (1946)

Dead Yellow Women (1947)

Nightmare Town (1948)

The Creeping Siamese (1950)

Woman in the Dark (1952)

A Man Named Thin (1962)

The Big Knockover, collection of Continental Op stories, edited and introduction by Lillian Hellman (1966)

The Continental Op: More Stories from "The Big Knockover" (1967)

The Continental Op, short stories (differs from similarly titled collections above), edited by Steven Marcus (1974)

Dashiell Hammett's Secret Agent, short stories (1990)

Crime Stories and Other Writings, ed. Steven Marcus (2001)

Lost Stories: 21 Long-Lost Stories by the Creator of Sam Spade, the Maltese Falcon, and the Thin Man, edited by Vince Emery (2005)

Other Literary Works

Creeps by Night, short fiction edited by Hammett (1931, rpt. 1983)

Secret Agent X-9, comic strip (1934, rpt. 1983)

Watch on the Rhine, screenplay from Lillian Hellman's play (1943)

The Battle of the Aleutians, history (1944)

Letters

Selected Letters of Dashiell Hammett, Richard Layman and Julie M. Rivett, eds., with intro. by Josephine Hammett Marshall (2001)

Archive

The Dashiell Hammett Collection, at the Harry Ransom Center, University of Texas at Austin

Stage Adaptations

The Maltese Falcon (2005); The Long Beach Shakespeare Company, adapted and directed by Martin Pope

The Maltese Falcon (2007), The Long Beach Shakespeare Company, adapted by Helen Borgers; this version was presented in April 2008 in Huntsville, Alabama, as part of a week of *Falcon*-related events.

Films

The Maltese Falcon (also known as *Dangerous Female*), Warner Bros. (1931).

Satan Met a Lady (based on *The Maltese Falcon,* though names of characters and the object sought were changed), a light comedy starring Warren William; Warner Bros. (1936).

The Maltese Falcon, starring Humphrey Bogart; Warner Bros. (1941).

The Black Bird, spoof starring George Segal as "Sammy" Spade, Jr.; Columbia (1975).

Radio

"The Maltese Falcon," *Screen Guild Theater* (1943): CBS, 30-minute version, starring Humphrey Bogart, Mary Astor, Sidney Greenstreet, and Peter Lorre.

"The Maltese Falcon," *Lux Radio Theatre* (1943): CBS, 60-minute version, starring Edward G. Robinson as Spade.

"The Maltese Falcon," *Academy Award Theatre* (1946): CBS, 30-minute version, starring Bogart, Astor, and Greenstreet.

"The House in Cypress Canyon" (December 5, 1946): CBS, 30 minutes, starring Howard Duff.

"The Khandi Tooth Caper" (January 10, 1948): CBS, 60 minutes, starring Duff.

The Adventures of Sam Spade (1946): ABC, 13 30-minute episodes, starring Duff.

The Adventures of Sam Spade (1946–1949): CBS, 157 30-minute episodes, starring Duff.

The Adventures of Sam Spade (1949–1950): NBC, 51 30-minute episodes, starring Duff.

The Adventures of Sam Spade (1950–1951): NBC, 24 30-minute episodes, starring Steve Dunn.

The Adventures of Babe Lincoln (ca. 1950): CBS (unaired), starring Howard Duff.

Charlie Wild, Private Eye (Sept. 24, 1950); NBC premiere only, with Duff in guest appearance ("Charlie Wild" was basically Sam Spade renamed).

"The Maltese Falcon," BBC Radio 4 (2001), starring Tom Wilkinson, Jane Lapotaire, and Nickolas Grace.

Comics

The Maltese Falcon, artist Rodlow Willard (1946); Feature Books 48, David McKay Publications.

Sam Spade Wildroot Hair Tonic Ads (1950s); artist Lou Fine (single-page comic strips appearing in comic books, magazines, and newspapers as tie-in with NBC radio series, *The Adventures of Sam Spade,* also sponsored by Wildroot).

Manga

"Detective Conan," vol. 21: contains Sam Spade profile in Gosho Aoyama Mystery Library.

Spinoffs

Kandel, Susan. *Sam Spade in the Green Room.* New York: Morrow, 2006.

Gores, Joe. *Spade & Archer.* New York: Alfred A. Knopf, 2009.

WORKS CITED

Brower, Charles. "Dashiell Hammett," *Dictionary of Literary Biography,* v. 226. Edited by George Parker Anderson and John B. Anderson. Detroit: Gale, 1988: 188–208.

Desilva, Bruce. "Novelist Resurrects Sam Spade." *The Forum* (Fargo, ND), March 8, 2009: B1.

Fearon, Peter. *The Origins and Nature of the Great Slump, 1929–1932.* Atlantic-Highlands, NJ: Humanities, 1979.

Fecher, Charles. *Mencken: A Study of His Thought.* New York: Knopf, 1978.

Freeman, D. "Sam Spade's San Francisco." *Saturday Evening Post* 264 (March/April 1992): 78–84.

Goulart, Ron, ed. *The Hardboiled Dicks: An Anthology and Study of Pulp Detective Fiction.* Los Angeles: Sherbourne Press, 1965.

Graff, Keir. "Another Look at the Maltese Falcon." *Booklist* 104 (May 1, 2008): 16.

Gray, W. Russel. "Jimmying the Back Door of Literature: Dashiell Hammett's Blue-Collar Modernism." *Journal of Popular Culture* 41 (October 2008): 762–783.

Griffiths, Janette. "Sam Spade's San Francisco." http://ezinesarticles.com/?Sam-Spades-San-Francisco," accessed 6/13/2008.

Hammett, Jo. *A Daughter Remembers.* New York: Carroll & Graf, 2001.

Haycraft, Howard. Ed. *The Art of the Mystery Story.* New York: Simon & Schuster, 1946.

Herbert, Rosemary. *Whodunit? A Who's Who in Crime and Mystery Writing.* New York: Oxford University Press, 2003.

Hyams, Joe. *Bogie: The Biography of Humphrey Bogart.* New York: New American Library, 1966.

Johnson, Diane. *Dashiell Hammett: A Life.* New York: Random House, 1983.

Johnson, Paul. *Modern Times,* rev. ed. New York: HarperCollins, 1991.

Keating, H.R.F. *Crime and Mystery: The 100 Best Books.* New York: Carroll & Graf, 1987.

King, Laurie R. *A Monstrous Regiment of Women.* New York: St. Martin's Press, 1995.

Layman, Richard. *Discovering the Maltese Falcon and Sam Spade.* San Francisco: Vince Emery Productions, 2005.

———. *Shadow Man: The Life of Dashiell Hammett.* New York: Harcourt Brace Jovanovich, 1981.

Layman, Richard, and Julie M. Rivett, eds., *Selected Letters of Dashiell Hammett* with intro. by Josephine Hammett Marshall, 2001. Cited as *Selected Letters*

Lehman, David. *The Perfect Murder: A Study in Detection*. New York: Macmillan, 1989.

Leitch, Thomas. "Goodbye Miss Marple, Farewell Sam Spade." *Kirkus Reviews* 70 (December 15, 2002): 1781.

Linder, Daniel. "Hammett's *The Maltese Falcon*." *Explicator* 60 (Fall 2001): 35–38.

Luhr, William, ed. *The Maltese Falcon: John Huston, Director*. New Brunswick, NJ: Rutgers University Press, 1996.

Madden, David. *Tough Guy Writers of the Thirties*. Carbondale and Edwardsville, IL: Southern Illinois University Press, 1968.

Margolies, Edward. *Which Way Did He Go?* New York: Holmes and Meier, 1982.

Marling, William. *The American Roman Noir: Hammett, Cain, and Chandler*. Athens, GA: University of Georgia Press, 1995.

———. "The Hammett Succubus." *Clues* 3 (1982): 66–75.

Mellen, Joan. *Hellman and Hammett*. New York: HarperCollins, 1996.

Metress, Christopher. *The Critical Response to Dashiell Hammett*. Westport, CT: Greenwood Press, 1994.

Montagne, Renee. "Profile: Anniversary of Dashiell Hammett's novel '*The Maltese-Falcon*.'" Morning Edition (NPR): 02/14/2005.

Murphy, Bruce F. *The Encyclopedia of Murder and Mystery*. New York: St. Martin's Press, 1999.

Nolan, William. *Dashiell Hammett: A Casebook*. New York: McNally and Loftin, 1969.

———. *A Life on the Edge*. New York: Congdon & Weed, 1983.

Queen, Ellery. *In the Queens' Parlor*. New York: Simon and Schuster, 1957.

Sperber, A.M., and Eric Lax. *Bogart*. New York: William Morrow, 1997.

Symons, Julian. *Bloody Murder*. 3rd edition. New York: The Mysterious Press, 1992.

Thompson, George J. *Hammett's Moral Vision*. San Francisco: Vince Emery Productions, 2007.

Ward, Greg. *The Timeline History of the USA*. New York: Barnes & Noble, 2005.

Wolfe, Peter. *Beams Falling: The Art of Dashiell Hammett*. Bowling Green, OH: Bowling Green University Popular Press, 1980.

FURTHER READING

Abrahams, Paul P. "On Re-reading *The Maltese Falcon*." *Journal of American Culture* 18 (Spring 1995): 97–108.

Davis, J. Madison. "The 10 Greatest Crime Novels of All Time?" *World Literature Today* 80 (January/February 2006): 6–8.

Delaney, Bill. "Hammett's *The Maltese Falcon*." *Explicator* 63 (Spring 2005): 167–169.

Dillon, David. Review of *Sons of Sam Spade,* by David Geherin. *Library Journal* 105 (January 1, 1980): 103.

Fletcher, Connie. Review of *Dashiell Hammett: Lost Stories. Booklist,* May 1, 2005: 1524.

Gardiner, Dorothy, and Katherine Sorley Walker, eds. *Raymond Chandler Speaking*. Boston: Houghton, 1962.

Gates, David. "Becoming Sam Spade." Review of *Spade & Archer*. *The New York Times Book Review,* February 8, 2009: 12–13.

Geheron, David. *Sons of Sam Spade: The Private-Eye Novel in the 70s*. New York: Ungar, 1980.

Gores, Joe. *Hammett: A Novel*. New York: Putnam, 1975.

Grams, Martin, Jr. *The Radio Adventures of Sam Spade*. Churchville, MD: OTR Publishing, 2007.

Hellman, Lillian. *Scoundrel Time*. Boston: Little, Brown, 1976.

———. *An Unfinished Woman*. Boston: Little, Brown, 1969.

———, ed. *The Big Knockover*. Boston: Little, Brown, 1966.

———, ed. *Dashiell Hammet*. Boston: Little, Brown, 1966.

"Humphrey Bogart: The Peak Years." http://www.moderntimes.com/mystique, accessed 7/17/2008.

Johnson, Patricia E. "Sex and Betrayal in the Detective Fiction of Sue Grafton and Sara Paretsky." *Journal of Popular Culture* 27 (Spring 1994): 97–106.

Layman, Richard, ed. *Dashiell Hammett: A Descriptive Bibliography*. Pittsburgh: University of Pittsburgh Press, 1979.

Malmgren, Carl D. "The Crime of the Sign: Dashiell Hammett's Detective Fiction." *Twentieth Century Literature* 45 (Fall 1999): 371–385.

Penzler, Otto. "Hard-Boiled Heaven." *New York Sun*, February 14, 2005. http://www.nysun.com/article/9177, accessed 7/17/2008.

Pierce, J. Kingston. "Let's Talk about the Black Bird." http://www.januarymagazine.com/features/hammettintro.html, accessed 7/17/2008.

Reeves, W.J. "The Mutation of the Maltese Falcon." *American Notes and Queries* 18 (October 1979): 21–25.

Rimoldi, Oscar. "The Detective Movies of the 30s & 40s." *Films in Review* 44 (July/August 1993): 224–234.

Torgerson, Douglas. "The Image of the Maltese Falcon: Reconsidering an American Icon." *European Journal of American Culture* 26 (2007): 199–215.

Wright, William. "Why Lillian Hellman Remains Fascinating." *New York Times* (November 3, 1996), http://www.writing.upenn.edu/~afilreis/50s/hellman-today.html, accessed 7/27/2008.

WEB SITES

http://www.bogieonline.com/houseofsquibbthemaltesefalcon.htm (Old Time Radio adaptation of *The Maltese Falcon,* starring Humphrey Bogart, Mary Astor, and Sidney Greenstreet)

http://www.thrillingdetective.com/spade_sam.html (Thrilling Detective Web site)

http://www.bogieonline.com (The online resource for Humphrey Bogart fans)

http://www.pbs.org/wnet/americanmasters/database/hammett_d.html (A portrait of Dashiell Hammett)

"Listen, there's got to be more action . . . ," by Chester Gould, 1942. © Tribune Media Services, Inc. All Rights Reserved. Reprinted with permission.

Dick Tracy:
The First Comic Strip
Police Detective Hero

Crime Does Not Pay!

—Dick Tracy's motto

Since its debut on October 4, 1931, the *Dick Tracy* comic strip has become "a popular culture phenomenon of incredible impact and import," inspiring countless spinoffs—comic books, radio and television programs, movies, toys, games, dolls—and leaving "its square-jawed impression on America and the world." *Dick Tracy* has enjoyed remarkable longevity: bought by only 22 newspapers in 1932, *Dick Tracy* appeared in 695 newspapers in the winter of 1967, and a generation later it was still being seen in about 250.

> In 1995, Dick Tracy appeared on one of 20 Comic Strip Classics U.S. commemorative postage stamps.

Dick Tracy comics and spinoffs still enjoy sizeable sales worldwide. The name "Dick Tracy" has become as famous a synonym for "detective" as Conan Doyle's Sherlock Holmes, and Tracy's creator Chester Gould has significantly influenced other American creative talents working in popular culture.

HISTORICAL/CULTURAL CONTEXT

Dick Tracy was born in the violent, precarious, terrifying onset of America's Great Depression. At that time, Gould remarked, "no cartoon had ever shown a detective character fighting it out face-to-face with crooks via the hot lead route" (Walker 226), and readers immediately and enthusiastically responded, welcoming reassurance that "Crime Does Not Pay," Tracy's motto. The American public was suffering from the nationwide crime wave that resulted from the economic cataclysm striking America at the end of the Roaring Twenties. One major cause of the 1929 stock market crash was the phenomenal U.S. growth in productivity between 1919 and 1929—an enormous 6.4 percent per year increase in capital investment, accompanied by inflation caused by attempts at economic stabilization. As a result, working-class families had to struggle to keep up with the new prosperity, bankers had to work harder to inflate the economy, margin trading ominously swelled, and badly planned investment trusts were cobbled together supposedly to allow the "little man" to get a piece of the action. By the autumn of 1929, the stock market had become "an engine of doom, carrying to destruction the entire nation and, in its wake, the world" (Johnson 241).

The Great Bull Market of the 1920s, a speculative financial boom, peaked on September 3, 1929, and began to slide, plummeting by 10 percent on Black Thursday, October 24, when 13 million stock shares were sold. Blind panic reigned on Wall Street, and on Black Tuesday, October 29, called by economist John Kenneth Galbraith "the most devastating day in the history of markets," 16 million more shares were sold and prices dropped by 30 percent, wiping out $32 billion. In June 1932, general stock indexes hit a tenth of their 1929 high and by the next summer, industrial production and personal incomes had dropped by half in four years; from 1929 to 1934, unemployment rose from 3.2 percent to 26.7 percent (Johnson 246)—from 3 million to 15 million persons out of work (Ward 241).

The Great Depression proved to be the worst economic and social disaster in American history; 28 percent of American men, women, and children—34 million individuals—had no income at all and a massive drought turned the Great Plains into the Dust Bowl. Cities agonized, too: because landlords could not collect rent, they could not pay taxes, and city relief systems collapsed. Chicago owed its teachers $20 million, and over 300,000 New York children, 20 percent of them suffering from malnutrition, could not be taught for lack of funds; 1,500 colleges had gone bankrupt or closed by 1933. The public lavatories outside New York's City Hall were "a common stew . . . revolting, disgusting, enough to render a man forever speechless with pity" (Wolfe 414).

Organized crime took advantage of America's "common stew" of misery. When they left their homeland in the late 19th and early 20th centuries, Sicilian immigrants brought their feudal traditions of justice through direct action by organized groups of brigands to their new urban American homes. The Mafia, a name given to Sicilians who spurned all legal authority and operated under strict conditions of secrecy, controlled gang activities when Congress passed the 18th Amendment mandating the prohibition of liquor in December 1917. That "Noble Experiment" began formally in 1920, supposedly enforced by the Volstead Act prohibiting the manufacture, sale, and transportation of all alcoholic beverages, but in practice, the Volstead Act triggered a national tidal wave of crime. Bootlegging, illegal dealing in liquor, almost immediately became a major criminal activity for Mafia-related gangs. By 1920, Chicago became the crime capital of the United States, where gangsters like Al Capone, who five years later at age 26 became Chicago's crime boss, used bootlegging profits to build substantial criminal organizations that branched out during the 1930s into gambling, drug dealing, prostitution, labor racketeering, and other illicit activities.

Prohibition "created the greatest criminal bonanza in American history" (Daniel Boorstin, quoted in Ward 237), funding "beer barons, rumrunners and speakeasies" (Gould 32). Liquor, smuggled from Canada or Mexico or home brewed as urban "bathtub gin" or backwoods "white lightning," supplied "speakeasies" that blossomed in every U.S. city. New York's 16,000 pre-Prohibition saloons swelled to 32,000 speakeasies, and the government lost an estimated $11 billion in liquor tax revenues while the bootleggers wallowed in vast illegal profits. Al Capone, whose Chicago mob controlled the bootlegging trade, earned about $60 million per year (equivalent to nearly a billion of today's dollars) between 1925 and 1929 (Ward 238). In

1929, after 215 unsolved murders and the St. Valentine's Day Massacre when five of Capone's hit men killed seven of Bugs Moran's gang and several innocent bystanders in a Chicago garage, Capone retired to Florida, living in luxury until sentenced in 1931 to 11 years' imprisonment in "that palatial island rendezvous known as Alcatraz" (Gould, quoted in Sheridan 122) for tax evasion. In the "Roaring Twenties," the general population seemed to view hoodlum capers "almost with detachment" (Gould vii), but after losing their jobs because of the 1929 stock market crash, many law-abiding citizens began to resent the mobsters who were reaping huge ill-gotten gains and thumbing their noses at the law.

Crime and corruption gradually wore down public and political support for Prohibition. In 1929, President Herbert Hoover created the Wickersham Commission to investigate the connection between Prohibition and crime, and his successor Franklin Roosevelt signed legislation abolishing Prohibition in 1933, declaring, "I think this would be a good time for a beer" (quoted in Ward 237). The damage Prohibition had caused by allowing the rise of organized crime, however, continued to mount.

In the early 1930s,

> The newspapers were filled with horror stories: . . . a 28-year-old man dropping dead of starvation on the sidewalks of midtown Manhattan; a sanitationman [sic] committing suicide by jumping into an incinerator because his salary was too meager to support his family . . . machine guns rattled, illicit beer trucks roared down dark streets, and the hooch gangs were giving Chicago coppers a bad time. (Gould vii)

In Brooklyn a grape truck driver was found slain with a hatchet. "Lucky" Luciano assembled an interstate crime "Syndicate" with powerful political connections and a lethal enforcement arm of professional killers called Murder, Inc. The notorious bank robber and murderer John Dillinger, "Public Enemy No. 1," rampaged through the Midwest in 1933, terrorizing the populace with numerous hit-and-run bank jobs and 16 killings before being gunned down the next year on a Chicago street by J. Edgar Hoover's FBI agents. G-men also killed "Pretty Boy" Floyd and "Baby Face" Nelson in 1934, shot down "Ma" Barker and one of her infamous gang in 1935, and cracked down on Murder, Inc. in 1940 to 1941. Despite these early successes and Sen. Estes Kefauver's 1950 to 1951 government investigations, U.S. organized crime continued to flourish, supported largely by the Mafia, which supplemented its profits and "laundered" them through legal "front" operations.

Organized crime provided a major source of terrifying raw material in the development of American popular culture during the 1930s and 1940s. In 1920, the year Prohibition began, so did *Black Mask,* a pulp magazine popularizing crime fiction and introducing hard-boiled American detectives in stories reflecting the United States' "violent and disillusioned spirit" following World War I. From 1920 to 1951, *Black Mask* perfected the hard-boiled style and cultivated authors like Erle Stanley Gardner, Dashiell Hammett, and Raymond Chandler, appealing to a wide range of readers, including Presidents Woodrow Wilson and Harry Truman and even Al Capone. Hollywood also followed the public's thirst for seeing thugs like Capone brought to justice. In 1931, the year Capone was tried for tax evasion, over 50 gangster and detective movies appeared, including *Little Caesar, Public Enemy,* and *The Maltese Falcon;* by 1935 over 150 more had been cranked out, though the Hays Office, responsible for enforcing the motion picture industry's code of conduct, prohibited films depicting Dillinger's life. In the wartime 1940s, colorful real-life gangsters began to disappear, but the allure of fictional crime remained, providing material for numerous novels, movies, and comic strips—the first and foremost of which was Chester Gould's *Dick Tracy.*

AUTHORSHIP

The first fictional private detective, Edgar Allan Poe's Chevalier M. Auguste Dupin, appeared in "The Murders in the Rue Morgue" (1841) when most American cities did not even have police departments and even Scotland Yard's Detective Department had not yet been established. Both Dupin and Sherlock Holmes, whose immensely popular adventures appeared between 1887 and 1927, generally dismissed the police as unimaginative plodders, lacking the intellectual brilliance that distinguished both Dupin and Holmes. "The funnies" familiar to American newspaper readers at first featured ludicrous figures like "The Yellow Kid," Richard Felton Outcault's bald-headed, flap-eared, buck-toothed street urchin. However, in the 1900s American comic strips with speech balloons, panel borders, regularly appearing characters, and continuing story lines began exploiting the public's desire for detection and adventure that Poe and Conan Doyle had stoked and "provided cheap thrills for children of all ages" (Walker 185). C.M. Kahles's *Hairbreadth Harry* (1906), Gus Mager's *Sherlocko the Monk* (1910), and *Hawkshaw the Detective* (1913) all featured comic sleuths, while Roy Crane's *Wash Tubbs* and Harold Gray's *Little Orphan Annie* (both 1924) "involved their protagonists in a continuous series of perilous episodes" (Broes 97). Chester Gould, however, "was the first to create a real [police] detective hero, to treat crime seriously and to depict violence openly if not with relish" (Broes 97 and Hoppenstand 248).

Born November 20, 1900, in Pawnee, Oklahoma, Gould grew up loving to draw. In a 1970 interview, he observed that his father, a newspaper printer who eventually owned a small weekly paper, probably had sparked his interest in cartooning. Gould Senior had asked his seven-year-old son to draw some men at a Pawnee County political meeting. The results, posted in the window of the Pawnee *Courier Dispatch*, earned young Gould considerable attention—"the thing," he claimed, "that definitely turned me into this business" (Galewitz vii). His father wanted him to study law, but at

17 Chester Gould won $10, a considerable sum then, in a cartoon contest sponsored by *The American Boy* magazine. He sent in $20 for 20 lessons from the W.L. Evans School of Cartooning, Cleveland, Ohio, his only formal training in this field. He drew cartoons for the *Daily Oklahoman* and the *Tulsa Democrat* during his two years at Oklahoma A & M, but he was determined to go to Chicago, then the capital of both U.S. crime and newspaper cartooning. He arrived in the Windy City on September 1, 1921, with $50 in his pocket, and shortly after received a horrified letter from his "dear mother": "Dear Son. I've just read in the newspaper about those gangsters in Chicago who have been shooting and robbing people for no reason at all, and YOU with $50 in your pocket! Come home at once!" (quoted in Gould xi).

Gould hated to disappoint his mother, but he stayed in Chicago, graduating from Northwestern University in 1923 with a degree in commerce and marketing while taking night school art courses. He stacked groceries at an A & P for about a month until he landed an artist's job on Chicago's *Evening Journal*, doing an occasional cartoon and helping cover stories about beer-baron machine gun shootouts. He commented,

> . . . this era . . . planted the idea of DICK TRACY [capitals in original] in my head. The revelations of fixed juries, crooked judges, bribery of public officials and cops . . . showed the crying need for a strong representative of law and order who would take an eye for an eye and a tooth for a tooth. Tracy was that man. (Gould xi)

In 1926, Gould married Edna Marie Gauger, a "lively, attractive girl . . . no frothy little attempt to make believe" and "someone he could believe in." Their only child, Jean, recalled that her father cherished Edna's "inner strength and beauty and her ability to always see the positive side of life" in a marriage lasting nearly 60 years (O'Connell 66, 108).

For about 10 years, Gould worked for five of Chicago's six papers, trying out about 60 different cartoon strips—"the beautiful girl strip, the office boy, the smart aleck, the oddball, the believe-it-or-not cartoon, even a comic feature on sports. But none of them quite clicked" (Gould, quoted in Galewitz xvii), though Gould did achieve modest success with the comic *Fillum Follies* (1924). In June 1931, during the "last stage . . . of big time gangsterism in Chicago," Gould said a 61st idea suddenly occurred to him: "perhaps we ought to have a detective in this country that would hunt these fellows up and shoot 'em down" (quoted in Galewitz viii), voicing the sentiments simmering in most good citizens since "gangland, with its coterie of killers, fixers and go-betweens, was in full bloom during the scarlet days of prohibition" (Gould, quoted in Sheridan 121). Gould drew six strips featuring a new symbol of law and order, "Plainclothes Tracy," a sharp-featured Holmesian private detective battling "Big Boy," a "thinly disguised caricature of Chicago crime boss Al Capone" (Walker 226) and sent them to Capt. Joseph Medill Patterson, the canny head of the *Chicago Tribune-New*

York News Syndicate distributing comic features. Two months later Patterson informed Gould that Tracy had "possibilities."

When Gould interviewed at Patterson's office, Patterson changed the detective's name to "Dick Tracy" because plainclothes detectives were familiarly known as "dicks." Patterson suggested that Tracy join the police force after the father of Tracy's fiancée, whom Patterson named Tess Trueheart, was brutally shot down by thugs who kidnapped her. He urged Gould to "'show the bullets going into the body,' which became a trademark of the strip." Patterson then hired Gould, who went down to the lobby, "bought a cigar and a Coke and broke out in a cold sweat" (*Thirties* viii, xii). After struggling for a decade, he had finally achieved his goal.

Chester Gould, described in 1944 as an "affable, well-adjusted man who drinks bourbon neat, smokes nine good cigars a day, and plays poker whenever he gets the chance" (Walker 226), lived for most of his life on a farm near Woodstock, Illinois, tirelessly producing *Dick Tracy* until he retired in 1977. His daughter Jean called him "a private person in the public eye"; he cared deeply about his fans, reading every piece of fan mail he received and answering most of them himself, and he took considerable pains to ensure the accuracy of *Dick Tracy*, according to Jean Gould O'Connell, who taped her father's recollections in 1983 and celebrated his clear memory and strong will "filled with compassion, self esteem and a sense of humor" in *Chester Gould: A Daughter's Biography of the Creator of Dick Tracy*. Gould frequently visited the Chicago police, met J. Edgar Hoover at the FBI headquarters in Washington, D.C., hired a retired Chicago policeman for weekly conferences on new developments in crime fighting, and at Patterson's suggestion studied crime detection at Northwestern University's School of Criminology, which even Chicago police officers attended. About two months after its October, 4, 1931, debut in the now-defunct *Detroit Mirror*, a tabloid owned by the Tribune Company, *Dick Tracy* took off "like wildfire," earning Gould numerous national awards, over a dozen awards from police associations, and in 1979 the first Edgar awarded to a cartoonist and comic strip by the Mystery Writers of America.

> During the 1945 New York newspaper deliverers' strike, Mayor Fiorello H. LaGuardia read a complete *Dick Tracy* comic strip over the radio.

Gould never wavered from his conviction that "Crime Does Not Pay." He made it Tracy's motto, and he worked hard to keep it before the American public. Gould believed that "A comic strip has to follow contemporary thinking to be popular . . . you have to please the young and the old . . . the biased . . . you have to try to get the people that don't read the comics. . . . There is no end for what you set for yourself. . . . The pressure is always there" (quoted in O'Connell 101). He averaged two all-night working sessions a week with his Bristol board and Gillott dip pen, the only one he ever used.

In 1971, Gould told an interviewer he took his few detractors "with a grain of salt," believing that people who deplored the "horrible things" he put into *Dick Tracy* "were the types who couldn't wait . . . to see how a particular thing turned out" (Galewitz ix). He also insisted on what he felt was "the basic reality of all humanity: 'we all build our lives around heroes,'" boys picking hero types that win out "over danger and risk," and girls yearning for "the prince and all the money" (quoted in Galewitz ix).

In the same interview, Gould explained the methods he used in *Dick Tracy*. To create convincing suspense, he never outlined each story line, believing that if he did not know the outcome, the reader couldn't, either. Although Gould never acknowledged the influence of the "tough dicks" of pulp fiction, Dick Tracy nonetheless fit that hard-boiled pattern in many respects. Gould instead claimed that his principal literary influences were his boyhood loves, Sherlock Holmes and Edgar Allan Poe's stories. Gould also insisted he "followed the newspapers almost exclusively" (*Thirties* viii), intensely focusing on the omnipresent war on crime. He relied heavily on melodramatic action, chance encounters, and opportunely overheard conversations, salting his characters' dialogue heavily with dialect and slang.

Gould quickly developed his detective "from a rather shaky young man on his first assignment to the professional bloodhound of Chief Brandon's police force" (Gould, quoted in Sheridan 122). Gould illustrated his belief that "the ugliest thing in the world is the face of a man who has killed seven nurses—or who has kidnapped a child" (Galewitz xi) by creating unmistakably villainous grotesque characters whose exaggerated features reflected their crimes. In the wake of the 1932 Lindbergh kidnapping, Gould introduced "Junior," ostensibly just a waif rescued and adopted by Dick Tracy, but actually the character that rescued the strip by attracting "the young, the old, and all in between," making Gould's stories more convincing and markedly improving his artwork (Gould ix).

Major Villains in *Dick Tracy*, 1933–1949 (*Celebrated Cases* 287)

Stooge Viller, 1933	The Brow, 1944	Shoulders, 1948
Mole, 1941	Vitamin Flintheart, 1944	Sketch Paree, 1949
Littleface, 1941	Flattop Sr., 1944	
B-B Eyes, 1942	Shakey, 1945	
Pruneface, 1943	Breathless Mahoney, 1946	
Mrs. Pruneface, 1943	Mumbles, 1947	

During World War II, Gould tried hard "to fight the headlines, which were pretty sensational," by keeping Tracy tracking fantastic criminals on the Home Front to furnish "relief from the damn headlines" (quoted in Galewitz xii). He also introduced many new gadgets like the famous 2-way

Dick Tracy's Scientific Arsenal (*Celebrated Cases* 291)

2-Way Wrist Radio

Battery-powered TV camera with self-light

Atom light to thwart bank robbery

The Voice-of-Graf voice printing device

2-Way Wrist TV

wrist radio, first seen in the strip in 1946. Gould originally sketched the 2-way wrist radio and TV on October 17, 1945, when television was in its infancy, so he used only the radio part of the device at first. Gould noted in 1978 that a few years after the Army's walkie-talkie made the wrist radio more plausible, he incorporated the TV aspect in 1964, which "has been a vital part of Tracy's gear to this very day" (Gould xii) (decades before Blackberries). Other "outrageous" Gould ideas catalyzed by Diet Smith in the strip were 1948's "Portable Teleguard," a predecessor to surveillance television cameras; 1954's "Electronic Telephone Pick-Up," foreshadowing caller ID; 1956's Floating Portable TV, predecessor to the camcorder; 1962's Magnetic Space Coupe; and 1968's Magnetic Police Space Car (O'Connell 135).

Chester Gould modeled the character Pear-Shape Tone after himself.

When postwar federal laws cracked down on major criminals, crimes like kidnapping diminished, and Gould revamped Tracy's supporting cast by retiring Tracy's first boss Chief Brandon and replacing him with Pat Patton, originally a comic figure. As Tracy's new sidekick, Gould introduced Sam Catchum, based on his own friend Al Lowenthal. He also used "increasingly violent and bizarre" means of slaying both crooks and cops, like freezing policemen alive in refrigerator trucks and having criminals torch rival cleaning-fluid-doused villains (Goulart 73).

The Name "Dick Tracy"

The name "Dick Tracy" inspired "Dick Grayson," Batman's first Robin; Al Capp built "Fearless Fosdick" into his *Li'l Abner* comic strip; and "Duck Twacy" appeared in the 1946 Daffy Duck Loony Tunes cartoon *The Great Piggy Bank Robbery*.

On the positive side, Dick Tracy began to inspire fellow cartoonists. Gould also introduced Dick Tracy's famous Crime Stoppers Club in his strip in 1947, and shortly afterward, he developed a real Crime Stoppers Club for children in the Goulds' home town of Woodstock, Illinois. Other communities quickly followed, and in 1976, Albuquerque, New Mexico, police officer George McAleese asked Gould's permission to use the name "Crimestoppers" [sic] for an adult organization that by 1982 involved over 300 U.S. communities in "one of the most effective citizen-law enforcement, anti-crime programs in existence," eventually including thousands of such U.S. and international programs (O'Connell 142–143).

In the 1950s, Gould worked topicalities like television into *Dick Tracy,* concentrating so heavily on Tracy's home life with Tess Trueheart, whom Tracy married on Christmas Eve, 1949, after an 18-year courtship, and their daughter Bonnie Braids that some episodes took on a soap opera flavor, with the Tracys living in an unconvincingly opulent house and riding around in a Cadillac—on the hero's police salary.

The unrest of the 1960s and 1970s gave Gould's *Dick Tracy* a more moralistic tone. He reflected in 1974, "You reap what you sow. I think we're sowing a bad seed in America right now. . . . We're not instilling the kind of character that made America. We have removed religion. Moral values have deteriorated" (quoted in O'Connell 160). He deplored the rise in American crime and the tendency to "coddle the criminal," and in one strip he made Tracy wonder, "With the milksop backing the cop gets, should he quit his profession?" Tracy typically concluded, however, "For myself, I'll stick around till these 'kiss-the-crook' and 'kick-the-victim' are banished from high places," and Gould put the command "Law and Order FIRST" next to Tracy's head on every piece of mail that left his house from the 1970s until his death in 1985 (O'Connell 162–163).

Some observers felt Gould also "got quirky" in the 1960s (Hughes 50). He launched his "Space Period," venturing into speculation which he refused to categorize as "science fiction." He postulated a "Space Coupe" driven by magnetic propulsion to reach lunar colonies and provided Tracy's police force with air cars to pursue moon-based villains, declaring, "we're going to have to protect what we find up there. . . . There is going to be a very definite need to exercise power" (quoted in Galewitz xi), but his fans hated this new direction.

Gould returned to Earth in the 1970s, attempting to update Tracy with a moustache and longer hair and Groovy Grove, a hippie-style sidekick and romantic interest for Lizz the Policewoman. Groovy turned off older readers who shared Gould's conservative opinions, like Tracy's complaints about the growing emphasis on the rights of the accused: ". . . under today's interpretation of the laws, it seems it's the police who are handcuffed!" Gould's audience also found his story lines increasingly tangential, just when newspapers were reducing the space they devoted to comics, severely restricting Gould's plotlines. According to Max Allan Collins, Gould's admirer since the age of eight and his successor on the strip, "The editors at the *Tribune* had decided Chet's increasingly idiosyncratic stories were killing the strip [he even incorporated the family dogs into some episodes]; they made him an offer that essentially gave him more *not* to do the strip than to do it," and Gould took it (Hughes 50, italics in original).

After Gould retired from *Dick Tracy* on Christmas Day, 1977, too proud to ever tell his family that he had been asked to leave the strip, Collins and Gould's assistant Rick Fletcher, who died in 1983, took over the strip, with Gould remaining briefly as a story consultant. Collins terminated the Space Period and put Tracy back into street police work, blew up Moon Maid to fans' applause, killed off Groovy Grove, and allowed Tracy to reluctantly come to terms with America's justice system, softening the strip's original direction. To rejuvenate *Dick Tracy*, Collins updated the strip with topical issues like computer-assisted embezzlement, air hijacking, and a punk-rock robber. He also revived one of Gould's "classic" villains per year and reemphasized Gould's popular B.O. Plenty, Gould's own favorite among Tracy's supporting cast, B.O.'s wife Gravel Gertie, and their daughter Sparkle Plenty as comic relief.

Relations among Gould, Fletcher, and Collins soon deteriorated, however, and after Fletcher bad-mouthed the strip to a reporter, Collins reluctantly removed Gould's name from *Dick Tracy*'s byline. Gould died on May 11, 1985, and Dick Locher, Gould's assistant in the 1950s and 1960s and a Pulitzer Prize-winning editorial cartoonist, returned to *Dick Tracy* with Locher's son John, who died in 1986. In 1992, after Collins had worked on the strip for 15 years, a new *Tribune* editor that Collins described as "a jerk" fired Collins because Collins told him so (Hughes 50). After Collins and Fletcher left the strip, *Dick Tracy* "sank back into mediocrity but for a while they breathed new life into a venerable warhorse" (Flagg). Mike Kilian, a *Chicago Tribune* staff writer and columnist, worked with Locher until Kilian died on October 27, 2005. Since January 9, 2006, Locher has drawn and authored *Dick Tracy*, retaining Gould's original conservative crime-busting orientation while updating gadgetry and variations of crime.

PROFILE OF DICK TRACY

Tracy's Background

Gould envisioned Dick Tracy as a modernized and idealized Sherlock Holmes, "if Holmes were a young man living today, dressed as a modern G-man and bearing the traditional characteristics" of a square chin and hooked nose (Gould, quoted in Sheridan 123). Gould's Tracy joined the police force at 34, without

> a soft line in his character or appearance . . . [a] true-blue, indomitable, granite-featured figure. . . . [He is] that tall, four-square man, with his jutting (meat-chopper bulldozer) chin, his grim mouth and tight-lipped smile, his eagle's beak of a nose, . . . and his vigorous, slangy, crisply emphatic speech. (Galewitz xviii)

Tracy, whose birthday is celebrated on October 4, does not drink, gave up smoking early in his career, and never, never swears. Gould said that

Tracy, who does not age in the strip, is always "extremely human—even to the point of having him do the wrong thing at the wrong time . . . none of us is a super specimen all the time, not even Dick Tracy" (Sheridan 123), a technique called "stereotype revitalization," where the author adds a frailty and/or significant touches of human complexity to a stereotypical figure (Cawelti 11–12), like Tracy's demonstrations of love and affection, his sudden angry outbursts, occasional errors of judgment, and a few occasions of physical awkwardness, as when he once fell out of a tree. Little is known about Tracy's parents or his youth, but Gould gave him a small family of his own: his "closest pal and devoted disciple, Junior"; his wife, Tess True-heart, a "woman of moods"; their child, Bonnie Braids, born in the back of a police car in 1950; his loyal and dependable assistant, Pat Patton, later Tracy's Chief of Police; and Tracy's first boss, Chief Brandon. After Tracy and Tess were married, Lizz the Policewoman entered the strip because Gould felt "you can't handle a woman prisoner without a policewoman" (quoted in Galewitz xiv), reflecting the growing numbers of women involved in both crime and law enforcement. Tracy's extended family eventually included Moon Maid, the Moon Valley humanoid chieftain's daughter who married Junior Tracy in 1968, and their daughter Honey Moon Tracy, born with antennae and magnetic hands but later phased out after Collins took over the strip and definitively ended Tracy's Space Period. After Collins killed off Moon Maid in 1978, Junior married Sparkle Plenty, a long-haired blond beauty with whom he had a daughter, Sparkle Plenty Jr.

Dick Tracy's Career

In 1931, Joseph Patterson realized that Chester Gould's basic concept of private eye "Plainclothes Tracy" had one serious flaw: Tracy as a freelance gangbuster could be accused of "championing vigilantism, combating one sort of lawlessness with another" (Harvey 105). Thus Tracy's activities needed legal validation; Tracy could not remain an ordinary citizen who heroically rescued Tess and hauled in her abductors. He had to become an incorruptible career policeman, a symbol of relentless law and order. Gould agreed, characterizing Tracy as "An individual who could toss the hot iron back at them [the gangsters] along with a smack on the jaw thrown in for good measure" (Gould, quoted in Sheridan 122). Though Tracy could—and did—make mistakes, he never deviated from that characterization until Gould's successors modulated him and his methods in the 1980s.

In pioneering the police-procedural detective strip, Gould explained that "I try to keep the detective deduction angle the main theme of underlying interest. Pursuit, deduction, and action are the ingredients that I stress" (quoted in Goulart 75). Under Patterson's direction, Gould established the successful "essential Tracy" formula in his first episode: in apprehending criminals, Tracy always gets his man or woman, surviving brutal treatment himself before he does in the crook who is wading justice.

This formula carefully balances conventions and inventions; conventions include recognizable period history and established police procedure, and inventions include scientific technologies and innovations in police work. Gould also defined Tracy as "a no-nonsense crime fighter whose superior deductive powers are satisfyingly amplified with a two-fisted modus operandi" (quoted in Harvey 107); he never materially changed him, though Gould made Tracy battle a wide variety of villains. Early in his career, Gould had met Al Valanis, a young Chicago police officer who after his retirement in 1953 became Gould's technical advisor, meeting weekly with Gould on new police techniques and lab work. The successive phases of Tracy's career thus were shaped by contemporary issues and characters that Gould found provocative, from the relatively conventional organized gangsters and crime bosses of the 1930s through the more exotic megalomaniac villains he created in the 1970s.

From a sociological viewpoint, Dick Tracy's career can be seen as a long-running morality play, in which good always triumphs over evil and police expertise always brings criminals to justice. Both the criminals and their crimes substantially changed, however, once Gould retired. Whereas in the earlier decades of Tracy's career he employed not only handcuffs and fisticuffs but almost any lethal weapon he could find. However, by 1989, with *Dick Tracy* appearing in over 600 domestic and 50 foreign newspapers, "police violence was both minimal and reactive; . . . the majority of offenses pictured were crimes against the American economic system, rather than violent crime, and offenders were disproportionately white, middle-aged males" (Mooney and Fewell 89).

In contrast to the murders, robberies, and assaults that in the 1980s were proliferating in prime-time television, the offenses pictured in the 1980s *Dick Tracy* strips were mostly nonviolent, including counterfeiting, illegal wire taps, drug trafficking, burglary, illegal toxic waste disposal, and theft, with the low incidence of "street crimes" responsible for "the underrepresentation [in the strip] of young, Black, low socioeconomic offenders." Criminals and lawmen both were of medium height, disproportionately white, male, and middle-aged, but the criminals were bald and endomorphic, unlike the muscular policemen who still sported most of their hair (Mooney and Fewell 93). Although the types of crimes depicted in Gould's *Dick Tracy* and strips produced by his successors differ, both the 1930s street thugs and the more contemporary "bad guys" threaten the social order, and so throughout *Dick Tracy* "the ends of social control and order maintenance justify all means of law enforcement" (Mooney and Fewell 96). After nearly eight decades, *Dick Tracy* still reflects the world as "a sinful, corrupt, degrading place . . . [and] in such a world there must be eternal vigilance . . . the power of evil to corrupt the good and to destroy man and his democratic institutions is a central tenet of this view" (Berger 123).

Dick Tracy's Strengths

Chester Gould made Dick Tracy an "absolutely honest and incorruptible defender of the faith with his Rock of Gibraltar sense of duty . . . [an] iron-willed man who, ahead of his time, was never uptight, who never blew his cool" (Ellery Queen, quoted in Galewitz xviii). Tracy survived countless physical assaults (27 bullet wounds in his first 24 years) and by far more hair-breadth escapes from inescapable situations than any of his competitors. Gould not only endowed Dick Tracy with physical courage and a talent for the knockout punch, he gave him a brilliant Holmesian deductive intellect, shown especially in his ability to discover and utilize technical crime-fighting innovations, like ballistics, handwriting analysis, psychological analysis, fingerprinting, and closed-circuit television surveillance. Tracy also relies on hunches based on the careful observation of minute details to carry out the consequences of his unequivocal moral conviction that "crime doesn't pay, and a life of crime will put you in daily communion with . . . gargoyles of criminality" (Harvey 107).

To portray this philosophical concept visually, Gould's cartooning style displayed his mastery of dramatic contrast. His "deceptively simple" geometric figures (Harvey 107) depicted the strict moralistic concept of absolute good versus absolute evil principally in black and white, and mostly black at that; and like the mob-ridden city streets after Black Tuesday, each of his panels has a large black area. Tracy always wears a black suit, and many ceilings, walls, streets, buildings, and furniture around him are black. Gould allowed no graduated shades of gray in his drawings or ethical ambiguities in his stories, but the effect of his solid black-laced panels is not foreboding; it results in "a stark rendition of reality . . . an exercise in black and white both graphically and philosophically" (Harvey 108).

Poet and critic Donald Phelps insists, "always pay attention to the blackness. To, that is, the identity, the singular vitality, of the black. . . . This blackness is not darkness . . . but the supplanting of light by a vigorous, surface-rending presence . . . [in a] mosaic of street naturalism and exotic-touched rodomontade . . . as marinated in a rancid sort of glamour" (1–2). So immense a "surface-rending" social-order-threatening "presence" collectively adds up to "Evil" represented by the prevalence of black. It requires an equally powerful hero, defining Tracy's stature as a hero and the enormous moral, physical, and intellectual strengths he musters against them. Evil, for Gould, wears a multitude of faces, so that Tracy must devise and employ different strategies and different tactics, making him "the world's first procedural detective of fiction . . . [and] illustrating the techniques of contemporary crime detection" (Harvey 107). When Gould retired, however, in contrast to his black-white pairing of his larger-than-life hero and his equally powerful group antagonist of grotesque villains, many felt the subsequent "Gould-Fletcher-Collins" Dick Tracy became "darkness . . . the savagery of the Gould design fearfully tethered" that Gould's successors tempered into "the most cordial, the most amenable of lobotomies" (Phelps 1–2).

Dick Tracy's Adversaries

Very little cordiality appeared in Gould's original *Dick Tracy,* vividly described by Jay Maeder as

> a dark and perverse and vicious thing, sensationally full of blood-splashed cruelty from its first week, the single most spectacularly gruesome feature the comics had ever known; there has never been another newspaper strip so full of the batterings, shootings, knifings, drownings, torchings, crushings, gurglings, gaspings, shriekings, pleadings and bleatings that Chester Gould gleefully served up as often as he possibly could. (Quoted in Walker 226)

Gould defended *Dick Tracy*'s unprecedented emphasis on violence against the misgivings of newspapers hesitating to buy the strip by claiming that "The law [American, at least] is always armed"—implying that the criminals bring the "hot lead route" to perdition on themselves (Sheridan 122), a sentiment Gould's fans, fed up with crime and criminals, heartily endorsed.

Gould's individual villains illustrate the myriad grotesque facets of evil. Against his "extremely human" Tracy (Sheridan 122), Gould posed unnatural-looking villains, employing "a comic-book genius for drawing grotesquely caricatured faces and heads," and deforming each criminal to reveal his or her special criminal orientation to the world. He also invented "grotesquely Dickensian character-names" to match his caricatures, sometimes spelling familiar words backwards to name a thug, exemplifying the inversion of Good that typifies Evil.

Gould's ghouls' gallery includes the criminally insane Selbert Depool ("Looped" spelled backwards); Jerome Trohs ("Short" spelled backwards) and Mamma, a miniature mobster and his gargantuan mother; Breathless Mahoney, a femme ultra-fatale; Shoulders, a lady killer; and Pruneface, a

---

"Breathless Mahoney" was also shameless, as these two Mae Westian scraps of dialogue show:

Big Boy Caprice:	"Around me, if a woman don't wear mink, she don't wear nothing."
Breathless Mahoney:	"Well, I look good both ways."

***

Dick Tracy:	"You know, it's legal for me to take you down to the station and sweat it out of you under the light."
Breathless Mahoney:	"I sweat a lot better in the dark."

disfigured Nazi spy who experiments with nerve gas. The goofy criminal hillbillies B.O. Plenty and Gravel Gertie reformed and over several decades humorously counterpointed Tracy's adventures. Probably Gould's most popular wartime villain was Flattop, a freelance hit man whose head was shaped like the deck of an aircraft carrier. Hired to kill Tracy, Flattop eventually perished in a spectacular shootout, and fans allegedly went into public mourning. In his earlier strips, Gould patterned some criminal figures after certain movie personalities of the 1930s, like Clark Gable, Greta Garbo, James Cagney, and Claudette Colbert. The perpetually sneering screen presence of Edward G. Robinson, famous for playing gangland figures like "Little Caesar," inspired some of Gould's most repellent caricatures.

Dick Tracy's Romantic Interest

"Gould was no bumpkin off the truck when it came to depicting love and romance in his strip" (Roberts 63). After rescuing Tess Trueheart from the kidnappers who murdered her father, Tracy courted her for 18 stormy years. Tess could be "brash, stubborn, independent, and foolish" and a problem for Tracy, but she also was "intelligent, charming, reasonable, and impossibly patient." She even rescued Tracy several times, and until 1955 when Lizz the Policewoman entered the strip, Tess was its only female embodiment of law and order. In 1932 she hurled Tracy's engagement ring into a river and nearly married Edward Nuremoh ("homerun" spelled backwards), but seven years later she dumped Nuremoh and returned to Tracy, for whom she turned into "a fiery blond goddess" (Roberts 63–64). Their wedding on Christmas Eve, 1949, culminated Tess' attempts to get Tracy through a marriage ceremony uninterrupted by 2-way wrist radio calls of duty. She and Tracy shared the joys of parenting Bonnie Braids, born in 1950, and Joseph Flintheart Tracy, born in 1979. Two decades later, Tess, sick and tired of her lonely life as a police "widow," filed for divorce in a Kilian-Locher sequence beginning February 7, 1994, while Tracy was attending the FBI Academy in Washington, a reflection of the high stress-related divorce rate among real-life police officers.

Dick Tracy's Associates

Besides Tess Trueheart, Dick Tracy's "family" included "Junior" Tracy, Chief Brandon, and Pat Patton. Possibly patterned after Charles Dickens's poverty-stricken orphans like Oliver Twist, nine-year-old then-nameless "Junior" first appeared in 1932, stealing a pocket watch from Pat Patton. In a popular "rags to riches" subplot, Dick Tracy cleaned him up, gave him a home and unfailing faith, and Junior became "what many children would liked to have been—a child protégé of the most likable detective ever . . . making it big as a law-abiding citizen" (Roberts 66). Junior, whose appeal snared the strip's youngest readers, had a poignant relationship with Miss Model Jones in the 1950s before marrying Moon Maid in the 1960s.

Dick Tracy's first authority figure, Chief Brandon, encouraged Tracy in the early and mid-1930s, but his role diminished as Tracy's independence grew. Through most of the 1940s Brandon remained in the background until retiring in 1948 due to his guilt over a mistake that cost Diet Smith's young protégé inventor Brilliant his life. "The episode essentially closing this subplot was ample proof of Gould's ability to provide complexity and continuity to his storylines"; he eventually brought Brandon back as the operator of a greenhouse named "Lawn Order" (Roberts 62). Pat Patton, a little overweight, hot-tempered, and perpetuating "the stereotype of the Irish [beat] cop," was a suitable counterpart to Tracy as his sidekick, friend, and comic relief. Patton's "human frailty and humorous character" lightened the series, toning down the violence and realism of the police procedure (Roberts 62). Patton, not Tracy, succeeded Brandon as Chief of Police because Tracy, an action character, had to remain a street cop, not a desk-bound pencil pusher. Patton and Sam Catchem, who joined the series on December 24, 1948, play a dual Watson to Tracy's Holmes. One other lawman shared their crime fighting; G-man Jim Trailer, as the FBI agent counterpart to the policeman Tracy, was probably responsible for J. Edgar Hoover's personal fondness for the *Dick Tracy* strip.

Dick Tracy's current cartoonists are keeping up this tradition: Dick Tracy appeared as a guest at Dagwood and Blondie's 75th anniversary party in the comic strip *Blondie,* and Brenda Starr met Dick Tracy in a special comic strip published in the July 31, 2004, issue of *The Sunday Chicago Tribune Magazine.*

DICK TRACY'S IMITATORS

Until *Dick Tracy* appeared in 1931, comic strips had concentrated on either exotic adventures or domestic intrigues. *Dick Tracy* "brought the excitement of adventure to its readers' front doors when Gould's cop began fighting contemporary crime in everyone's home town . . . the beginning of raw violence on the comics page" (Harvey 107). In the 1930s, Tracy's main competitors were the pulps' "masked avengers" (Phelps 9), but within two years, six *Dick Tracy*–inspired strips were on the market, and others soon followed, including Norman Marsh's *Dan Dunn* (1933); *Secret Agent X-9* (1934), written by Dashiell Hammett and drawn by Alex Raymond, who later drew *Flash Gordon;* and Alfred Andriola's *Charlie Chan* (1938). Al Capp even created *Fearless Fosdick* as a comic within his popular *L'il Abner* strip, delighting Gould, who claimed he was pleased to be the world's only cartoonist "who had a great comic strip artist for a press agent—absolutely free" (Sheridan 122).

MEDIA ADAPTATIONS

Dick Tracy almost immediately inspired radio programs, film serials, and early feature films. Starting on NBC's New England stations in 1934, 15-minute *Dick Tracy* radio episodes aired for CBS from February 4, 1935, to July 11, 1935, and then went to Mutual from September 30, 1935, to March 28, 1937. NBC brought 30-minute episodes of *Dick Tracy* sponsored by Quaker Oats to prime time from April 29, 1939, to September 30, 1939, and ABC Blue Network aired 15-minute episodes sponsored by Tootsie Rolls from March 15, 1943, to July 16, 1948; *Dick Tracy* then moved to 30-minute Saturday episodes on ABC from October 6, 1945, to June 1, 1946. "The sound effects of squealing tires, explosions, and gunfire added great excitement to the already thrilling stories," and Quaker Oats box-top premiums like codebooks and badges were "pretty exciting stuff before television" (O'Connell 113).

The first live action Dick Tracy Republic Studios movie serial starred Ralph Byrd in *Dick Tracy* (1937), followed by *Dick Tracy Returns* (1938), *Dick Tracy's G-Men* (1939), and *Dick Tracy vs. Crime* (1941). In the serials, only Tracy, portrayed as a California FBI agent (G-Man), and Junior appear from Gould's original comic strip cast, although characters analogous to Pat Patton, Tess Trueheart, and others were created. Because of a contract interpretation, Gould received payment for only the first of these serials. RKO then produced four *noir*-ish Dick Tracy Grade B feature films: *Dick Tracy, Detective* (1945) and *Dick Tracy vs. Cueball* (1946), both starring Morgan Conway, and *Dick Tracy's Dilemma* (1947) and, the most famous, *Dick Tracy Meets Gruesome* (1948), both starring Ralph Byrd and Boris Karloff, forever famous from the horror film *Frankenstein*, as "Gruesome."

Played by Ralph Byrd on television, Gould's hero preserved law and order on a short-lived live action ABC *Dick Tracy* series (1950 to 1951) that was much criticized for its violence. It featured some of Gould's familiar villains like Flattop, Shaky, and Breathless Mahoney as well as "good guys" Sam Catchem, Tess Trueheart Tracy, Junior, and Pat Patton. Only a few episodes were filmed in 1952, due to Byrd's unexpected death.

Two television cartoon series featured Dick Tracy. UPA produced 130 five-minute cartoons from 1960 to 1961 with Tracy voiced by Everett Sloane and Mel Blanc, famous for Bugs Bunny, voicing many of the other characters, like "Hemlock Holmes," a Cockney police bulldog with a voice resembling Cary Grant's. The Keystone Kop-like "Retouchables," a police squad parodying J. Edgar Hoover's famous "Untouchables," backed up Hemlock. This series inspired Mattel Toys' various Dick Tracy toy weapons for budding "Crime Stoppers" as well as toy Dick Tracy Wrist Radios. In the mid-1970s, the series was pulled from syndication because of ethnic stereotypes but it returned to television in 1990 and in 2006 appeared on DVD and pay-per-view digital cable channels. A pilot by 1966 *Batman* series producer William Dozier for a live action Dick Tracy television series starring Ray MacDonnell never made it to the small screen, because *Batman*'s ratings were sinking and neither ABC nor NBC wanted to risk a *Dick Tracy* fiasco. A 1971 Dick Tracy Filmation cartoon series was featured in *Archie's TV Funnies*. In 2003, Film Roman and Classic Media proposed a new *Dick Tracy* television series, but it has not yet materialized.

In 1980, producers Art Linson and Floyd Mutrux bought the rights to the *Dick Tracy* comic strip and work with Paramount and Universal began on screenplays for a feature film. Max Allan Collins recalled that early scripts were "terrible," "paper-thin," and "uncomfortably campy" (Hughes 51). Almost every popular 1980s leading man was considered to play Tracy, including Clint Eastwood, Harrison Ford, Richard Gere, Tom Selleck, and Mel Gibson. Warren Beatty, interested in playing Tracy since 1983, got the part, but he wanted $5 million plus 15 percent of the gross. Universal refused, and Beatty left the project. When the *Dick Tracy* rights lapsed in 1985, Beatty "swooped in to pick them up for himself," telling Barbara Walters, ". . . as a kid I had a lot of affection for the strip . . . I thought it would be fun to make a picture that . . . dealt in primary emotions and primary colours [sic]." He added to Mike Bonifer, "There's something quaint about 1939/1940 crime fighting . . . something about it moved me . . . there probably was a *naïveté* about America in that period, about good and evil, law and order. It's just before America took over. . . . Just before our loss of innocence as a country" (quoted in Hughes 52).

Beatty directed and starred in the surreal 1990 *Dick Tracy* movie for Disney, with Collins as a consultant and Dick Tracy expert. Beatty chose to shoot the film entirely in-studio, combining animation and live action in only the blazing seven comic-strip colors which carry brilliantly over into contemporary symbolism (Simon 50). He used many of Gould's most notable characters, with competent actors including Al Pacino, Charlie Korsmo, Michael J. Pollard, Dustin Hoffman, James Caan, Dick Van Dyke. Beatty's then-girlfriend Madonna, widely considered outclassed by them, played torchy nightclub singer Breathless Mahoney. All characters were swathed in "some of the most remarkable make-up ever put on film" (Hughes 53) and lavishly costumed by Oscar-winner designer Milena Canonero, Madonna in particular oozing from "the sexiest imaginable outfits" with "a come-hither look in every part of her largely visible anatomy" (Simon 49). The album *I'm Breathless: Music from and Inspired by Dick Tracy*, included Madonna's "Vogue" and "Hanky Panky," two top-ten hits both unused in the film, and Stephen Sondheim's "Sooner or Later (I Always Get My Man)," sung by Madonna in *Dick Tracy*, won the Oscar for Best Song.

Critics generally felt that Beatty's *Dick Tracy* was "a victory of style over substance" (Hughes 57), with a "clunking script," leaden dialogue, and "dismal performances" (Hughes 59). *Variety* declared, "though it looks ravishing, Warren Beatty's long-time pet project is a curiously remote, uninvolving film" (Hughes 57–59). Collins, who novelized the movie, agreed with a critic who compared it to "a lovely restored period automobile—[but] when you raise the hood, there's no engine" (Hughes 60). On the other hand, film critic Roger Ebert believed that overall, *Dick Tracy* ". . . is one of the most original and visionary fantasies I've seen on a screen" (Hughes 58). The film received four Golden Globe nominations and seven Academy Award nominations, and Disney's enormous marketing efforts, a reported $54 million, paid off with gross profits of $103 million overall. In 1994 to 1995, Disney also produced ice shows featuring Dick Tracy.

A $30 million lawsuit filed in 2005 by Warren Beatty against the Tribune Company continues over the rights to the Dick Tracy character. Beatty planned to make a second Tracy feature film, but the Tribune Company also intended to make Tracy the centerpiece of a television series. In 2010, a judge ruled that Beatty maintained rights to the character.

Since May 2005 Warren Beatty, who reportedly wants to make a sequel to his 1990 film, and the Tribune Company have been locked in a legal battle over rights to the character Dick Tracy. The film *Dick Tracy* inspired the 1990 return of UPA's cartoon series as well as a comic book miniseries, *True Hearts and Tommy Guns*, produced by Disney. Previous Dick Tracy comic books had included Sig Feuchtwanger's giveaway comic (1947) in boxes of Quaker Oats; Dell's (1948 to 1961) 145-issue comic books; and Blackthorne's 99-issue comic books began in 1986.

DICK TRACY'S ENDURING APPEAL

The didactic element of *Dick Tracy* has been discussed only by Garyn Roberts, in *Dick Tracy and American Culture: Morality and Mythology, Text and Context* (1993). Blending history, sociology, and psychology with literary analysis, Roberts contends that *Dick Tracy* is much more sophisticated than most observers think; that Gould was as skilled in his accomplishment as Arthur Conan Doyle or Agatha Christie; and that Gould intended *Dick Tracy* to present "a moral dialogue about the individual's responsibility to society" (Hoppenstand 248).

In that moral dialogue, power—its uses in the hands of the righteous crime-busting detective and its abuses by fiendish criminals—sums up Chester Gould's *Dick Tracy,* a dark mélange of

fast-action story lines that could kick the breath out of you, arrestingly stylized artwork that was both super-realistic and weirdly cartoonish, a famous rogues' gallery of villains, an unrelievedly grim Calvinist conscience that informed every move every one of its characters ever made—and always the pathological mayhem. (Jay Maeder, quoted in Walker 226)

Gould's public still finds it all irresistible, and Dick Tracy has came to share "a place in the history of detective fiction hitherto occupied in solitude by Conan Doyle's Sherlock Holmes" (Harvey 104).

Dick Tracy "proposed a *new* standard of precision . . . such as only those artists, major and minor, who are entitled to be taken with full seriousness, ever deal with . . . presenting the terms and figures of darkness in the imagery of a superhuman, murderous daylight" (Phelps 9, italics in original). In implementing this "new standard," Gould harked back to the delicious didactic horror of medieval religious mystery plays, seen especially in their Herod and Pilate masks. Gould may be seen as "a lineal heir" of Jacobean playwrights Webster and Ford, who built their terrifying dramas of unspeakable crime and implacable revenge against "pestilential atmospheres" and the sense of "stumbling through a miasma" which detective and criminals share. To make these elements even more powerful, Gould counterpointed them with humor "of the battlefield or the plague-smitten community" whose "very crudity and frankness is a relief"—especially as seen in the grungy hillbilly B.O. Plenty clan that Gould based on earthy Oklahoma pioneers he had known in his youth.

Gould disparaged his artistic ability, declaring that "Drawing has always been an uphill fight" and "I have never been a good artist" (Bainbridge 46). Current art critics disagree. Claiming that Gould's art resembles the 18th-century satirist Hogarth's in minuteness and the Spanish master Goya's in ruthless caricature, Donald Phelps feels Gould developed specific drawing techniques to illustrate the *Dick Tracy* criminal element's "violation and perversion of nature": "the rigid patterning, the tightly braced bodies; the compulsive passion of the contorted faces; the angular, spasmodic gestures" that affront nature so fiercely that nature's revenge demands "the most ferociously attenuated death sequences, the most broodingly exact depictions of decay and death agony" of any comic strip (Roberts 13–14). *New York Times* art critic John Russell has called Gould "a workman of a very high order in a craft that is much harder than it looks. . . . [His] images [are] tokens of a time when issues were clear—when law was law, order was order, and the best man won out in the end" (Russell 20.4).

In America's 1930s, bedeviled by criminals, frustrated by Prohibition, tormented by financial reverses, ordinary citizens applauded Dick Tracy's fearless, uncompromising war on crime for its "strictly retributive justice," wreaked on the ungodly in fast-paced, action-filled episodes about gangsters, ghoulishly attractive to the public who generally scorned them, though some considered them "modern day Robin Hoods in opposition to a decadent or dying socioeconomic order." Readers could vicariously participate in *Dick Tracy*'s criminal-driven violence, "safe in the realization that it was that of a comic strip world which in no way could impinge on their own lives" (Broes 117). Then, *Dick Tracy* was "a popular culture sensation during an era when Americans needed a square jaw and broad shoulders to lift itself out of dark and dangerous times . . . reflecting and affecting the way Americans thought and behaved" (Hoppenstand 914). Robert Storr, Dean of Yale University's School of Art, concurs: "The original Dick Tracy was an earnest caricature of American manhood facing hard times and legions of bad guys," and adds: "For some, he still is" (*CA Online*). Roberts lists elements of *Dick Tracy*'s appeal still attractive today: crime detection, idealized father-like hero, a child protégé, romance between hero and lady, unique criminals, villain-created dangers and situations, authentic urban settings, idealized family atmosphere, appropriate humor, accurate police procedure, reflections of actual events, ingenious death traps, sensational violence, and legitimate scapegoats (Roberts 11).

In the decades since *Dick Tracy* first appeared, the United States has been bedeviled by World War II; the Korean War; the Cold War; the social, racial, and gender upheavals of the 1960s; the Vietnam War; the AIDS epidemic; the computer revolution; the Gulf Wars; and international terrorism—all threatening societal shifts that lead readers to seek reassurance that "Crime Does Not Pay." Today, readers still take comfort that Dick Tracy will persevere and succeed, "a ritual that enacts the myth" of Good tri-

The world's largest Dick Tracy mural is at 503 Harrison Street, Pawnee, Oklahoma, painted in 1990 by Tulsa artist Ed Melberg, and "Dick Tracy Days" took place in 1994 in Woodstock, IL, Chester Gould's home.

umphing over Evil" (Roberts 11). Commenting on Beatty's 1990 *Dick Tracy* film, James Bowman observes that "this film shows how even Hollywood's political exoticism yields to nostalgia for that better world . . . in which villains recognizable by their ugliness are invariably destroyed by the guardians of decency" (Bowman 31). *Dick Tracy* in its various transformations and adaptations is still confirming that "Crime Does Not Pay," providing "excitement and continuity and a weird coherence" to hundreds of thousands of people (Russell 20.4).

PARALLEL CHRONOLOGY

Major Events Related to Dick Tracy	World Events
	1841 First fictional private detective, Poe's M. Auguste Dupin
	1887–1927 Sherlock Holmes stories published by Conan Doyle

Major Events Related to Dick Tracy	World Events
Nov. 20, 1900 Chester Gould born	1906 *Hairbreadth Harry* appears
	1910 *Sherlocke the Monk* appears
	1913 *Hawkshaw the Detective* appears
	1914–1918 World War I
1917 First narrative comic strip, *The Gumps*	
	Dec. 1917 Congress passes 18th Amendment (Prohibition)
	Jan. 1919 18th Amendment ratified
	Jan. 1920 Prohibition begins; organized crime revives; Chicago becomes crime capital; *Black Mask* magazine begins, popularizing crime fiction
1921 Gould arrives in Chicago	
1923 Gould graduates from Northwestern University	
1924 Gould's *Fillum Fables* appears	
	1924 *Little Orphan Annie* appears; J. Edgar Hoover becomes FBI Director
	1925 Al Capone takes over as Chicago crime boss
	1927 First public television demonstration; first "talkie," *The Jazz Singer*
	1928 Democrat Al Smith opposes Prohibition; Walt Disney introduces Mickey Mouse
	Feb. 14, 1929 St. Valentine's Day Massacre; Capone retires to Florida
	1929 Pres. Hoover creates Wickersham Commission to investigate connection between Prohibition and crime
	Oct. 29, 1929 U.S. stock market crash
1930s Gould uses racial stereotypes for humor in *Dick Tracy;* introduces bullet-proof vest and lie detector	1930s Over 200 gangster films made in U.S. alone
Oct. 4, 1931 *Dick Tracy* debuts in *Detroit Mirror;* Tracy saves and courts Tess Trueheart	1931 Capone jailed for income tax evasion; Empire State Building dedicated
1932 Gould uses a child abduction episode; introduces Dick Tracy, Jr.	1932 Lindbergh's infant son kidnapped; Bonus March suppressed; New Deal announced
	1933 Prohibition repealed; Hitler becomes Chancellor of Germany;

(Continued)

Major Events Related to Dick Tracy	World Events
	drought turns Great Plains into Dust Bowl
1934 Tracy slays first villain, Spaldoni	**July 22, 1934** FBI agents shoot John Dillinger in Chicago; "Pretty Boy" Floyd and "Baby Face" Nelson also killed and G-men become national heroes; U.S. Hays Office prohibits movies from depicting films on Dillinger's life
1935 *Dick Tracy* appears on front page of *New York Sunday News;* Gould uses character "Cut Famon" resembling Capone	**1935** Social Security Act goes into effect; "Ma" Barker killed in Florida shootout
1935–1937 Mutual Broadcasting *Dick Tracy* radio series	
1936–1937 Gould uses story of Purple Cross Gang in longest comic episode of the 1930s	
1936–1941 Four multi-part *Dick Tracy* movie serials by Republic	
1937–1939 NBC *Dick Tracy* radio series	
1938 *Dick Tracy* takes on European flavor, using poison gas and concentration camp motifs	**1938** Hitler and Chamberlain sign Munich Pact ("Peace in Our Time")
	1939 World War II begins
1940s Gould begins to use grotesque villains	**1940s** Colorful gangsters are disappearing
1943 Gould creates most popular villain, Flattop Jones	**Dec. 7, 1941** Japanese attack Pearl Harbor; U.S. enters war
1943–1944 ABC Blue Radio *Dick Tracy* series	**1944** D-Day invasion of Europe
Mid-1940s *Dick Tracy* has established readership of 27,000,000; Tracy fights homegrown criminals like rustics Gravel Gertie and B.O. Plenty; violence in the strip becomes more sadistic	
1944–1948 ABC radio *Dick Tracy* series	
1945–1947 Four RKO *Dick Tracy* movies	**1945** Atomic bombs dropped on Japan; end of World War II
1946 Gould introduces 2-Way Wrist Radio	

Major Events Related to Dick Tracy	World Events
	1946 Churchill's "Iron Curtain" speech; first United Nations General Assembly convenes
1947 First *Dick Tracy* comic book; Gould introduces Sparkle Plenty	**1947** U.S. announces Marshall Plan
1948–1961 *Dick Tracy* comic book series	
Dec. 24, 1949 Dick Tracy marries Tess Trueheart	
1950–1951 ABC-TV's *Dick Tracy* television series	**1950** Korean War begins; anti-Communist fervor rises, fueled by Sen. McCarthy
1951 Daughter Bonnie Braids born to Dick and Tess	**1951** Senate Kefauver Hearings reveal organized crime activities
1953 Gould introduces TV police lineup	**1953** USSR leader Stalin dies
Mid-1950s Tracy's policewoman Lizz paves way for women detectives in fiction and film	**1955** Disneyland opens; U.S. sends military "advisers" to Vietnam
	1956 USSR launches *Sputnik,* first earth satellite, triggering Space Race
	1957 Creation of NASA
1960s *Dick Tracy* ventures into science fiction; advent of the Space Coupe	**1960** John F. Kennedy elected President
1961 *Dick Tracy* animated cartoon series by United Productions of America	**1961** First USSR and then first U.S. astronaut enter space
	1962 Cuban Missile Crisis; U.S. aircraft spray Agent Orange in Vietnam
	1963 Assassination of Pres. John F. Kennedy; Betty Friedan's *The Feminine Mystique*
1964 Tracy Jr. meets and marries Moon Maid; 2-Way Wrist TV introduced	
1965 HoneyMoon—"first child born in outer space"	**1965** U.S. begins bombing of North Vietnam; first U.S. combat troops arrive there; Watts riots
	1967 Race riots and antiwar marches in U.S.
	1967 Tet offensive in Vietnam; assassinations of Robert Kennedy and Martin Luther King

(Continued)

Major Events Related to Dick Tracy	World Events
	1968 "Pentagon Papers" leaked to press
	1969 Neil Armstrong walks on the Moon
	1972 Watergate saga begins
	1973 U.S. involvement in Vietnam ends
1977 Gould ceases drawing *Dick Tracy* and retires	
1977–1983 Richard Fletcher and Max Collins continue the *Dick Tracy* comic strip	
1983–1992 Dick Locher and Max Collins continue the *Dick Tracy* comic strip	
May 11, 1985 Chester Gould dies	
1986–1999 Blackthorn Pub. Comic book series begins	
1990 *True Hearts and Tommy Guns,* Disney comic book series	
1990 Warren Beatty directs and stars in *Dick Tracy* (feature film)	
1992–2005 Collins fired from strip and Mike Kilian joins Dick Locher	
May 2005 Warren Beatty-Tribune Company lawsuit over rights to character "Dick Tracy" begins	
Jan. 9, 2006–Present Dick Locher both develops story line and draws the *Dick Tracy* comic strip	

DICK TRACY COMIC STRIP COLLECTIONS

Max Collins. *Dick Tracy Meets Angeltop.* New York: Ace, 1980.

———. *Dick Tracy Meets the Punks.* New York: Ace, 1980.

———, ed., with Dick Locher. *Dick Tracy's Wartime Memories.* Park Forest, IL: Ken Pierce, 1986.

———. *The Dick Tracy Casebook: Favorite Adventures, 1931–1990.* New York: St. Martin's Press, 1990.

———. *Dick Tracy: The Secret Files.* New York: St. Martin's Press, 1990.

————. *Dick Tracy's Fiendish Foes: A 60th Anniversary Celebration.* New York: St. Martin's Press, 1991.

MEDIA ADAPTATIONS

Radio

Actors: Bob Burlen was Dick Tracy's first radio voice, in 1934; Barry Thompson, Ned Wever, and Matt Crowley later played Tracy on the radio.

1934: NBC's New England stations; 15-minute weekday episodes

Feb. 4, 1935–July 11, 1935: CBS; 15-minute afternoon episodes, four times weekly

Sept. 30, 1935–Mar. 24, 1937: Mutual Broadcasting Company; 15-minute afternoon episodes

Jan. 3, 1938–Apr. 28, 1939: NBC; 15-minute afternoon episodes

Apr. 29, 1939–Sept. 20, 1939: NBC; 30-minute evening episodes

Mar. 15, 1943–July 16, 1948: ABC Blue Network; 15-minute episodes

Oct. 6, 1945–June 1, 1946: ABC Blue Network; 30-minute Saturday episodes

Film Serials

Dick Tracy (1937), 15 episodes: Dick Tracy's live action debut, starring Ralph Byrd as Tracy. Aside from Tracy and Tracy Jr. no other characters from the strip appear in this serial or its sequels, all produced by Republic

Dick Tracy Returns (1938), 15 episodes

Dick Tracy's G-Men (1939), 15 episodes

Dick Tracy vs. Crime Inc. (1941), 15 episodes

Feature Films

Dick Tracy (1937), feature version of serial, starring Ralph Byrd

Dick Tracy, Detective (1945), RKO, starring Morgan Conway

Dick Tracy vs. Cueball (1946), RKO, starring Morgan Conway

Dick Tracy's Dilemma (1947), RKO, starring Ralph Byrd

Dick Tracy Meets Gruesome (1947), RKO, starring Ralph Byrd, with Boris Karloff as the villain

Television Live Action Series

Dick Tracy (1950–1951), ABC, starring Ralph Byrd

Cartoons

The Dick Tracy Show (1960–1961), UPA, 130 5-minute cartoons, as a juvenile version of *The Untouchables;* with Tracy voiced by Everett Sloane and Mel Blanc voicing many other characters; withdrawn from syndication in mid-1970s but brought back in 1990 to coincide with release of feature film; in 2006 appeared on pay-per-view digital cable channels and DVD.

Dick Tracy segments featured in Filmation's *Archie's TV Funnies* (1971).

Classic Media and Film Roman produced an animated Dick Tracy cartoon series in 2006.

Television Live Action Pilot

Dick Tracy (1967), pilot for a live-action Dick Tracy series, starring Ray MacDonnell, but not purchased by ABC or NBC

Feature Film

Dick Tracy (1990), starring Warren Beatty, who also directed the movie, budgeted at $47 million. Stephen Sondheim's song "Sooner or Later (I Always Get My Man)" sung by Madonna won an Oscar for Best Song; the film grossed $104 million in the U.S. and $55 million abroad.

Comic Books

Dick Tracy (1947), giveaway in boxes of Popped Wheat cereal.

Dick Tracy (1948–1961), 145-issue comic book series, begun by Dell but published by Harvey Comics after issue number 25.

Dick Tracy (1986), 99-issue series by Blackthorne Publishing.

True Hearts and Tommy Guns (1990), 3-issue miniseries by Disney as film tie-in.

Graphic Novels

Collins, Max Allan, and Rick Fletcher. *Dick Tracy: The Collins Casefiles,* vols. 1 and 2. New York: Checker, 2003 and 2004.

Spinoffs

Role-Playing Game

Dick Tracy: The Roleplaying Game, by Cynthia Miller and Sabrina Belle; uses pen and paper and cannot be played by computer or e-mail.

Cell Phone Watch

An M 300 GSM Cell Phone Watch with a one-inch OLED screen has batteries that last 80 minutes, 99 speed-dials, and Bluetooth for a headset.

Dick Tracy Dolls

From the late 1940s through the 1960s, the Ideal Toy Company produced "Sparkle Plenty," "Bonny Braids," and "Little Honey Moon," dolls based on the *Dick Tracy* comic strips.

WORKS CITED

Bainbridge, John. "Chester Gould." *Life* (August 14, 1944): 43–46.

Berger, A.A. *The Comic Stripped American.* New York: Walker, 1973.

Bowman, James. "Tricky Dick." *The American Spectator* 23 (September 1990): 30–35.

Broes, Arthur T. "*Dick Tracy:* The Early Years." *Journal of Popular Culture* 25 (Spring 1992): 97–122.

Cawelti, John. *Adventure, Mystery, and Romance: Formula Stories as Art and Popular Culture.* Chicago: University of Chicago Press, 1976.

"Chester Gould." "Contemporary Authors Online." http://web2.infotrac.galegroup.com.

Flagg, Gordon. Review of *Dick Tracy: The Collins Casefiles,* vol. 2, ed. Max Allan Collins and Rick Fletcher. New York: Checker, 2004.

Galewitz, Herb, ed. *The Celebrated Cases of Dick Tracy, 1931–1951.* New York: Bonanza Books, 1970.

Goulart, Ron. *The Adventurous Decade.* New Rochelle, NY: Arlington House, 1975.

Gould, Chester. *Dick Tracy: The Thirties: Tommy Guns and Hard Times.* Edited by Herb Galewitz. Secaucus, NJ: Wellfleet, 1990.

Harvey, Robert C. *The Art of the Funnies.* Jackson, MS: University Press of Mississippi, 1994.

Hoppenstand, Gary. Review of *Dick Tracy and American Culture: Morality and Mythology, Text and Context. Journal of Popular Culture* (Spring 1996): 248.

Hughes, David. *Comic Book Movies.* London: Virgin Books, 2003.

Johnson, Paul. *Modern Times,* rev. ed. New York: HarperCollins, 1991.

Mooney, Linda A., and Carlo-Marie Fewell. "Crime in One Long-Lived Comic Strip." *American Journal of Economics and Sociology* 48 (January 1989): 89–101.

O'Connell, Jean Gould. *Chester Gould: A Daughter's Biography of the Creator of Dick Tracy.* Jefferson, NC: McFarland, 2007.

Phelps, Donald. *Reading the Funnies.* Seattle, WA: Fantographic Books, 2001.

Roberts, Garyn G. *Dick Tracy and American Culture: Morality and Mythology.* Jefferson, NC: McFarland, 1993.

Russell, John. "Gallery Season Opens in All Its Variety, Opens Uptown and Down." *New York Times,* October 1, 1982: Section C, 20.4.

Sheridan, Martin. *Comics and Their Creators: Life Stories of American Cartoonists.* Rev. ed. Westport, CT: Hyperion Press, 1977.

Simon, John. "Cartoon Before the Horselaugh." *National Review* 42 (23 July 1990): 48—50.

Walker, Brian. *Comics before 1945.* New York: Harry A. Abrams Inc., 2004.

Ward, Greg. *The Timeline History of the USA.* New York: Barnes & Noble, 2005.

Wolfe, Thomas. *You Can't Go Home Again.* 1934; rpt. New York: HarperCollins, 1998.

FURTHER READING

Bonifer, Mike. *Dick Tracy: The Making of the Movie.* New York: Bantam, 1990.

Brennan, Steve. *Hollywood Reporter,* international ed., 377 (February 18, 2003): 89.

Collins, Max Allan, and Dick Locher, eds. *The Dick Tracy Casebook: Favorite Adventures.* New York: St. Martin's Press, 1990.

Copeland Vargo, Beth. "Dick Tracy's Dolls." *Doll Reader* 29 (October 2001): 74.

Gould, Chester. *Dick Tracy's Secret Detective Methods and Magic Tricks.* Whitefish, MT: Kessinger, 2007.

Herbert, Rosemary. *Whodunit? A Who's Who in Crime and Mystery Writing.* New York: Oxford University Press, 2003.

Keel, Beverly. "Happy Birthday, Dick Tracy." http://americanprofile.com, accessed 11/1/2007.

"75 Years of Continuous Crime-Stopping." http://mystericale.com/index, accessed 11/1/2007.

Murphy, Bruce. *The Encyclopedia of Murder and Mystery.* New York: St. Martin's Press, 1999.

Shprintz, Janet. "Beatty Battles Tribune over Tracy Pic Rights." *Daily Variety Gotham,* May 16, 2005, http://www.variety.com, accessed 11/1/2007.

Spurgeon, Tom. "Dick Tracy and the Attached Sub-Rider." http://www.comicsreporter.com/index, accessed 11/1/2007.

Swirski, Peter. "Bulworth and the New American Left." *Journal of American Culture* 28 (September 2005): 293–301.

"Wife of Dick Tracy Is Filing for Divorce." *Editor and Publisher* 127 (February 5, 1994): 32.

WEB SITES

http://www.chestergould.org/ (The Chester Gould Dick Tracy Museum)

http://www.comicspafe.com/dicktracy (The Dick Tracy comic strip)

http://www.toonopedia.com/tracy.htm (Don Markstein's Toonopedia: *Dick Tracy*)

http://www.checkerbpg.com/docs/dtl_gn.html (*Dick Tracy* graphic novels)

http://www.comics.org (Grand Comics database)

Photograph from "The Golden Spiders: A Nero Wolfe Mystery," (A&E) TV Movie, March 5, 2000. Directed by Bill Duke. Shown from left: Maury Chaykin (as Nero Wolfe) and Timothy Hutton (as Archie Goodwin). Courtesy A&E Television Networks/Photofest.

Nero Wolfe:
The Armchair Sleuth

Compose yourself, Archie. Why taunt me? Why upbraid me? I am merely a
genius, not a god.

—Nero Wolfe, *Fer-De-Lance*, 1934

The rotund and reclusive curmudgeon Nero Wolfe and his investigator/
bodyguard/secretary Archie Goodwin are second only to Holmes and Watson as a great detective double-act. Wolfe and Goodwin appear in about
80 novels, novellas, and short stories, "the most outstanding achievement
in the mystery field in the post-Holmes era" (*CA Online*). Nero Wolfe's
40-year career, "one of the longest and most successful of any series detective" (Murphy 532) has sold over 100 million books and continues in audio
versions, a recent television series, and a Wolfe Pack of enthusiasts "prepar-
ing, ingesting and washing down food" (Winn 246) and roaming the Internet. The 2000 Bouchercon, the world's largest mystery convention,
nominated the Nero Wolfe stories as Best Mystery Series of the Century and
Rex Stout as the century's Best Mystery Writer, and many commentators
believe Nero Wolfe "remains unchallenged in the field of American deductive investigators" (Landon Burns, in Herbert 211).

HISTORICAL/CULTURAL CONTEXT

Most of Nero Wolfe's cases are set in New York City, and all of them occur
within or close to the time Rex Stout was writing them, from 1933 to 1974,
four decades of substantial turmoil in the United States. Stout felt both
America and the detective genre were facing nothing less than the possibility
of extinction, and "As he worked to save the genre, he was engaged in the
larger labor of saving the existing social order which that genre shadowed
forth, by urging on it, even as he upheld it, those reforms it had to under-
take if it was to be healed of corruption and made fit for salvation"
(McAleer xxvii).

When Stout began to write about Nero Wolfe and Archie Goodwin in the
early 1930s, one of the gravest threats the United States faced was its apparent inability to resolve its critical social ambivalence. On the one hand,
Jeffersonian democracy fostered the "melting pot" racial fusion theory welcoming all "huddled masses yearning to breathe free," but on the other,
fears of "degeneration" of the Anglo-Saxon, German, Scotch-Irish, and
Dutch stock that had founded the United States had encouraged xenophobic
organizations like the Ku Klux Klan and by 1914 had virtually halted
unlimited immigration. A gulf also seemed to be widening between East
Coast "highbrows" whose WASPish values had dominated American intel-
lectualism and "middle America," the "silent majority" (Johnson 207–208).
Early 20th-century arts reflect the tensions caused by these core societal
issues, but eventually new trends in music, painting, and literature emerged
and changed American popular culture forever.

The nation's "vast debate . . . about the nature and purpose of American society" ("Who was an American? What was America for?") (Johnson 203) paralleled an alarming increase in corruption and crime. World War I's patriotic xenophobia resulted in the 1921 Quota Law

Where's the beer?
—Nero Wolfe's first words in
Fer-de-Lance

that barred Japanese completely, favored northern and western Europe over eastern and southern Europe, and ended mass immigration to America. To no avail, H.L. Mencken, then one of America's most powerful journalists, denounced the policy's author, Attorney General Mitchell Palmer, as "the most eminent living exponent of cruelty, dishonesty, and injustice" and accused the State Department of becoming an unprecedented "system of espionage" that cynically violated human rights, "filled the public press with inflammatory lies and fostered the worst poltrooneries of sneaking and malicious wretches" (Mencken in *Baltimore Evening Sun,* 27 September 1920, quoted in Johnson, 206).

Prohibition, that misguided American attempt to legislate public morality under the Volstead Act of 1920, also encouraged racial minorities—mostly Jews, Irish, and Italians—to consolidate themselves into wide-ranging crime organizations. Enforcement of Prohibition proved impossible and public morality abruptly and dramatically declined. As one example of nationwide hypocrisy around 1930, Detroit alone held over 20,000 speakeasies, and in one bacchanalian entertainment testified to by journalist Walter Ligger before the U.S. House Judiciary Committee in February 1930, "The governor of Michigan, the chief of police of Detroit, the chief of the State Police, politicians, club men, gamblers, criminals, bootleggers . . . and four judges of the circuit of Michigan" enjoyed one "drunken revel, at which naked hoochy-koochy dancers appeared" (quoted in Johnson 211). Even after Congress repealed the Volstead Act in 1933, minority-dominated crime families flourished through the 1930s, "damaging social morals and the civilized cohesion of the community" (Johnson 212).

Joyce's *Ulysses* appeared in 1922, *le jazz hot* and banana-skirted Josephine Baker wowed Paris audiences, and disturbing post-Picasso "isms" exploded in chic art galleries.

During the "Roaring Twenties" well-heeled Americans had reveled in spectacular economic affluence and exciting, even shocking, new literature, art, music, and theatre, but in late October 1929, reality set in. The Stock Market Crash initially wiped out $32 billion in the United States alone, and by 1932 specific stocks like General Motors and U.S. Steel stood at a tenth of their 1929 high. U.S. industrial production and personal income plummeted by half in four years, and unemployment jumped from 3 million to 15 million. In the depth of the Great Depression, 1930 to 1933, farmers could not sell crops, factories and industries closed, and retail stores went bankrupt; by 1932 nearly every U.S. bank had closed, and the following year saw 1,500 U.S. colleges bankrupt or closed. U.S. book sales fell by 50 percent in 1932, because as author John Steinbeck complained, "When people are broke, the first things they give up are books" (quoted in Johnson 246).

"Serious" literature still existed, however. Critic Edmund Wilson observed that even during the Depression, "One couldn't help being exhilarated at this sudden unexpected collapse of the stupid gigantic fraud. It gave us a new sense of freedom . . . a new sense of power" (Wilson 498). Writers, who often support public planning efforts, began to clamor for governmental changes to bring America out of its misery. Rex Stout joined and eventually led their professional organizations, playing an active part in mid-20th-century political activity.

John Dewey in 1922 warned Eastern highbrows that the American Middle West, "the prairie country, has been the centre of active social philanthropy and political progressivism . . . the element responsive to appeals for . . . more nearly equal opportunities for all." Later, Midwestern popular culture helped America crawl back slowly from the Depression. Movies offered temporary escape from the grim here and now, and popular literature, especially the inexpensive "pulp" magazines on poor quality paper and cheap ink thrived. As Dewey also commented in 1922, "democracy by nature puts a premium on mediocrity" (quoted in Johnson 208).

Democracy allowed some American radicalism, too. America, the strongest and most inventive of the capitalist economies, refused to produce the proletarian revolution Karl Marx thought was the inevitable result of capitalism, but during the Great Depression, many American intellectuals began to repudiate "the virtues of capitalist enterprise and embraced those of collectivism." Having lost faith in U.S. business leaders, some American intellectuals suddenly discovered the Soviet Union (USSR) and extolled the USSR's five-year plans. Even the quintessentially American comedian Will Rogers remarked, "Those rascals in Russia, along with their cuckoo stuff have got some mighty good ideas. . . . Just think of everybody in a country going to work" (Johnson 259–260).

The U.S. Communist Party "failed to become a new expression of American radicalism and became a mere U.S. appendage of Soviet policy" (Theodore Draper, quoted in Johnson 213), but occupied first with the 1930s economic woes and then World War II, many Americans failed to realize that "the devils had taken over" in the Soviet Union (Johnson 261). Dominating a totalitarian regime that cannibalized its own people, Soviet leader Josef Stalin sacrificed 5 million peasants to forced collectivization. According to the KGB's own records and chronicled in Aleksandr Solzhenitsyn's magisterial *The Gulag Archipelago* (1974–1976),

> *Nothing is more admirable than the fortitude with which millionaires tolerate the disadvantages of their wealth.*
>
> —Nero Wolfe

they were only a small part of the 100 million Soviet citizens annihilated by Communist totalitarianism between 1930 and 1945.

Subtlety chases the obvious in a never-ending spiral and never quite catches it.
—Nero Wolfe

After the uneasy wartime alliance between the Western Allies and Stalin's Soviet Union had dissolved, the Iron Curtain dropped over Eastern Europe and the Cold War set in, and between 1950 and 1954, Wisconsin Senator Joseph McCarthy led a nationwide witch hunt directed at U.S. Communists and Communist sympathizers. McCarthy's attempted smears against the Truman administration contributed to electing popular General Dwight Eisenhower to the presidency in 1950, and in 1953 as Chairman of the Senate Subcommittee on Investigations, McCarthy did incite national panic about "Communist subversion." However, the following year, McCarthy's own staff accused him of allowing some of its members to blackmail the U.S. Army. In December 1954, the Senate censured McCarthy, who died in disgrace three years later at age 48.

Enormous changes were jolting American society. Women and ethnic minorities working in wartime factories had become accustomed to a freer and more affluent lifestyle; the new Interstate Highway System increased mobility to pursue the American Dream; the Supreme Court declared racial segregation illegal in 1954; and television—spiced with the gyrating Beatles and hip-swivelling Elvis Presley—was invading nearly every house in the country. By 1968 these dramatic transformations had pushed the country's traditional social fabric to the brink of collapse. Widespread racial riots and violent protests against the Viet nam War, the orgiastic "Summer of Love," the national energy crisis, the Kennedy and King assassinations, the women's movement, and the Watergate scandal, together crescendoed into unprecedented national malaise by 1975. Rex Stout died that year; but his detective fiction still deplores corruption and social injustice and urges reform to preserve his vision of what America's social order ought to be.

AUTHORSHIP

Rex Todhunter Stout was a child of the American Midwest, born to fifth-generation Quaker parents in Noblesville, Indiana, on December 1, 1886. His maternal grandmother Emily McNeal Todhunter adjudicated all family problems, a plump, physically indolent omnivorous reader who cherished atlases, dictionaries, flowers, and her own special chair. Stout once said he left Indiana at age one because he was already "fed up with Indiana politics" (quoted in *CA Online*). He grew up in Kansas, proudly exhibited by his parents as a child mathematical genius; he became state spelling champion at 13 and later dropped out of the University of Kansas after two weeks. He joined the U.S. Navy in 1905, serving for two years on Teddy Roosevelt's presidential yacht *Mayflower* as a pay yeoman and making about $400 a month playing whist, enough to tour the United States after discharge. He settled in New York City in 1912 and wrote 32 pulp stories and four novels in the next four years, and regularly "spen[t] himself penniless," he told *Contemporary Authors*.

In 1916, Rex Stout married Fay Kennedy and he and his brother John Robert Stout founded the Educational Thrift Service, a savings plan eventually enrolling over 2 million school children. It made Stout about $400,000, and now financially secure, he left the firm in 1927 to devote himself to writing. In 1929 he began building his home, "High Meadow," near the New York-Connecticut border; he and Fay divorced in 1931, and the following year he married fabric designer Pola Hoffman, with whom he had two daughters. Stout enjoyed agricultural experiments; at one time he tended over 300 houseplants and grew gigantic vegetables, like a 210-pound pumpkin he force-fed on evaporated milk. He once trained a jumping pig, and he even attempted to replicate the taste of wild grouse by raising chickens on nothing but blueberries.

Between 1929 and 1933 Stout also tried out the life of an expatriate American writer in Paris, where he produced four serious psychological suspense novels. Realizing that he was "a good storyteller but would never make a great novelist," he then turned to detective fiction, thinking, "You just tell stories and you don't have to worry about making new comments on life and human beings. That's when I started Nero Wolfe for *American Magazine*" (quoted in *CA Online*). For his first Wolfe novel, *Fer-de-Lance* (1933), though, Stout developed a significant psychological approach to the detective novel, using a self-punishment formula that satisfied his audience's desire to make the criminal inflict his own punishment, compressing "judgment and punishment into one decisive moment" in a projection "of common ideals of justice, power, and responsibility" (Beiderwell 21). After *Fer-de-Lance,* Stout never looked back. He created other fictional sleuths, notably Tecumseh Fox and Alphabet Hicks, but after 1941, he concentrated on Nero Wolfe and Archie Goodwin fiction.

Stout's heavy writing schedule made him "a wonder of the publishing world" (McAleer 266). He wrote quickly, usually starting with "a slip of paper with the names of the people, their ages and what they do, and that's all the outline I have." About 40 days later he had his story done. He never revised, rewrote, or reread any of his books, since he felt "writing is a sort of explosion . . . [so] there is no use going around looking at the debris" (quoted in *CA Online*). Few initially realized that Stout's political activities helped shape his fiction, but soon those activities propelled him into controversy. Stout's hope for worldwide peace caused him to denounce Hitler's *Mein Kampf* as "the most immoral book ever written," and since he felt it would be immoral to do nothing to combat Nazism, he "stepped out from behind his fictional characters to become a defender of the social order he believed in, and the nemesis of those agencies that menaced it" (McAleer 265).

In 1940, Stout worked with the Friends of Democracy, an organization founded three years earlier to battle extremism of both the right and the left, and that April, with the Nazis sweeping through Europe, Stout became a charter member of the Committee to Defend America (eventually called the Fight for Freedom Committee [FFC]) which defied "America First" isolationism and militantly advocated aid to Britain through lend-lease, opening FFC members like Stout, who was doing all he could to "wake people up to the danger" to charges of being warmongers (quoted in McAleer 279).

Shortly before the Japanese attacked Pearl Harbor, Stout became involved with the Freedom House project, a "vital affiliation" he continued throughout his life (McAleer 281). Freedom House arose from the merger of several groups advocating war against Hitler as a concrete means of promoting the principles of freedom. Stout told *Cue* magazine in October 1941, "No one can rest now . . . Everything else must be put aside . . . until that man [Hitler] and machine are destroyed" (quoted in McAleer 282). In 1942, Stout became Head of the Writers' War Board, which adopted the controversial position that the German people were responsible for Hitler's aggression. When Stout declared, "'A man who tells you he hates evil but not the doer of evil is kidding either you or himself and in any case is gibbering'; Nero Wolfe himself might be speaking" (quoted in McAleer 305).

After the war ended, Stout opposed the use of nuclear weapons and became a vocal proponent of civil rights, world government, and the United Nations, while his output of fiction and his involvement with the U.S. Authors' League steadily grew. He served twice as the League's president and successfully battled with publishers to increase royalties for writers. Beginning in 1949 he settled into producing one Wolfe novel and a collection of three novellas per year. When Senator Joseph McCarthy began his anti-Communist activities in 1950, Stout immediately helped formulate the League's condemnation of the blacklisting of writers. Even though he himself loathed Communism, he hoped that reason might prevail over the mounting Red Scare hysteria. His insistence on steering the League "between the Scylla of McCarthyism and the Charybdis of Communism," however, earned Stout the animosity of FBI Director J. Edgar Hoover, then promoting "wiretapping, bugging of offices and residences, and monitoring of people's mail" (quoted in McAleer 449). Hoover even personally put Stout on the FBI's General Watch List. The FBI never formally investigated Stout, but a 12-page confidential FBI memo branded him a Communist in 1952 and indicated that FBI files contained 500 references to him. Stout shot back with *The Doorbell Rang* (1965), where Nero Wolfe creates what Stout called "a hell of a stink about the FBI and J. Edgar Hoover," whom Stout considered "a megalomaniac" and "an enemy of democracy" (quoted in McAleer 446–447). Subsequently an FBI Special Agent named Jones critiqued *The Doorbell Rang* for the Bureau, accusing Stout of "sensationalism" against the FBI "to improve sales" (Mitgang 228).

The Doorbell Rang reveals how thoroughly Stout's writing and political activity reinforced one another: "The Wolfe saga all along had served him as a vehicle

I carry this fat to insulate my feelings. They got too strong for me once or twice and I had that idea. If I had stayed lean and kept moving around I would have been dead long ago.

— Nero Wolfe

for stringent social commentary" (McAleer 450). It never stopped doing so, though as Rex Stout aged, his writing slowed down; his last Wolfe novellas appeared in 1964 and between 1969 and 1973 he wrote no Wolfe novels at all. Just after publication of his last Wolfe novel, *A Family Affair,* Stout died at High Meadow on October 17, 1975. His passionate commitment to human freedom had fueled his lifelong goal of a healing fusion of the dangerous ambiguities he had witnessed in American society, a fusion he illustrated in "the most original and plausible Holmes-and-Watson pair" (Symons 1972, 123): his unprecedented combination in detective fiction of an eccentric genius sleuth and a hard-boiled private eye: Nero Wolfe and Archie Goodwin.

PROFILE OF NERO WOLFE, VIA ARCHIE GOODWIN

Rex Stout claimed, "Nero Wolfe just appeared. I haven't the faintest idea where he came from. . . . I really don't know who he is and I don't give a damn so long as he's an interesting guy. . . . Wolfe, Archie, the brownstone—I haven't the slightest idea how I thought of them" (quoted in McAleer 234, 542 n3). Stout suspected, however, that "my subconscious has a very strong feeling toward them," and those closest to Stout, like Mark Van Doren, his most enduring friend, believed that while Archie is Stout himself, "There are times when Nero equals Rex." Stout's daughters felt that Archie was Stout's "spontaneous self" and Wolfe was his "achieved self" (quoted in McAleer 245).

Reflecting Stout's perception of the ambiguities of American society, too, Nero Wolfe and Archie Goodwin arose from two disparate developments of mystery fiction, from the old world and the new. Starting with Sherlock Holmes, the classic British "genius detective" utilized minute observation, crystalline deduction, staggering intellect, photographic memory, and leaps of brilliant intuition. In fact, the physical resemblance between Wolfe and Sherlock Holmes's corpulent and sedentary spymaster brother Mycroft led Christopher Morley and Bernard DeVoto to suspect Mycroft was Wolfe's father, a notion that in turn sparked John D. Clark's 1956 thesis, later promulgated by William S. Baring-Gould but never confirmed by Stout, that Wolfe was the illegitimate son of Sherlock Holmes and "*the* Woman" Irene Adler, conceived during one of Holmes's travels in Montenegro. Contemporary novelist John Lescroart went a step farther in *Son of Holmes* and *Rasputin's Revenge,* both reissued in 2003, hinting that their main character Auguste Lupin, son of Sherlock Holmes and Irene Adler, becomes Nero Wolfe. Although the British "genius detectives" pursued their criminal quarries to produce their own thrills of the hunt, however, Nero Wolfe worked for money, giving a "thin lining of steel" (Keating 58) to his extremely solid flesh.

Nero Wolfe's Personal Background

Since Wolfe cherished his privacy, he sometimes obscured facts about his early life, though Stout dropped a few hints in the novels. In *Over My Dead Body* (1939), Stout identified Wolfe's homeland as Montenegro, a tiny Balkan nation which in modern times was a part of Communist Yugoslavia. Italians call Montenegro's chief mountain "Monte Nero" and the surname of Wolfe's childhood friend and purported twin brother, the restauranteur Marko Vukcic, means "little wolf" in Serbo-Croatian, allowing speculation that "Nero Wolfe" may be an alias (McAleer 393). Clues in the novels show that Wolfe was born in Montenegro around 1892 and prior to 1908 had traveled in Europe, Asia, and Africa. He spied for Austria from 1913 to 1916, changed sides during World War I, and in 1917 to 1918, he walked 600 miles to join the American Expeditionary Force, on the way killing about 200 Germans. Between 1918 and 1921 he traveled in Europe, eventually returning to the Balkans and adopting a daughter in 1920 or 1921. Wolfe had a "lost period" like Holmes's "Great Hiatus"; Wolfe's was 1922 to 1928, and when he resurfaced in 1930, he was "not penniless." (Bernard DeVoto conjectured that in the "lost period" Wolfe had been involved in something so desperate that "his true identity must be forever concealed," accounting for Wolfe's falsely claiming to the FBI in *Over My Dead Body* that he had been born in the United States.) Detailed house plans for the New York brownstone that Wolfe bought in 1930 appear at "Rex Stout House" (Stout used various street numbers for it in his novels). Wolfe turned its rooftop into orchid rooms, hired Archie Goodwin, and became a private investigator.

Nero Wolfe's Career

Nero Wolfe's cases, like almost everything readers learn about Wolfe himself, are seen through Archie Goodwin's keen ironic eyes, and each case takes place at the time when Stout was creating it (see Muffy Barkocy for a complete listing). Stout hoped Nero Wolfe would "live forever" (Murphy 532), so Wolfe remains 58 and Archie 34 during their 40-year career from the Depression to the threat of nuclear holocaust. For Stout and his readers, "The confident certainties of Wolfe's exploits served as an antidote to the pressing uncertainties of the real world" (Van Dover 2003, 3).

Wolfe summarized his work as an "intellectual mercenary" (Hilliard and Smith) in *Too Many Crooks:* "I entrap criminals, and find evidence to imprison them or kill them, for hire." In *Death of a Doxy,* he described his personality: "I am what I call tenacious and Mrs. Goodwin calls pigheaded" (168), readily acknowledging his income came "from the necessities, the tribulations, and the misfortunes of my fellow beings." Archie Goodwin often "goads and prods and generally annoys Wolfe until at last the great man gives in and undertakes—with the worst possible grace—whatever case Archie has decided he should tackle" (*Too Many Clients*, 76).

Wolfe's cases usually follow a stock formula: someone brings him a problem or crime; Wolfe uses Archie and his day-work leg men, Saul Panzer, Fred Durkin, Orrie Cather, and occasionally others, to search out facts, suspects, witnesses, and accomplices, which they present to Wolfe in detail. Sometimes Wolfe and Archie cooperate with the police and at other times they delightedly befuddle the NYPD's Inspector Cramer. Wolfe ponders the information, at length interviews those connected with the case; and "while seldom giving Goodwin a hint about what he is thinking . . . narrow[s] the list of suspects while never varying his daily personal routine" (Landon Burns, in Herbert 211). In his signature confrontation scenes, which Inspector Cramer attends and calls "charades," Wolfe then uses his intellectual and intuitive gifts to wreak justice on the criminal, often at the villain's own hand; ". . . self-punishers relieve the state and its law-abiding citizens of active responsibility [and] confession powerfully marks an individual's surrender to the severe judgment of the state" (Beiderwell 17). Wolfe has a low opinion of judges; he once declared that the ideal judge had "the kind of

---

Nero Wolfe's Weekday Schedule

ca. 7:30 A.M.	Breakfast
9–11 A.M.	Plant rooms with Theodore Horstmann
11 A.M.–1 P.M.	Business or reading
1:15 P.M.	Lunch
2–4 P.M.	Business or reading
4–6 P.M.	Plant rooms
7:15 or 7:30 P.M.	Dinner

---

daring mind that glories in deciding an issue without understanding it" (*The Second Confession*, 84).

Weighing about a seventh of a ton because he once starved and wants never to be hungry again, and consuming five to six quarts of beer daily, Wolfe rarely leaves his elegant brownstone's "eccentric coziness [that] makes it—far more than Poirot's art-deco [sic], Wimsey's clubman magnificence or 221 Baker Street [*sic*] with its reek of chemicals—a place where one might really like to live" (Langford). Considering automobiles as whim-driven demons, he trusts only Archie to drive him; "He would sooner cut his throat than step into a taxi" (*Private Lives* 204). Wolfe's passions included his 10,000 priceless orchids and his private Swiss chef Fritz Brenner's exquisite cuisine. He also had an unquenchable reading habit, often reading three books on any given day. Wolfe habitually ranked his favorite books by various types of bookmarks. Among those receiving slivers of gold were Lincoln Barnett's *The Treasure of Our Tongue;* Jane Austen's *Emma;* Robert Ardry's *African Genesis;* and five versions of the Bible in four different languages. Wolfe quotes Shakespeare more often than any other writer and keeps a complete set in his office; Stout himself had read all Shakespeare's plays between ages 7 and 12; he memorized all of Shakespeare's sonnets and at age 86 could quote them perfectly (Winnifred Louis, "Wolfe's Reading List"). Wolfe rigidly limits his detective work to six hours a day: 2 to 4 P.M., 6 to 7 P.M., and 9 P.M. to midnight. He claims, "I do not soil myself cheaply" so he demands outrageously high fees—as much as $100,000; his budget for staff, food, books, orchids, taxes, and luxurious incidentals ran to $10,000 per month in the 1930s.

Wolfe and Archie carried out their most widely acclaimed investigations against the backdrop of the Depression and the gathering clouds of World War II. In this bleak world, relieved only slightly by speakeasies and 20-cent movies, Wolfe drove the villain to suicide; unemployment results in suicide, too, in *The League of Frightened Men* (1935), praised as one of the best mystery novels of all time; and international instability and hatred of fascism shadowed *The Rubber Band* (1936). Wolfe reluctantly left his brownstone in *Too Many Cooks* (1937), a juicy treatment of elite gastronomy and racial prejudice introducing Marko Vukcic, a master chef and possibly Wolfe's twin brother. In another rare excursion, *Some Buried Caesar* (1939), Stout's favorite Wolfe novel, Wolfe dealt with the possible barbecuing of a $45,000 Guernsey bull and Archie met Lily Rowan, a fabulously wealthy socialite who became his principal romantic interest.

During World War II, *Over My Dead Body* (1940) "begins the long line of pleasant entertainments in which Wolfe and Archie exploit the familiar formulas" (Van Dover 2003, 13) and Wolfe vents Stout's fervent anti-Nazi, anti-financier, and anti-FBI sentiments. During the war, Wolfe assisted the government by nosing out domestic enemies gratis. The novella *Black Orchids* (1942) reveals both Wolfe's greedy orchidomania and Archie's interest in model Anne Tracy, as well as some unforgettably horrid images, as when Archie's inspection of the victim's fatal head wound felt "like sticking your finger into a warm apple pie."

Wolfe made substantial sacrifices for his work and his adopted country. In *Not Quite Dead Enough* (1942), he decided to enlist in the army, exercising four hours a day and giving up bread, cream, sugar—and beer; Archie returned to New York as an Army Intelligence major to find nothing in the brownstone pantry but oranges, prunes, lettuce, tomatoes, and applesauce. After the war, Wolfe went on another strenuous diet, losing 117 pounds as a disguise (*In the Best Families* (1950)), but in *Murder by the Book* (1951), Wolfe resumed his sedentary comfort while Archie tracked a killer across the United States. In *The Black Mountain* (1954), however, Wolfe somehow performed "improbably vigorous activities in Yugoslavia . . . without having a heart attack" (Murphy 533).

Wolfe probably reached his detecting peak in his duel of wits with criminal mastermind Arnold Zeck, Wolfe's Professor Moriarty, in the trilogy *And Be a Villain* (1948), *The Second Confession* (1949), and *In the Best Families* (1950), which opens with Wolfe volunteering to take a case so he can pay his upcoming taxes, emphasizing his animosity toward governmental intrusion into personal finance. Later notable Wolfe novels include *The Golden Spiders* (1953) involving the mistreatment of immigrants; *A Right to Die* (1964), the sequel to *Too Many Cooks* dealing with the civil rights movement and assaulting American racism; and *The Doorbell Rang* (1965), Wolfe's pillorying of the FBI's unethical tactics under J. Edgar Hoover. *Death of a Dude* (1969) took Wolfe and Archie to Montana, where Stout had vacationed since 1923. This novel includes references to the Vietnam War, the Berkeley protests, and Solzhenitsyn's groundbreaking indictment of Stalinism, *The First Circle*. Stout's last Nero Wolfe novel, *A Family Affair* (1975), uses the Watergate Affair as "a powerful and pervasive context for the drama"; Wolfe declared, "I would have given all of my orchids—well, most of them—to have an effective hand in the disclosure of the malfeasance of Richard Nixon" (quoted in Van Dover 2003, 61). Wolfe also solved a crisis in his own "family" and forced the suicide of the perpetrator as he had done in *Fer-de-Lance*, but at a wrenching personal price. In *A Family Affair*, Rex Stout insisted on the triumph of individual integrity over societal expedience, and Wolfe's last words showed he knew the cost: "Will you bring brandy, Archie? . . . We'll try to get some sleep."

Stout never revealed Wolfe's last days, but Julian Symons' clever fictional interview "In Which Archie Goodwin Remembers" suggests that after making his will, Wolfe vanished into the Montenegrin mountains on a mysterious mission to coordinate an anticommunist uprising, leaving Archie wistfully thinking of Wolfe "out there, hunting dragonflies up on the roof of Yugoslavia" (Symons 1981, 61). Ken Darby, on the other hand, suggests that Wolfe moved to Alexandria, Egypt, where he produced a beard to "keep all predatory widows at pay" (unpaginated Preface).

Nero Wolfe's Strengths

Archie Goodwin loved watching Wolfe's lips pushing "out and back again" while he was contemplating a new case: ". . . something was happening so fast inside of him and so much ground was being covered, the whole world in a flash, that no one else could ever really understand it, even if he had tried to his best to explain, which he never did" (*Fer-de-Lance* 4–5). Wolfe insisted that "The brain can be hoodwinked but not the stomach" (*Blood Will Tell*, 159), and he never doubted his own capabilities. As he told Archie, "You can't be expected to see what I'm accomplishing; if you could do that, you could do the job yourself" (*Some Buried Caesar* 87). He also informed Archie that he, Wolfe, felt phenomena, while Archie collected facts. Wolfe's intellectual ability, impenetrable to ordinary pragmatic minds, synthesized information at lightning speed and near-instantaneously drew intuitive conclusions. Archie often felt that Wolfe "never seemed to realize that . . . I could do my part with a little more intelligence if I knew what was making the wheels go around." Wolfe put the issue as plainly as God did to Job: Archie and all lesser beings are incapable of understanding, let alone carrying out, the process of creation: Wolfe also had a bellow that "would stop a tiger ready to spring" (*Homicide Trinity,* 113). "Must I again demonstrate that while it is permissible to request the scientist to lead you back over his footprints, a similar request of the artist is nonsense, since he, like the lark or the eagle, has made none? Do you need to be told again that I am an artist?" (*Fer-de-Lance* 55).

Stout masterfully plays Wolfe's erudition, his wide-ranging interests, and his mastery of the English language off against Archie's wisecracking Americanisms in "the best dialogue in mystery fiction" (*Private Lives* 201). Wolfe shredded the third edition of a dictionary that allowed abbreviations like "ad" for "advertisement" and the use of "contact" as a verb, though he reserved his most stringent linguistic formality for suspects and relaxed somewhat with his associates and innocent bystanders. Wolfe dominates visually by favoring the colors yellow and black (though Archie would like to see him do it with pink and green) and calls himself "a born actor" (*Fer-de-Lance* 161); and he employs a withering formality with women, even making the considerable effort of standing when one enters or leaves a room. He is "a tough guy . . . swathed in layers of urbanity and fat" (Murphy 532).

Nero Wolfe's Prejudices

Women in general, hysterical women especially

Germans during World War II

J. Edgar Hoover

Richard Nixon during Watergate

The 3rd edition of Webster's Dictionary

Radio

Television

Nero Wolfe's Foibles

Wolfe's reclusive habits force him to depend on others for basic information. He refuses to interrupt his daily schedule or leave his house except in the most dire circumstances. He detests traveling in any kind of motorized vehicle, becoming "frantic with fear" in *Too Many Cooks* "because he was alone on the train and it might begin to move" (*Cooks* 1). His chronic inertia, which Archie considers laziness, often forces Archie to prod him into action.

The Kanawha Spa Dinner

Oysters Baked in the Shell

Terrapin Maryland

Beaten Biscuits

Pan-Broiled Young Turkey

Rice Croquettes with Quince Jelly

Lima Beans in Cream

Avocado Todhunter

Sally Lunn

Pineapple Sherbet

Sponge Cake

—*The Nero Wolfe Cookbook*, 187–188

Wolfe suffers from inexplicably paralyzing relapses that his associates simply must endure, lasting "from one afternoon up to a couple of weeks," with Wolfe either retreating to bed on bread and onion soup or concocting arcane recipes with Fritz Brenner, oblivious to everything but eating. "He ate a whole sheep that way in two days, once, different parts of it cooked in twenty different ways" (*Fer-de-Lance* 75–76). Wolfe can "dehydrate" even Archie "with a look" (*Omit Flowers* 48). He tends to be unforgivably grumpy, he treats clients condescendingly and even rudely, and he seemingly does not like women at all. Archie puts it pungently: "Nero Wolfe is investigating the murder . . . with his accustomed vigor, skill and laziness. He will not rest until he gets the bastard or until bedtime, whichever comes first" (*The Golden Spiders* 39). Despite these negative traits, however, "this notoriously taciturn character stands as one of fiction's most memorable Great Detectives" (Landon Burns, in Herbert 211).

Nero Wolfe's Master Criminal Opponent

Just as a knight of old needed to prove himself against an equally formidable opponent, Great Detectives need Master Criminals to demonstrate their mettle. Nero Wolfe's would-be nemesis was villainous mastermind Arnold Zeck, the only man Wolfe feared, not because of what Zeck might do to him but of "what he may someday force me [Wolfe] to do to keep from hurting him." Zeck surfaced first in *And Be a Villain* (1948) as a "disembodied voice" warning Wolfe off a lurid poisoning case. Stout claimed that when he wrote this novel, he didn't "plan or even consciously contemplate, subsequent appearance or appearances of Zeck" (McAleer 594), but Zeck became increasingly malignant, though still disembodied, in *The Second Confession* (1949). Zeck's illegal and morally repulsive activities included

"Narcotics, smuggling, industrial and commercial rackets, gambling, waterfront blackguardism, professional larceny, blackmailing, [and] political malfeasance" (quoted in Van Dover 2003, 23), and membership in the Communist Party, which Wolfe, Archie, and Rex Stout all despised. In this novel, Zeck warned Wolfe not to investigate a potential crime by sending him a teargas-boobytrapped packet of gourmet sausage and then ordered his minions to machine gun Wolfe's rooftop plant rooms. In *In the Best Families* (1950), Wolfe abandoned his brownstone and went into disguise, allowing Fritz Brenner and gardener Theodore Horstmann to find other employment, and having Archie establish his own detective agency, but eventually Wolfe and Archie engineered the demise of Zeck and his cohorts. Most commentators feel that Zeck is no Moriarty, only "an oversized gangster . . . tough-talking, but gullible, vulnerable, and banal," and that his climactic confrontation with Wolfe lacks the epic quality of the Great Detective's Good versus Evil faceoff with Moriarty at the Reichenbach Falls. When Wolfe faced Arnold Zeck, "The reader is more affected by the reactions of the detective than by the actions of the criminal— even those of a criminal mastermind. This suggests both the special strength and the special weakness of the Wolfe series" (Van Dover 2003, 26).

> *I'm chiefly cut out for two things, to jump up and grab something before the other guy gets his paws on it, and to collect pieces of the puzzle for Wolfe to work on.*
> —Archie Goodwin

Nero Wolfe's Associates

Stout once commented that people think they like reading about Wolfe but what they really like is Archie (Murphy 211). Archie Goodwin hailed from Ohio and the early American pulp hard-boiled private eye tradition. Archie "went to college two weeks, decided it was childish, came to New York and got a job guarding a pier, shot and killed two men and was fired, was recommended to Nero Wolfe, . . . was offered a full-time job by Mr. Wolfe, took it, still have it" (*Fourth of July Picnic* 149). He's "a tough, handsome guy with a photographic memory, a .32 under his well-tailored suit (and sometimes an extra .38 in his overcoat pocket) and a well-developed appreciation for the ladies . . . a smart and tenacious operative with a good right hook, and a decent and personable man" (Hilliard and Smith 2). Archie works for Wolfe "for fun" (*Fer-de-Lance* 15) and readily acknowledges Wolfe's genius. Where Wolfe is startlingly intuitive, Archie pragmatically believes "a lie isn't a lie if it is a reply to a question the questioner has no right to ask" (*Plot It Yourself* 174), and though sharp-witted, Archie is no genius, just an ordinary guy using "a combination of forcefulness (fist and gun), endurance, and perseverance" (Van Dover 2003, 4). Archie shares Stout's own "brightness, cockiness, . . . directness, and sharpness of speech" (McAleer 235), and he can effectively track, punch and shoot villains. He carries on an often mentioned but seldom actually glimpsed affair with the

You know, son, you have one or two good qualities. In a way I even like you. In another way I could stand and watch your hide peeling off and not shed any tears. You have undoubtedly got the goddamndest nerve of anybody I know except Nero Wolfe.

—Inspector Cramer to Archie Goodwin

rich, lissome Lily Rowan whose Tammany Hall father made millions installing New York sewers. Archie plays poker every week with Saul Panzer, showing that he knows both how to hold 'em and when to fold 'em. To refute his own hint that "there seemed something sexually ambiguous about the household of Nero Wolfe and Archie," Julian Symons extrapolates Archie's vehement retrospective comments about love in or out of the brownstone, "telling" Symons, "that's between the girls and me and the four-poster." In Stout's novels Archie never was infatuated enough to marry one, though Ken Darby in *The Brownstone House of Nero Wolfe* conjectures that Archie and blonde, blue-eyed Lily later married and took up residence at her Montana ranch. As for Archie's relationship with Wolfe, Archie insisted, "[It] was father and son, if you can understand anything that simple" (Symons 1981, 51)—with all the tensions and all the redeeming though seldom-voiced affection of a father-son relationship.

Nero Wolfe's large supporting cast includes his domestic staff, his relatives and friends, his hired hands, and contacts with police and other professionals. Fritz Brenner, Wolfe's French-speaking Swiss master chef, knew Wolfe before Archie did and devotedly runs Wolfe's household with Rolex-timed precision. Theodore Horstmann, Wolfe's prima donna orchid nurse, barely tolerates Archie; during Horstmann's absences, Wolfe's friend Lewis Hewitt cares for the priceless collection. "Headstrong, gullible, over-sanguine, and naïve," Marko Vukcic was possibly Wolfe's twin brother, a master chef with "a warm eye for women" who owned the upscale New York Rusterman's Restaurant, which Wolfe inherited and operated as a trustee after Vukcic's murder. Marko posthumously received Wolfe's ultimate compliment: "the insult would be to smear his corpse with the honey excreted by my fear of death" (*Golden Spiders*

When the day finally comes that I tie Wolfe to a stake and shoot him, one of the fundamental reasons will be his theory that the less I know the more I can help. . . . He merely can't stand to have anyone keep up with him at any time on any track.

—Archie Goodwin

21). Carla, Wolfe's adopted daughter, appeared in only *Over My Dead Body* and *The Black Mountain*; her surname is the Montenegrin name for the "black mountain" which gives that small Balkan country its own name. She and Marko Vukcic belonged to a guerrilla group called "The Spirit of the Black Mountain," fighting for Montenegro's independence from Communist Yugoslavia.

Wolfe frequently employed various private detectives for specialized duties. Saul Panzer, Fred Durkin, and Orrie Cather, his chief investigators, are three of the only nine or 10 people to whom Wolfe willingly offers his hand. Wolfe and Archie consider that Panzer, small, nondescript, usually unshaven, and near-invisible on the job, is "the best operative south of the North Pole." Fred is steady and dependable because "he knows what he doesn't know" (*Might as Well Be Dead* 63), but Archie never liked Orrie Cather; handsome and "born with the attitude towards all attractive women that a fisherman has toward all the trout in a stream." Cather wanted Archie's job and Archie knew it. Other operatives occasionally working for Wolfe are Johnnie Keems; Del Bascom, who operates a large detective agency Wolfe sometimes subcontracts with when he needs more personnel; and Theodolinda ("Dol") Bonner and Sally Colt, two of the first female fictional private eyes, useful to Wolfe when he needs women detectives' talents.

Among Wolfe's police contacts, red-faced, cigar-chomping NYPD Inspector Cramer, the main character in Stout's novel *Red Threads*, and Sergeant Purley Stebbins most frequently figure in Wolfe's cases, usually as the butt of Wolfe's disdain for official authority. Wolfe particularly loathed the obnoxious Lt. George Rowcliffe for executing a search warrant on his brownstone home, and Wolfe and Archie enjoyed adversarial relationships with District Attorneys like Westchester County's Cleveland Anderson, notable for blatant stupidity.

Wolfe's professional friends and associates include Wolfe's old friend attorney Nathaniel Parker, who shares many of Wolfe's intellectual pursuits; Dr. Vollmer, another longtime friend of Wolfe's whom Wolfe called whenever a dead body turned up; and Len Cohen, the *Gazette*'s senior journalist, who traded Archie background information on suspects and prospective clients in return for scoops when Wolfe nailed his murderous prey.

Nero Wolfe and Women

Nero Wolfe kept his distance from women. John McAleer has suggested regarding Stout's mother that emotional distance and Puritanism make children either hyperachievers or self-destructive. Wolfe himself once hinted that a woman had injured him so fiercely that he never wanted to leave himself vulnerable again. Perhaps she was a Montenegrin woman that he might have married, the only person, he said, from whom he "skedaddled, physically." Wolfe did not "disapprove of them [women]" (*The Rubber Band* 94), but he also observed that "All women are [hysterical]. Their moments of calm are merely recuperative periods between outbursts" (*Too Many Cooks* 137). Archie's lover Lily Rowan claimed to be "the only woman in America who has necked with Nero Wolfe, concluding, "Nightmare, my eye. He has a flair" (*In the Best Families* 97). Wolfe referred in turn to her as "rich, intemperate and notorious." To Julie Jacquette, one of the few women to capture Wolfe's attention, Wolfe admitted, "I had the impression that your opinions of our fellow beings and their qualities are somewhat similar to mine" (*Death of a Doxy* 92), but according to Archie Goodwin, ". . . as far as Wolfe's concerned you might

You can't know what a woman is like until you see her at her food.

—Nero Wolfe

add the word celibacy to your vocabulary. . . . it's the only answer you're going to get" (Symons 1981, 51).

Archie's opinions about women are far more entertaining. Having suffered a jilting in his youth, Archie divides girls into "clingers, divers, or laggers, and I don't know which is the worst" (*Where There's a Will* 43), and as a character in *The Silent Speaker* noted, "Any girl who needed a rest would go anywhere with Mr. G., because she wouldn't have to use her mind" (51). He's got "nothing against maturity [in women] as long as it's not overdone" (*Golden Spiders* 34), but he's often a little cynical: "No man with any sense assumes that a woman's words mean to her exactly what they mean to him" (*Mother Hunt* 137), and while he and Lily Rowan enjoy one another's company, Lily knows what men are for and what they're not for. She rejects marriage just as strongly as Archie does, and he doubts if he'd go to his own.

ADAPTATIONS

Novels

After Stout's death in 1975, his heirs authorized Robert Goldsborough to continue the series, beginning with *Murder in E Minor* (1986), which Goldsborough wrote as a gift for his mother shortly after Stout's death, and continuing with six more modestly successful cases. His last Wolfe novel, *The Missing Chapter* (1994), deals with the murder of a mediocre continuator of a popular detective series.

Movies

Two early Nero Wolfe films by Columbia Pictures, *Nero Wolfe* (1936), adapted loosely from *Fer-de-Lance*, and *The League of Frightened Men* (1937), thoroughly turned Rex Stout off allowing cinema versions of his work. He objected to Lionel Stander's performance as a gunslinging Dead-End-Kid Archie and refused to sell the movie rights to any of his books or stories.

Radio and Audio

Early radio versions of Wolfe's cases received poor ratings. In *The Adventures of Nero Wolfe* (1943 to 1944), with Santos Ortega as Wolfe; *The Amazing Nero Wolfe* (1945 to 1946), with Francis X. Bushman as Wolfe; and *The New Adventures of Nero Wolfe* (1950 to 1951), with Sydney Greenstreet overacting as Wolfe. A succession of actors played Archie with pedestrian results. *Rex Stout's Nero Wolfe* (1982), for the Canadian Broadcasting Company, successfully offered 13 one-hour episodes based on Wolfe novellas and stories.

Contemporary audio versions of the Nero Wolfe canon read by Michael Pritchard have received stellar reviews. They transport listeners "back not only to the upscale New York City of the 1950s, but also to an era when wit and literacy flourished in the mystery genre. . . . a relatively recent but completely vanished world of glamour, greed and human weakness (Review 30).

Television

A 1977 pilot based on *The Doorbell Rang* received an excellent review in Leonard Maltin's annual movie guide, but due to the death of its star Thayer David, Paramount delayed the proposed series for four years. William Conrad then starred as Wolfe, with Lee Horsley as Archie in NBC's *Nero Wolfe* drama series only loosely based on Stout's stories and set in contemporary New York. After disappointing ratings the series lasted only 13 episodes.

In 2000, A&E Television brought out the first of its historical repertory company Wolfe telefilms, *The Golden Spiders,* starring Maury Chaykin as Wolfe and Timothy Hutton, so enraptured with his role as an elegantly flippant Archie, that he continued on as the show's executive producer and occasional director. Despite brilliant acting, nearly 1,000 masterfully designed 1960s and 1970s period costumes per season, critical acclaim, and the Wolfe Pack's fervent approval, high production costs of $1.1 million an episode, a licensing fee of $700,000, and low overall ratings caused A&E to cancel the series after only two seasons. DVD versions of the show have proved popular, however, and both Chaykin and Hutton have professed interest in reviving the series. Abroad, West Germany produced a 1961 Wolfe miniseries, *Zu Viele Küche (Too Many Cooks)*; the Italian network RAI broadcast black-and-white Nero Wolfe telefilms in 1969 to 1971; and in Russia, *Pola Ya Ne Umer,* the first of five Nero Wolfe telefilms written by Vladimir Valutsky, who also wrote the Russian Sherlock Holmes series, appeared in 2001 to 2002.

THE ENDURING APPEAL OF NERO WOLFE AND ARCHIE GOODWIN

Conceived during the Great Depression and over five decades commenting on some of America's most perilous challenges, Rex Stout's Nero Wolfe fiction became "a unique, and personal, view of history . . . through Wolfe and Archie, we see the effects of the Depression, World War II, the Civil Rights Movement, Women's Liberation, and Watergate" (Kiser). Nero Wolfe's cases remain a valuable and entertaining reflection of those societal upheavals, history lessons spicily coated in the wit and linguistic brilliance of a master wordsmith and liberal thinker.

As a craftsman, Stout adhered faithfully to the guidelines that Edgar Allan Poe laid down for detective fiction: "everything must converge on a single effect," and how the detective arrives at the criminal's identity outweighs who that criminal is (John McAleer, quoted in *CA Online*). Further, "The puzzle [of each work] and its solution are impeccably fair. . . . the reader

knows all that Archie does and can even make an informed guess at the specific thing that was strikingly suggestive to Wolfe but not to the other"
(Frank Jellinek, quoted in *CA Online*). Stout also advanced the art of the
detective story by echoing the ambiguities of American society in pairing
Nero Wolfe, the immigrant armchair genius detective who made astronomi-
cally good, with Archie Goodwin, a brash Huckleberry Finn out of the
dawn of American hard-boiled private eyehood.

Philosophically, Nero Wolfe's principle of judging people on a person-to-
person basis regardless of race (though not, perhaps, regardless of gender)
upholds the general theme that makes his stories universally appealing: In the
face of human dignity and weakness, never make assumptions. Stout himself
put those contradictions and ambivalences of human nature, the timeless tension between reason and feeling, into the context of detective fiction:

> You know goddam [sic] well why, of all kinds of stories, the detective story is
> the most popular. It supports, more than any other kind of story, man's
> favorite myth, that he's Homo sapiens, the rational animal. And of course the
> poor son-of-a-bitch isn't a rational animal at all . . . the most important
> function of the brain is thinking up reasons for the decisions his emotions
> have made. (Quoted in *CA Online*)

The secret of Nero Wolfe's popularity lies in the fun he and Archie share
with their readers, reassuring and comforting them that reasons for bedevil-
ing human emotions do exist:

> We crowd around his desk dying to know
> What at last the great detective says.
> *Sit down! And shut those women up!* he says.
> In the end there is nothing we won't know. (Buffington 126)

PARALLEL CHRONOLOGY

Major Events Related to Nero Wolfe	World Events
ca. 1880 Nero Wolfe born in Montenegro (conjectured from Stout's initial stories where Wolfe is about 56; in another, Wolfe claimed to have been born in the U.S. in the early 1890s)	
1886 Rex Stout born, Noblesville, IN	
1887 The Stouts move to Kansas	**1887** *A Study in Scarlet,* first Sherlock Holmes novel
1892 Hypothesized affair between Sherlock Holmes and Irene Adler in Montenegro, resulting in birth of	**1892** *A Scandal in Bohemia* with Irene Adler, by Arthur Conan Doyle

Major Events Related to Nero Wolfe	World Events
Nero Wolfe; no evidence exists Rex Stout considered this	
ca. 1894–ca. 1908 Wolfe travels in Europe, Africa, Asia	
1905 Rex joins U.S. Navy	
1909 Rex settles in New York	
1910 Rex makes first sale, a poem	
1912 Rex begins writing for pulps	
1913 First novel published (serial)	
1913–1916 Wolfe spies for Austria	
ca. Summer 1914 Wolfe changes sides	**Aug. 1914** Outbreak of World War I
1916 Rex Stout marries Fay Kennedy; founds Educational Thrift Service (ETS)	
1917–1918 Wolfe fights against Germans and Austrians, walks 600 miles to join American expeditionary force	
	Nov. 1918 Armistice of World War I
1918–1921 Wolfe moves around; then returns to the Balkans and adopts daughter	
	1920 Congress passes the Volstead Act (Prohibition)
	1921 U.S. Quota Law passed, limiting immigration
1922–1928 Wolfe's "lost years"	
1926 Stout, now well-to-do, leaves ETS	
1929 Stout publishes first book	**1929** U.S. stock market collapse, start of Great Depression; appearance of first "hard-boiled" detective, Race Williams, in pulp magazine *Black Mask*
1930 Stout and wife are divorced; Wolfe comes to America "not penniless"	
1931 Stout builds home, High Meadow, in New York-Connecticut; Wolfe buys brownstone on West 35th St., New York; hires Goodwin, begins private detective career	**1931** The Empire State Building is dedicated
1930–1933 Various cases described in short stories	
1932 Stout marries Pola Hoffman	**1932** Franklin D. Roosevelt elected president

(Continued)

Major Events Related to Nero Wolfe	World Events
June 7–21, 1933 Events of *Fer-de-Lance*	**1933** Hitler appointed Chancellor of Germany; first Nero Wolfe novel published; Congress repeals Prohibition
Nov. 2–Nov. 12, 1934 Events of *The League of Frightened Men* (published 1935)	**1934** FBI agents shoot John Dillinger, Public Enemy No. 1
Feb. 1935 Archie is convinced to carry a gun	**1935** Social Security Act is made law
	1936 Nazi Germany occupies the Rhineland
Apr. 5–Apr. 9, 1937 Events of *Too Many Cooks* (published 1938)	
1938 Wolfe acquires first knowledge of X	
Nov. 1938 Events of *Over My Dead Body,* where Wolfe learns he has an adopted daughter (published 1940)	
	1939 Germany invades Poland; beginning of World War II
1941 Stout helps found the Fight for Freedom Committee and Freedom House; a Thurs. or Fri. in March, events of *Black Orchids* (published 1942)	**Dec. 7, 1941** Japanese attack on Pearl Harbor; U.S. enters the war
1945 Stout is president of Authors' League	**1945** U.S. drops atomic bombs on Japan; end of World War II
April 1946 X's second call to Wolfe	**1946–1980s** The Cold War between Communist bloc and Free World
Mar. 18–Apr. 5, 1947 Events of *Too Many Women* (published 1947)	
1948 X telephones Wolfe twice	
1949 Stout organizes Writers' Board for World Government; X phones again, blasts Wolfe's plant rooms	**1949** USSR tests their first atomic bomb
1950 *In the Best Families* published; Arnold Zeck dies	**1950–1953** Korean War
	Nov. 1950 Passage over Pres. Truman's veto of McCarran Internal Security Act barring Communists from working in defense industries, becoming naturalized citizens, and if citizens, from using passports
	1950–1954 Sen. Joseph McCarthy conducts investigations into possible

Major Events Related to Nero Wolfe	World Events
	Communist infiltration of U.S. public life
1951 Stout condemns McCarthyism	**Mar. 12, 1951** Kefauver Hearings disclose widespread U.S. crime and corruption
	Apr. 5, 1951 Julius and Ethel Rosenberg sentenced to death for passing nuclear secrets to the USSR
May 19–May 29, 1953 Events of *The Golden Spiders* (published 1953)	**June 1953** Rosenbergs executed; McCarthy engineers barring of J. Robert Oppenheimer, former head of the Manhattan Project, from access to classified material
1954 Wolfe visits native Montenegro	**Mar. 1954** U.S. explodes first hydrogen bomb
Mar. 11–Mar. 19, 1954 Events of *The Black Mountain* where Wolfe's adopted daughter plays a role (published 1954)	
	May 17, 1954 Supreme Court outlaws segregation
	Dec. 1954 McCarthy publicly censured
Apr. 12–Apr. 19, 1955 Events of *Before Midnight* (published 1955)	
Apr. 9–Apr. 16, 1956 Events of *Might As Well Be Dead* (published 1956)	**1956** USSR puts down Hungarian revolt
	Oct. 4, 1957 USSR launches *Sputnik*
	1958 U.S. launches first satellite
May 18–June 3, 1959 Events of *Plot It Yourself* (published 1959)	
	1960 John F. Kennedy elected U.S. President
Apr. 25–May 1, 1961 Events of *The Final Deduction* (published 1961)	**1961** Abortive Bay of Pigs invasion
	1962 Cuban Missile Crisis
	Nov. 22, 1963 Pres. John F. Kennedy assassinated
Jan. 5–15, 1965 Events of *The Doorbell Rang* (published 1965)	**Feb. 1962** U.S. begins bombing in Vietnam
	Apr. 4, 1968 Martin Luther King assassinated
June 4–30, 1969 Events of *Please Pass the Guilt* (published 1973), first new Wolfe novel in four years	**June 4, 1968** Robert F. Kennedy assassinated

(Continued)

Major Events Related to Nero Wolfe	World Events
	July 20, 1969 Neil Armstrong becomes first man to walk on the moon
	June 3, 1971 Pentagon Papers published
	1973 Withdrawal of U.S. troops from Vietnam; Watergate hearings
	Aug. 8, 1974 Richard Nixon resigns as president
Oct. 29–Nov. 7, 1974 Events of *A Family Affair* (published 1975), last Wolfe novel by Stout	**Nov. 21 1974** Freedom of Information Act passed, increasing public's right of access to government files
Oct. 27, 1975 Stout dies in Danbury, Connecticut	
1977 John McAleer's definitive biography, *Rex Stout,* published	
1980 Definitive bibliographies published by McAleer and Guy Townsend	
1981 William Conrad stars as Wolfe in NBC's drama series lasting only 8 months	
1987–1994 Seven Wolfe novels by Robert Goldsborough published	
2000–2001 A&E brings out Wolfe telefilms with Maury Chaykin and Timothy Hutton	
2008 Bantam reissues *Fer-de-Lance* and *The League of Frightened Men* in one volume	

WORKS BY REX STOUT

Nero Wolfe Mystery Novels

Fer-de-Lance. New York: Farrar & Rinehart, 1934.

The League of Frightened Men. New York: Farrar & Rinehart, 1935.

The Rubber Band. New York: Farrar & Rinehart, 1936, republished 1960 by Curl (New York) as *To Kill Again.*

The Red Box. New York: Farrar & Rinehart, 1937.

Too Many Cooks. New York: Farrar & Rinehart, 1938.

Some Buried Caesar. New York: Farrar & Rinehart, 1930.

Over My Dead Body. New York: Farrar & Rinehart, 1940.

Where There's a Will. New York: Farrar & Rinehart, 1940.

Black Orchids (two novellas, *Black Orchids* and *Cordially Invited to Meet Death*). New York: Farrar & Rinehart, 1942.

Not Quite Dead Enough (two novellas, *Not Quite Dead Enough* and *Booby Trap*). New York: Farrar & Rinehart, 1944.

The Silent Speaker. New York: Viking, 1946.

Too Many Women. New York: Viking, 1947.

And Be a Villain. New York: Viking, 1948.

Trouble in Triplicate (three novellas, *Before I Die, Help Wanted, Male,* and *Instead of Evidence*). New York: Viking, 1949.

The Second Confession. New York: Viking, 1949.

Three Doors to Death (three novellas, *Man Alive, Omit Flowers,* and *Door to Death*). New York: Viking, 1950.

In the Best Families. New York: Viking, 1950.

Murder by the Book. New York: Viking, 1951.

Curtains for Three (three novellas, *The Gun with Wings, Bullet for One,* and *Disguise for Murder*). New York: Viking, 1951.

Triple Jeopardy (three novellas, *Home to Roost, The Cop Killer,* and *The Squirt and the Monkey*). New York: Viking, 1952.

Prisoner's Base. New York: Viking, 1952.

The Golden Spiders. New York: Viking, 1953.

The Black Mountain. New York: Viking, 1954.

Three Men Out (three novellas, *Invitation to Murder, The Zero Clue,* and *This Won't Kill You*). New York: Viking, 1954.

Before Midnight. New York: Viking, 1955.

Three Witnesses (three novellas, *The Next Witness, When a Man Murders,* and *Die like a Dog*). New York: Viking, 1956.

Might as Well Be Dead. New York: Viking, 1956.

Three for the Chair (three novellas, *A Window for Death, Immune to Murder,* and *Too Many Detectives*). New York: Viking, 1957.

If Death Ever Slept. New York: Viking, 1957.

Champagne for One. New York: Viking, 1958.

And Four to Go (four novellas, *Christmas Party, Easter Parade, Fourth of July Picnic,* and *Murder Is No Joke*). New York: Viking, 1958.

Plot It Yourself. New York: Viking, 1959.

Three at Wolfe's Door (three novellas, *Poison a la Carte, Method Three for Murder,* and *The Rodeo Murder*). New York: Viking, 1960.

Too Many Clients. New York: Viking, 1960.

The Final Deduction. New York: Viking, 1961.

Gambit. New York: Viking, 1962.

Homicide Trinity (three movellas, *Eeny Meeny Murder Mo, Death of a Demon,* and *Counterfeit for Murder*). New York: Viking, 1962.

The Mother Hunt. New York: Viking, 1963.

Trio for Blunt Instruments (three novellas, *Kill Now, Pay Later*; *Murder Is Corny*; and *Blood Will Tell*). New York: Viking, 1964.

A Right to Die. New York: Viking, 1964.

The Doorbell Rang. New York: Viking, 1965.

Death of a Doxy. New York: Viking, 1966.

The Father Hunt. New York: Viking, 1968.

Death of a Dude. New York: Viking, 1969.

Please Pass the Guilt. New York: Viking, 1973.

A Family Affair. New York: Viking, 1975.

Collections of Short Nero Wolfe Fiction

Justice Ends at Home and Other Stories, edited by John McAleer. New York: Viking, 1977.

Death Times Three. New York: Bantam, 1985.

Under the Andes. New York: Penzler Books, 1985.

An Officer and a Lady, and Other Stories. New York: Carroll & Graf, 2000.

Target Practice. Thorndike, ME: G.K. Hall, 1998.

Three at Wolfe's Door. New York: Bantam, 1995.

Other Novels by Rex Stout

How Like a God. New York: Vanguard, 1929.

Seed on the Wind. New York: Vanguard, 1930.

Golden Remedy. New York: Vanguard, 1931.

Forest Fire. New York: Farrar & Rinehart, 1933.

The President Vanishes, 1934; rpt. New York: Pyramid, 1967.

O Careless Love! New York: Farrar & Rinehart, 1935.

The Hand in the Glove: A Dol Bonner Mystery. New York: Farrar & Rinehart, 1937.

Mr. Cinderella. New York: Farrar & Rinehart, 1938.

Double for Death: A Tecumseh Fox Mystery. New York: Farrar & Rinehart, 1939.

Mountain Cat, 1939, repub. as *The Mountain Cat Murders*. New York: Dell, 1943.

Red Threads (an Inspector Cramer mystery). New York: Farrar & Rinehart, 1939.

Bad for Business (a Tecumseh Fox mystery). New York: Farrar & Rinehart, 1940.

The Broken Vase: A Tecumseh Fox Mystery. New York: Farrar & Rinehart, 1941.

Alphabet Hicks: A Mystery, 1941; repub. as *The Sound of Murder*. New York: Pyramid, 1965.

Corsage (a miscellany). Florence, SC: Rock, 1977.

Under the Andes. New York: Mysterious Press, 1985.

Cookbook

The Nero Wolfe Cookbook (with others). New York: Viking, 1973.

OTHER WOLFE NOVELS

Nero Wolfe Novels by Robert Goldsborough, all published by Bantam Books, New York.

Murder in E minor, 1986

Death on Deadline, 1987

The Bloodied Ivy, 1988

The Last Coincidence, 1989

Fade to Black, 1990

Silver Spire, 1992

The Missing Chapter, 1994

"August Lupa" Novels by John Lescroart

(Lescroart strongly implies that Lupa is the son of Sherlock Holmes and Irene Adler.)

Son of Holmes. New York: New American Library, 1986 (reissued 2003)

Rasputin's Revenge. New York: New American Library, 1987 (reissued 2003)

ADAPTATIONS

Movies

Nero Wolfe (adapted from *Fer-de-Lance*), Columbia Pictures (1936); Edward Arnold as Nero Wolfe, Lionel Stander as Archie Goodwin

The League of Frightened Men, Columbia Pictures (1937); Walter Connolly as Nero Wolfe, Lionel Stander as Archie Goodwin

Radio

The Adventures of Nero Wolfe (1943–1944); ABC, 34 20-minute episodes; Santos Ortega as Nero Wolfe, John Gibson as Archie Goodwin; Louis Vittes as scriptwriter; no Stout story material used.

The Amazing Nero Wolfe (1945–1946), MBC; Francis X. Bushman as Nero Wolfe, Elliot Lewis as Archie Goodwin; no Stout story material used.

The New Adventures of Nero Wolfe (1950–1951), NBC; 26 30-minute episodes; Sydney Greenstreet as Nero Wolfe; various actors played Archie Goodwin.

Rex Stout's Nero Wolfe (1982), CBS; 13 60-minute episodes; Mavor Moore as Nero Wolfe, Don Francks as Archie Goodwin (released on audiocassette by Durkin Hayes Publishing (DH Audio).

Television (U.S.)

"The Fine Art of Murder" (December 9, 1956), 40-minute segment (*Omnibus*) with Rex Stout and hosted by Alistair Cooke, showing a homicide as various authors would treat it fictionally.

Nero Wolfe (1979), Paramount Television; telefilm; (based on *The Doorbell Rang*), Thayer David as Nero Wolfe, Tom Mason as Archie Goodwin.

Nero Wolfe (1981), Paramount Television, 24-week series on NBC-TV; William Conrad as Nero Wolfe, Lee Horsley as Archie Goodwin, set in contemporary New York.

The Golden Spiders (March 2000), Jaffe/Brownstein Films with A&E Television (*A Nero Wolfe Mystery* telefilm).

A Nero Wolfe Mystery (2001–2002), A&E Television series, Maury Chaykin as Nero Wolfe, Timothy Hutton as Archie Goodwin, set in 1940s to 1960s; on DVD.

Foreign Television

Zu viele Küche (*Too Many Cooks*) (1961); NWRV-Hamburg, German miniseries

RAI (an Italian network) (1969–1971); broadcast black-and-white Nero Wolfe telefilms; 10 episodes available on DVD

Pola Ya Ne Umer (2001–2002); first of five Russian Nero Wolfe television movies, written by Vladimir Valutsky, writer of the previous Russian Sherlock Holmes series

Comic Strip

Nero Wolfe Comic Strip: written by John Broome (credited to Rex Stout), art by Mike Roy.

ARCHIVE

Rex Stout's manuscripts, personal papers, and the most complete collection of his published works are held in the Burns Rare Book Library at Boston College.

WORKS CITED

Beiderwell, Bruce. "State Power and Self-Destruction; Rex Stout and the Romance of Justice." *Journal of Popular Culture* 27 (Summer 1993): 13–22.

Buffington, Robert. "Sunday Evening with Nero Wolfe." *Sewanee Review* 114 (Winter 2006): 126.

Congdon, Don. *The Thirties: A Time to Remember.* New York: 1962.

Darby, Ken. *The Brownstone House of Nero Wolfe, as Told by Archie Goodwin.* Boston: Little, Brown, 1977.

Herbert, Rosemary. *Whodunit? A Who's Who in Crime and Mystery Writing.* New York: Oxford University Press, 2003.

Hilliard, Don, and Kevin Burton Smith. http://www/thrillingdetective.com/wolfe.html, accessed 7/8/2007.

Johnson, Paul. *Modern Times,* rev. ed. New York: HarperCollins, 1991.

Keating, H.R.F. *Crime and Mystery: The 100 Best Books.* New York: Carroll & Graf, 1987.

Kiser, Marcia. "Nero Wolfe: A Social Commentary on the U.S." http://www.thrillingdetective.com/non_fiction/e002.html, accessed 7/8/2007.

Langford, David. "A Stout Fellow." http://www.ansible.co.uk/writing/rexstout/html, accessed 7/8/2007; originally published in *Million* Magazine, 1992.

McAleer, John. *Rex Stout: A Majesty's Life.* Millennial Ed. Rockville, MD: James A. Rock, 2002.

Mitgang, Herbert. *Dangerous Dossiers: Exposing the Secret War Against America's Greatest Authors.* New York: Donald I. Fine, 1988.

Murphy, Bruce. *The Encyclopedia of Murder and Mystery.* New York: St. Martin's Press, 1999.

Penzler, Otto. *The Private Lives of Private Eyes, Crimefighters & Other Good Guys.* New York: Grosset & Dunlap, 1977.

Review of *If Death Ever Slept* (sound recording). *Publishers Weekly* 249 (April 1, 2002): 30.

"Rex Stout." Contemporary Authors Online. http://web2.infotrac.galegroup.com.

Symons, Julian. "In Which Archie Goodwin Remembers," in *Great Detectives: Seven Original Investigations.* New York: Abrams, 1981: 42–61.

———. *Mortal Consequences.* New York: Harper & Row, 1972.

Van Dover, Kenneth. *At Wolfe's Door: The Nero Wolfe Novels of Rex Stout,* 2nd ed. Rockville, MD: James A. Rock, 2003.

———. *Murder in the Millions.* New York: Continuum, 1984.

Wilson, Edmund. "The Literary Consequences of the Crash," in *The Shores of Light.* New York: Farrar, Straus and Young, 1952.

Winn, Dilys. *Murder Ink.* New York: Workman, rev. ed., 1984.

FURTHER READING

Anderson, David R. *Rex Stout.* New York: Ungar, 1984.

Baring-Gould, William S. *Nero Wolfe of West Thirty-fifth Street.* New York: Viking, 1969.

Barkocy, Muffy. "Nero Wolfe's Cases." http://www.things.org/~muffy/pages/books/rex_stout/bibliography.html, accessed 7/12/2007.

Barzun, Jacques. *A Birthday Tribute to Rex Stout, December 1, 1965.* New York: Viking, 1965.

Bergman, Anne. "On the Horizon: A&E." *Daily Variety* 269 (November 28, 2000): A16.

Bourne, Michael. "An Informal Interview with Rex Stout." *Corsage: A Bouquet of Rex Stout and Nero Wolfe.* Rockville, MD: James A. Rock, 1977.

DeVoto, Bernard. "Alias Nero Wolfe." *Harper's Magazine,* July 1954, pp. 8ff.

Forbes, Malcolm S., Jr. "Neo Nero Wolfe." *Forbes* 151 (March 1, 1993): 26.

Gotwald, Frederick G. *The Nero Wolfe Handbook.* Self-published essays; 1985, rev. 1992, 2000.

"The House on 35th Street: Nero Wolfe & Archie Goodwin at Home." http://john claytonsr.com/Wolfe/Intro.htm, accessed 7/8/2007.

Kaye, Marvin. *The Archie Goodwin Files.* New York: Wildside Press, 2005.

———. *The Nero Wolfe Files.* New York: Wildside Press, 2005.

Killen, Michael. "Actress Plays Multiple Roles in 'Nero Wolfe' Series. *Chicago Tribune* April 12, 2002.

http:/geocities.com/Athens/8907/wolfe_rl.html?20078, accessed 7/8/2007.

Louis, Winnifred. "Wolfe's Reading List" (modified 3 February 2001). http://www.geocities.com/Athens/8907/wolfe, accessed 7/8/2007.

Martinez, Jose A. "Hutton Handles Dual Role on 'Wolfe.'" *Multichannel News* 22 (April 9, 2001): 20.

Mason, M.S. "Cracking the Case of Sherlock Holmes." *Christian Science Monitor* 92 (March 3, 2000): 17.

McAleer, John. *Royal Decree: Conversations with Rex Stout.* Ashton, MD: Pontes Press, 1983.

McBride, O.E. *Stout Fellow: A Guide through Nero Wolfe's World.* iUniverse, 2003.

Oxman, Steven. "*The Golden Spiders:* A Nero Wolfe Mystery." *Daily Variety* 266 (March 2, 2000): 9.

Prescott, Jean. "Actress Adds More than Dimples to A&E Series 'Nero Wolfe.'" *The Sun Herald* (Biloxi, MS): April 11, 2002.

———. "Tim Hutton Settles into Archie Goodwin's Skin in 'Nero Wolfe.'" *The Sun Herald* (Biloxi, MS): April 16, 2001.

"Rex Stout House." http://www.things.org/muffy/pages/books/rex_stout/house .html, accessed 7/8/2007.

Rimoldi, Oscar. "The Detective Movies of the 30s and 40s." *Films in Review* 44 (May/June 1993): 165–175.

Rogers, Michael. "Nero Wolfe: The Complete First Season." *Library Journal* 129 (December 1, 2004): 178.

Sobczak, A.J. Review of *Silver Spire. Magill Book Reviews,* December 1, 1992.

Spiesman, Anthony. "Nero Wolfe Consultation." *Murder Ink.* New York: Workman, 1977.

Teachout, Terry. "A Nero as Hero." *National Review,* August 12, 2002: 51–52.

"The Psychology of Rex Stout, Nero Wolfe and Archie Goodwin." http://abelard .org/nero_wolfe.php, accessed 7/8/2007.

Townsend, Guy M. "Rex Stout." *The St. James Guide to Crime and Mystery Writers.* Detroit, MI: St. James Press, 1996.

———, and John McAleer, *The Work of Rex Stout: An Annotated Bibliography and Guide.* San Bernardino, CA: Borgo Press, 1995.

Upstead, R. Thomas. "A&E Cans 'Nero Wolfe.'" *Multichannel News,* August 26, 2002: 2.

Ward, Greg. *The Timeline History of the USA.* New York: Barnes & Noble, 2005.

WEB SITES

http://www/nerowolfe.org (The Wolfe Pack, official site of the Nero Wolfe Society)

http://www.danlhos.com/wolfe/ (The Nero Wolfe Database, with all plot and character summaries)

http://www.geocitiers.com/Athens/8907/nero.html (Winnifred Louis; complete annotated bibliography plus Wolfe fan site)

Matt Rawle as Zorro on poster from *Zorro the Musical* (London). (© Robbie Jack/CORBIS.)

Zorro:
The Masked Avenger

Justice for All!

—Zorro's Motto

Zorro!

> Just say the name and images flood your mind: the devilishly simple mask, the
> dashing black cape, the fiercely rearing steed . . . moonlit assignations with
> smitten señoritas and a righteous demand for justice from a sneering
> Gobernador . . . narrow escapes, swashbuckling battles and always, finally,
> the triumph of Good over Evil. . . . the ability of the story to win us over is
> nothing short of astonishing. (Taccone 74)

Zorro, "the Fox," has become "an intergenerational, cross-cultural icon"[*]
(Curtis 10).

Since 1919, the dashing masked Hispanic avenger created by Johnston
McCulley has fascinated readers of pulp fiction, enraptured moviegoers,
and captivated television audiences throughout the world, slashing Zs on
villains and wooing a succession of beauteous dark-eyed damsels, Everyman's quintessential high-stakes hero, and Everywoman's dream of passionate romance. McCulley loved history, and he drew on deep roots of
European Spanish culture, roots that anchored the traditions of Alta California, the northernmost part of Spain's first Viceroyalty in the New World
and later a province of Mexico: Spain's geographic insularity and history of
invasions; its often savage Roman Catholicism; and *españolismo,* traits of
temperament that shaped and still dominate Hispanic literature.

HISTORICAL/CULTURAL CONTEXT

Bordered by the Mediterranean Sea, the Atlantic Ocean, and the Bay of Biscay
and separated from Europe by the formidable Pyrenees, Spain, a poor land of
few natural resources, experienced several foreign conquests in its earliest history. The Phoenicians established trading colonies there by the 11th century
BCE; the Carthaginians conquered most of Spain in the 3rd century BCE only to
be vanquished themselves by Rome during the Punic Wars, 264 to 146 BCE.
Spain became Romanized and integrated into the Roman Empire, adhering to
Roman law and many Roman cultural norms even after being overrun by Germanic tribes starting in 409 CE. Spain's fiercely Christian Visigothic kingdom,
established in 415, collapsed when a Moslem army from North Africa defeated
its king in 711, beginning a 700-year domination of Spain by the Moors.

Arabic translations of Greek and Roman studies at Moorish universities
in Spain gradually filtered classical thought into the rest of Europe, helping
dispel the Dark Ages. Within Spain, the Moors established prosperous cities,

---

[*]Note: For datings, see Matthew Baugh's "The Legacy of the Fox: A Chronology of
Zorro."

fine architecture, and well-regulated agriculture and industries, but they were divided among themselves and could not control the entire Iberian peninsula. Resentment against foreign overlords bred bitter resentment, and in 1094 Spain's national hero, Rodrigo Díaz de Bivar, "El Cid," the "*Compeador*" or "Champion," reconquered Moorish Valencia, ruling there as the prototype of the noble, chivalrous, and generous Castilian warrior commemorated in *The Song of the Cid,* Spain's 12th-century national epic. The Moors never conquered Asturias, and as the Christian territories of Leon, Castile, and Aragon became more powerful, Moorish influence waned. After centuries of bitter conquests, defeats, and reconquests, Christians had regained almost all of Spain by 1400. In 1469 Ferdinand of Aragon married Isabella of Castile, uniting most of Spain, and Granada, the last Moorish stronghold in Spain, fell in 1492, the year Columbus discovered America. A new Spain was born.

Known as "*Los Reyes Catolicos*" ("The Catholic monarchs"), Ferdinand and Isabella championed the work of the Spanish Inquisition, established in 1478 by Pope Sixtus IV to stamp out heresy. The medieval Holy Office of the Inquisition, begun in 1233, could employ judicial torture, but it usually left executions to secular authorities. Spanish Christianity, however, had developed a tradition of intolerance under its Visigothic rulers, "the most zealous of European Catholics, savagely intolerant of heretics and unbelievers," who had already in the early 7th century persecuted Jews so cruelly that even some members of the clergy had tried unsuccessfully to intercede (Horton and Hopper 323). Centuries later, the Spanish Inquisition, originally directed to spy out Moslem and Jewish *conversos* thought to be insincere about their new Christianity and extort financial proof of their conversion, became a kind of thought police. Fearsomely organized by the Grand Inquisitor Torquemada, firmly backed by Spanish monarchs, and not abolished until 1820, the Spanish Inquisition employed vicious means of torture, often including death by burning in *autos da fé* (acts of faith), from which no Spaniard was safe.

Spanish literature vividly represents *españolismo,* the defining characteristics of the Spanish temperament: stoicism, physical courage, fierce individualism often carried to the point of egotism, and enormous disdain for the foreigner. In addition, Spanish *hidalgos* (noblemen), whose first names carried the honorific "Don," prided themselves on their elaborate etiquette, their grandiose behavior and grandiloquent language, their personal courtesy, and their hypersensitivity to "points of honor," especially their extreme concern for the reputations of their women. A woman whose honor had been impugned in the slightest degree had only two choices, marriage or the convent, and her male relatives were honor bound to seek physical revenge. Spanish literature has given the world two remarkable examples of *españolismo:* Don Juan, first seen in Tirso de Molina's *The Trickster of Seville* (1630), whose "scorn for women, convention, and even death highlights Spanish individualism, rebellion against the mundane, and passion for living one's life with a flair"; and Cervantes' gallantly befuddled Don Quixote, the embodiment of Spain's refusal to come to terms with reality (Horton and Hopper 326).

Don Juan and Don Quixote appeared during the 17th-century Golden Age of Spanish literature, which paradoxically followed Spain's downfall from its apex of power in the 1500s. The gold and silver and other riches of the New World had catapulted Spain to unprecedented wealth, but its thirst to extend Spanish Catholicism throughout Europe led to disaster. The Spanish Netherlands revolted against the Inquisition in 1581 and Philip IV's Invincible Armada, defeated by the English in 1588, bankrupted the country. The Thirty Years' War (1618 to 1648) between Catholics and Protestants further diminished Spanish prestige, and with its economy hopelessly ruined and its ordinary people desperately impoverished, Spain tottered toward total humiliation. In 1808, Napoleon set his brother Joseph Bonaparte on the Spanish throne, and the Latin American wars of independence (1810 to 1825) resulted in the loss of most of Spain's former empire.

As a part of that empire, Mexico, conquered for Spain by Cortes in 1519, became independent in 1821, established its first constitution on the U.S. model in 1824, and elected Antonio Santa Anna president in 1833. California, which had become a part of the Mexican republic in 1821, revolted against Mexican rule in 1835 and became a short-lived republic in 1846; after the Mexican-American War (1846 to 1848), Mexico ceded California to the United States. A year later the Gold Rush erupted, paving the way for statehood in 1850.

Spain's colonization of California by sword and cross had begun in 1769, when Franciscans led by Father Junipero Serra began to establish 21 missions about 30 miles apart—a day's horseback travel—along the dusty *El Camino Real* ("The Royal Road") near the California coast from San Diego in the south to Sonoma in the north. The missions, built with savagely exploited Indian labor and situated on the choicest arable land with good water supplies, flourished so well they later caused significant resentment; they dominated California's early history, generally divided into the Days of the Missions, the romantic Spanish Period (1769 to 1821) and the Days of the Ranchos, the turbulent Mexican Period (1822 to 1848).

The Spanish also built presidios, or frontier forts, usually located at the entrances to chief ports, to protect the missions from Indians and foreign invaders; "military towns" grew up around the presidios, eventually developing into colonial centers. Indian converts, called "neophytes," did most of the menial work for minimal pay—"a string of beads, a dish of porridge, shoes, or a bit of cloth" (Rolle 62–63).

In addition to the missions and the presidios, "civil pueblos," the first real municipalities of California, were founded; the earliest were San José (1777) and Los Angeles (1781). Each centered on a rectangular plaza, with the council house, church, storerooms, the jail, and private houses facing it; bullfights might even have taken place there. Settlers received valuable inducements, like five-year tax exemptions, but they had to provide military service and work their land, which they could not sell. The powers of the alcalde (mayor), who served without pay, were almost unlimited.

For wealthy New World hidalgos and their families, California life in the Days of the Missions was "one continuous round of hospitality and social amenities, tempered with vigorous outdoor sport." California had no hotels then, and every door was open to guests. The name "California" comes from episodes of a 16th-century Spanish romance relating to Amazons, reflecting the relatively emancipated role women played in early California society.

> No white man had to concern himself greatly with work, and even school books were a thing apart. Music, games, dancing, and sprightly conversation . . . constituted education. . . . men and women . . . were expert horsemen, could throw a lasso, and shoot unerringly, even the women. . . . When foreign ships came, there were balls and the gayest of festivals. (Chapman, quoted in Curtis 63)

The aristocratic Spanish settlers also devoured fanciful chivalric romances full of days of swordplay and nights of love and noble revenge, the tales that so deranged poor Don Quixote.

By the Days of the Ranchos, however, the wealth and power that the "haves" of California accumulated led to abuse of the "have nots." In 1810, when the South American independence movements began, Spanish trading ships ceased visiting California ports and the towns, missions, and presidios were left on their own. Trade at the missions in hides and tallow became California's chief economic support, and corruption flourished. As one villain in *Zorro Rides Again* admitted, "I buy hides from the native scum and pay them what I please. The neophytes [natives] are too holy to complain" (quoted in Curtis 66). Between 1822 and 1834, Californians suffered from north-south rivalries within the state as well as from harsh treatment under ruthless Mexican governors who imposed death penalties for minor offenses and exiled people without trials. Although the Spanish had originally intended that the missions should be turned into civilian towns after a decade, no secularization took place for 65 years, and enormous resentment against the Franciscan friars who had built up the wealthy missions led to their persecution.

California rebelled against Mexico and created a short-lived republic, but after the Mexican-American War, the United States paid Mexico $15 million for Alta California; "the Californians became an alien culture in their own land, and a culture clash of eminent proportions developed." Maria Amparo Ruiz de Burton, the first Spanish-Mexican woman writer in the Southwest, observed in her novel *The Squatter and the Don* (1885), "It cannot be denied that the Californians have reason to complain. The Americans must know it: their boasted liberty and equality of rights seem to stop when it meets a Californian. . . . And now we have to beg for what we had the right to demand" (quoted in Ruiz 660).

Because the Protestant American Yankees looked down on the Roman Catholic Californios (persons of Spanish birth or background who settled there during the Spanish and Mexican eras), some Californios responded by becoming *bandidos* like Domingo Hernandez, who collected valuables and human ears from travelers along *El Camino Real*; Joaquin Murieta; and Tiburcio Vasquez, who was widely revered as "an avenger who refused to submit to the American conquest" (Curtis 73–74). Some Chicano scholars, in fact, contend that Vasquez "was feared by the Anglos for his revolutionary potential, and Vasquez himself stated that "Given $60,000 I would be able to recruit enough arms and men to revolutionize Southern California" (Burciaga 8).

From these elements—Spanish history, Spanish literature, and *españolismo;* the romantic traditions of Spanish California; the abuses and outrages wreaked on the innocent by unscrupulous overlords; the legends about Robin Hood-like *bandidos*—Johnston McCulley built his most enduring creation: El Zorro—the Fox, the first cross-cultural hero and defender of the common man.

AUTHORSHIP

Born on February 2, 1883, in Ottawa, Illinois, Johnston McCulley was "a wizard as a history student . . . [who] began writing historical and period serials in high school" and soon began turning out "pulp" fiction under various pen names. Best known for his 65 stories about Zorro and the scripts for the 1957 to 1959 *Zorro* television series, he had also been a special correspondent in the United States and abroad, a screenwriter, and the author of 20 mystery novels and over 100 Western-genre short stories. His interest in California's history led him eventually to move into his daughter Maurine's home in the Lake Arrowhead region of California's San Bernardino Mountains, according to the back copy of the Penguin Signet paperback edition of McCulley's *The Caballeros*. Shortly before his death in 1958, he assigned the Zorro film rights to Mitchell Goetz, a Hollywood agent. Goetz's descendent John Goetz now directs Zorro Productions with his wife, the official Zorro historian Sandra Curtis.

After World War I the United States "was eager for escapist fantasy and the popular romance of the Old West" (Curtis 12). At 36, Johnston McCulley was already seasoned at writing for the "pulps," inexpensive magazines aimed at a popular audience craving exotic locales, high adventure, and gorgeous heroines. In 1919 he sold his first Zorro tale as a serial called *The Curse of Capistrano,* which appeared in novel form in 1920 and is now known as *The Mark of Zorro,* to *All-Story Weekly,* the best of the pulps, which had just published *Tarzan of the Apes.* From then on, McCulley and Zorro, by far his most enduring creation, remained inseparable.

McCulley's "Zorro formula" resembles the dual-identity theme popularized by Baroness Orczy in her highly successful 1905 novel *The Scarlet Pimpernel,* later made into a stage play and a film, though McCulley's knowledge of its versions has not been established. The "Pimpernel," named for a British flower, was the alter ego of English nobleman Sir Percy Blakeney, who saved French aristocrats from the Reign of Terror in France. Curtis sees "remarkable parallels": both heroes are aristocratic, young, handsome, and rich. As Don Diego de la Vega and as Sir Percy, they yawn their way through their "cover" appearances, enjoying fine horses, elegant clothes, and vast estates. As Zorro and the Pimpernel, fighting for the helpless, each leaves a "trademark"—Zorro's "Z" sword strokes and the Pimpernel's primrose. Each first appears in an inn on a rainy night and each persuades a group of young noblemen to follow him. The Pimpernel's wife, Marguerite St. Just, calls Sir Percy an "empty-headed nincompoop," just as Zorro's first beloved, Lolita Pulido, deplores Don Diego as "a laughing stock," but both women praise their heroes' strength, bravery, and the loyalty they inspire in their followers. Both women firmly stand by their men in their darkest hours, "preferring death to betrayal" (Curtis 23). The heroes' motives differ strikingly, however, since the Pimpernel acts out of his yen for dangerous sport, while Zorro spent years training for his self-imposed mission of saving the unfortunate from persecution.

> *So, inside the peacock we find a hawk.*
>
> —The Governor

McCulley may have used real-life sources for his dashing hero and perhaps some "grandiose dream" might have existed of uniting such bands "to liberate Alta California from the gringo usurpers, but such dreams never came to pass" (MacLean 69). One such dreamer was Tiburcio Vasquez (ca. 1835 to 1875), slightly built, typically Castilian with dark hair and light skin, from a respectable middle-class Californio family. His outlaw career began with a brawl in a fandango hall where a lawman was fatally stabbed; widely blamed for the killing, Vasquez did six years (interrupted by one escape) in San Quentin for horse stealing, then another three and a half years for cattle rustling, after which he gathered a gang and robbed stagecoaches. He was hanged for murder around the age of 40, insisting on his innocence to the end. Legend insists "this Don Juan of the Gabilans had many *dulcianas* (sweethearts), scattered from San Jose to San Diego," who sincerely believed that "Vasquez was the victim of prejudice and racial persecution" (MacLean 87).

Less concrete are tales about Joaquin Murieta, "California's greatest legendary badman" (McCulley xviii) whose dubious Robin Hood-like story was published in 1854 by a hack newsman, John Rollin Ridge. Murieta, known as an archfiend or as *el bandido magnifico* depending on one's viewpoint, may have led a robber band terrorizing Central and Southern California for three years in the 1850s. Murieta's real-life nemesis, Captain Love, a former Texas Ranger, in 1853 captured and killed Murieta and pickled his head, adorned by a fierce black moustache, in a glass jar, but the jar and head were lost in the great San Francisco earthquake and fire of 1906.

Still more tenuous is a claim by the "Honourable Society of the Irish Brigade" that behind Zorro's mask was an Irish soldier of fortune from Wexford, William Lamport, who battled French forces in Spanish Flanders in the 1640s, went to Mexico and fought for the poor and native Indians, and became the leader of the Mexican independence movement. He was arrested in the bed of the wife of the Spanish Viceroy of Mexico and in 1659 the Inquisition led him to the stake as a heretic, but he burst his bonds and strangled himself before the flames could reach him ("Real Zorro").

A Zuni proverb insists, "There are no truths, there are only legends." These early outlaw legends share a common theme, the pursuit of justice by "champions fighting for the downtrodden in an unjust culture plagued by rigid class distinctions." Johnston McCulley was "notoriously close-mouthed about the inspiration for Zorro," but just as he fused historical elements of both California's Spanish Period and its Mexican Period into the setting of his Zorro tales, he probably also integrated the story of the Scarlet Pimpernel and the tales about Vasquez and Murieta, and perhaps even those about William Lamport, into his creation of Zorro, "an intrinsic part of New World Culture" (Alexander 48).

PROFILE OF DON DIEGO DE LA VEGA/EL ZORRO

Baugh observes that because of the large number of Zorro-related works, numerous inconsistencies appear even in McCulley's own Zorro stories. Baugh also notes that most film and television versions follow the original Disney *Zorro* series, set in the 1820s, but he believes Zorro's adventures should be anchored by the serial *Zorro's Fighting Legion*, set in 1824, making Diego become Zorro in 1806, as is shown in the film *The Mask of Zorro*.

Masked Avengers (Based on Baugh's Chronology)

Don Diego de la Vega	Zorro	Various sources	Various years
Don Cesar de la Vega	Don Q	*Don Q, Son of Zorro* (movie)	1925
James Vega	Zorro	*Zorro Rides Again* (movie serial)	1937
Jeff Stewart	Zorro	*Son of Zorro* (movie serial)	1947
Ken Munson	Zorro	*The Ghost of Zorro* (movie serial)	1949
Alejandro Murieta	Zorro	*The Mask of Zorro* (movie)	1998

Personal Background and Career of Don Diego de la Vega/Zorro

In Isabel Allende's novel *Zorro* (2005), which departs substantially from McCulley's account of Don Diego's parentage, she claimed that Don Diego's father, Don Alejandro de la Vega, traced his hidalgo ancestry all the way back to Spain's 11th-century epic hero El Cid, who vanquished the Moors of Valencia and became the prototype of the courteous, generous, courageous Spanish grandee. In 1781, the year that the pueblo of La Reina de Los Angeles was founded, Don Alejandro and his wife Dona Chiquita de la Cruz arrived in California. Their son Diego was born the following year, at the beginning of California's Romantic years as a Spanish colony, and after the boy's mother died, Don Alejandro, soon to become alcalde (mayor) of Los Angeles, sent the boy to Madrid to be educated. Lolita Pulido, daughter of the noble but impoverished Pulido family, was born in 1788.

When Diego returned to California in 1806, he discovered that the corrupt Luis Quintero had replaced his father as alcalde. With Captain Juan Ramon, the vicious commander of the presidio, Quintero was brutally exploiting the peasants, the friars, and the Indians. Now 24, Diego adopted a cover identity as a harmless dandy while he became "Zorro," "the Fox," outwitting and defeating Quintero and Ramon in *The Mark of Zorro.* Later Zorro tales preserved Zorro's secret identity. Just before Diego's marriage to Lolita, Ramon, bent on revenge, allied himself with Bardosa the pirate, and Zorro had to fight them both in McCulley's *The Further Adventures of Zorro.* Because Lolita's health was precarious, she then returned to Spain for three years while Diego as Zorro battled the evil Capitan Monastario in most of the short fiction McCulley published in *West* magazine and in the Disney television series.

Around 1807, Don Diego foiled his conniving maternal uncle, Estevan de la Cruz, who had arrived in Los Angeles to make a dishonest fortune. Two years later, Diego traveled to Spain to fetch Lolita home, but he also shared an adventure with the Three Musketeers and their companion D'Artagnan, as recounted in the New World *Zorro* television series, and to duel with the vampire Dracula in the Topps Comics miniseries *Dracula vs. Zorro.* Diego and Lolita returned to California, where he retired as Zorro to prepare for their wedding, but he had to resume the mask to thwart a false and criminal "Zorro" and prove himself innocent of the imposter's crimes in McCulley's *Zorro Rides Again.*

Lolita died of a fever only one season after their marriage. The grieving Diego rode again as Zorro in McCulley's *The Sign of Zorro,* where he met and later married Panchita Canchola and again semi-retired as the Fox. Panchita died in 1811 bearing Diego's son Cesar de la Vega. The following year, Zorro battled with his old nemesis Capitan Monastario in the Topps Comics *Zorro's Renegades* series, and in 1815, he carried on increasingly exotic adventures in the Young Adult titles *Zorro and the Jaguar Warriors* (1998), *Zorro and the Dragon Riders* (1999), and *Zorro and the Witch's Curse*

(2000). Zorro appeared in 1820s adventures in *Zorro: The Dailies—The First Year*, and in 1824 he organized a legion of masked caballeros to thwart a plot against Mexican president Guadalupe Victoria, as portrayed in the Republic serial *Zorro's Fighting Legion*. When Diego returned to Los Angeles, as Zorro he battled another heinous presidio commander, Rafael Montero, the scourge of the pueblo, while as Diego he became Montero's rival for the lovely Esperanza, who appears in the 1998 film *The Mask of Zorro*.

Around 1830, Don Diego made his son Don Cesar his "apprentice Zorro," as seen in the television series *Zorro and Son,* where Don Cesar is incorrectly called "Don Carlos." (Baugh conjectures that in this year Joaquin Murieta, who appears with his younger brother Alejandro in the movie *The Mask of Zorro*, was baptized.) About two years later, Don Cesar became enmeshed in a tangled intrigue in Spain; Don Diego joined him there and cleared him of an archduke's murder in the film *Don Q, Son of Zorro* before returning to California to marry Esperanza. The wicked commander Montero believed Diego was Zorro, but he could not prove it. Elena, the daughter of Diego and Esperanza, was born the following year.

During California's revolt against Mexico in 1835, Montero clashed yet again with Zorro. Esperanza was killed, Diego was imprisoned, the de la Vega hacienda was burned, and Montero took Elena and fled to Spain, to raise her there as his own daughter, as recounted in the prelude to the film *The Mask of Zorro*. Around this time, Jeff Stewart, Diego's second cousin and grandson of Don Estevan de la Cruz, was born. Don Cesar married Dolores de Muro (from *Don Q*) and learned incorrectly that Diego, Esperanza, and Elena had perished in the fire at the de la Vega hacienda, so Don Cesar remained in Spain with Dolores.

Diego himself escaped from prison in 1853, the year Captain Love killed Joaquin Murieta, though Alejandro survived and Montero returned to California with dreams of seizing power. In *The Mask of Zorro*, Diego trained Alejandro Murieta to become the next Zorro; together they defeated Montero and Love, although Don Diego, the original Zorro, was fatally wounded in that confrontation.

The spirit of Zorro could not die, however. Alejandro, the new Zorro, first adopted the alter ego of Alejandro del Castillo y Garcia in *The Treasure of Don Diego,* and when Don Diego's will was revealed at the end of that novel, Alejandro changed his name to de la Vega and inherited his father's vast estate, pursuing adventures in the novels *Skull and Crossbones* and *The Secret Horseman* and marrying Elena later in 1853. Their son Joaquin, born the next year, grew up to be called "Ken" to escape the stigma of a Spanish name, and he later became the hero of the serial *The Ghost of Zorro*. Don Cesar's sons Don Ramon de la Vega and Don Manuel de la Vega were born between 1855 and 1860, and in 1865, Jeff Stewart adopted Zorro's mask after returning from the Civil War, as shown in the Republic serial *Son of Zorro*. Successive Zorro relatives include Joaquin "Ken"

Mason, who fought outlaws in 1875 in *The Ghost of Zorro* Republic serial; and Barbara Meredith, Diego's great-granddaughter, who became "The Whip" in 1889 to defeat outlaws attempting to stop Idaho from becoming a state in the Republic serial *Zorro's Black Whip*. In 1910, James Vega was born, Don Ramon's son and thus Don Diego's great-grandson. ("James" is the English version of "Diego.")

James Vega appeared in the adventures of the serial *Zorro Rides Again,* set in 1935, as the last living descendent of Don Diego to bear the surname Vega.

Strengths and Weaknesses of Don Diego/Zorro

In the captivating paradox of the dual identity hero, the apparent weaknesses of one "cover" the strengths of the other. Johnston McCulley's fascination with early California history exposed him to *españolismo,* that unique cultural synthesis that defines the Spanish hidalgo and provides most of his allure: stoicism, physical courage, ferocious individualism, disdain for the foreigner, elaborate etiquette in behavior and language, hypersensitivity to "points of honor," and enormous concern for the safety and chastity of his women. Each of these qualities appears positively in one persona of McCulley's dual hero and is perceived negatively in the other, convincingly maintaining the secret of Zorro's identity. McCulley probably had these qualities in mind when he began to create his most memorable character, as *The Mark of Zorro* shows.

Stoic philosophy, stressing virtue, endurance, and self-sufficiency, took firm root in Spain under Roman rule and endures today in Ernest Hemingway's ideal, reinforced by his admiration for Spanish bullfighting, of *duende*—"grace under pressure." From start to finish of his first adventure, Zorro consistently demonstrates remarkable stoicism and physical courage. In his solitary entrance, masked, with eyes that glitter "ominously," to punish Sergeant Gonzales for brutally beating a native, Zorro holds a roomful of able-bodied men at bay while he engages the sergeant "in the proper manner," and humiliates him (McCulley 16–17), and he declares, "I fight it out alone!" when he and Lolita seem to be facing death (McCulley 253). Zorro endures pain and physical hardships with a smile, and even beset by his foes, he can declare, "I care not, so that I die fighting as a caballero should" (McCulley 251). For the stoic, self-sufficiency resides in self-control; Zorro is always master of his emotions, even at the climactic moment when, loving Lolita passionately, he still tries to convince her to forget him and reap all the benefits of marriage to Don Diego: ". . . it would be folly for you to let my disaster influence your life" (McCulley 252).

At the same time and at every opportunity, Zorro's alter ego the handsome but medium-sized Don Diego displays different courage and stoic behavior, one that his adversaries fatally fail to recognize. At the outset, he

I fight it out alone!

—Zorro

insists that he does not have "the reputation for riding like a fool at risk of my neck, fighting like an idiot with every newcomer, and playing the guitar under every woman's window like a simpleton" (McCulley 8), which his listeners take for laziness. His trademark yawn evidences his apparent boredom with physical and even romantic activity: ". . . he disliked action. He seldom wore his blade, except as a matter of style and apparel. He was damnably polite to all women and paid court to none" (McCulley 9), and he prefers sitting in an ornate carriage to riding his fine horse. To Lolita's disgust, Diego even spares himself the effort of serenading her, telling her he will send a servant to do it instead. Diego's apparent weaknesses, like Zorro's mask and cape, successfully disguise the real man beneath them.

Diego and Zorro share a fierce individualism, evidenced in the frequent use each makes of the pronoun "I." By choice, Zorro fights alone; he sees his work of punishing unjust oppressors as his personal mission, and he generally carries it out by engineering a duel, a one-on-one clash in which he first overcomes, then humiliates, his opponent while dominating the opponent's supporters. Zorro even manages to rescue Lolita and her family from prison with minimal help from a band of young caballeros, riding off with her alone while they attend to her parents. Those around Diego mistake his individualism for selfish avoidance of effort, never suspecting that what appears to be his desire "to rest in peace without hearing of violence and bloodshed" (McCulley 118) actually allows him to function as Zorro. Diego's powerful self-control is evident to his readers, though not to Captain Ramon and his minions when Diego forces himself to watch as his friend Fray Felipe endures a savage whipping.

McCulley equipped his Californios with elaborate Hispanic etiquette and formalities of speech. With his enemies and his friends alike, Zorro expresses himself with delicious irony; when rescue appears to be near for Sergeant Gonzales, Zorro declares, "I regret it, for I will not have the time to give you the punishment you deserve" (quoted in McCulley 21). To his deaf and dumb servant Bernardo, Diego speaks as politely as he does to his own father, indicating his respect for all human beings regardless of their station, which most of his society sees as foolish, if not downright weak. For both Diego and Zorro as Spanish caballeros, "blood" in the sense of noble ancestry is also fundamental to their personalities. Although this concept can be carried to silly and egotistical extremes, as Lolita's father Don Carlos does, for Zorro it signifies his responsibility as an aristocrat to care for the people beneath him; for Diego, it means fulfilling his familial duty to marry and carry on his father's name and position.

Regard for personal honor spurs both Diego and Zorro to great deeds. Zorro's dashing exploits are easy to admire, even by most of his enemies, while Diego's passive-appearing actions, as "cover" for Zorro's activities, demand as much, if not more, exertion of principle and character. After

Zorro whips the fat landlord for his treachery, he taunts his adversaries, but politely: "There are not enough of you to make a fight interesting, *señores*" (quoted in McCulley 156). Diego, on the other hand, drinks for a little while with the same group Zorro had taunted, then sits aside and listens, "as if such foolishness bored him" (McCulley 164), quietly planning to use them for his own purposes. Both men deeply respect Lolita's honor; Zorro rewards Ramon's attempt to kiss her with a well-planted boot, while Diego's elegant language subtly warns the governor that imprisoning Lolita and her parents may lead to his downfall: "Men of good blood hate to see such a thing, and there may be murmurings" (McCulley 197), a warning which the arrogant governor fails to recognize.

As McCulley first portrayed him, the gallant deeds of Zorro the Fox demonstrate by action the quintessential inheritance of "blood" that defined the caballero, which even most of his enemies must acknowledge. Diego, by his passive-appearing behavior, lulls their suspicions effectively by using their own desire to think him a fool against them, a stratagem requiring as much courage, cool self-control, wit, and insight as Zorro's swashbuckling deeds do: together Diego/Zorro represent *españolismo* at its dashing acme.

Opponents of Diego/Zorro

In his first Zorro novel, McCulley gave his dual hero three opponents, each reflecting a different aspect of official corruption. Diego's friend, beer-swilling Sergeant Pedro Gonzales, with his trademark "Meal mush and goat's milk!," plays the buffoon, futilely lurching in pursuit of Zorro. Captain Ramon, more intelligent and thus more sinister, not only attempts to compromise Lolita's honor, but falsely accuses Diego and his powerful father Don Alejandro of treason in a letter to the governor. The governor himself epitomizes the hypocritical, self-serving politician; confronted by Diego over the imprisonment of the Pulidos, the slippery governor insists, "Look at what I was forced to do today! I am called upon to put in prison a man of good blood, and his lady wife and tender daughter. But the state must be protected" (McCulley 196), illustrating how effectively the politician avoids responsibility by using the grammatical "divine passive."

Associates of Diego/Zorro

Because of their fierce individualism, neither Diego nor Zorro needs or wants a Dr. Watson-like partner. Instead, minor characters strengthen the hero's desire to protect the innocent. McCulley ignored the severe historical role Spanish Catholicism played in subjugating the natives and instead focused on the courage and goodness of the individual Franciscan friar. In *The Mark of Zorro*, Fray Felipe, falsely accused of improper dealings in hides, helps Diego/Zorro as best he can, voicing the pain of 20 years' injustice under harsh overlords: "They began taking our mission lands from us. . . . They robbed us of worldly goods. And not content with that they now are persecuting us. . . . The mission-empire is doomed, caballero" (McCulley 143). Diego's humble native servant Bernardo, unable to hear or speak, personifies the plight of the Indians under the governor's cruel regime. Zorro's closest assistant in his first adventure is his noble horse, here unnamed but later called "Tornado," able to understand and obey his master's coded whistles and willing to charge at crowds of mounted enemies at the touch of Zorro's spurs.

Diego/Zorro and Romance

In Californio culture, women were held as inviolate as possible until marriage. They were wooed romantically, with serenades and well-chaperoned activities, while their parents engineered alliances with noble families of equal or better "blood." The clothing of the period reflected the relative positions of noble men and women; a man's fiesta outfit included deerskin shoes embroidered with gold or silver, velvet breeches and jacket, similarly adorned, a red satin sash around the wearer's slender waist, and a wide sombrero with silver or gold cord, tipped jauntily to one side, and his horse was nearly covered with embroidered trappings, its saddle and bridle mounted in solid silver. Compared to men's dress, women's clothing was colorful but plainer, trimmed in lace with pearl necklace and earrings, flounced scarlet petticoats, and blue satin shoes. An ideal wife was deeply respected for her piety and fidelity, but subservient to her husband in all things.

Parental authority among Californios was so profound that a father could legally flog his married children. Obedient to his father's demand that he marry to carry on the de la Vega name and fortune, Diego nonetheless chooses an unconventional woman, one who complements his dual role in his society. As daughter of a noble family now the target of the governor's animosity, the gorgeous Lolita Pulido matches Zorro in "blood," in audacity, in defense of her honor, and even in horsemanship. At first as disgusted with Don Diego's apparent languor and ineffectuality as she is enraptured by Zorro's daring kiss on her "pink, moist palm," Lolita gradually begins to respect Diego for his compassion, his tact, and his love of poetry, while she defies her Roman Catholic faith to seize a dagger and threaten suicide rather than accept a dishonorable escape from what appears to be certain death beside Zorro. Once Zorro reveals himself as Don Diego, Lolita declares, "I had fancied that I loved Señor Zorro, but it comes to me now that I love the both of them" (McCulley 265); Zorro, personifying the passionate, mysterious, bold lover, and Diego, the cultured, wealthy, devoted swain, together provide Lolita—and a host of female fans—with an irresistible romantic hero.

Major Portrayers of Zorro	
Douglas Fairbanks, Sr.	George Hamilton
Tyrone Power	Duncan Regehr
Guy Williams	Antonio Banderas and
Alain Delon	Anthony Hopkins

ZORRO'S DEVELOPMENT IN POPULAR MEDIA

Since 1919, each successive generation has found a popular image of Zorro that satisfies its own needs, so the Fox has undergone several transformations as he moved from fiction to popular films, television, comics, and theater, chronicled in detail by Sandra Curtis in *Zorro Unmasked* (1998), the most thorough and reliable historical guide to Zorro lore available.

Douglas Fairbanks Sr., the silent screen actor who first portrayed Zorro, liked to entertain friends with tall tales about California's legendary *bandido* Tiburcio Vasquez, but whether Johnston McCulley used such tales in either his initial Zorro story or the 64 that followed is not known. McCulley did take liberties with history for local color; he mingled historical periods, flavored his stories with Spanish words, created a presidio for Los Angeles that never existed, and may have drawn on *bandido* stories for his later Zorro fiction. McCulley's original hero and his supporting cast received their first transformation on the large silver screen.

Popular as McCulley's first Zorro novel was in 1919, Zorro's legacy might not have survived without the "remarkable athletic and comic talents" of Douglas Fairbanks Sr. in portraying the silent film Zorro (Curtis 25). Fairbanks, obsessively devoted to physical fitness, had been successfully playing acrobatic comedic roles in topical social farces and had just married America's silent screen sweetheart Mary Pickford when he came across McCulley's *The Curse of Capistrano*. Playing Zorro would allow Fairbanks to combine his athletic prowess with "a classically romantic, heroic figure" (Curtis 24) from a titillating historical period. He wrote, produced, and starred in the film he called *The Mark of Zorro* (1920), and according to his son Douglas Fairbanks Jr. ". . . it turned out to be the most successful movie he had ever made . . . his trademark for years to come" (quoted in Curtis 30).

Fairbanks' portrayal of Zorro showcased his athleticism, especially his fencing, but he won more praise as a wistful, languid, and comic Don Diego, flaunting an elegant lace handkerchief and embellishing the role with magic tricks, recalling the comic hero of the classic Spanish author Tirso de Molina's *The Trickster of Seville*. Fairbanks's adaptation of McCulley's novel, centered on "avenging Lolita's honor" (Curtis 43), added many humorous touches and climaxed with Zorro's rescue of Lolita from Ramon, never revealing Zorro's true identity.

In 1925, Fairbanks played both Don Cesar, Zorro's son, and a gray-haired Don Diego in the film *Don Q, Son of Zorro*. Cesar, in Spain to travel and study, was falsely accused of murdering an archduke, and his father Diego had to come to clear his name. Fairbanks gave Zorro two new capabilities, mastery of the Australian stock whip and dancing the fandango, and audiences and critics alike loved *Don Q*'s light comic spirit. According to Curtis, "no actor has imbued the California defender of justice with such panache or given Diego such a contrasting, humorous persona" (53).

The first talking Zorro film, Republic Pictures' *The Bold Caballero* (1936), starring Robert Livingstone, significantly departed from McCulley's original Zorro formula. As adapted by Wells Root from a suggestion by McCulley, Diego incited a peons' revolt to undo a wicked commandant who had usurped Zorro's signature "Z."

During the Great Depression, Republic Pictures (known familiarly as the "Thrill Factory") aimed to provide its increasingly sophisticated audiences with escapist entertainment involving fast-paced action, slick photography, spectacular stunts devised and enacted by Yakima Canutt, exciting music, and rousing story lines. Each 19-minute episode of Republic's seven serialized Zorro adventures ended with a spectacular cliffhanger: *Zorro Rides Again* (1937), *Zorro's Fighting Legion* (1939), *Zorro's Black Whip* (1944), *Son of Zorro* (1947), *Ghost of Zorro* (1949), *Don Daredevil Rides Again* (1951), and *Man with the Steel Whip* (1954). Notable Zorros from these serials included John Carroll, Reed Hadley, George Turner, and Clayton Moore, who later starred as the Lone Ranger. Several new "signature behaviors" also appeared in *Zorro's Fighting Legion* before being used in the Disney television series: Zorro's white horse, Phantom, reared with his rider for the first time and he and Zorro leapt a gorge to escape pursuers; Zorro swung from chandeliers; and he neatly sliced an adversary's waistband so that his trousers comically fell down.

In 1940, Twentieth Century Fox remade *The Mark of Zorro* with Tyrone Power as Diego/Zorro and Basil Rathbone as his nemesis Captain Esteban. Power, a reigning Hollywood heartthrob and a gifted professional actor with aspirations to classical drama, appeared longer in this film as Diego than he did as Zorro. Because Twentieth Century Fox had dubbed the film into six Spanish idioms to capitalize on the Hispanic hero, Power enjoyed immense success in Latin America for this role, where Diego learned that his father lost his position as alcalde (mayor) through the machinations of Captain Esteban. Zorro, while wooing Lolita, had to restore justice to the pueblo while Diego shone with magic tricks and deft dialogue. Given its many departures from McCulley's original plot and the excising of Sergeant Gonzales, Bernardo, and the whole Pulido family, and considering that Power was more actor than athlete, critics either loved or hated this version of *The Mark of Zorro*. One commentator even believes that "The 'straight' or 'cover story' of Tyrone Power's Diego masks the secret of a queer textuality coexisting with heterosexual discourse in the caped crusader's oeuvre" (Williamson 3).

Twentieth Century Fox reshot *The Mark of Zorro* in 1974 as a pedestrian television movie, with Frank Langella as a "somber and humorless" hero, Ricardo Montalban as Esteban, and Gilbert Roland as Don Alejandro, who seemed to have become the real hero of this film, rallying the caballeros and sending the wicked usurper back to Spain (Curtis 115). Tepid swordplay and weak casting seemed to have blunted the Vega sword in this adaptation.

Zorro's Basic Equipment

Australian stock whip	Horses Tornado (black)
Black cape	and Phantom (white)
Black mask	Sword

Zorro and his rearing black stallion Tornado exploded into baby boomers' homes via the black-and-white Disney television series that began on October 10, 1957, the first to present a Hispanic role model/hero figure. It starred Guy Williams, a hitherto unknown model and actor of Italian descent and an excellent professionally trained fencer, like his father and uncles. When Williams interviewed for the part, his wife Jan recalled, ". . . he came home . . . so excited about it, because it . . . absolutely fit his personality and background and everything about him" (quoted in Curtis 125). The Zorro series was "the biggest-budget western production of its time" (Swanson 268), its set alone costing over $100,000. For Zorro, Walt Disney originally wanted Britt Lomond, a highly ranked college and amateur fencer, but writer-director Norman Foster convinced Disney to use Williams as Zorro and Lomond as Captain Monasterio. Williams thus became not only an American television idol but a national hero in Argentina, where he died in 1989. The cast also included Henry Calvin as McCulley's stout and jovial Sergeant Garcia, Diego's source for information on his enemies' movements; Gene Sheldon as a short Bernardo, now a clever magician and mime; and George J. Lewis, the only Hispanic cast member, as Don Alejandro. Disney dropped the character of Fray Felipe, the Catholic moral conscience of the series, after four episodes of the first season.

Changes in the portrayal of Diego/Zorro again reflected changes in American society. Walt Disney himself supervised the initial episodes closely, insisting that Diego should be "nonviolent and studious, but . . . not a wimp" (quoted in Curtis 134), because 1950s audiences would be bored by a silly fop. Zorro's mission followed McCulley's lead in blaming outsiders, not the Roman Catholic Church, for mistreating the Indians, and Zorro's lethal sword was limited to minimal killings, usually dispatching only those who had seen Don Diego's handsome face behind Zorro's black mask.

Cancelled on May 20, 1959, the Disney series, like Zorro, refused to die. *Zorro*'s theme song ("Out of the night . . .") sold a million copies during the series' two-year run, and over 500 licensed Zorro products generated enormous additional income for Disney and a tidy fortune for Williams, who received 2.5% of all such product sales. Disney combined several episodes of the series into two feature films for foreign markets, *Zorro the Avenger* (1959) and *The Sign of Zorro* (1960). Republic re-released two of its serials, and Twentieth Century Fox also re-released Tyrone Power's *The Mark of Zorro*. Disney made four one-hour Zorro color specials for 1960 to 1961, syndicated its original series for 1965 to 1967, and featured it on the Disney cable channel in 1983. In 1992, it became the only television series to be colorized, so that "the fox so cunning and free" still wins audience's hearts worldwide (Curtis 144). The original Disney *Zorro* series "serves as a model for much that is right and much that is wrong with children's television. It often propounded positive values and altruistic behavior, but it was ultimately one of the first of a long line of productions used solely to deliver a huge number of children to advertisers" (Cooper).

Other television Zorro productions included Filmation's 1980 animated series, incorporating an educational message at the close of each episode, and the 1981 five-episode CBS live-action series *Zorro and Son,* using slapstick humor and off-color wordplay. After considerable startup difficulties, the international New World co-production *Zorro,* filmed in Spain, aired 88 episodes over four seasons on the Family Channel, starring the imposing 6′5″ Canadian actor and fencer Duncan Regehr, whose screen love interest was a beauteous tavern owner and staunch advocate for justice. Spinoffs of this series included a Marvel Comics series and seven novels published in Europe by Sandra Curtis. Licensing of Zorro merchandise picked up again, and Zorro even advocated drug education and crime prevention. The U.S. Arts and Entertainment Network's 1996 one-hour feature "The History of Zorro" for its Biography Series traced the Fox's career with interviews of individuals involved with each stage of the character's development, and Telemundo's 2007 "telenovela" *Zorro: La espada y la rosa* (*Zorro: The Sword and the Rose*) confronted Zorro with vengeful natives, carefree gypsies, feuding relatives, and plenty of love and lust.

Foreign filmmakers, principally in France, Italy, and Spain, have continued to produce many Zorro films. One of the more successful foreign Zorros was played by French star Alain Delon in a 1974 film retaining basic features of McCulley's original novel. *Zorro, The Gay Blade* (1980), an outrageous spoof on Tyrone Power's *The Mark of Zorro,* starred George Hamilton not only as Diego/Zorro, but Diego's "flamingly gay twin, Bunny Wigglesworth" (Curtis 150).

Midsummer 1998 saw Tristar's blockbuster film *The Mask of Zorro,* produced by Steven Spielberg and shot in Mexico City. This serious cinema treatment "plumbed the depths of human anguish across twenty years of tragic loss, thievery, imprisonment, and greed, emerging with measured triumph in rescue, love, and redemption," uniting Anthony Hopkins's "elevated star quality" as an aged Diego with sexy Majorca-born Antonio Banderas (Curtis 187) as his spiritual heir and the new Zorro, Alejandro Murieta. Banderas considers Zorro a classic hero who learns to practice "discipline, respect, and centering oneself" (quoted in Curtis 202); and he told Mark Fineman of the *Los Angeles Times* that Zorro conveys "an important message . . . for the entire Hispanic community. He fought for justice. He fought against poverty. This is an especially important model for kids, especially today and especially here in Mexico" (quoted in Curtis 202). New Zealand director Martin Campbell envisioned a Merlin–King Arthur-type relationship that would pass Zorro's noble mission to a new generation, seeing this Zorro as "the perfect hero . . . he doesn't go out and kill as many bad guys as he can—he cleverly disables them, embarrasses and makes fools of them" (quoted in Curtis 213). Zorro here lives to free the enslaved peasants, and Elena, his love interest, equals him in swordsmanship and passion. Though not as well received as its predecessor, the 2005 sequel *The Legend of Zorro* fuses the legends of Joaquin Murieta and Zorro, as Diego faces a troubled marriage and problems with his dysfunctional family when religious fanatics threaten California's statehood and force him to spend too much time as Zorro.

> Don Diego: *"Do you know how to use that thing?"*
>
> Alejandro Murieta: *"Of course! The pointy end goes into the other man."*
> —*The Mask of Zorro*, 1998

Other Zorro-related ventures—comics, animation, stage productions, games, toys, and other merchandise—sold well, like the Topps Comics 1993 to 1994 series, in which writer Don McGregor gave Zorro a darker side, shown through moral dilemmas, and endowed his villainous adversaries with complex motivations. McGregor's Zorro knew "he couldn't save people from their own destructive instincts" (Curtis 234). *TV Guide* (October 25–31, 1997) praised Warner Brothers' 1997 weekend cartoon series for clever 1990s twists: a "feisty female character who shares Zorro's secret," Batman-type gadgetry, "larger-than-life bad guys," and "slam-bang action." In radio, critics praised the BBC's five-part Radio Four Zorro series based on McCulley's first Zorro novel as "an excellent comic-book caper" (quoted in Curtis 244).

Recently Playmates has spun off a dark, brooding Zorro action figure, Heinz Foods sells a Zorro-related salsa, and Zorro introduced Citroen's ZX model car. TOR Books is producing a series of adult Zorro novels by Jerome Preisler, and Santillana is publishing English and Spanish versions of yet another Zorro series. The official Zorro Web site, http://www.zorro. com, premiered in November 1996, and Vintage Library's republications of some of McCulley's original Zorro stories are available at http://www.vintagelibrary. com.

> Zorro: *"You blackmail my soul, no?"*
>
> Fray Felipe: *"Hell yes."*
> —*The Legend of Zorro*, 2005

Theatrical productions of Zorro tales have begun to appear, with swash-buckling swordplay particularly thrilling young audiences in U.S. children's theatre. Other theatrical adaptations include Mexico City's family show *Zorro, El Musical* (1994); Ken Hill's London production *Zorro, the Musical* (1995), "breezy high camp with low agitprop" (quoted in Curtis 243); and a gently satiric Zorro play (1996) in West Palm Beach, Florida, reminding audiences how closely love and justice are linked.

Recent fictional revisionist treatments of Zorro warp the original swash-buckling "masked avenger" concept into trendy psychological theories. In Chilean feminist author Isabel Allende's *Zorro* (2005), she comments on the colonial and postcolonial Americas to her substantial international middle-brow audience through her technique of Magical Realism. Allende's female narrator traces Zorro's parentage—his father Don Alejandro de la Vega marries a rebellious young native woman—to a mission in Monterey, where Diego and Bernardo, his Indian "milk brother," grow up steeped in Californio lore and *okahué*, the Indians' code of honor and courage. Later, in Spain, Diego joins a secret society dedicated to upholding the rights of the oppressed, and transforms himself into Zorro. Newly conscious of his dual identity, "one part Diego de la Vega, elegant, affected, hypochondriac, and the other part El Zorro, audacious, daring, playful," Diego/Zorro "writes his own story in sweat, blood, tears, and signs it . . . Z for Zorro!" (Cheuse 28). Here, however, "Zorro's motivation is sexual desire or love as much as it is justice (Swanson 271). He begins in Barcelona "as a mere stripling with protruding ears and a high-pitched voice" and like a latter-day Don Quixote, he ends up in California, loveless and balding (Swanson 271, 381).

Allende, chosen by John Goetz to write a serious novel about the Fox, portrayed her 21st-century Zorro "not as some arbitrary superhero but as a product of circumstances, influences, and practical social and moral education." This ambiguous and "human, all-too-human" Zorro conveys the "sense of the real nature of the (Latin) American experience and the issues it raises" to those outside it (Swanson 268, 275). Allende's hero vacillates between his Indian warrior heritage and his descent from El Cid. "A third Zorro" even pops up, the narrator Isabel de Romeu (Swanson 373–375), who presents her writing as an adventure, paralleling the pen and the sword. Allende's *Zorro* inspired a 2007 action-filled children's book, *Young Zorro,* showing Diego and Bernardo as brother Indian and Anglo vaqueros on Don Alejandro's rancho, where they jointly help solve cattle rustlings and murders.

Zorro in Hell, premiering in 2006, departed even more from McCulley's legendary Zorro by offering Richard Montoya, Ric Salinas, and Herbert Siguenza, "three fearless comedians" of the San Francisco group Culture Clash "the task of tearing apart the myth of the legendary Masked Man as an insult to Chicano culture" (Taccone 74), but in the course of researching Zorro's complex career, Culture Clash's opinion of Zorro changed, and

"*Zorro in Hell* morphed from a cheeky satire to a bold piece of agitational propaganda." Its Zorro is "more akin to Everyman," with a fragile psyche, a mixed-race heritage, and a "virtually permanent state of confusion"; his heroism comes not from high-born gifts but from simple humanity (Taccone 75).

ZORRO'S LASTING APPEAL

Sergeant Gonzales might say, "Meal mush and goat's milk!" to such latter-day transformations of Zorro into watered-down victims of unfortunate heredity or social injustice. Legend, drawn from his Hispanic roots, sets the Fox apart from the other dual-identity crime fighters he has helped to inspire, like Superman, Batman, Wonder Woman, and Spider-Man. Zorro carries out his self-appointed righteous cause of "justice for everyone" with a unique combination of unquenchable zest, pure joy in humiliating the ungodly, and the irresistible passion of the cross-cultural Latin lover, making him "the hero of Latinos and Anglos alike" (Alexander 47). Attempting to explain Zorro's appeal as a victim of racial prejudice, a woozily confused Everyman (Taccone 76), or even—*ay, caramba!*—a superhero draped in same-sex drag (Williamson 3) is impossible. The real Zorro, the masked avenger as he leapt from Johnston McCulley's first pages, is no flawed real-life hero but the mighty stuff of legend lying at the innocent child's heart beating within nearly every human breast.

The legendary Zorro that inspired Douglas Fairbanks's demanding athleticism, Tyrone Power's grace and gifts, 6'3" Guy Williams's fabulous smile and fearsome fencing, and the masterful performances of Hopkins and Banderas represents "the big brothers many of us never had, defenders who stand up for our rights, and protectors against a callous and all-too-often ruthless world" (Alexander 49). Zorro wears both his black mask and his mask as Don Diego so everyone can ride with him, defy unjust authority with him, punish the wicked, and save the downtrodden with him as Don Quixote wanted to do, and with the best qualities of Don Juan, either win true love or be wonderfully won. Contemporary novelist Arturo Perez-Reverte acknowledges that Zorro is no mere adolescent fantasy but the incarnation of an elemental human belief that each of us, like the fox, "so cunning and free," can improve our world. Perez-Reverte's epigraph for his second Captain Alatriste novel, *Purity of Blood* (1997) (English translation 2006), a swashbuckling adventure set in late 1500s Madrid, conjures up, as Zorro continues to do, that romantic world of imagination out of the Golden Age of Spain, where everyone, deep down, at least for a little while, might most like to be:

> Glory and honor . . .
> . . . and swords flashing on every corner.
>
> —Tomás Borrás, *Castillo*

PARALLEL CHRONOLOGY

Major Events Related to Zorro	World Events
1769 California colonized by Spain; San Diego is founded by Fr. Junipero Serra, as first of 21 Spanish missions in California	
1769–1821 The Days of the Missions (the Spanish Period)	
	1776 U.S. Declaration of Independence
	1776–1783 U.S. Revolutionary War
1781 Founding of Los Angeles; Don Alejandro de la Vega and his wife come to California	
1782–1810 The Romantic Period of California	
1782 Don Diego de la Vega is born; after his mother dies, he is sent to Madrid to be educated	
1784 King of Spain grants private ranchos	
	1787 U.S. Constitution establishes federal system
1788 Lolita Pulido is born	
	1789 The French Revolution
	1800 Mexican independence movement begins, led by two priests, executed in 1810 and 1814
	1803 U.S. Louisiana Purchase
1806 Diego returns to California; his father has been replaced and peasants, priests, and two priests executed	
1806–1809 Lolita returns to Spain for health	
1809 Diego goes to Spain for Lolita; encounters Three Musketeers and Dracula; returns to California and retires as Zorro; marries Lolita, who dies after one season	
1810–1814 Indians are being exploited; Diego poses as a harmless dandy and battles injustice as El Zorro; his marriage to Lolita is foiled; Disney series shows Diego/Zorro's adventures at this time	

Major Events Related to Zorro	World Events
1810 Diego rides again as Zorro; marries Panchita	
1810 Trade opens along Pacific Coast; Spanish ships cease visiting California northward from South America	1810 Independence movement spreading
	1810–1825 Spanish-South American Wars of Independence
1811 Panchita dies bearing son, Don Cesar de la Vega	
1812 Diego rides again as Zorro; events of Topps comics series	1812–1814 War of 1812
	1819 Simon Bolivar proclaims United States of Colombia
1820s Setting of the original Walt Disney Zorro series and the Fairbanks film, the Topps comic series, and all television versions	
1821 California becomes part of Mexican republic	1821 Mexico gains independence from Spain; brief Mexican empire
1822–1848 The Days of the Ranchos (the Mexican Period)	
1822 Rivalries between north and south California began	
1824 Events of *Zorro's Fighting Legion;* Zorro meets Esperanza (who is in movie *Mask of Zorro*)	1824 First Mexican Constitution; all South American colonies liberated from Spain
1830 Diego takes on Don Cesar as "apprentice Zorro"	
1832 Events of movie *Don Q, Son of Zorro*	
1833 Diego marries Esperanza	1833 Antonio de Santa Anna emerges as Mexican President
1834 Secularization begins in California; Indians virtually enslaved; padres losing their power; daughter Elena born to Diego and Esperanza	
1835 California revolts against Mexican rule; Esperanza killed; Diego imprisoned; around this date Jeff Stewart born (Diego's 2nd cousin); Don Cesar marries Dolores and stays in Spain	
	1836 Texas declares independence from Spain
1840s–1850s U.S. judicial system considers Tiburcio Vasquez an outlaw	

(Continued)

Major Events Related to Zorro	World Events
1846 California becomes republic	**1846–1848** Mexican-American War
1848 California ceded to United States; gold strike at Sutter's mill; gold rush begins	**1848** Treaty of Guadalupe Hidalgo; U.S. also claims Texas and areas that became New Mexico and Arizona
1850 California becomes a state; Foreign Miner's Tax imposed	
1850s Joachin Murieta terrorizes Calaveras County	
1853 Murieta killed; Diego escapes from prison, trains Alejandro Murieta to be next Zorro; Diego fatally wounded (*The Mask of Zorro*); events of novel *The Treasure of Don Diego;* Elena and Alejandro marry	
1854 Joaquin, son of Alejandro and Elena, born; later takes name "Ken" and becomes hero of series *The Ghost of Zorro*	
ca. 1855 Don Ramon de la Vega born to Don Cesar	**1857** 2nd Mexican Constitution
	1861–1865 U.S. Civil War
	1864 Napoleon III of France imposes Maximilian as Emperor of Mexico
1865 Jeff Stewart returns from Civil War, takes name of Zorro; events of serial *Son of Zorro*	
	1869 Transcontinental railroad completed
ca. 1871 Barbara Meredith born, Don Diego's great-granddaughter	
1875 Joaquin "Ken" Mason, Diego's grandson, takes name of Zorro; events of serial *The Ghost of Zorro*	
	1876–1910 Dictatorship of Porfirio Diaz in Mexico
1883 Johnston McCulley born	
1889 Barbara Meredith takes on Zorro-like disguise as "the Whip"; events of serial *Zorro's Black Whip*	
	1898 Spanish-American War
1905 Baroness Orczy publishes *The Scarlet Pimpernel*	
1910 James Vega, Diego's great-grandson, born	**1910–1940** Mexican Revolution to overthrow Diaz dictatorship; early revolutionaries included Emiliano Zapata and Pancho Villa; Catholic

Major Events Related to Zorro	World Events
	Church opposes reconstitution of Mexican political authority
1919 Publication of *The Curse of Capistrano* (5-part serial);	
1920 Film, *The Curse of Capistrano*	
1922 6-part serial, *The Further Adventures of Zorro;* published as *The Mark of Zorro* (1924)	
	1928–1930 War of the Cristeros (Mexico); Christian peasants protest against "godless state"; defeated at Battle of Reforma (1930)
ca. 1935 James Vega takes guise of Zorro as last to bear family name "Vega"; events of serial *Zorro Rides Again*	
1936 First talking Zorro film	
	1940–1946 Mexican consolidation and reconciliation
1947 "Zorro Races with Death"	
1957–1959 *Zorro* television series (Disney)	
1958 Johnston McCulley dies	
1959 *The Mask of Zorro,* McCulley's last of 65 Zorro stories	
1994 *Mask of Zorro* exhibit at Gene Autry Western Heritage Museum	
1996 A&E Network: "The History of Zorro" in its Biography Series	
1998 *The Mask of Zorro* (film)	
2005 Isabel Allende's *Zorro* (novel); *The Legend of Zorro* (film)	

SELECTED PRIMARY SOURCES

Novels

Allende, Isabel. *Zorro.* Translated by Margaret Sayers Peden. New York: Harper, 2005.

McCulley, Johnston. *The Mark of Zorro.* 1920; Rpt. ed. New York: TOR, 1998.

Selected Short Fiction

McCulley, Johnston. *Zorro.* Pulp Adventures, 1947.

———. *Zorro: The Master's Edition, Volume One.* Pulp Adventures, 2000

———. *Zorro: The Master's Edition, Volume Two.* Pulp Adventures, 2002

Selected Young Adult Novels and Short Fiction

Adkins, Jan. *Tales of Zorro.* New York: HarperCollins, 2003.

———. *Young Zorro: The Iron Brand.* New York: HarperCollins, 2005.

Bergantino, David. *Zorro and the Dragon Riders.* New York: TOR, 1999.

Lauria, Frank. *Skull and Crossbones.* New York: Minstrel Books, 1999.

———. *The Lost Temple.* New York: Minstrel Books, 1999.

McCay, William. *The Treasure of Don Diego.* New York: Minstrel Books, 1998.

———. *The Secret Swordsman.* New York: Minstrel Books, 1999.

Preisler, Jerome. *Zorro and the Jaguar Warriors.* New York: TOR, 1998.

Whitman, John. *Zorro and the Witch's Curse.* New York: TOR, 2000.

Selected Comic Books/Graphic Novels

Walt Disney's Comics and Stories (1990) (also by Dell), #275–#278 Marvel, 12-issue tie in with the Duncan Regehr television series.

Topps Comics, *Dracula versus Zorro* (1993), followed by 11-issue Zorro series.

Reprint Collection of Comics

Alex Toth. *Zorro: The Complete Classic Adventures by Alex Toth.* New York: Image Comics, 1998.

McGregor, Don, and Sidney Lima, *Scars, Drownings,* and *Vultures* (Zorro graphic novels #1, #2, and #3, respectively). New York: Papercutz, 2006.

Veritus, Thomas Yeates. *Zorro: The Dailies* (written by Don McGregor and illustrated by Sidney Lima). Berkeley, CA: Image Comics, 2001.

Computer Games

The Shadow of Zorro (PC)

The Mask of Zorro (Game Boy Color)

Zorro (Apple II)

The Destiny of Zorro (Wii)

Television Series

Zorro (1957–1959); Walt Disney Studios; live action, 78 episodes

The New Adventures of Zorro (1981); Filmation; animated series, 13 episodes

Zorro and Son (1983); Walt Disney Studios; live action, 5 episodes

Zorro (1989–1992); New World Productions; live action, 89 episodes

The Legend of Zorro (1992); Mondo TV; animated series, 52 episodes

The New Adventures of Zorro (1997); Warner Bros International; animated series, 26 episodes

Foreign Adaptations of Zorro

Zorro: la Espada y la Rosa (2007); Telemundo; shown across the United States entirely in Spanish with English closed-captioning

Beginning in 2006 BKN International AG, a global animation company, produced 22-minute modern-day Zorro-themed adventures for a "Generation Z" audience; 100 episodes were viewed in the Philippines alone in 2009.

Audio Presentation

Zorro, by Isabel Allende, read by Blair Brown. New York: HarperCollins, 2006.

U.S. Zorro Films

1920: *The Mark of Zorro*, United Artists; Douglas Fairbanks, Sr.

1925: *Don Q, Son of Zorro*, United Artists; Douglas Fairbanks, Sr.

1936: *The Bold Caballero*, Republic; Robert Livingstone

1937: *Zorro Rides Again*, Republic; John Carroll (12-part serial)

1939: *Zorro's Fighting Legion*, Republic; Reed Hadley (12-part serial)

1940: *The Mark of Zorro*, Twentieth Century Fox; Tyrone Power

1944: *Zorro's Black Whip*, Republic; Linda Sterling (12-part serial)

1947: *Son of Zorro*, Republic; George Turner (12-part serial)

1949: *Ghost of Zorro*, Republic; Clayton Moore (12-part serial)

1958: *Zorro, the Avenger*, Disney; Guy Williams

1958: *The Sign of Zorro*, Disney; Guy Williams

1972: *The Erotic Adventures of Zorro*, RFA; Douglas Frey

1974: *The Mark of Zorro*, Twentieth Century Fox; Frank Langella

1980: *Zorro the Gay Blade*, Mel Simon; George Hamilton

1998: *The Mask of Zorro*, TriStar/Amblin; Antonio Banderas and Anthony Hopkins

2005: *The Legend of Zorro*, TriStar/Amblin; Antonio Banderas

Numbers of Foreign Zorro Films

Belgium: 1

Italy/France: 2

Italy/Spain: 11

Italy: 12

Mexico: 6

Spain/France: 1

Spain: 3

Selected Theatrical Productions

1994: *Zorro, El Musical*   Mexico City production

1995: *Zorro, the Musical*   London production by Ken Hill

2007: *Zorro in Hell*   San Francisco "Culture Clash" production

2008: London's West End production of *Zorro, the Musical* by Zorro Productions and AKA Productions, co-written by Isabel Allende and co-composed by John Cameron of *Les Miserables* fame, paved the way for nine confirmed productions of Zorro, in France, Germany, Holland, and other countries.

WORKS CITED

Alexander, Marc. "Zorro Behind the Mask." *Américas* 59 (Jan.–Feb. 2007): 45–49.

Baugh, Matthew. "The Legacy of the Fox: A Chronology of Zorro." http://www.pjfarmer.com/woldnewton/Zorro.htm, accessed 6/4/2007.

Burciaga, José Antonio. "Tiburcio Vasquez: A Chicano Perspective." *The Californians* (May–June 1985): 8–13.

Cheuse, Alan. Review of *Zorro*, by Isabel Allende. *World Literature Today,* Jan.–Feb. 2006: 27–28.

Cooper, John. "Zorro." http://www.museum.tv/archives/etv/Z/html/Zorro/Zorro.htm, accessed 6/22/2007.

Curtis, Sandra R. *Zorro Unmasked: The Official History.* New York: Hyperion, 1998.

Horton, Rod W., and Vincent F. Hopper. *Backgrounds of European Literature.* Englewood Cliffs, NJ: Prentice-Hall, 1975.

MacLean, Angus. *Legends of the California Bandidos.* Fresno, CA: Pioneer Publishing, 1977.

McCulley, Johnston. *The Mark of Zorro*, new ed. New York: TOR, 1998.

"The Real Zorro." http://home.earthlink.net/~rggsibiba/html/sib/sib6.html, accessed 6/22/2007.

Rolle, Andrew. *California: A History,* 4th ed. Wheeling, IL: Harlan Davidson, 1987.

Ruiz, Vicki L. "*Nuestra America*: Latino History as United States History." *Journal of American History* (December 2006): 655–672.

Swanson, Philip. "Z/Z: Isabel Allende and the Mark of Zorro." *Romance Studies* 24 (Nov. 2006): 365–277.

Taccone, Tony. "*Culture Clash*'s Zorro in Hell." *TheatreForum* (Winter/Spring 2007): 74–76.

Williamson, Catharine. "'Draped Crusaders': Disrobing Gender in *The Mark of Zorro*." *Cinema Journal* 36 (Winter 1997): 3–16.

FURTHER READING

Allende, Isabel. *Zorro*. New York: Harper, 2005.

Atienza, Juan Garcia. *The Knights Templar in the Golden Age of Spain*. Rochester, VT: Destiny Books, 2001.

Bunner, H.C. *Zorro*. Whitefish, MT: Kessinger Publishing Co., 2005.

Chapman, C.E. *A History of California: The Spanish Period*. New York: Macmillan, 1921.

Cotter, Bill. "Zorro: A History of the Series." http://www.BillCotter.com/Zorro/history-of-series.htm., accessed 6/22/2007.

Dooley, Gerry. *The Zorro Television Companion: A Critical Appreciation*. New York: McFarland, 2005.

Dubrow, Rochelle. *A Guide to Zorro Collectibles*. Albany, GA: Bear Manor Media, 2008.

Hofstede, David. *Hollywood Heroes: Thirty Screen Legends from King Arthur to Zorro*. London: Anness Publishing, 1994.

Kaplan, Paul. "Zorro's Bar Mitzvah." *Library Journal* 132 (5 May 2007): 127.

Lane, Antoinette G. *Guy Williams: The Man behind the Mask*. Boalsburg, PA: Bear Manor Media, 2005.

Nedaud, Marcello. *Zorro and Old California*. Lakewood, WA: Eclipse Books, 1990.

Ronan, Gerard. *The Irish Zorro: The Extraordinary Adventures of William Lamport*. Cooleen, Ireland: Brandon Book Publishers, 2004.

Schon, Isabel. "From Aztecs to Zorro." *Book Links*, January 2007: 50–54.

Thomas, Hugh. *Rivers of Gold: The Rise of the Spanish Empire, from Columbus to Magellan*. New York: Random House, 2003.

Yenne, Bill. *The Legend of Zorro*. Lombard, IL: Mallard Press, 1991.

WEB SITES

http://www.zorro.com (The official site for Zorro)

http://www.pjfarmer.com/woldnewton/Zorro.htm (A Zorro Chronology)

http://www.geocities.com/thezorrolegend (Summaries of all Zorro versions)

http://www.newworldzorro.com (Comprehensive guide to New World *Zorro* television series)

http://www.comics.org/search.lasso? (Database for Zorro comics)

http://www.billcotter.com/zorro (Guide to Disney Zorro television)

Selected Bibliography

Arnstein, Walter. *Britain Yesterday and Today*, 5th ed. Lexington, MA: Heath, 1988.

Barzun, Jacques, and Wendell Hertig Taylor. *A Catalog of Crime*, rev. ed. New York: Harper, 1989.

Benvenuti, Stefano, and Gianni Rizzoni. *The Whodunit: An Informal History of Detective Fiction*. New York: Macmillan, 1979.

Bourgeau, Art. *The Mystery Lover's Companion*. New York: Crown, 1986.

Brunsdale, Mitzi. *Gumshoes: A Dictionary of Fictional Detectives*. Westport, CT: Greenwood, 2006.

Carr, John C. *The Craft of Crime: Conversations with Crime Writers*. Boston: Houghton, 1983.

classiccrimefiction.com/authorsf.htm.

Collins, Max Allan. *The History of Mystery*. Portland, OR: Collectors Press, 2001.

Cox, J. Randolph. *Masters of Mystery and Detective Fiction: An Annotated Bibliography*. Pasadena, CA: Salem Press, 1989.

Craig, Patricia, and Mary Cadogan. *The Lady Investigates: Women Detectives & Spies in Fiction*. New York: St. Martin's, 1981.

DeAndrea, William L. *Encyclopedia Mysteriosa*. New York: Prentice Hall, 1994.

Dene, Kate, ed. *The Deadly Directory*, rev. ed. New York: Deadly Serious Press, 2004.

Gorman, Ed, Martin H. Greenberg, and Larry Segriff. *The Fine Art of Murder*. New York: Carroll & Graf, 1993.

———, Lee Server, and Martin H. Greenberg, eds. *The Big Book of Noir*. New York: Carroll & Graf, 1998.

Goulart, Ron. *The Dime Detectives*. New York: Mysterious Press, 1988.

Grape, Jan, Dean James, and Ellen Nehr, eds. *Deadly Women*. New York: Carroll & Graf, 1998. http://www.measuringworth.com/calculatora/uscompare/result.php.

Haigh, Christopher, ed. *The Cambridge Historical Encyclopedia of Great Britain and Ireland*. Cambridge, UK: Cambridge University Press, 1985.

Haycraft, Howard, ed. *The Art of the Mystery Story*. New York: Carroll & Graf, 1946, 1974.

Herbert, Rosemary, ed. *The Oxford Companion to Crime & Mystery Writing*. New York: Oxford University Press, 1999.

———. *Whodunit? A Who's Who in Crime and Mystery Writing*. New York: Oxford University Press, 2003.

Holman, C. Hugh. *A Handbook to Literature*, 3rd ed. New York: The Odyssey Press, 1972.

Horton, Rod W., and Vincent F. Hopper. *Backgrounds of European Literature*. Englewood Cliffs, NJ: Prentice-Hall, 1975.

Hubin, Allen J. *Crime Fiction III: A Comprehensive Bibliography, 1749–1995* (CD-ROM version). Oakland, CA: Locus Press, 1999.

———, ed. *The Armchair Detective, 1967–1997* (30 vols.).

Irons, Glenwood, ed. *Feminism in Women's Detective Fiction*. Toronto: University of Toronto Press, 1995.

Johnson, Paul. *Modern Times: From the Twenties to the Nineties*, rev. ed. New York: HarperCollins, 1991.

Keating, H.R.F. *Crime and Mystery: The 100 Best Books*. New York: Carroll & Graf, 1987.

———, ed. *Whodunit? A Guide to Crime, Suspense, and Spy Fiction*. New York: Van Nostrand Reinhold, 1982.

Lehman, David. *The Perfect Murder: A Study in Detection*. New York: Macmillan, 1989.

Levinson, Richard, and William Link. *Stay Tuned, an Inside Look at the Making of Prime-Time Television*. New York: St. Martin's Press, 1981.

Mann, Jessica. *Deadlier Than the Male*. New York: Macmillan, 1981.

McBride, Jim. *In Cold Blood*, 4th ed. Toronto: Crime Writers of Canada, 1997.

Meyers, Richard. *TV Detectives*. San Diego: A.S. Barnes, 1981.

Mottram, James. *Public Enemies: The Gangster Movie A–Z*. London: Botsford, 1998.

Murphy, Bruce F. *The Encyclopedia of Murder and Mystery*. New York: St. Martin's Press, 1999.

Nichols, Victoria, and Sarah Thompson. *Silk Stalkings*. Lanham, MD: Scarecrow Press, 1998.

Ousby, Ian. *Bloodhounds of Heaven: The Detective in English Fiction from Godwin to Doyle*. Cambridge, MA: Harvard University Press, 1976.

Pederson, Jay P., ed. *St. James Guide to Crime & Mystery Writers*, 4th ed. Detroit, MI: St. James Press, 1996.

Penzler, Otto. *The Private Lives of Private Eyes, Crimefighters, & Other Good Guys*. New York: Grosset & Dunlap, 1977.

———, and Mickey Friedman. *The Crown Crime Companion: The Top 100 Mystery Novels of All Time*. New York: Crown, 1995.

Pronzini, Bill, and Marcia Muller. *1001 Midnights*. New York: Arbor House, 1986.

"Rex Stout." Contemporary Authors Online. http://web2.infotrac.galegroup.com.

Routley, Erik. *The Puritan Pleasures of the Detective Story*. London: Gollancz, 1972.

Steinbrunner, Chris, and Otto Penzler. *Encyclopedia of Mystery & Detection*. New York: McGraw-Hill, 1976.

Stine, Kate. *The Armchair Detective Book of Lists*. New York: Otto Penzler Books, 1995.

Swanson, Jean, and Dean James. *Killer Books.* New York: Berkley, 1998.

Symons, Julian. *Bloody Murder: From the Detective Story to the Crime Novel,* rev. ed. New York: Mysterious Press, 1992.

———. *Criminal Practices.* London: Macmillan, 1994.

———. *Great Detectives: Seven Original Investigations.* New York: Harry N. Abrams, 1981.

———. *Mortal Consequences.* New York: Harper & Row, 1972.

———. *Great Detectives: Seven Original Investigations.* Illustrated by Tom Adams. New York: Harry N. Abrams, 1981.

Van Dover, Kenneth. *Murder in the Millions.* New York: Continuum International Publishing Group, 1984.

Ward, Greg. *The Timeline History of the USA.* New York: Barnes & Noble, 2005.

Wilkie, Brian, and James Hurt. *Literature of the Western World.* 2 vols. Upper Saddle River, NJ: Prentice Hall, 2001.

Winks, Robin. *Murder Ink,* rev. ed. Edited by Dilys Winn. New York: Workman Publishing, 1984.

Winks, Robin W., ed. *Mystery and Suspense Writers: The Literature of Crime, Detection, and Espionage.* New York: Scribner's, 1998.

Winn, Dilys. *Murderess Ink.* New York: Workman, 1979.

Woods, Paula, ed. *Black Mystery Crime and Suspense Fiction of the 20th Century.* New York: Doubleday, 1995.

Index

Note: Page numbers in italics denote figures and tables.

ABOUT THE AUTHOR

MITZI M. BRUNSDALE, Ph.D., is Professor of English at Mayville (N.D.) State University. She has written *Student Companion to George Orwell* (Greenwood 2000) and *Gumshoes: A Dictionary of Fictional Detectives* (Greenwood 2006), as well as *Sigrid Undset: Chronicler of Norway*; *Dorothy L. Sayers: Solving the Mystery of Wickedness*; *James Joyce: A Study of the Short Fiction*; and *James Herriot*.